THE BIOLOGY OF HABITATS SERIES

The Biology of Deserts

THE BIOLOGY OF HABITATS SERIES

This attractive series of concise, affordable texts provides an integrated overview of the design, physiology, and ecology of the biota in a given habitat, set in the context of the physical environment. Each book describes practical aspects of working within the habitat, detailing the sorts of studies which are possible. Management and conservation issues are also included. The series is intended for naturalists, students studying biological or environmental science, those beginning independent research, and professional biologists embarking on research in a new habitat.

The Biology of Rocky Shores
Colin Little and J. A. Kitching

The Biology of Polar Habitats
G. E. Fogg

The Biology of Lakes and Ponds
Christer Brönmark and Lars-Anders Hansson

The Biology of Streams and Rivers
Paul S. Giller and Björn Malmqvist

The Biology of Mangroves
Peter J. Hogarth

The Biology of Soft Shores and Estuaries
Colin Little

The Biology of the Deep Ocean
Peter Herring

The Biology of Lakes and Ponds, second edition
Christer Brönmark and Lars-Anders Hansson

The Biology of Soil
Richard D. Bardgett

The Biology of Freshwater Wetlands
Arnold G. van der Valk

The Biology of Peatlands
Håkan Rydin and John K. Jeglum

The Biology of Mangroves and Seagrasses, 2nd Edition
Peter J. Hogarth

The Biology of African Savannahs
Bryan Shorrocks

The Biology of Polar Regions, 2nd Edition
David N. Thomas et al

The Biology of Deserts
David Ward

The Biology of Caves and Other Subterranean Habitats
David C. Culver and Tanja Pipan

The Biology of Alpine Habitats
Laszlo Nagy and Georg Grabherr

The Biology of Deserts

David Ward

OXFORD

UNIVERSITY PRESS

OXFORD
UNIVERSITY PRESS

Great Clarendon Street, Oxford OX2 6DP

Oxford University Press is a department of the University of Oxford.
It furthers the University's objective of excellence in research, scholarship,
and education by publishing worldwide in

Oxford New York

Auckland Cape Town Dar es Salaam Hong Kong Karachi
Kuala Lumpur Madrid Melbourne Mexico City Nairobi
New Delhi Shanghai Taipei Toronto

With offices in

Argentina Austria Brazil Chile Czech Republic France Greece
Guatemala Hungary Italy Japan Poland Portugal Singapore
South Korea Switzerland Thailand Turkey Ukraine Vietnam

Oxford is a registered trade mark of Oxford University Press
in the UK and in certain other countries

Published in the United States
by Oxford University Press Inc., New York

© David Ward 2009

The moral rights of the author have been asserted
Database right Oxford University Press (maker)

First published 2009

British Library Cataloguing in Publication Data
Data available

Library of Congress Cataloging in Publication Data
Ward, David, 1961, June 15–
    The biology of deserts / David Ward.
       p. cm.
    ISBN 978–0–19–921147–0—ISBN 978–0–19–921146–3   1. Desert ecology.   I. Title.
    QH541.5.D4W36   2009
    577.54—dc22   2008027746

Typeset by Newgen Imaging Systems (P) Ltd., Chennai, India
Printed in Great Britain
on acid-free paper by
CPI Antony Rowe, Chippenham, Wiltshire

ISBN 978–0–19–921146–3 (Hbk)   978–0–19–921147–0 (Pbk)

10 9 8 7 6 5 4 3 2 1

To my wife, Megan, who contributed to this book in so many ways,

and

to my mother, Maureen, and to my late father, Neville, for instilling in me a desire to learn.

Preface

Deserts are difficult to define. They vary greatly in their aridity, from close to 0 mm of rainfall annually to more than 500 mm. They range in temperature from more than 50°C to far less than 0°C. Most of all, they are distributed across the globe in so many places that it is difficult to define exactly where they are and what makes a desert what it is. I have used the term 'desert' in the broadest sense of the word, but have tried to keep away from neighbouring topics such as savannas and grasslands. I have usually used the term to include all 'arid' and 'semi-arid' habitats, or where the term 'xeric' seemed to fit. Most of all, I have tried to focus on the studies that use the term prominently, especially where I am familiar with the system.

The amount of research done varies greatly among deserts, and often there is a difference in the issues that are focused on in a particular region. North Americans have done more work of interest in terms of evolutionary studies and population and community ecology. Israeli scientists have done a lot of research on population and community ecology, as well as ecosystem and conservation ecology. Researchers in Russia (and allied states) and China have mostly been concerned with applied issues, as have researchers in many Arab states and Iran and India. Researchers in Australia have focused a lot on rangelands as well as on plant, lizard and small mammal diversity. Southern Africans have focused on a range of issues, especially on animal physiology and plant diversity, but very little has been done on plant physiology and population and community ecology. In contrast, German researchers have extensively studied desert plant physiology in the Sahara, Middle East and in the Namib and Kalahari deserts. South Americans have conducted studies on a wide range of desert issues, with a focus on population ecology. Clearly, if we each learned a bit from each other, we could gain a lot more insight into how desert systems work. It is not possible to assume that if a trend has been demonstrated elsewhere, it will work the same way in all deserts. I believe that we need to consider how we might replicate studies in different deserts (e.g. plant and animal physiology studies) and expand the number of deserts in which we study competition, facilitation, predation, parasitism and plant–animal interactions (as well as ecosystem studies).

In this book, I have decided to focus on an evolutionary approach to deserts because I believe that this is what makes them so interesting.

Deserts are indeed laboratories of nature. I realize that evolution means different things to different people. Here, I use the term very broadly, covering phylogenetic constraints, optimization, Evolutionarily Stable Strategy models, and convergence, among other things. This is not to say that there is no coverage of other issues. I believe that I would be doing a disservice if I were to focus on evolutionary issues alone, so I do cover ecosystem approaches, desertification and conservation issues, to name but a few. However, there are other excellent books published on community and ecosystem approaches such as Gary Polis' (1991) 'Ecology of desert communities', Walt Whitford's (2002) book on 'Ecology of desert systems', and many others covering specific deserts. I particularly like John Lowell's (2001) book titled 'Desert ecology: an introduction to life in the arid southwest'. Clearly, its focus is on North American deserts, but it covers a tremendous range of issues. These are all very good books; it will be hard to find a niche among them.

There are many people that I would like to thank. Most of all, I thank my wife, Megan Griffiths-Ward, for her help in copy-editing (and Maureen Ward and Betsy Griffiths) and in so many other ways. I am most grateful to the Biology Department at Tufts University during my sabbatical there, and to my host Colin Orians, for his assistance and collegiality. Our friends, Randi Rotjan and Jeff Chabot, were very kind to us during our sabbatical in Boston, as were Elizabeth and Jonathan Griffiths in New Jersey. I thank my colleagues at the Blaustein Institutes for Desert Research in Sede Boqer, Israel, including my long-time collaborator and friend, David Saltz, as well as Zvika Abramsky, Yoav Avni, Yoram Ayal, Burt Kotler, Boris Krasnov, Yael Lubin, Ofer Ovadia, Berry Pinshow, Uriel Safriel, Moshe Shachak, Jura Shenbrot, Josef Plakht, Eli Zaady, and Yaron Ziv. I pay special thanks to my technician of many years, Iris Musli. I am indebted to my many Israeli students, especially Gil Bohrer, Keren Or, Natalia Ruiz, Madan Shrestha, and Sergei Volis. In South Africa, I am very grateful to my research assistant Vanessa Stuart, my German collaborator, Kerstin Wiegand, as well as to Rob Slotow and my students, especially to Tineke Kraaij, Mari-Louise Britz, Khanyi Mbatha, and Michiel Smet, as well as to Katrin Meyer, Aristides Moustakas, and Jana Förster. I would also like to thank Joh Henschel, Steve Johnson, Boris Krasnov, Yael Lubin, Gordon Orians, Scott Turner, Olle Pellmyr, and Jane Waterman for their assistance and clarifications, and for reviewing parts of this manuscript. Last, but definitely not the least, I would like to thank my editor, Ian Sherman, and his assistant, Helen Eaton, at Oxford University Press for their inspiration and assistance.

Contents

PREFACE   vii

1 Introduction   1

  1.1 General introduction   1
  1.2 What creates a desert?   2
  1.3 Deserts have low precipitation and high variability
      in precipitation   2
  1.4 How old are deserts?   3
  1.5 Deserts are created by a lack of precipitation and not
      high temperatures   4
  1.6 Aridity indices   5
  1.7 What denies rainfall to deserts?   7

2 Abiotic factors   11

  2.1 Precipitation   11
  2.2 Temperature   19
  2.3 Geology   20
  2.4 Fire   27

3 Morphological and physiological adaptations of desert plants to the abiotic environment   29

  3.1 Classifications of desert plants   29
  3.2 Types of photosynthesis   34
  3.3 Biological soil crusts   39
  3.4 Annual plants   40
  3.5 Grasses, forbs and shrubs/perennials   48
  3.6 Geophytes   51
  3.7 Stem and leaf succulents   56
  3.8 Halophytes   60
  3.9 Phreatophytes   62

4 **Morphological, physiological, and behavioural adaptations of desert animals to the abiotic environment** 66

4.1 Evaders and evaporators 68
4.2 Adaptations to handle unique situations 84
4.3 Endurers 87
4.4 Removing the effects of phylogeny 92

5 **The role of competition and facilitation in structuring desert communities** 102

5.1 Plant communities 102
5.2 Competition between animals 107
5.3 Indirect interactions: keystone species, apparent competition, and priority effects 118

6 **The importance of predation and parasitism** 124

6.1 Direct mortality 124
6.2 Predation risk 125
6.3 Isodars 126
6.4 Spiders 129
6.5 Scorpions 131
6.6 Visually hunting predators 132
6.7 Snakes, scent-hunting predators 133
6.8 Keystone predation 135
6.9 Animal parasites and parasitoids 137

7 **Plant–animal interactions in deserts** 145

7.1 Herbivory 145
7.2 Pollination 158
7.3 Seed dispersal and seed predation 167
7.4 Are these coevolved systems? 170

8 **Desert food webs and ecosystem ecology** 177

8.1 Do deserts have simple food webs? 177
8.2 The first supermodel—HSS 179
8.3 Interactions among habitats—donor–recipient habitat interactions 183
8.4 Effects of precipitation, nutrients, disturbances and decomposition 184

9   **Biodiversity and biogeography of deserts**   192

    9.1   Are deserts species-poor? α, β, and γ diversity patterns   193
    9.2   Productivity–diversity relationships in deserts   199
    9.3   Convergence and divergence of desert communities   202
    9.4   Large-scale patterns in desert biogeography   208

10   **Human impacts and desertification**   217

    10.1 The sensitive desert ecosystem: myth or reality?   217
    10.2 Pastoralism is the most important use of desert lands   222
    10.3 Military manoeuvres threaten some desert habitats
         and protect others   237
    10.4 Pumping aquifers: a problem of less water and more salinity   239
    10.5 An embarrassment of riches: oil extraction in desert
         environments   240
    10.6 When is it desertification? The importance of reversibility   242

11   **Conservation of deserts**   246

    11.1 Are deserts worth conserving?   246
    11.2 Conservation of desert species or habitats   246
    11.3 The 3 Rs: reintroduction, recolonization, and revegetation   256
    11.4 The coalface of evolution—genotype by environment
         interactions   261
    11.5 Who gets to pay for this conservation and how is it
         controlled?   264
    11.6 Conclusions   267

    REFERENCES   269
    INDEX   317

1 Introduction

'Nothing in biology makes sense except in the light of evolution'

Dobzhansky (1964)

1.1   General introduction

Deserts are defined by their arid conditions. A consequence of this aridity is that most of the area occupied by desert is barren and monotonous, leading many people to view it as a wasteland. In contrast, biologists have long seen deserts as laboratories of nature, where natural selection is exposed at its most extreme. Generations of scientists have focused on the numerous unique adaptations of plants and animals for surviving the harsh desert environment. Indeed, such studies have made the adaptations of desert organisms some of the best-known examples of Darwinian natural selection. In this book, I will introduce the reader to the major constraints facing organisms in desert environments and also consider how organisms have evolved to circumvent these constraints.

More recently, researchers have shifted their attention to the biotic interactions among desert organisms. I will attempt to convince the reader that, while the abiotic environment defines deserts and imposes strong selection pressure on the organisms that live there, the biotic interactions among the organisms in deserts are no less exciting or intricate than those of other environments. Indeed, it is the relative simplicity of desert ecosystems that makes them more tractable for study than more complex environments. I will also emphasize the myriad ways in which organisms exploit the enormous spatial and temporal variations in deserts, leading to the creation of unique assemblages with surprisingly high diversity.

Finally, the book will examine the sensitivity of the desert environment to disturbances and the effects that human beings have had on deserts. It will focus on the paradox that deserts have been particularly important habitats for humans in spite of their aridity and how changing resource use patterns are placing these unique ecosystems under threat.

1.2   What creates a desert?

Deserts are defined by their aridity, yet differ enormously in their abiotic characteristics. The variation among deserts is probably greater than for any other biome, largely because deserts are so widely spaced on the planet and have arisen for very different reasons. For example, North American continental deserts are far hotter and wetter than African and Middle Eastern deserts (Louw and Seely 1982). The Kalahari and Namib deserts in southern Africa mostly experience summer rainfall and are dominated by grasses, while the adjacent succulent Karoo desert experiences winter rainfall and is dominated by succulents. In contrast, Middle Eastern deserts experience winter rainfall and are dominated by annual forbs (mostly Asteraceae). The coastal Namibian and Chilean desert systems are driven by fog, while run-off from winter floods controls plant production in Middle Eastern deserts. Australian deserts are limited by phosphorus (Beadle 1981; Stafford Smith and Morton 1990), while nitrogen is the most limiting nutrient in other deserts (Ezcurra 2006).

1.3   Deserts have low precipitation and high variability in precipitation

It is critical to consider deserts both as resource-poor environments and as places where there are enormous variations in environmental quality in space and time. Ward *et al.* (2000a) have shown that there is a strong negative correlation between the coefficient of variation (c.v.) in annual rainfall and its median value in arid systems (Fig. 1.1a and b). Le Houérou (1984) noted that in the north of the Sahara, the c.v. of annual rainfall increased from 25–30% in the 400–500 mm zone to 70–80% in the 100 mm belt. In a study on North American deserts, Davidowitz (2002) has shown that

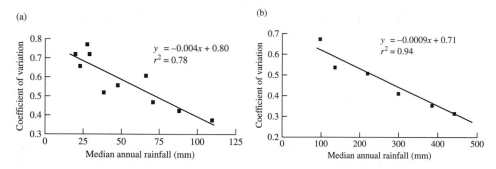

Fig. 1.1   Strong negative correlation between the coefficient of variation (c.v.) in annual rainfall and its median value. (a) Negev desert, Israel. (b) Namib desert, Namibia.

this trend is generally true there as well. Coefficients of variation of mean annual rainfall in specific places may be as much as five times higher than in mesic places. However, he warns that this is not universally true. Indeed, there may be places in North America where there is no difference in c.v. between xeric and mesic sites. Nonetheless, this variation in environmental quality leads to high local species diversity and allows deserts to be exploited by a wide variety of organisms that are more common in mesic environments (see Chapters 3, 4, and 8).

1.4   How old are deserts?

One may be tempted to assume that deserts have always been so. However, fossils found in deserts such as those discovered in the Gobi desert by Roy Chapman Andrews in the 1920s, the *Lystrosaurus* fossils in the Karoo desert (Kitching 1977; Rubidge 2005), the ammonite fossils in the Arabian desert (Parnes 1962), and the soft-bodied Ediacaran fossils of the Great Basin desert (Hagadorn and Waggoner 2000) indicate that these were once shallow seas, deltas or even, in the case of the Arabian desert, areas of the former Tethys Sea when the world was a single continent known as Pangaea (Parnes 1962). Plate tectonics has resulted in major changes in the positions of the continents and, consequently, in the positions of the deserts (Wegener 1966).

Many, if not most, deserts are reasonably young, although they do vary considerably in age, persistence through geological time and the types of habitats occurring on their borders. This, in turn, affects the types of flora and fauna that deserts are likely to attract (Kelt *et al.* 1996). It is generally agreed that the Miocene (23.5 million to 20,000 years BP) was a time of global desertification (Axelrod 1950; Alpers and Brimhall 1988; Singh 1988; Bristow *et al.* 2007).

The deserts of central Asia (Gobi, Taklamakan, Turkestan) are considered old Cretaceous (144–58 million years BP), although they were not widespread until the Miocene (Sinitzin 1962). The exception in this region is the Thar desert of India, where most sand landscapes were developed due to human activities in historical times (Wadia 1960; Prakash 1963). The Taklamakan desert in southern China formed about 5 million years ago (Sun and Liu 2006). The permafrost (permanently frozen ground) in the Gobi desert is much more recent (Owen *et al.* 1998), being only about 15,000–22,000 years old.

Australian deserts have only been arid for about a million years at most (Ollier 2005), and perhaps only experienced a sharp increase in aridity about 350,000 years ago (Hesse *et al.* 2004). The Atacama in South America is about 25 million years old at the oldest (Dunai *et al.* 2005), although estimates indicate that about 10–15 million years old may be more appropriate (Prellwitz *et al.* 2006). Also in South America, the Patagonian desert is about 25 million years old (Dunai *et al.* 2005).

Although the Sahara is the largest desert in the world (about 9 million km²), it was formed only about 7 million years ago (Schuster *et al.* 2006). In contrast, the Namib desert is believed to be the world's oldest desert. It is claimed to have been arid for at least 55 million years and, perhaps, as much as 80 million years BP (Ward *et al.* 1983). The convergence of the Benguela upwelling and the hot interior have maintained, and perhaps increased, this aridity in recent times but they did not generate the aridity. The region, isolated between the ocean and the escarpment, is considered to be a constant island of aridity surrounded by a sea of climatic change (Ward *et al.* 1983; Armstrong 1990). The arid conditions probably started with the continental split of West Gondwana 130–145 million years ago when this area shifted to its present position along the Tropic of Capricorn (Ward *et al.* 1983). This lengthy dry period has had a profound influence on the region's biodiversity. The region has remained a relatively stable centre for the evolution of desert species. This has resulted in a unique array of biodiversity with high levels of endemism and numerous adaptations to arid conditions (Barnard *et al.* 1998), and may explain why so few species are shared between the Namib and the Sahara (Shmida 1985) (see Chapter 9).

1.5 Deserts are created by a lack of precipitation and not high temperatures

What makes a desert is not a particular temperature but rather a lack of precipitation. The Arctic and Antarctic polar regions have large barren stretches that can be considered desert. Similarly, the Great Basin desert does not have the extreme temperatures of the Sonoran desert or the Sahara. Most deserts lie in two belts between the Equator and the tropics of Cancer and Capricorn. In the Northern Hemisphere, the arid belt includes the Sahara, Arabian and Iranian deserts, and the Gobi and central Asian deserts, as well as the deserts of the North American Southwest. In the Southern Hemisphere, it includes the Namib and Kalahari deserts, the deserts of Peru and Chile, and the Australian deserts (Fig. 1.2).

Until fairly recently, a desert was considered a place that received less than 250 mm of rainfall. If distributed evenly over the entire year, 250 mm of annual rainfall can be sufficient to maintain a grassland, yet when concentrated in one or two months, deserts may exist because plants can use only a certain amount of rain at a time. Rain that falls in torrents usually runs off or sinks into the ground before it can be used. Thus, flash floods can create far more than 250 mm of rainfall but they are not accessible to desert organisms because most of the rainfall is not absorbed by the soil, leaving the ground nearly as dry as it was without rain. Furthermore, some deserts (deemed 'cold' deserts) receive precipitation as snow and ice, which can exceed the 250 mm threshold, but that precipitation is again not

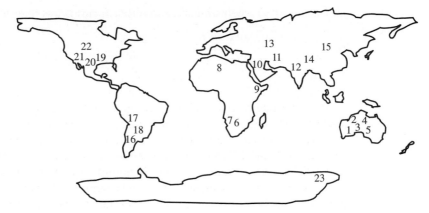

Fig. 1.2   Map of deserts of the world. Names of deserts: 1 = Victoria desert; 2 = Great Sandy desert; 3 = Gibson desert; 4 = Simpson desert; 5 = Sturt's Stony desert; 6 = Kalahari desert; 7 = Namib desert; 8 = Sahara; 9 = Somali-Chalbi desert (also known as the Ogaden desert); 10 = Arabian desert; 11 = Iranian desert; 12 = Thar desert; 13 = Turkestan desert; 14 = Taklamakan desert; 15 = Gobi desert; 16 = Patagonian desert; 17 = Atacama-Sechura desert; 18 = Monte desert; 19 = Chihuahuan desert; 20 = Sonoran desert; 21 = Mojave desert; 22 = Great Basin desert; 23 = dry valleys of Antarctica. (Modified from Page 1984.)

accessible to organisms. Here, I will include mean annual rainfall values up to 500 mm where appropriate to include regions that border on deserts but that are not grasslands or savannas. While the main deserts are indicated in Figure 1.2, there are many smaller areas containing deserts (e.g. the Turkana desert of Kenya and the Karoo of South Africa) that are not specifically illustrated. Indeed, deserts make up about 40% of the world's biomes (Ezcurra 2006).

Rainfall alone is insufficient to describe desert conditions, so some scientists have devised systems that relate potential evaporation to precipitation (Thornthwaite 1948; Geiger 1961). Thus, in the Atacama and Namib deserts, two of the driest places on Earth, the sun's energy can evaporate 200 times as much rainfall as the area receives in an average year. The aridity index is thus 200 (Page 1984) and both areas are classified as 'hyperarid'. At the other end of the scale, the Great Basin desert in North America has an index that ranges from 1.5 to 4. This region is known as 'semi-arid' and can support a wide diversity of life forms.

1.6   Aridity indices

At the beginning of the 20th century, Köppen (1931; modified by Geiger 1961) developed a concept of climate classification where arid zones were defined as areas where annual rainfall (R, in cm) is less than $R/2$, where

$R = 2 \times T$ if rainfall is in the cold season,
$R = 2 \times T + 14$ if rainfall occurs throughout the year, and
$R = 2 \times T + 28$ if rainfall occurs in summer, with T = mean annual temperature (in °C).

This was one of the first attempts at defining aridity that shows the effects of the thermal regime and the amount and distribution of precipitation in determining the native vegetation in a particular area. It also recognized the significance of temperature in allowing colder places such as northern Canada to be recorded as humid with the same precipitation as subtropical deserts because of the lower potential evapotranspiration in colder places. In the subtropics, the difference between rain falling in warm and cold seasons recognizes the greater potential impact of rain in winter because of its effects on plant growth. Athens, Greece (mean annual rainfall = 372 mm), gets most of its rainfall in winter and is considered to have a humid climate with roughly the same rainfall as Kimberley, South Africa (mean annual rainfall = 390 mm), where most rain occurs in the summer. The most frequently used climate classification map of Köppen (1931) was presented in its latest version by Geiger (1961) (Fig. 1.3) for the second half of the 20th century.

A more widely used index of aridity was developed by Thornthwaite (1948) as $AI_T = 100 \times d/n$, where the water deficiency d is the sum of the monthly differences between precipitation and potential evapotranspiration for those months when normal precipitation is less than normal evapotranspiration and n is the sum of monthly values of potential evapotranspiration for the deficient months (later modified by Huschke 1959).

A number of other aridity indices have since been developed. The United Nations Environment Programme (1992) defined aridity as AI_U = P/PET,

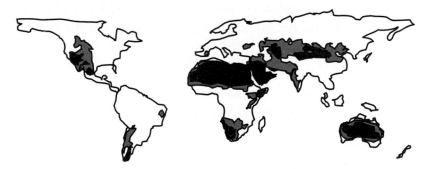

Fig. 1.3   Climate classification map of Wladimir Köppen (1931) was presented in its latest version by Rudolf Geiger (1961). Black = extremely arid; Grey = arid to semi-arid. (Modified from Peel *et al.* 2007.)

where P refers to precipitation and PET refers to potential evapotranspiration. PET and P must be expressed using the same unit (e.g. in mm), and the resulting index is therefore dimensionless. Table 1.1 indicates the boundaries between hyperarid, arid, semi-arid, and dry sub-humid and the percentage land area of the Earth that they occupy.

1.7 What denies rainfall to deserts?

Four factors influence the lack of rainfall in deserts (Page 1984; Milich 1997):

1. The most constant of these is the global circulation of the atmosphere, which maintains twin belts of dry, high-pressure air over the fringes of the tropics, known as Hadley cells (Milich 1997). Air is fluid (Vogel 1994), and is kept in continuous motion by solar energy. When the sun's radiation reaches the earth, most passing through the atmosphere, it is absorbed by land and water and is then re-radiated as heat. Most solar radiation is absorbed in the tropics, where the sun is virtually directly overhead in summer and winter. As tropical air warms, it expands, becoming lighter than the surrounding air and rises, carrying with it huge volumes of water vapour from the warm ocean surface. As the moist air rises, it cools and spreads laterally, northwards and southwards. The cooling reduces its capacity to hold water and moisture begins to condense and fall in huge torrents of tropical rain. After further cooling and having been stripped of its water content, the increasingly heavy air sinks as it travels towards the Poles and is compressed by the continuing flow of sinking air. This compression causes the air to warm again. This warm, dry, high-pressure air mass presses down at the tropics and then much of it flows back to the Equator into the low-pressure void left by the rising tropical air. The deserts of the subtropics are where the high-pressure air descends.

2. Circulation patterns in the sea also contribute to aridity when cold coastal waters (on the west coasts of North America, South America, and

Table 1.1 Classification of deserts according to their level of aridity, following the scheme of United Nations Environment Programme (1992).

Classification	Aridity index	Global land area (%)
Hyperarid	AI < 0.05	7.5
Arid	0.05 < AI < 0.20	12.1
Semi-arid	0.20 < AI < 0.50	17.7
Dry Sub-humid	0.50 < AI < 0.65	9.9

The last column indicates the percentage of land area that is currently occupied by these various categories. AI = aridity index.

Africa) chill the air, reducing its moisture-carrying capacity. Prevailing winds blowing along the coastline tend, because of the earth's rotation, to push surface currents seawards perpendicular to the wind. Because there is no surface water upcurrent to replace the water being driven out to sea, very cold water is drawn upward from near the ocean floor. This vertical movement of the ocean is known as an upwelling (Fig. 1.4). Air masses crossing these stretches of very cold water are chilled and their capacities to hold water vapour are diminished. The condensing moisture forms dense fog banks along the coast, leaving little or no rain to fall on the land. The Atacama and Namib deserts are largely formed by these processes (Armstrong 1990). Some parts of these deserts can go for years without rain, although abrupt changes in the upwelling area (known as El Niño effect, which occurs in the Pacific Ocean off South America) can cause the trade winds to change and warm water to surge shoreward. This can cause incredible rains to fall. For example, in

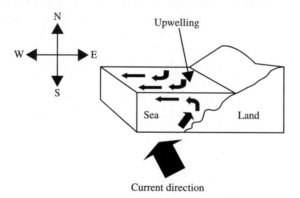

Fig. 1.4   A fog desert is created by vertical movement of the ocean known as an upwelling, which chills the air. These deserts usually form on the west coasts of southern continents. (Following Ezcurra 2006. With kind permission of United Nations Environment Programme.)

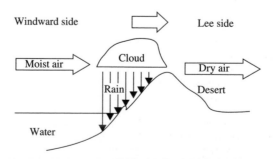

Fig. 1.5   A schematic diagram of a rain shadow desert.

1934, about 800 mm of rain fell at Walvis Bay in the Namib desert, even though the mean annual rainfall there is 11 mm (Ward *et al.* 1998).

3. Even moisture-laden winds may not be able to carry rain if it is in a rain shadow (also known as *relief* desert) created by a mountain range (Fig. 1.5). The Great Basin desert and the deserts of Afghanistan and Turkestan are examples of deserts created by this process.
4. If the distance to the interior of a continent is too great (e.g. China's Taklamakan and Gobi deserts) then water is limited. By the time that westerly winds have blown across central Asia, the winds would have travelled over thousands of kilometres of land and, hence, would have lost most of their moisture.

Many of these factors may work in tandem to create deserts (Table 1.2).

Arid lands are not entirely restricted to the subtropics. There are very cold deserts in China (Taklamakan and Gobi deserts), Turkmenistan and Kazakhstan (Turkestan desert), and the southern tip of South America (Patagonian desert). The Great Basin desert is also very cold in the winter. Relatively warm air at about 60°N and 60°S rises and flows towards the

Table 1.2 Reasons for the formation of deserts across the world.

Continent	Desert	High pressure	Midcontinent	Rain shadow	Upwelling
Australia	Sturt's Stony	X	X	X	
	Victoria	X	X		
	Gibson	X	X	X	
	Simpson	X	X	X	
	Great Sandy	X	X		
Asia	Gobi		X		
	Taklamakan		X		
	Thar	X			
	Iranian	X	X	X	
	Turkestan		X		
	Arabian	X			
Africa	Somali-Chalbi	X			
	Kalahari	X			
	Namib	X			X
	Karoo	X		X	
	Sahara	X			X
South America	Patagonian			X	
	Monte	X			
	Atacama-Sechura	X			X
North America	Chihuahuan	X			
	Sonoran	X			
	Mojave	X		X	
	Great Basin			X	
Poles	Antarctic	X			
	Arctic	X			

Poles. As this air cools, it releases little moisture as rain or, more frequently, as snow. It then sinks and moves outwards to complete the circular flow (also known as a Hadley cell).

At the Poles, there are regions that can also be classified as deserts by virtue of their low precipitation. They seldom receive more than 75–100 mm of precipitation and less than 120 mm of rain (Page 1984). Within the Arctic and Antarctic circles, there are barrens, which are ice-free rocks or sediments deposited by glaciers and where the weak snowfalls are swept away by fierce winds. Parts of northern Greenland, the northern slope of Alaska, some northern Canadian islands and a section of Antarctica also fall into this category. The cold that characterizes these polar barrens produces permafrost, which may extend as far below the surface as 300 m. When there is an annual cycle of freezing and thawing, this permafrost may be overlain by an active layer that, when it thaws in summer, may create pools.

2 Abiotic factors

There are a number of abiotic factors that have important impacts on the desert environment. Clearly, the most important of these abiotic factors is rainfall or, in some cases, other sources of precipitation such as fog, snow, and ice. Temperature is another important factor, having both positive and negative effects. I also consider the role of geology, particularly in terms of the effects on soils, which in turn is important for plant life and to a certain extent animal life (e.g. those living in burrows). The last abiotic issue that I cover is fire. As this book focuses on the biology of deserts, there will be some issues that I will not cover, but I believe that sufficient knowledge will be gained to serve for the understanding of subsequent chapters.

2.1 Precipitation

2.1.1 Rainfall

It is widely known that deserts are defined by their low mean rainfall, although it is just as important to measure the temporal variability in annual rainfall (see Fig. 1.1). Similarly, spatial variation in rainfall is high. For example, Sharon (1972) has shown that the correlation coefficient for rain gauges in the Negev desert (Israel) may vary from 0.95 at distances less than 1 km to as little as 0.15 at distances greater than 23 km (Fig. 2.1). In the Namib desert, Sharon (1981) has also shown that there are weak correlations between rain gauges. He found that convective storms are not randomly scattered in space, but rather tend to cluster at distances of 40–50 km and 80–100 km from one another, with no preferred locations of, or directions between, storms. It is this high variability that leads to the high biodiversity that occurs in some desert areas. For example, α diversity of plants (diversity in a particular place) in Middle Eastern deserts is several times higher than that of the world's richest biome, the fynbos of South Africa (Naveh and Whittaker 1979; Ward and Olsvig-Whittaker 1993).

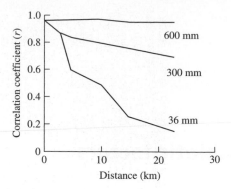

Fig. 2.1   Spatial variation in rainfall in desert (36 mm), semi-arid (300 mm) and mesic (600 mm) areas. Correlation coefficients are based on daily rainfall variation over 3 years. (Modified from Sharon 1972.)

Rainfall in deserts tends to fall in pulses (Sharon 1972; Chesson *et al.* 2004; Sher *et al.* 2004). These pulses can vary considerably in their magnitude and timing. They can fall in summer or in winter, and can vary considerably in the amount of rain that falls. Short precipitation pulses may be sufficient for annual plants but perennial plants need far longer periods of rain for effective growth (Chesson *et al.* 2004). Pulses may be local in scale but are, nonetheless, driven by large-scale global and atmospheric factors such as the position of the jet stream, polar boundary shifts, El Niño Southern Oscillation events, and even longer-term ocean cycles (Ezcurra 2006).

The erosion and scouring effects of torrential downpours can be marked in desert landscapes. In sandy deserts, rain usually drains away and changes in the landscape are reasonably small. In contrast, downpours in rocky deserts drain rapidly into adjacent *wadis* (Arabic; also known as *arroyos* in Spanish), which are ephemeral rivers (Fig. 2.2). These wadis can be heavily affected by downpours, and they frequently are subjected to flash floods because there is little or no vegetation to hold the water back. Such flash floods carry sand and gravel and later rocks and boulders with them, adding to the erosive power of water as it rushes down the slope. This is known as the threshold of critical power, which is the power needed to cause water to flow (Bull 1981) (Figs. 2.3 and 2.4). At the end of most wadis lies an alluvial fan (called a *bajada* in Spanish) (Fig. 2.5) made up of sand and stone. At this point, the critical power threshold (Bull 1981) is no longer exceeded as the water moves into a more open landscape. The torrent subsides and most of the sand, stone, and boulder contents are dropped into the alluvial fan (McAuliffe 1994). The substrate is coarser, with larger rocks on the upper bajada and finer stones and gravel at the lower elevations (McAuliffe 1994). The water may pass into a *playa*, which

Fig. 2.2   Augrabies waterfall in the arid Northern Cape province, South Africa. The Orange River runs through here, dropping over 190 m *en route* to the sea.

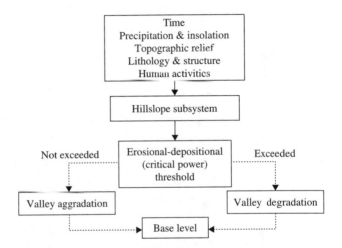

Fig. 2.3   Basic elements of a fluvial system. Feedback mechanisms are indicated by dashed lines and arrows. (From Bell 1979. With kind permission of the Geological Society of America.)

is a water body with no exit. During wet cycles, shallow playa lakes may last for a few months, a few years or even longer. Some playa lakes may last for considerably longer; for example, the Salton Sea, in California (USA), has been around since 1906 (Page 1984). In some areas, wadis may feed into rivers or lakes (e.g. Negev desert wadis feed into the Dead Sea and some Sonoran desert wadis feed into the Colorado River and Simpson desert wadis feed into Lake Eyre) or even into the ocean (e.g. Sonoran desert wadis empty into the Pacific Ocean in certain areas). Poorly drained

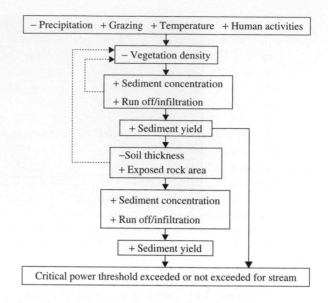

| − Precipitation | + Grazing | + Temperature | + Human activities |

− Vegetation density

+ Sediment concentration
+ Run off/infiltration

+ Sediment yield

−Soil thickness
+ Exposed rock area

+ Sediment concentration
+ Run off/infiltration

+ Sediment yield

Critical power threshold exceeded or not exceeded for stream

Fig. 2.4   Increases (+) and decreases (−) in elements of an arid hillslope subsystem. Self-enhancing feedback mechanisms are shown by dashed lines. (From Bell 1979. With kind permission of Geological Society of America.)

Fig. 2.5   Alluvial fan in Jordan (viewed from above).

patches and larger playas may become alkaline (salty) through accumulation of soluble chemicals (see below).

2.1.1.1 Oases

No desert is totally dry, although one may have to travel great distances to find water. Somewhere underground there is a continuous supply of flowing water. Its source is the rain that seldom falls, perhaps hundreds of kilometres away. A common source for an oasis is the rain that falls on the windward side of a mountain and soaks into a porous rock called an aquifer. This groundwater seeps down the tilted aquifer until it is stopped by an impermeable rock at a fault, where hydraulic pressure forces it to the surface. An oasis can also occur at a site where the erosive forces of wind and sand have created a basin lower than the elevation at which the rain fell. Water in the saturated portion of the aquifer flows along the sloping course until it intersects with the desert surface at what is called an artesian well.

Oases can also be saline. If the water moves slowly through an aquifer it may leach out large amounts of salt from the rock. Only a few plants can survive in the marshes surrounding these salty springs. Narrow oases can also form along rivers such as the Nile River in Africa, and the Rio Grande and Colorado River in North America. These rivers form in more tropical (e.g. Nile) or temperate regions (e.g. Colorado).

2.1.1.2 Fog

Some deserts are coastal [e.g. Namib (Namibia), Atacama (Chile and Peru), western part of the Sahara and Baja California section of the Sonoran deserts] and, although rainfall is very low, fog coming off the sea is sufficient to drive these systems. The Atacama desert is considered to be the driest desert in the world, and it has been claimed that it did not receive any rain from 1570 until 1971 (Flegg 1993). In Namib desert fog water, Eckardt and Schemenauer (1998) have studied with regard to ion concentrations and ion enrichment relative to sea water and compared these values with the values obtained for Chilean and Omani deserts. Where the World Health Organization (WHO) standard allowable maxima are 6–8.5 pH, 250 ppm SO_4, 45 ppm NO_3, 250 ppm Cl, 200 ppm Ca and 125 ppm Mg, the mean values for the Chilean (Schemenauer and Cereceda 1992a), Omani (Schemenauer and Cereceda 1992b) and Namib deserts (Eckardt and Schemenauer 1998) under fog conditions were 4.7, 7.4, and 6.3 for pH; 12.3 ppm, 3.4 ppm, and 3.2 ppm for SO_4; 1.6 ppm, 4.7 ppm, and 3.4 ppm for NO_3; 8.7 ppm, 44.7 ppm, and 4.8 ppm for Cl; 1.0 ppm, 15.7 ppm, and 1.2 ppm for Ca; and 0.7 ppm, 2.9 ppm, and 0.4 ppm for Mg, respectively. That is, the fogwater values for these chemicals are far lower than the values that WHO allows as maxima and are definitely suitable for collection schemes.

The high levels of fog in coastal desert fog zones provide habitats extremely favourable for lichen growth (Rundel 1978; Beckett 1998). Much of this moisture is unavailable to vascular plants, allowing a large biomass of lichens (Fig. 2.6) to occur in areas with little or no vascular plant cover.

2.1.1.3 Run-off

High run off from desert slopes (Fig. 2.7) is another factor that leads to high spatial patchiness in some deserts, such that run-on areas (usually in wadis) may have sufficient water availability to maintain important

Fig. 2.6   Foliose lichen, Namib desert, Namibia.

Fig. 2.7   Hillslope system on a limestone hillside in the Negev desert, Israel.

crops. The importance of run-off in desert ecosystem function has been
particularly well studied in the Middle East, where people (most notably,
the Nabateans; Fig. 2.8) exploited its availability from as early as 300 BC.
The Nabatean people grew grapes at the beginning of the Common Era
(AD 0) in the Negev desert (with a probable effective mean annual rainfall
of about 400 mm; this is the minimum required to grow crops) under conditions that did not differ from today's conditions (mean annual rainfall
of 90 mm) (Evenari *et al.* 1982).

Howes and Abrahams (2003) have modelled run-off and run-on processes
in a desert shrubland in the Chihuahuan desert (North America). Run-on
infiltration can supply between 3% and 20% of water flow to shrubs, while
the remainder arrives by direct precipitation on the shrubs (Martinez-Meza
and Whitford 1996). Shrubs often occur on microtopographic mounds a

Fig. 2.8 Khazneh (Treasury) in the capital city of the Nabatean people (100 BC to AD 200) at Petra, Jordan.

few centimetres high, which means that run-on infiltration will not occur unless the flow is sufficiently deep (Howes and Abrahams 2003). The most favourable conditions for run-on infiltration are an initially wet soil and low-intensity rainfall events. Run-on infiltration is generally more effective for shrubs that have grasses at their bases (see also Abrahams *et al.* 1995) than bare soils, because of the greater penetration of the soil by the dense matrix of roots that promote infiltration via the creation of macropores in the soil. Howes and Abrahams (2003) consider run-on infiltration to be ineffective in the summer months when rain falls because of monsoonal events from the Gulf of Mexico that saturate the surface of the soil. In the latter case, the rain passes by the shrubs and empties into the arroyos (wadis). Abrahams *et al.* (1995) have shown that the increased run-off (and erosion) can result in stripping of the surface soils, the formation of desert pavement (*reg*; see below under *Geology*) in intershrub areas, and the development of rills (small channels or streams, usually created by soil erosion) (see below under *Geology*).

2.1.1.4 *Saline soils*

Soils that form in desert climates are predominantly mineral soils with low organic matter content. However, the repeated accumulation of water in certain soils causes salts to precipitate out. When the water table rises to within about 2 m of the ground level, water may begin to rise to the surface by capillary action. When a rising water table intersects with salts that were previously held below the root zone, the salt will dissolve, and be carried up to the surface, concentrating in the upper layers of the soil as water is evaporated. Most playa lakes will consequently be highly saline.

Salinity is typically measured as electrical conductivity (EC), in deciSiemens m^{-1}. Seawater is typically 50–55 dS m^{-1}. When soil salinity exceeds about 2 dS m^{-1}, agricultural crops will generally fail. Salinity disrupts the ion exchange mechanism between soil moisture and plant cells. As a result, plant cells dry out, plants wilt and, therefore, salinity steadily rises. Harmful quantities of nutrients or trace minerals (such as boron, copper, manganese and zinc) can also damage or kill a plant. Salinity changes the electrochemical balance of soil particles. It also destroys physical soil properties, reduces its draining capacity, and increases evaporation and soil erosion.

One form of saline soil is created by gypsum. Eckardt *et al.* (2001) considered that gypsum primarily precipitates at isolated points, such as inland playas. Deflation of evaporitic-rich gypsum dust from these playas contributes to the formation of gypsum duricrusts on the coastal gravel plains of the Namib desert surrounding these playas. Duricrusts are formed when dew creates hardened soil layers, usually consisting of calcium carbonate and aluminium-rich or silica-rich compounds, which act as protective caps on ridges. Eckardt and Schemenauer (1998) tested whether Namib desert fog water carries exceptionally high concentrations of sulphate, which may be responsible for the formation of gypsum deposits in the desert [the chemical formula of gypsum is $CaSO_4 \cdot 2(H_2O)$]. It appears that fog is not an efficient sulphur source for the formation of gypsum deposits, unless rare deposition events with high concentrations of marine sulphur compounds occur. They proposed that, following primary marine aerosol deposition, both inland playas and coastal sabkhas (salty plains where sand is cemented together by minerals left behind from seasonal wetlands) generate gypsum which goes through the process of playa deflation and gravel plain redeposition, thereby contributing to the extensive soil crusts found in the Namib desert region.

There is some variability among deserts in terms of soil salinity (Pankova and Dokuchaev 2006) (Table 2.1). For example, the Mongolian part of the Gobi desert is a stony desert in the centre of Asia with a dry climate that is largely affected by its great distance from the ocean. The mean annual precipitation is about 35 mm, and in some years the desert remains absolutely dry. Strong winds, particularly in the spring, and deep soil freezing in the winter (permafrost) are typical of the Mongolian Gobi. Although flat interfluvial areas account for 90% of the total area in the Gobi desert, about 3–5% of soils (derived from the clayey red-coloured deposits of the Cretaceous–Palaeogene age) are saline. The salt transfer by wind into the adjacent regions leads to soil salinization, even if the soils are developed from non-saline deposits. In the Trans-Altai Gobi, extremely arid soils

Table 2.1 From the FAO/UNESCO soil map of the world, the following percentages of salinized areas can be derived (Brinkman 1980).

Continent	% Salinized area
Africa	69.5
Middle East	53.1
Asia	19.5
South America	59.4
Australia	84.7
North America	16.0
Europe	20.7

are widespread. They are saline at the surface and are underlain by rocks without salts. Saline takyrs (flat or sloping deep clayey soils that act as natural catchments) and solonchaks (highly soluble salt accumulation within 30 cm of the soil surface), often in combination with saline sandy soils, are formed in these depressions. In wet years, during rainfall in the mountains, the mudflows reaching the depressions form temporary lakes. This is the zone of surface run-off accumulation. When the lakes dry out, the surface transforms into solonchaks. In the Ekhiin-Gol natural oasis, the solonchaks may contain up to 40–70% of salts in the surface horizons; the salt content decreases in the deeper layers (50–200 cm). Thus, while the main area of the Mongolian Gobi is occupied by non-saline soils, soil salinization is restricted to the areas of surface run-off accumulation in closed depressions and to natural oases where there is discharge of deep saline groundwater.

2.2 Temperature

The effects of temperature in deserts are widely known. However, little emphasis has been placed on the large differences among deserts in ambient temperature (and seasonality) and how these differences affect the organisms that live there. As mentioned in Chapter 1, the central parts of North American deserts have far higher temperatures and evaporation than African and Middle Eastern deserts, for example, leading to more extreme conditions.

2.2.1 Hot deserts

The highest air temperature ever recorded was 57°C in Azizia in the Libyan part of the Sahara in September 1922 (Page 1984). Temperatures on the soil surface can be considerably higher, as much as 75–80°C (Ward and Seely

1996a). However, the temperature of winter nights in these deserts may fall below freezing point and daytime maximal temperatures may exceed 40°C. The major deserts in this category include the Sahara, Namib, Kalahari, Arabian, Iranian, Sonoran, Mojave, Chihuahuan, and Australian deserts.

2.2.2   Cold deserts

Cold deserts have hot summers counterbalanced by relatively or extremely cold winters (Flegg 1993). For example, for half the year, the Gobi desert lies below 0°C. In the arid parts of Antarctica, mean winter temperatures may be as low as –30°C, while, in summer, diurnal temperatures will exceed 5°C for only a few weeks (Flegg 1993). Most cold deserts lie in the Northern Hemisphere (with the exception of the Patagonian desert) and away from the tropics, because only great distances from the ocean makes them both hot in the summer and cold in the winter. The Patagonian desert is the exception here because it does not occur far from the ocean. Rather, it is the fact that it is in a rain shadow and because it is relatively close to Antarctica that makes it so cold. Cold deserts include the Great Basin, Patagonian, Turkestan, and Gobi deserts (Page 1984; Flegg 1993).

2.3   Geology

Many deserts have very high spatial variation in geological substrates and, consequently, soil type. Deserts can also have shifting habitats created by dune systems, which leads to the formation of unique vegetation forms and their associated fauna (Louw and Seely 1982). Yet other deserts are highly saline (see above). Limestone deserts may support high densities of organisms, such as snails, otherwise associated with mesic ecosystems (e.g. in the Negev desert) (Shachak et al. 1981).

As indicated above, plant productivity in deserts can be nutrient-limited. Nitrogen is the key limiting nutrient in most deserts (Jones and Shachak 1990; Schlesinger et al. 1990, 1996; Schlesinger and Pilmanis 1998; Cross and Schlesinger 1999), phosphorus is the most limiting nutrient in Australian deserts (Beadle 1981), while nitrogen, phosphorus, and potassium are limiting in sand dune communities in Africa's Namib and Kalahari deserts (Robinson 2001; Aranibar et al. 2004). In the Negev desert, for example, nitrogen inputs are often low, soil nitrogen pools small, and losses from run off, erosion, volatilization, and denitrification can be high. Jones and Shachak (1990) have found an unusual but important source of soil nitrogen in the central Negev highlands of Israel, a limestone rock desert with patches of soil. Snails feed on endolithic lichens that grow within the rock, ingesting both rock and lichens, and depositing their faeces on the soil under the rocks. Snails transfer between 22 and 27 mg N m^{-2} per year to soil, which constitutes about 11% of total soil nitrogen inputs, at least 18% of net soil inputs, and a minimum of 27% of the nitrogen annually accumulated by endolithic lichens from dust.

Soil nutrients and organic matter tend to be concentrated in the upper 2–5 cm of the soil with the greatest amounts underneath the canopies of individual desert shrubs in 'islands of fertility' (Caldwell *et al.* 1991; Schlesinger and Pilmanis 1998; Cross and Schlesinger 1999; Schlesinger *et al.* 2000, 2006). These resource islands harbour greater concentrations of water, soil nutrients and microorganisms than adjacent soils (Cross and Schlesinger 1999; Schlesinger *et al.* 2006). Moreover, the distribution of soil nitrogen, phosphorus, and potassium is strongly associated with the presence of shrubs in desert habitats because organic matter from the plants accumulates there (Schlesinger and Pilmanis 1998; Cross and Schlesinger 1999; Aranibar *et al.* 2004). Shrubs concentrate the biogeochemical cycle of these elements in 'islands of fertility' that are localized beneath their canopies, while adjacent barren, intershrub spaces are comparatively devoid of biotic activity (Schlesinger and Pilmanis 1998).

Desert animals building their burrows in soil, such as isopods (which also consume it), termites, ants, and rodents, change the chemical and physical qualities of the soil (including porosity, water-holding capacity, infiltration rates, redistribution of nutrients, and organic matter) and they can affect soil erosion and redeposition (Whitford 2002). For example, Shachak *et al.* (1976) have shown that the isopod *Hemilepistus reaumuri* in the Negev desert highlands has an annual soil turnover of 28.5–105.7 g m^{-2}.

Thus, this variability in substrate type, while generally of lesser importance than rainfall and temperature, may play a key role in determining where desert organisms can live because rainfall and temperature vary relatively little within a particular area of a desert but substrates can vary considerably.

2.3.1 Desert landscapes

There are five major types of desert landscapes that are commonly recognized (Flegg 1993).

2.3.1.1 Sand

The sand desert landscape that is not as common as is often perceived, and probably accounts for as little as 15–20% of deserts. Bagnold (1941) found that the wind must reach a particular speed before sand grains begin to roll along the surface. When a rolling grain encounters a stationary one, the collision may knock the other grain forward or propel it into the air. A fast-moving grain that strikes a pebble or another large obstacle may bounce into the air (Page 1984). However, the flight of any single sand grain is usually short-lived. Even in the worst sandstorms, individual

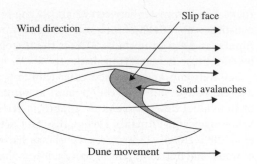

Fig. 2.9   Schematic diagram of a barchan dune. (This U. S. National Park Service file [Date accessed: 12 June 2008] is licensed under the Creative Commons Attribution ShareAlike 2.5 License.)

grains seldom reach heights greater than 1 m. When the sand grain lands, it knocks other sand grains around. If the wind continues to blow, the air near the surface is soon filled with bouncing sand grains, with larger particles rolling along the ground. If a stream of moving sand encounters an obstruction, the air flow is disrupted. In front of the obstacle and to a larger degree just behind it, wind velocity drops and sand grains pile up (Bagnold 1941). The accumulation behind the obstruction is initially the larger of the two piles, but later they coalesce into one mound, which is the beginning of dune formation (Lancaster 1995). The shape it takes depends on wind velocity and sometimes by the amount of sand available. Dunes may form in a number of ways:

Barchan dunes—these usually are formed on the margins of deserts where the wind direction is generally more uniform and the amount of sand is moderate. The tips of the crescent (Fig. 2.9) point downwind and are lower than its centre, where air flow is impeded most and sand accumulates in larger quantities. Some of these dunes can be rather high. The complex transverse megadunes, which resemble the barchan dunes in terms of wind direction and amount of sand, range in height between 180 and 350 m and may reach as much as 400 m in the Badain Jaran desert (part of the Alashan desert, in turn part of the Gobi desert) (Dong *et al.* 2004).

Seifs or longitudinal dunes—where sand is more plentiful, a steady wind creates transverse dunes shaped similar to long waves with crests perpendicular to the wind and with gentle windward slopes (lee slopes are often called the slip face) (Fig. 2.10). Bristow *et al.* (2005) consider this to be the most abundant type of desert dune. Bristow *et al.* (2007) have shown that longitudinal dunes (also known as linear dunes) are not fixed in space and may move considerably (about 300 m or more) under certain wind conditions. Bristow *et al.* (2007) have also shown that longitudinal dunes in the Namib desert may undergo several phases of construction. One dune

Fig. 2.10   Longitudinal dunes, Namib desert. (Photograph courtesy of Megan Griffiths.)

Fig. 2.11   Star dunes, Namib desert. (Photograph courtesy of Megan Griffiths.)

had a hiatus of about 2,000 years and took a total of about 5,700 years to construct to its current height. Seif and longitudinal dunes may exceed 40 m in height and may extend for hundreds of kilometres, as much as 250–400 km (e.g. in the Sahara, Namib desert, Thar desert in India, and the western part of the Great Australian desert). Where wind directions are less well defined, both barchan and seif systems may merge into areas of complete sand cover (Flegg 1993).

Star dunes—if the sand is confined to a basin, and the wind periodically radically changes its direction, the resulting dunes will become complex in shape and may be called star dunes (Fig. 2.11).

Loess—It is an important form of wind-blown silt deposit, which even on the least windy days can form a fog of dust (Pye 1987). It consists mostly of quartz, feldspar, mica, clay minerals and carbonate grains in varying proportions (Pye 1984). Strong winds can carry these dust particles many thousands of kilometres. White dust in the summer and red dust in the winter can spread from the Sahara and the Arabian deserts over the Mediterranean Sea even reaching as far as Sweden (Page 1984). The highest dust storm frequencies occur in the arid and semi-arid regions of the world, with a mean frequency of 80.7 days when visibility at eye level is less than 1,000 m being recorded in the Seistan Basin of Iran (Middleton 1986). Pye (1987) has noted that the frequency of dust storms shows a weak negative relationship with mean annual precipitation, with areas receiving 100–200 mm rainfall having markedly higher dust storm frequencies. Goudie (1983) suggested that this may be because infrequent stream run-off limits dust supply or because strong winds associated with storm fronts and cyclonic disturbances are rare in these areas. In contrast, the higher dust storm frequencies could be related to greater fluvial activity, greater dust supply and more frequent strong winds. Pye (1987) believes that it is more likely that recent cultivation is a more important source of dust on desert-margin soils.

The Loess Plateau in China (also known as the Huangtu Plateau) contains some of the most impressive loess deposits recorded anywhere. It covers about 640,000 km^2 around the Huang He (Yellow River). Liu *et al.* (1981) recorded that dust that had been transported from the deserts of northwestern China to Beijing (more than 3,000 km) contained greater than 90% of its particles that were less than 30 μm in size. The initial desertification in the Asian interior is thought to be one of the most prominent climatic changes in the Northern Hemisphere during the Cenozoic era (65 million years ago until the present). However, the dating of this transition is uncertain, partly because desert sediments are usually scattered, discontinuous and difficult to date. Guo *et al.* (2002) reported nearly continuous aeolian deposits covering the interval from 22 to 6.2 million years ago, on the basis of palaeomagnetic measurements and fossil evidences. Over 230 visually definable aeolian layers occur in the Huangtu Plateau as brownish loesses interbedded with reddish soils. Soil and loess can be distinguished because soil is reddish in colour and contains organic matter and many finer particles, while loess is paler and grainier. When strong winds blow from the desert, loess is brought into the region, while soil accumulates when it is wet or a different wind blows. Guo *et al.* (2002) indicate that large source areas of aeolian dust (and energetic winter monsoon winds to transport the material) must have existed in the interior of Asia by the early Miocene epoch, 22 million years BP, which is at least 14 million years earlier than previously thought. Regional tectonic changes and ongoing global cooling are considered by Guo *et al.* (2002) to be probable causes for these changes in aridity and circulation in Asia.

2.3.1.2 Stone

Stone substrates usually have relatively level gravel surfaces. This is known as desert pavement (also known as *reg*—Fig. 2.12), which is a dense cover of rocks too large to be carried away by wind or water. Silt, sand and smaller pebbles have been removed by a gradual erosive process called deflation (Page 1984). After a long time, the remaining stones settle into a coarse mosaic, resembling a street paved with cobblestones (hence the name *desert pavement*), which presents a shield against further erosion.

Desert pavement is frequently coated with desert patina (also known as *desert varnish*), which is a black or brown coating on the outer surface of the rocks (Fig. 2.13). This gives a similar veneer to the rocks of various different compositions, created by oxides of iron and manganese and deposited by wind and water from rain and dew. This process takes thousands of years. In the Sinai desert, thousands of square kilometres are covered with reg.

2.3.1.3 Rock

Rock desert landscapes normally have bare rock surfaces, with a huge pavement kept clear of sand and gravel by the wind.

Fig. 2.12   Reg, Negev desert.

Fig. 2.13   Desert patina with an ibex engraved on the thin outer surface of iron/manganese in the Negev desert.

2.3.1.4 Plateaux

Rocky plateau landscapes are often deeply dissected by ephemeral rivers (wadis). In some cases, notable repetitions of anticlines and synclines occur. This occurs in a desert landform known as *mountain-and-basin* desert (Ezcurra 2006). An anticline is a trough-like upfold of the earth while a syncline is a trough-like downfold (Strahler 1976). In a few cases, anticlines may erode through the soft rock at the top, creating a wadi along its length. Such an anticline is known as an erosional cirque (Ben-David and Mazor 1988; Plakht 1996) or *makhtesh* (Hebrew) (Fig. 2.14). They are only known from the western edge of the Arabian desert in Israel, Jordan, and Syria (Plakht 1996).

2.3.1.5 Mountain

Mountain desert landscapes are bare arrays of rocky peaks, such as in the Sinai portion of the Arabian desert and the granitic areas of the Namib desert (Fig. 2.15). These mountainous deserts constitute a second landform (see *mountain-and-basin landform* under *Plateaux* above) called a *shield* desert, which has very old igneous rocks. This includes the Sinai desert, as well as the Australian and southern African deserts and the Sahara. Unlike the mountain-and-basin deserts, wind is a more effective force than water in shield deserts. Note that the Australian deserts are, topographically speaking, extremely flat (Stafford Smith and Morton 1990); therefore, mountains are found only in a few places. Nonetheless, the mountains that occur consist of old igneous rocks.

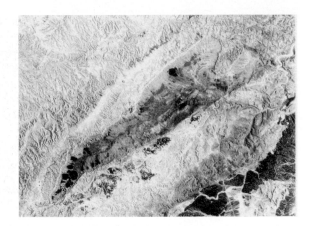

Fig. 2.14   Satellite photograph of Makhtesh Ramon, a Negev desert erosion cirque. The dark objects are basalt hills.

Fig. 2.15   Granitic hills of the Namib, near Spitzkoppe. (Photograph courtesy of Megan Griffiths.)

2.4   Fire

Generally, fire is not considered as an important factor in desert ecosystems because fuel loads are generally too low (McPherson 1995; Higgins *et al.* 2000; Meyer *et al.* 2005). However, McPherson (1995) considered three conditions for fires to spread, namely, an ignition source, sufficient fine fuel, and the fuel must be sufficiently dry to burn. All of these conditions occur in the North American desert grasslands (McPherson 1995). Clearly, there is sufficient fine fuel from the grasses and the fuel is dry enough to burn. Lightning storms prior to the onset of monsoon rains in June or July provide opportunities for fires to ignite in desert grasslands of North America (McPherson 1995). Humphrey (1958) reviewed historical fire accounts dating back to 1528 in the North American desert grasslands and considered fires critical to the maintenance of these grasslands by preventing them from succeeding towards shrubs and trees.

In Australia, spinifex grasslands (mostly *Triodia* species) and many woody desert plants are renowned for their ability to burn (Stafford Smith and Morton 1990; Orians and Milewski 2007). Spinifex plants have high resin contents and they have low levels of nutrients (which means that consumption rates by herbivores are low) and decomposition rates of ligneous litter are also low. Thus, litter and standing biomass accumulate rapidly in some areas of Australian deserts (Stafford Smith and Morton 1990). Fires may range in intensity from ground fires that consume litter and small plants to stand-destroying fires that kill all plants such that they are unable to resprout from underground storage organs (Orians and Milewski 2007). Meyer *et al.* (2005) found that fires can also occur in arid regions of South Africa and may, paradoxically, kill off larger trees and leave smaller trees behind. The effects of fires may be increasing in many parts of the world, including deserts, as a consequence of the increase in shrub or bush encroachment (see Chapter 10).

3 Morphological and physiological adaptations of desert plants to the abiotic environment

Some of the most interesting adaptations of plants to their environments are shown by desert plants. One need to only think of the cacti of North and Central America, *Welwitschia mirabilis* of the Namib, and the Mesembryanthema (Aizoaceae) of the Karoo in South Africa to realize that deserts contain a uniquely adapted flora. Geophytes and other plants with special storage organs may be considered to be pre-adapted to desert conditions, while trees and shrubs with deep root systems are able to exploit deep aquifers in an otherwise dry environment. Many annual plants do not have clear morphological or physiological adaptations to the desert environment but thrive there by germinating immediately after the infrequent rains and completing their life cycles before the onset of the summer heat. This chapter will also examine the various ways in which mesic plants have been able to exploit resource variability to survive in extreme desert environments.

3.1   Classifications of desert plants

There are several ways to approach the study of desert plants and their relationships with their abiotic environments (cf. Shantz 1927; Raunkiaer 1934; Evenari 1985; Danin and Orshan 1990; Smith *et al.* 1997). For example, Shantz (1927) classified desert plant strategies in terms of their abilities to tolerate or avoid drought:

1. *Drought escaping*—plants that grow only when water is available. These are usually annual plants that are ephemeral and restrict their growth to those periods, usually in the spring, when there is sufficient water for plant growth and reproduction.

2. *Drought evading*—these plants avoid periods of limited soil moisture by using morphological features such as deep roots (e.g. in riparian trees from southern Africa such as camelthorn, *Acacia erioloba*, and shepherd's tree, *Boscia albitrunca*, which have roots as deep as 68 m (Jennings 1974)), stem succulence (e.g. cacti in the Americas and euphorbs in Africa) and/or physiological features such as stomatal control of water loss and crassulacean acid metabolism (CAM) photosynthesis. Drought avoidance is characterized by stomata that close at higher water potentials, larger leaves with less vertical orientation and less ability for the accumulation of solutes and/or maintenance of high tissue elasticity (Smith *et al.* 1997). Inward contraction of elastic walls can cause a loss of volume, allowing for the maintenance of turgor pressure (Smith *et al.* 1997). Monson and Smith (1982) showed that maintenance or seasonal adjustment of low osmotic potentials was negatively correlated with drought avoidance (Fig. 3.1).

3. *Drought enduring*—plants that possess rapid gas exchange (with less stomatal control of water loss) and shed their leaves when droughts occur. This includes most desert shrubs, such as *Hammada scoparia* (Chenopodiaceae) in the Middle East.

4. *Drought resisting*—plants with moderate rates of gas exchange when water is plentiful but able to maintain some reduced level of gas

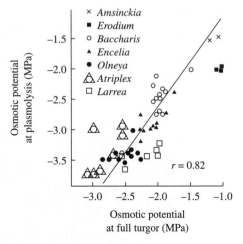

Fig. 3.1   Monson and Smith (1982) found a strong positive correlation between water potential at full turgor and water potential at plasmolysis (also called the turgor loss point), which indicated that maintenance of low osmotic potentials was negatively correlated with drought avoidance. The species involved were *Amsinckia intermedia* and *Erodium cicutarium* (both annual herbs), *Olneya tesota* (evergreen tree), *Larrea tridentata* (evergreen shrub), *Baccharis sarothroides* (evergreen tree or shrub), *Atriplex polycarpa* (evergreen halophyte shrub) and *Encelia farinosa* (drought-deciduous shrub). Note that the axes are reversed. (From Monson and Smith 1982. With kind permission of Springer Science and Business Media.)

exchange during periods of water stress. These plants are characterized by having stomata that close at low plant water potentials, small leaves with a tendency for vertical orientation, low hydraulic conductance of the xylem, and high capacity to accumulate solutes and/or maintain high tissue elasticity to ensure turgor maintenance (Smith *et al.* 1997). Only a few plants fall into this category, including the creosote bush *Larrea tridentata* and some plants in Middle Eastern deserts, such as *Zygophyllum dumosum* and *Anabasis articulata* (Fig. 3.2). Note that *drought tolerance* is a synonym for *drought resisting*. In addition, the terms *drought stress, water stress,* and *water deficit* are often used interchangeably.

One limitation to this categorization is that it does not accommodate the mistletoes (Loranthaceae and Viscaceae) (Fig. 3.3). These hemiparasitic plants are capable of photosynthesizing but do so at the expense of their hosts, from which they gain water and nutrients (Bowie and Ward 2004). Through passive water uptake, mistletoes open their stomata and transpire profligate amounts of water from the xylem to access nutrients such as nitrogen. Some mistletoes (e.g. *Plicosepalus acaciae* which grows on a number of plants, especially *Acacia raddiana* and *A. tortilis*) also take up water from the phloem using active water uptake, which does not require large amounts of water (Bowie and Ward 2004).

Raunkiaer (1934) developed an alternative classification system based on the strategy a plant uses to protect its perennating buds (growing points), noting that plants will maximize the survival of these buds during dry or cold seasons (not all of Raunkiaer's (1934) types are listed here because some are not pertinent to plants growing in xeric conditions):

Fig. 3.2   *Anabasis articulata* from the Negev desert, Israel.

Fig. 3.3   Hemiparasitic mistletoe, *Viscum rotundifolium*, from the arid Northern Cape province, South Africa.

Fig. 3.4   Annual plant, *Picris damascena*, from the Negev desert, Israel.

1. *Therophyte*—annuals (Fig. 3.4).
2. *Phanerophyte*—the surviving buds or shoot apices are borne on shoots which project into the air.
3. *Chamaephyte*—a perennial plant that sets its dormant vegetative buds just at or above the surface of the ground and that dies back periodically. Usually, the difference between the phanerophytes and chamaephytes is somewhat arbitrary but diffentiates trees (phanerophytes) and shrubs (chamaephytes).

Fig. 3.5   A geophyte, *Tulipa systola*, from the Negev desert, Israel.

4. *Cryptophyte*—plants whose buds develop underground or underwater. In the terrestrial case, they can be divided into:
   a. *Geophyte*—a perennial plant that propagates by underground bulbs, tubers or corms (Fig. 3.5).
   b. *Halophyte*—plants living in or near saline conditions.
5. *Hemicryptophyte*—the surviving buds or shoot apices are situated in the soil surface and die back during unfavourable conditions.
6. *Vascular hemiparasite*—parasitic plants that photosynthesize, e.g. mistletoes such as *P. acaciae* (Loranthaceae, Middle East) or root parasites such as *Santalum acuminatum* (Santalaceae, Australia).
7. *Vascular parasite*—plant that is entirely dependent on other plants, including root parasites such as *Orobanche* (Orobanchaceae) in the Negev desert (Fig. 3.6) and stem parasites such as *Cuscuta* (Cuscutaceae or Scrophulariaceae, depending on the classification).

Raunkiaer's classification system is probably most appropriate for buds escaping freezing rather than dry conditions (Danin and Orshan 1990; Smith *et al.* 1997). The limitation of this classification system in desert scenarios is that plant water and carbon relations during favourable seasons may be more important in determining the success of plants than the location of buds (Schulze 1982). For example, phreatophytes are deep-rooted plants (usually trees) that use the water table or some other permanent water supply. Nonetheless, Raunkiaer's (1934) system is widely used, although one needs to be aware of the fact that it is somewhat limited in its generality.

Overall, a structure–function classification is the most useful way to categorize desert plants (see also Danin and Orshan 1990; Smith *et al.* 1997).

Fig. 3.6   A root parasite, *Orobanche aegyptiaca*, growing on *Atriplex halimus* in the Negev desert, Israel.

3.2   Types of photosynthesis

Before embarking on the analysis of relationships between plants and their desert environments (reviewed in Table 3.1), it is important to consider some basics of photosynthesis that allow a plant to convert carbon dioxide into sugars (carbohydrates). There are three major types of photosynthesis:

1. *C₃ photosynthesis*—it is most common for plants to use the C_3 metabolic pathway, which means that CO_2 is attached to the 5-carbon sugar RuBP (ribulose bisphosphate) with the assistance of the enzyme RuBP carboxylase-oxygenase (also known as Rubisco), and will then be converted into sugar. There are two phosphoglycerate (PGA) sugar molecules produced by this form of photosynthesis. They are C_3 molecules, hence the name of this photosynthetic pathway. C_3 photosynthesis is a diurnal process. The ratio of CO_2 to O_2 is very low, resulting in a considerable amount of photorespiration, which results in a lower level of net photosynthetic efficiency than in C_4 plants (about one-third lower efficiency). C_3 photosynthesis is considered the most simple and least derived photosynthetic pathway (Ehleringer and Monson 1993). In spite

Table 3.1 Adaptive characteristics of the major structural/functional groups of plants in the deserts of North America. (After Smith *et al.* 1997.)

Adaptation	Structural/functional group					
	Annuals	Perennial grasses	Deep-rooted trees	CAM succulents	Deciduous shrubs	Evergreen shrubs
Small leaves	Typically not	Yes, but dense	Variable, usually small	No	Variable, many broad	Yes
Waxy cuticle, sunken stomata	No	No	No	Yes	Variable	Yes
Shallow roots	Yes	Variable, usually yes	No	Yes	Variable, usually yes	Variable
High root:shoot ratio	No	Variable	Variable	Mass: no Area: yes	Variable	Variable, often high
High water stress tolerance	No	Variable, some yes	No	Plant: yes Tissues: no	Variable, usually yes	Yes, very high
High heat tolerance	No	C_3: no C_4: yes	No	Yes, very high	No	Yes
Low photosynthetic and growth rates	No	No	No	Yes	No	Yes
High water-use efficiency	No	No	No	Yes	Variable	Yes
High nutrient-use efficiency	No	Variable	No	Yes	Variable	Yes
Opportunistic phenology	Yes	No	No	No	Variable	No

of the fact that this form of photosynthesis is energetically expensive, it occurs in many desert plants, especially dicotyledonous plants.

2. *C_4 photosynthesis*—the C_4 pathway is most commonly used by plants in arid environments (i.e. with high light levels and temperatures) that have a lot of water available to them in the summer. This form of photosynthesis also occurs diurnally. Here, CO_2 is converted into oxaloacetate (a C_4 sugar) by PEP carboxylase and then into a sugar (either malate or aspartate) by RuBP carboxylase (Rubisco) inside the bundle sheath cells. The PEP carboxylase is more efficient than Rubisco because it matches its substrate better, has greater velocity than Rubisco and effectively acts as a CO_2 pump. C_4 plants still use the C_3 method in their internal cells (typically the bundle sheath) but their external mesophyll cells use the C_4 method. There is a distinct spatial segregation of the bundle sheath cells where C_3 photosynthesis occurs and the exterior mesophyll cells where C_4 photosynthesis occurs. This is created by a structure known as Kranz anatomy (Ehleringer and Monson 1993). The

Rubisco reactions in C_4 plants take place under higher CO_2/O_2 levels and photorespiration is effectively eliminated.

3. *CAM (Crassulacean Acid Metabolism)*—this photosynthetic pathway is employed by many succulent plants such as aloes, cacti (Cactaceae), agaves (Agavaceae), euphorbias (Euphorbiaceae), ice plants (Mesembryanthema, Aizoaceae), and crassulas (Crassulaceae; from which the name of the photosynthetic pathway is derived). The CAM pathway is used in deserts that have high light levels, high temperatures, and low levels of moisture in the summer. Thus, one major difference between C_4 photosynthesis and CAM is that C_4 photosynthesis takes place when water is readily available while CAM is restricted to low water conditions. CAM photosynthesis takes place in two stages. The first stage takes place nocturnally when the stomata of the plant are opened. CO_2 enters the leaf through the open stomata and is fixed and stored as an acid (usually malic acid). The second stage of the CAM process takes place diurnally while the stomata are closed. The CO_2 is released from the malic acid and is then used to make sugar with the aid of RuBP carboxylase. While C_4 plants use a different *spatial* strategy for C_3 photosynthesis (Kranz anatomy), CAM plants have a different *temporal* strategy for C_3 photosynthesis (night vs. day).

CAM plants may also employ C_3 photosynthesis when conditions improve but never use C_4 photosynthesis. An interesting example of a switch between CAM (i.e. nocturnal photosynthesis) and diurnal photosynthesis occurs in *Agave deserti* (Agavaceae), which changes photosynthetic pathway when given supplemental water (Hartsock and Nobel 1976) (Fig. 3.7).

Compared with other pathways, C_4 photosynthesis requires two extra molecules of ATP to reduce a CO_2 molecule, which should make C_3 photosynthesis more light-use efficient. However, this only occurs at leaf

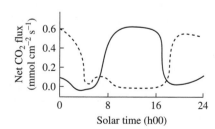

Fig. 3.7 Conversion in photosynthetic pattern (measured as CO_2 flux) from CAM (dashed line) to diurnal photosynthesis (solid line) in *Agave deserti* after watering. Soil water potentials were raised from -9 MPa to -0.01 MPa. Note the switch from nocturnal CO_2 flux under CAM conditions to diurnal CO_2 flux under watered conditions. (From Hartsock and Nobel 1979. With kind permission of Nature Publishing Group.)

temperatures below about 25–30°C (Ehleringer and Monson 1993). Above this temperature range, there is a negative effect of photorespiration on C_3 photosynthesis. Because there is no temperature constraint on C_4 and CAM photosynthesis, these two photosynthetic pathways have a greater light-use efficiency at high temperatures. C_4 photosynthesis is also more water-use efficient because the greater CO_2 pump activity of PEP carboxylase makes it mostly independent of CO_2 inside the leaf. Furthermore, changes in the degree of stomatal opening exert little influence on photosynthetic rates in C_4 plants over a broad range of stomatal openings. However, rates of transpirational water loss are directly proportional to the degree of stomatal opening in C_3 and C_4 plants. Therefore, water-use efficiency (the ratio of photosynthesis:transpirational water loss) is higher in C_4 plants than in C_3 plants. CAM plants have an even higher water-use efficiency because their stomata are only opened at night, when transpirational water loss is low. Thus, at equivalent rates of water loss, a C_4 or CAM leaf is expected to photosynthesize more than an adjacent C_3 leaf operating under the same set of environmental conditions (Ehleringer and Monson 1993).

One would expect that C_4 and CAM plants should occur under more arid conditions than C_3 plants. In the North American deserts, C_3 plants typically occur in the winter rainfall Mojave desert, C_3 and C_4 plants in the summer- and winter-rainfall Sonoran desert, and mostly C_4 plants in the summer rainfall Chihuahuan desert (Ludwig et al. 1988; Smith et al. 1997; Huxman and Monson 2003). In the Chihuahuan desert, Eickmeier (1978) found that, of 88 species, the dominant plants changed from CAM to C_4 to C_3 as aridity declined, although CAM plants tend to be somewhat bimodally distributed (Eickmeier 1978). CAM plants occupy the most arid sites along the Californian and Chilean coasts (Mooney et al. 1974). In semi-arid southwestern Madagascar, succulent CAM plants of the families Euphorbiaceae and Didiereaceae are predominant (Winter 1979). Along a gradient of desert to Mediterranean climate in the northern Sahara desert, $\delta^{13}C$ isotopes have been used to identify C_3 and C_4 plants. Typically, C_4 plants have higher values (−9 to −16‰) than C_3 plants (−25 to −32‰) (Winter et al. 1978; Ehleringer 1993). Winter et al. (1978) found that C_3 species predominate in the Mediterranean region and the C_4 species in the desert.

Contrary to expectation, Hattersley (1983) examined the distribution of C_3 and C_4 grasses relative to climate in Australia and concluded that C_4 species are most abundant where summers are hot and wet and decline with decreasing temperature and/or decreasing summer rainfall, whereas C_3 species are most numerous where the spring is cool and wet and decline with increasing temperature and/or decreasing spring rainfall. Similarly, in the cold-winter Great Basin desert, both C_3 and C_4 plants are common strategies (Caldwell et al. 1977). In the very hot and arid Death Valley of California, both C_3 and C_4 plants grow in close proximity (Mooney et al.

1975). It appears that C_3 and C_4 plants can coexist in deserts such as the Namib, Great Basin, and Negev (Vogel and Seely 1977).

Summer temperatures through most of Namibia are remarkably similar (around 30–40°C), except for the cooler temperatures (about 20°C) of the narrow Atlantic Ocean coastal region. While ambient temperature is relatively high, rainfall exhibits a gradient from about 10 mm to more than 600 mm per annum in a northeasterly direction. C_4 grasses are dominant throughout Namibia. In the central Namib desert, non-grass species are mostly C_3 (Vogel and Seely 1977). C_3 grass species have a limited distribution, making up about 18% of the grass species in the dry southwest with winter rainfall and about 15% of species in the mesic northeast. Clearly, C_3 grasses cannot be restricted by rainfall, being present at either end of the rainfall gradient. However, in the low rainfall areas of the southwest they tend to favour moist microhabitats (Ellis *et al.* 1980).

Nonetheless, it appears that plants with different types of C_4 photosynthesis differ in their responses to rainfall in Namibia. All C_4 grasses have Kranz anatomy and initially fix CO_2 in the mesophyll cells, which results in the formation of oxaloacetate and is converted into either malate and/or aspartate. Depending on the relative quantities of malate and aspartate formed, two distinct groups of C_4 plants are recognized (Gutierrez *et al.* 1974; Edwards *et al.* 2001):

1. Aspartate formers with an inner bundle (mestome) between the metaxylem elements and the Kranz sheath. There are two subtypes of aspartate former: those using PEP-carboxykinase (PEP-ck) and those using NAD-malic enzyme (NAD-me). PEP-ck species have centrifugally located chloroplasts that lie against the outer wall of the Kranz sheath cells while the NAD-me species have centripetally located chloroplasts.
2. Malate formers with a single chlorenchymatous or Kranz sheath and centrifugal chloroplasts formed around the vascular bundles. The malate formers lack well-developed grana in the chloroplasts and have a low mitochondrial frequency. Also, malate formers do not show a post-illumination CO_2 'burst' as the aspartate formers do.

Ellis *et al.* (1980) found that malate formers increased in abundance relative to rainfall (contrary to the expectation if they were true arid-zone plants), NAD-me aspartate species decreased in abundance with increasing rainfall, while PEP-ck aspartate-forming species were intermediate in their distributions. Thus, the type of C_4 distribution may be affected by climate, with NAD-me species more common in truly xeric areas.

There are also a number of interesting phylogenetic and biogeographic issues involved in explaining the patterns of photosynthesis observed today (Ehleringer and Monson 1993). For example, C_4 photosynthesis has evolved at least three times in the grasses (Poaceae) (Brown and Smith 1972) and at least twice in the widespread genus *Atriplex* (Chenopodiaceae). Brown and Smith (1972) have examined the presence of C_4 photosynthesis in the grasses and have shown that it is consistent with Wegener's (1966) notion of continental drift. For example, they showed that the tribes Eragrostoideae and Aristideae have Kranz anatomy (i.e. they are C_4 species) and are found in all the major deserts of the world, which can only be explained by the presence of a single continent of Pangaea. Johnson (1975) analyzed about 1,000 desert species in California and found that about 85% were C_3, 11% were C_4, and 4% were CAM. However, Johnson (1975) found that more than half the C_4 species were grasses (Poaceae). In the Crassulaceae, the group for which CAM is named, North American species exhibit only CAM recycling, which means that there is C_3 uptake of CO_2 with capacity to recycle respired CO_2 at night. However, full CAM ability has evolved at least twice in trans-Mexican species (Ehleringer and Monson 1993). Another interesting point is that C_4 dicotyledons do not follow the climate relationships that have been reported for C_3 monocotyledons. Stowe and Teeri (1978) found that the representation of dicot species in local floras of North America was more highly correlated with indices of aridity than indices solely describing temperature.

However, even C_3 species in those families that contained C_4 dicots exhibited significant correlations with aridity, suggesting a phylogenetic component independent of photosynthetic pathway. Assuming that C_3 photosynthesis was ancestral in these families, the results suggest a pattern of C_4 evolution in those North American dicot taxa predisposed to growth in arid habitats. Nonetheless, Evenari (1985), and Ehleringer and Monson (1993) after him, considers it an unresolved issue and assume that there must be a trade-off between photosynthetic ability and competition under conditions of high temperature (with C_3 plants being more effective and competitively dominant at lower temperatures and C_4 plants being dominant at higher temperatures because of their greater water-use efficiency). Should researchers have studied the different forms of C_4 photosynthesis, as Ellis *et al.* (1980) did (see above), they may have been able to understand whether it is the subtype rather than merely the type (i.e. C_3 vs. C_4) that differs.

3.3   Biological soil crusts

In arid and semi-arid parts of the world, autotrophic organisms occur in the open spaces between higher plants. These organisms are called biological soil crusts (Fig. 3.8) or, alternatively, cryptogamic, cryptobiotic, microbiotic or microphytic communities (West 1990). In general, the higher the vegetative cover of higher plants, the lower the cover by biological soil crusts. Biological soil crusts differ from mechanical and chemical crusts. Mechanical and chemical crusts are formed by clays or salts in the soils. Biological crusts, on the other hand, are formed from a combination of cyanobacteria, algae, lichens, mosses, bacteria, and fungi. Mechanical and chemical crusts tend to cause run-off of surface flow, increasing loss

Fig. 3.8   Biological soil crust.

of precipitation from an ecosystem (Savory 1988) while biological crusts increase infiltration, and thus have positive local effects. They may also increase nitrogen fixation (5–88% of nitrogen fixed by a cyanobacterium is released to neighbouring vascular plants) (Belnap and Harper 1995), reduce wind and water erosion, and contribute to local soil organic matter (Eldridge and Greene 1994).

Biological crusts may constitute as much as 70% of the cover of biological organisms in a particular community. Structurally, they form a low surface of 1–10 cm above ground. Below ground, they bind the soil or sand together by means of cyanobacterial filaments, fungal hyphae and moss and lichen rhizines (a root-like filament growing from moss, and lichens). These organisms are capable of withstanding desiccation and suspending respiration with no apparent negative effects (Belnap *et al.* 2001), unlike vascular plants that either regrow or die. These organisms are considered poikilohydric and often equilibrate their activities with that of atmospheric humidity or soil moisture content (Belnap *et al.* 2001). They can appear dark or black (especially cyanobacteria) until they photosynthesize, when they change colour (to green) within minutes. These organisms require relatively high levels of hydration to photosynthesize.

3.4   Annual plants

Annual plants live for one growing season or year and then survive until the following growing season as seeds. Smith *et al.* (1997) emphasized that desert annuals have little capacity for photosynthetic acclimation, unlike evergreen species, and are unable to handle severe drought. Some annuals are amphiphytic, that is, they may be annual or perennial depending on local environmental conditions (Orshan 1986; Danin 1996). For example, several species of the grass genus *Stipagrostis* (e.g. *S. plumosa*, *S. ciliata*, and *S. hirtigluma*) are perennial under moderate conditions but are annual when conditions become more extreme (Danin 1996). A few species of *Fagonia* are also capable of this behaviour (Orshan 1986).

Annuals can be classified as winter and summer annuals. Winter annuals have three features that differentiate them from summer annuals:

1. *Height*—they are usually shorter than summer annuals, keeping their leaves closer to the soil surface where the ambient temperatures are warmer during the cool winter.
2. *Basal rosette*—they keep their leaves in a single layer near the soil surface. These leaves are usually non-overlapping to maximize solar radiation in the afternoon.
3. *Leaf dissection*—leaves are highly dissected, perhaps because this decreases boundary layer effects, increasing CO_2 passage into the leaf for photosynthesis (Mulroy and Rundel 1977).

Summer annuals have the following features:

1. *Leaf size*—leaves are displayed along the entire vertical length of the stem and are smaller in size to reduce the heat load during the day, leading to more efficient cooling by convection.
2. *Height*—they keep their leaves as high as they can above the soil surface to reduce high ambient temperatures that can lead to inhibition of photosynthesis.
3. *Solar tracking*—leaves maintain their orientation to the sun throughout the day, which provides the plant with a high rate of carbon gain when growth is more limited by light availability than by precipitation or nutrient availability. Ehleringer and Forseth (1980) found that winter annuals in the Mojave desert show solar tracking in 28% of species but 75% of summer annual species in the Sonoran desert show solar tracking.

One means of achieving high photosynthetic performance is to load the leaves with high levels of crude protein (15–28%) and have a high leaf conductance; for this reason, desert annuals have the highest photosynthetic rates recorded in terrestrial plants (Werk *et al.* 1983). Another strategy is solar tracking, which allows plants to maintain maximum rates of photosynthesis throughout the day, while non-trackers reach a maximum for only a few hours of the day when the solar angle is high (Mulroy and Rundel 1977).

3.4.1   Desert versus mesic annual species

An effective way to establish the nature of adaptations is to make comparisons among congenerics or among races or populations of the same species. For example, *Machaeranthera gracilis* (Asteraceae) has both desert and foothills races in the Sonoran desert. The foothills race occurs in cooler and wetter pinyon-juniper and ponderosa pine woodlands and the desert race in the hotter and drier lowlands (Jackson and Crovello 1971). Plants of the desert race have higher photosynthetic rates than the foothills race, reach anthesis sooner after germinating, and allocate more biomass to reproduction (Anderson and Szarek 1981; Monson and Szarek 1981). Studies of conspecific desert and Mediterranean populations of several annual species (*Erucaria hispanica, Brachypodium distachyon, Bromus fasciculatus* and *Hordeum spontaneum* (wild barley), *Triticum dicoccoides* (wild emmer wheat), and *Avena sterilis* (wild oats)) demonstrate patterns similar to those observed in *M. gracilis*, with accelerated growth rates in desert forms compared with Mediterranean plants (Nevo *et al.* 1984; Aronson *et al.* 1990, 1992; Volis *et al.* 2004; Volis 2007). Desert populations exhibit greater sensitivity to late-season water stresses and have greater seed set and senescence of vegetative growth, resulting in higher reproductive allocation (Aronson *et al.* 1992; Boaz *et al.* 1994; Owuor *et al.* 1999; Volis *et al.* 2004). Volis (2007) found that both *H. spontaneum* and *A. sterilis* had earlier onset of flowering and produced more seeds that were smaller at the arid end of the rainfall gradient than at the Mediterranean end of the gradient. Similarly, more seeds per plant but of smaller size were also observed in the desert as compared with the Mediterranean population of an annual grass *Stipa capensis* (Aronson *et al.* 1990). These findings emphasize the importance of seed size as part of a plant's reproductive strategy (Leishman and Westoby 1994). The initial seedling size is positively correlated with seed size (Leishman *et al.* 2000). Although larger initial seedling size may be advantageous under competition or drought (Leishman and Westoby 1994), large seed size may trade-off with lower persistence in the seed bank due to seed predation (Gutterman 2002).

3.4.2   Seed germination and dispersal strategies

Some of the most unique desert adaptations involve annual plants (reviewed by Van Rheede van Oudtshoorn and Van Rooyen 1999; Gutterman 2000, 2002) (see Fig. 3.9; see also Stamp 1984 and Fig. 3.10). Gutterman (1994) indicated that there are two main strategies of dispersal to avoid massive seed consumption, a common problem in plants that reproduce annually and need to survive in the seed stage until the following year:

1. *Escape strategy*—seeds escape by being very small. For example, *Schismus arabicus* can produce 10,000 caryopses (seeds) per m^2, each weighing an average of 0.007 mg. *Spergularia diandra* may produce as many as 32,000 seeds per m^2, each weighing 0.018 mg.
2. *Protection strategy*—There are a number of different ways to protect a seed. For example, seeds could be maintained on the parent plant where it is covered by woody and/or dry material. Examples of this include the

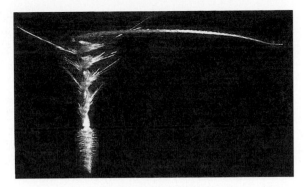

Fig. 3.9   *Erodium* twisting itself into the soil. (From www.harunyahya.com/books/science/seed/seed4.php. Date accessed: 14 February 2008.)

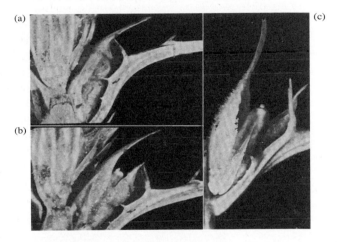

Fig. 3.10   *Blepharis* germination mechanism. (a) Closed. (b) Partly open. (c) Completely open and ready to disperse into the air. (From Gutterman 1993. With kind permission of Springer Science and Business Media.)

amphicarpous (two or more ways of preserving seeds) *Gymnarrhena micrantha* and *Emex spinosa* (Polygonaceae). Serotiny (preservation within a woody structure; also called bradyspory *sensu* Van Rheede Van Oudtshoorn and Van Rooyen (1999)) has been shown in a number of Namib desert plants (Günster 1992, 1993a, b) and in Negev desert plants (e.g. in *Asteriscus pygmaeus* (Asteraceae) by Gutterman and Ginott (1994)). However, Günster (1994c) has challenged the notion that the protection of the seeds of serotinous (bradysporic) plants is a driving force in the evolution of these species because she found no difference in insect predation of serotinous and non-serotinous plants.

Some plants are protected by myxospermy, which means that they are covered with a layer of mucilage and then attach themselves to the biological soil crust to avoid ant herbivory. Examples of such plants include *Plantago coronopus*, *Carrichtera annua* and *Reboudia pinnata* (Gutterman and Shem Tov 1997) (see Fig. 3.11). However, Zaady *et al.* (1997) found that seeds of these species did not germinate well under such conditions and rather need the soil crust to be broken up. Thus, it may be that avoiding ant herbivory is necessary for the seeds to endure the summer but breaking up the soil crust must occur the following winter for these winter annuals to germinate. Zaady *et al.* (1997) speculate that this may explain why germination occurs best when the seeds occur in the shallow holes formed by porcupine (*Hystrix indica*) diggings, which frees the seeds of attachment by their mucilage.

3.4.3   Why is long-range dispersal rare in desert plants?

Many authors have observed that there are few species of desert plants that show adaptations for long-distance dispersal (Zohary 1937; Van der Pijl 1972). One explanation has dominated with regard to the dispersal of desert plants, namely, the 'mother-site' theory of Zohary (1937). Consistent with Zohary's theory, Friedman and Stein (1980) contend that in deserts, where the number of suitable sites is limited, a plant that occupies the place that once supported its mother is likely to have a good chance of success. This assumes that competition is rare in deserts (Tilman (1988) disagrees with this assumption; see Chapter 5) and that the benefits of germinating in a particular site outweigh any purported costs. Such a theory may explain

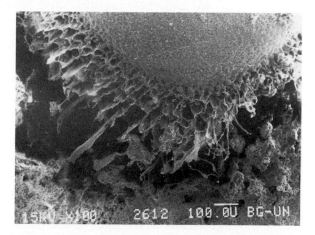

Fig. 3.11   *Carrichtera annua* seed with mucilage (upper section) to attach itself to loess. (From Gutterman 1993. With kind permission of Springer Science and Business Media.)

why adaptations for long-distance dispersal (*telechory*) are rare in desert plants. Two terms have been derived to describe adaptations associated with dispersal, namely, atelechory and antitelechory. Atelechory entails a lack of adaptations for dispersal and antitelechory describes adaptations to prevent dispersal (Zohary 1937).

Ellner and Shmida (1981) have contested the mother-site theory, although they do acknowledge that there are few adaptations for long-distance dispersal in desert plants (Tables 3.2 and 3.3). Ellner and Shmida (1981) argue that annuals do not rely on special moist microsites as they can be widely distributed across the desert in moist years. They also note that geocarpy and amphicarpy, which are adaptations to retain seeds in the same site, are rare or absent in deserts. Furthermore, fine-scale spatial distributions should be common among years but are not. Indeed, these authors show that their small 10 × 10 cm plots in the Judean desert have a relatively high temporal variance (0–66% similarity). This has also been shown by Ward *et al.* (2000a) on a larger spatial scale (0.1 ha) in the neighbouring Negev desert, where plants mostly have a <10% probability of appearing more than once in the same plot (see Fig. 7.1). Ellner and Shmida (1981) name

Table 3.2 Major dispersal types of the Israeli flora (modified from Ellner and Shmida 1981). The columns indicate the % of species with a particular dispersal type (numbers in parentheses indicate number of species involved). Columns 4 and 5 indicate the dispersal types of total numbers of species counted in 0.1 ha plots at a single site in 1980 (Sansan) and 1981 (Ein Gedi). Percentages of species have been recalculated for Mediterranean/semi-desert based on numbers of species with a particular dispersal type from Ellner and Shmida (1981).

Dispersal type	Mediterranean/ semi-desert	Desert	Sansan (open maquis)	Ein Gedi (desert)
Telechory	41.6 (574)	14.6 (88)	45.0	26.0
Atelechory	56.6 (780)	75.0 (453)	53.0	52.0
Antitelechory	1.8 (25)	10.4 (62)	2.0	22.0

Table 3.3 Dispersal types of the Goegap nature reserve in arid Namaqualand, South Africa. Numbers indicate the % of species with a particular dispersal type. Numbers in parentheses indicate the numbers of species involved. Note the difference in % values for atelechory and antitelechory for this study and the one mentioned by Ellner and Shmida (1981) (Table 3.2).

Dispersal type	Goegap
Telechory	47.6 (736)
Atelechory	8.1 (126)
Antitelechory	44.3 (685)

five possible reasons, excluding the 'mother-site' theory, why antitelechory might have evolved:

1. *Protection from predation*—consistent with Gutterman's (1994) model mentioned above, buried seeds and/or seeds attached to the mother plant are less likely to suffer from seed predation.
2. *Anchorage against surface run-off*—this is particularly important for slope-dwelling species because they may get washed into the wadis, even without specialized mechanisms for dispersal.
3. *Regulation of within-season timing of germination*—precipitation occurs rarely in deserts, so germination should be timed to coincide with these events.
4. *Spreading dispersal and germination over several years*—responses to early season rains can lead to high mortality if not followed by subsequent rains (Loria and Noy-Meir 1981). Selection should favour multiple germination events in the same species (*polyphenism*) (Cohen 1966, 1967).
5. *Enhancing water uptake by seeds and seedlings*—seeds that are buried in the soil can have reduced exposure to extreme heat and cold and have better access to water than unburied seeds.

Ellner and Shmida (1981) contend that atelechory has evolved because of the extremely low benefit to be derived from long-distance dispersal (i.e. possession of morphological features such as pappi and barbs; Fig. 3.12a and b) rather than a benefit of adaptive short-range dispersal. They suggested that antitelechory, on the other hand, is part of a group of characteristics that happen to have evolved for the purpose of regulation of the timing of germination to limit it to years after the mother plant has died. It is important to note that the mother-site theory of Zohary (1937) and Ellner and Shmida's (1981) theories are not mutually exclusive.

3.4.4 Delayed germination

Cohen (1967) addressed the question of why annual plants have delayed germination. Using mathematical models, he showed that the higher the probability of seed failure following a rain event, the smaller the optimal germinating fraction should be. Venable *et al.* (1993) found support for this model in the Sonoran desert, where each of the 10 species they studied had a greater germinating fraction in years of greater germination success (see also Adondakis and Venable 2004). A mechanism that could give rise to such a pattern could be as simple as having a germination fraction sensitive to conditions favourable for early growth and establishment (Van Rheede van Oudtshoorn and Van Rooyen 1999). Weather data at a local weather station in Arizona over the past 115 years indicated a significant correlation between December rainfall (a good predictor of germinating fraction) and February rainfall (a good predictor of realized fecundity) (Venable *et al.* 1993).

Fig. 3.12   (a) Pappi of a dandelion and (b) barbs (in Mexican devil's claw *Ibicella lutea*) used as dispersal mechanisms. (From www.harunyahya.com/books/science/seed/seed4.php. Date accessed: 14 February 2008.)

3.4.5   Seed heteromorphism

Seed heteromorphism is known in a number of deserts, including the Arabian desert (*E. spinosa* (Weiss 1980) and *G. micrantha* (Koller and Roth 1964)), Namib desert (e.g. *Geigeria alata*; Burke (1995)), and Sonoran desert (*Heterotheca pinnatum*; Venable *et al.* (1995)). The strategy of such plants is to simultaneously invest in two or more types of seeds. In *E. spinosa*, for example, one seed type is aerial and the other is subterranean. Aerial seeds are dispersed greater distances by wind, while subterranean seeds are dispersed locally (Weiss 1980). In most cases, local dispersal is more effective because there is little benefit to leaving an area that was successful for the mother plant for another area that may or may not be better (*sensu* Zohary 1937, 1962).

Venable (1985) developed a game theory model to consider the issue of seed heteromorphism and its effects on fecundity. The appropriate method of comparing fecundity is by the geometric mean (the nth root of the product of n values) and not by the arithmetic mean (sum of the numbers divided by n), because the geometric mean controls for very high or very low values. In the case of annual seed yields, the geometric mean can be increased by increasing the arithmetic mean seed yield or by reducing the variance (Gillespie 1977). Only one seed type is necessary to maximize the arithmetic mean but two morphs can reduce the variance. For example, there are two seed types and they have respective annual seed yields of 2,

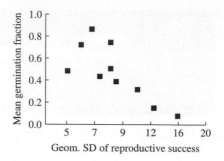

Fig. 3.13 Mean germination fraction of 10 species of desert annuals plotted against variation in *per capita* reproductive success (average number of germinating seeds). Germination is averaged over 14 years. Demographic variation is calculated over 22 years and is plotted as geometric SD (exp. SD [ln (per capita reproductive success)]). (Modified from Venable 2007. With the kind permission of the Ecological Society of America.)

5, and 8 seeds (morph 1) and 8, 5, and 2 seeds (morph 2). If the seed types represent different strategies and all seeds germinate and survive to reproduce, there will be 80 descendants of a single individual after 3 years (2 × 5 × 8 = 80 seeds). If they are morphs in a 1:1 ratio with a heteromorphic strategy, the arithmetic mean offspring fitness is 5 seeds per annum (arithmetic mean of 2, 5, and 8 = 5) or 125 seeds over three years. All strategies have a mean arithmetic yield of 5 seeds per annum but the heteromorphic strategy has the highest yield because they have a lower between-year variance (Venable 1985).

Venable (2007) has also addressed the notion of bet hedging in desert annuals. Bet hedging involves trading off short-term geometric mean fitness for long-term risk reduction. Using the 10 most common species in a 22-year study near Tucson, Arizona, Venable found that bet hedging does indeed occur; there was a significant negative correlation between the log-transformed SD and mean germination fraction (Fig. 3.13).

3.5   Grasses, forbs, and shrubs/perennials

3.5.1   Clonality

Vasek (1980) showed that creosote bushes *L. tridentata* (Zygophyllaceae) are clonal and are extremely long-lived. The oldest known *Larrea* occurred in Yuma, Arizona, occurred there about 10,850 ± 500 years BP. Assuming that the growth rate was 0.66 mm yr^{-1} from about 7,000 years ago and was double that prior to 7,000 BP, this would indicate that such a shrub would be at least 9,400 years old.

Bruelheide *et al.* (2004) have shown that clones of *Populus euphratica* in the Taklamakan desert can be larger than 100 m in radius, leading to a calculation of at least 4 ha occupied by a single clone, yet a perennial herb *Alhagi sparsifolia* (Fabaceae) sampled at the same site had clones that were >5 m but <100 m radius. However, Bruelheide *et al.* (2004) note that *P. euphratica* may even have >4 ha clones as no further spatial sampling was conducted.

3.5.2   Photosynthesis and stomatal opening

Kappen *et al.* (1976) showed in the drought-deciduous shrub *H. scoparia* (Chenopodiaceae) in the Negev desert that non-irrigated plants on hillslopes had a net photosynthetic rate of approximately 3 mg CO_2 g^{-1} h^{-1}, while non-irrigated wadi plants had a net photosynthetic rate of about 5 mg CO_2 g^{-1} h^{-1}. In contrast, irrigated wadi plants had a value of about 7 mg CO_2 g^{-1} h^{-1}. The mean midday water potentials of these same plants were −7 MPa (going as low as −9.1 MPa (−91 bars)), −7 MPa, and −5 MPa, respectively. Kappen *et al.* (1976) contended that the relatively high net rate of photosynthesis in mid-summer (July) occurred even under low (i.e. very negative) water potentials. These results may be explained by the fact that wadi plants have a prolonged period with less sensitive stomata in summer unlike the hillslope plants which had been under high water stress since spring (because hillslope plants occur where run-off is high and wadi plants occur where run-on is highest). This may lead to permanently low water potentials and low rates of net photosynthesis, resulting in the shedding of the plant's cortex in the wadis by the end of the dry season, and hence deciduousness (Kappen *et al.* 1976).

More extreme values of xylem and leaf water potential have been recorded at −16.3 MPa and −9.2 MPa by Kappen *et al.* (1972) in *Artemisia herba-alba*, also in the Negev desert. These values produced a low but nonetheless positive value of net photosynthesis of about 0.2 mg CO_2 g^{-1} h^{-1}. Similar values have been recorded for desert shrubs by Halvorson and Patten (1974), who recorded a water potential of −8.5 MPa in *Franseria deltoidea* (Fig. 3.14) in the Sonoran desert at noon. Before sunrise and after sunset, the values for Kappen *et al.*'s (1972) study on *A. herba-alba* were still very negative, being around −10 MPa for xylem and −5 MPa for the leaves. Donovan *et al.* (2001) have indicated that soil and leaf water predawn potentials may not equilibrate because either nighttime transpiration or apoplastic solute transport occurs (or both). Nonetheless, they can account for relatively small predawn disequilibria between soil water potentials and leaf water potentials of about −0.5 to −2.34 MPa in bagged plants that cannot transpire (Donovan *et al.* 2001). Values as extreme as those in *A. herba-alba* are difficult to explain.

3.5.3   Leaf pubescence

Sandquist and Ehleringer (1998) studied reflective leaf pubescence in a desert shrub, *Encelia farinosa* in the Sonoran desert. Leaf hairs have high

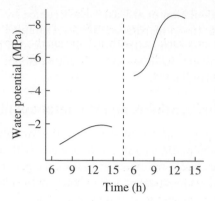

Fig. 3.14   Photosynthesis can be achieved even under extreme water stress conditions: Halvorson and Patten (1974) recorded a water potential of −8.5 MPa in *Franseria deltoidea*. (From Halvorson and Patten 1974. With the kind permission of the Ecological Society of America.)

(albeit once-off) construction costs and reduce photosynthetic efficiency by cutting down on photosynthetically active radiation. However, leaf pubescence reduces leaf temperature and plant water loss and is therefore considered adaptive in arid environments. Using three sites along a natural rainfall gradient, with mean rainfall values at 52, 111, and 453 mm per year, Sandquist and Ehleringer (1998) showed that drought-induced leaf loss was earliest at the high rainfall site but these plants also had higher leaf absorbance values. Higher absorbance increases the relative dependence on transpirational cooling and, perhaps more importantly, also allows for higher instantaneous carbon assimilation. Conversely, plants at the driest site had lower absorbance values and maintained their leaves for longer. Lower absorbance values, which are associated with greater leaf pubescence, reduced water consumption. These studies showed that a trade-off exists between carbon assimilation (wetter sites) and reduced water consumption. Plants from drier sites may also need to extend leaf longevity to maintain photosynthetic activity for longer into the dry season.

3.5.4   Fog—an unusual water source

Two plant species in the Namib desert, *Trianthema hereroensis* (Aizoaceae) and *Stipagrostis sabulicola* (Poaceae), are capable of using fog, at least as a supplementary source of water (Seely *et al.* 1977; Louw and Seely 1980). Using tritiated water (a commonly used tracer for water transport studies, where the hydrogen ions are replaced with tritium; the chemical formula is ^3H_2O), they showed that the succulent *T. hereroensis* can take up large amounts of this water sprayed on its leaves, indicating that they can use fog water in the same way (Seely *et al.* 1977). This strategy is unlikely to be effective because water taken up by the leaves is even more likely to evaporate from the leaves (Danin 1991; Von Willert *et al.* 1992). However, the perennial grass *S. sabulicola* has an extensive superficial root system, part of which lies within 1 cm of the substrate. This sand layer is often moistened with fog. Louw and Seely (1980) showed that when moistened to field capacity with tritiated water, this water was taken up by these roots. When the same plants were tested 7 weeks later, most of the photosynthates were transferred to the main vertical and lateral roots.

3.5.5 Grasses

Most species of plants in deserts are grasses (see Chapter 9). Grasses are usually C_4 species and show many of the classic adaptations of such plants (see Photosynthetic pathways above).

The distinctive Australian hummock grasslands consist largely of grasses of two genera, *Triodia* and *Plectrachne* (often called desert spinifex). The hummocks can be large, up to 1 m in diameter and about 30 cm tall (Specht and Specht 1999). The hummock grows outwards, leaving the centre senescent or dead. Hummock grasses typically occur where mean annual rainfall is between 125 and 350 mm. Unlike many other desert situations, where there is usually insufficient fuel for a fire, these Australian hummock grasslands are prone to fire.

Ryel *et al.* (1994) examined the factors that may lead to hummock or tussock formation (also called bunch grasses), a common desert grass formation. Tussock grasses are composed of essentially autonomous tillers (Welker *et al.* 1991). They compared the physiology of uniform tillers with those of bunch grasses of *Agropyron desertorum*, in the Great Basin desert of North America. When tussock density was low, they found that bunch grasses had 50–60% lower carbon gain, lower daily incident photon flux density, and lower net photosynthesis than equivalent uniformly distributed tillers because of light competition within tussocks. When tussock densities were high, they found that there was considerable variability in net photosynthesis, ranging from 7% to 96% relative to an isolated seedling. Ryel *et al.* (1994) hypothesized that the loss of net photosynthesis because of clumping is offset by the benefits of protecting their belowground resources from competition from competing seedlings.

3.6 Geophytes

The term 'geophyte' refers to plants that use underground organs for storage. Most plants in this category belong to the monocot families Iridaceae, Liliaceae, and Amaryllidaceae. The term 'geophyte' is used to consider a number of types of storage organ and includes bulbs, corms, rhizomes, and, in some cases, tubers. True bulbs, if cut in half vertically, reveal the components you would find in a bud, namely, flower and leaves (Fig. 3.15).

Fig. 3.15   Geophyte bulb, *Pancratium sickenbergeri*, from the Negev desert, Israel.

Examples of true bulbs include tulips, lilies, and narcissus. Alternatively, corms are solid, enlarged stem bases, such as anemones and crocus. Rhizomes are swollen stems that grow horizontally typically underground and send up leaves and flowers at intervals. Irises are the best-known rhizomes. The term 'tuber' is applied to any plant with underground storage parts that does not fit the above categories.

3.6.1   Hysteranthy and its consequences

Hysteranthous plants produce their flowers at different times from their leaves while synanthous plants produce flowers and leaves simultaneously. In Israel, only a few plant species flower in the autumn (about 10% of the native flora) (Zohary 1962). Most of them are hysteranthous geophytes. Dafni *et al.* (1981) have claimed that these species have adopted a new pollination strategy that avoids the conventional timing of pollination in the spring and thus avoids 'arms races' with other potential pollinators. However, Kamenetsky and Gutterman (1994) have shown that these hysteranthous plants may retain their seeds for several months, even as late as January the following year, and thereby avoid ant predation, which is a major source of seed predation. Clearly, the pollination and seed predation avoidance strategies are not necessarily mutually exclusive.

Boeken (1989, 1990) investigated the consequences of hysteranthy for two species in the genus *Bellevalia* (Hyacinthaceae (Dahlgren *et al.* 1985), or, alternatively, Liliaceae (Cronquist 1981) or Asparagaceae (Angiosperm Phylogeny Group 2003)) growing in the central Negev desert of Israel. Boeken (1989) showed that the reproductive state of a population of

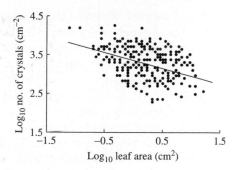

Fig. 3.16   Ruiz et al. (2002) showed that there was a trade-off between investment in defence ($\log_{10}$ number of crystals) and investments in growth (measured as $\log_{10}$ leaf area). (From Ruiz *et al.* 2002. With kind permission of Blackwell Publishing.)

Bellevalia desertorum was determined by the size of the plant and by the current conditions (rainfall) but not by previous conditions or previous reproductive activity. In contrast, he showed that *B. eigii* was affected by previous and current conditions and found that there was a negative effect of previous reproduction (Boeken 1990).

In a study of *Pancratium sickenbergeri* (Amaryllidaceae), Ward *et al.* (2000a) found a significant positive effect of rainfall in the previous season but none from the current season. Ruiz *et al.* (2002) tested the effects of simulated bulb herbivory by the Dorcas gazelle on *P. sickenbergeri* plants with a high level of herbivory. They removed 25%, 50%, and 75% of bulb tissues from the plant and left some as controls. Bulbs with an intermediate amount of tissue removed (50%) showed the highest regrowth capacity and fitness. The investment in calcium oxalate defences also increased in cut bulbs, although they also showed a trade-off between investments in storage and defence (Fig. 3.16) (and no trade-offs between growth and defence, growth and reproduction, or between reproduction and defence). Control plants grew less than cut plants, had lower levels of calcium oxalate but they stored more energy in the bulb and produced more flowers and fruits.

Ruiz *et al.* (2006a) also investigated the factors that controlled the production of a second inflorescence stalk in this species. Clipped plants had a greater probability of producing a second inflorescence, especially if cut in the emerging stage (rather than at anthesis). This indicated that there was a cost to compensation. Unlike the bulb-cutting study, the production of a second inflorescence stalk was related to resource availability (as indicated by rainfall) in all 3 years of the study. While the Ruiz *et al.* (2002) study provides results that are consistent with the hypothesis that plants may overcompensate after herbivory, these last-mentioned results (Ruiz *et al.* 2006b) are inconsistent with the hypothesis that herbivory is beneficial to plants and support the trade-off hypothesis that benefits of herbivory are attained at an evolutionary cost. A further study by Ruiz *et al.* (2006c) showed that the height of the inflorescence stalk was positively correlated with the amount of reserves stored by the bulb. There was an optimum height that was determined by maximizing visibility to pollinators and reducing visibility to herbivorous gazelles (gazelles consume lilies at the flowering, leaf, and bulb stages).

Boeken (1991) examined the factors that constrain above-ground emergence of the desert tulip *Tulipa systola* (Liliaceae) (Fig. 3.5) in the Negev desert. Between 10% and 70% of adults and between 40% and 80% of juveniles do not appear above ground in a given year. Most, however, appear the following year. The appearance of desert angiosperm species above ground is variable, and exemplified by the enormous variation in annual species (see above). Boeken (1991) showed that the failure to emerge above ground was due to insufficient root and shoot development and not simply a continuation of summer resting. He showed that the decreased availability of water, caused by a decline in rainfall, was responsible. He also showed that below-ground temperatures must be less than about 25°C, as was the case in another desert geophyte, *Sternbergia clusiana* (Amaryllidaceae) (Boeken and Gutterman 1986). Biomass and water availability limit below-ground shoot growth in *T. systola*. Emergent plants frequently experience great loss of biomass (as much as 30%). However, if they do not emerge, then they lose comparable amounts from the bulb.

3.6.2   Contractile roots

Galil (1980) has shown that lowering of the bulb may occur either by direct lowering or by combined lowering, where pioneer roots are used to lower the bulb. Pioneer roots grow downwards in the direction of proposed growth and subsequently make room for the bud-carrying organ. The most common type of pioneer root is the contractile root (Thoday 1926; Thoday and Davey 1932), which prepares the bulb by longitudinal contraction. In *Ixiolirion tataricum* (Amaryllidaceae) in the northern Negev desert of Israel, both direct lowering occurs (in the first year, with very little effect), followed by combined lowering, where the bud-carrying first leaf lowers into the tunnel created within the primary root as a result of core contraction (Galil 1983). The acting force must be growth pressure of the leaf itself, rather than any pulling effect of the contracting core. In abnormal seedlings that were sown in shallow pots (and which could not grow downwards), a second root quite frequently developed sideways, hampering the normal contraction of the core (Galil 1983).

In *P. sickenbergeri* (Amaryllidaceae) in the Makhtesh Ramon erosion cirque in the central Negev desert, there are important effects of lowering the bulb. The Dorcas gazelle, *Gazella dorcas*, consumes all or part of the bulb of about 58% of lilies (Ward and Saltz 1994), by digging in the sand

to remove the bulb (Fig. 3.17). In these populations, the lilies lower themselves into the sand by as much as 40 cm. In some populations where there
are no gazelles (presumably because of leopard predation), the lilies do not
lower their bulbs (Ward and Saltz 1994; Ward *et al.* 1997; Saltz and Ward
2000; Ruiz *et al.* 2002) (Fig. 3.18). Ruiz *et al.* (2006b) investigated whether
this was an effect of sand compaction (in more compacted substrates, such

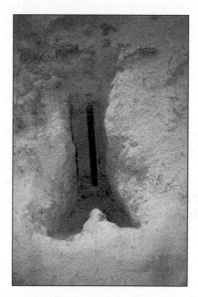

Fig. 3.17   Gazelles use their forelimbs to dig down to extract the bulb of *Pancratium sickenbergeri*. Length of ruler is 30 cm.

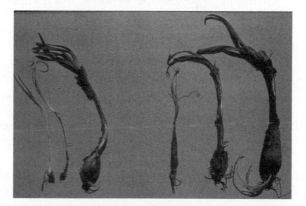

Fig. 3.18   Bulbs of *Pancratium sickenbergeri* with different stalk lengths. Uneaten bulbs (on the
right) pull themselves down with contractile roots. The bulbs on the left have been partially consumed and have to regrow from the depth they have reached. Consequently,
they are far more slender than the plants on the right.

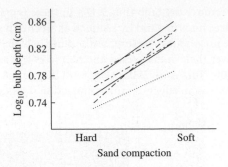

Fig. 3.19   Crossing reaction norms for $\log_{10}$ bulb depth versus sand type (hard and soft) in different populations of *Pancratium sickenbergeri* indicate that there are significant G × E
interactions. (From Ruiz *et al.* 2006. With kind permission of Oxford University Press).

as loess, bulbs do not grow as deeply) or a genetic effect, showing differences among populations. They found that there were effects caused by
sand compaction (sands that were more compacted had shallower bulbs)
but there were also genetic effects, indicating the effects of selection on
bulb depth (Fig. 3.19). This is known as a genotype by environment (or
G × E) interaction.

3.7   Stem and leaf succulents

This category may be divided into two non-phylogenetically related groups
of organisms, stem succulents (such as the Cactaceae and Euphorbiaceae
species) and leaf succulents (such as *Lithops* and *Aloe*). Many succulents
have CAM photosynthesis. However, this is not universally true (see Von
Willert *et al.* 1982).

3.7.1   Stem succulents

Here we consider three examples of stem succulent life histories:

1. *Welwitschia mirabilis* (Gnetales, Gymnospermae) (Fig. 3.20)—unlike
   most desert succulents, this species is a gymnosperm that is endemic
   to the narrow coastal strip of the Namib desert. Schulze and Schulze
   (1976) have considered this species to be capable of CAM photosynthesis
   on the basis of carbon isotope values. However, Von Willert *et al.* (1982)
   re-examined this in the field and have not found any evidence to support this claim. Von Willert *et al.* (1982) argue that this species has conventional C_3 photosynthesis. No evidence of nocturnal CO_2 uptake (as
   expected from CAM photosynthesis) was detected. Nonetheless, fairly
   high values of malate and citrate were found in the leaves of this plant
   (as expected with CAM photosynthesis), yet these did not exhibit any

Fig. 3.20   *Welwitschia mirabilis,* Namib desert.

diurnal-nocturnal pattern. Von Willert *et al.* (1982) found that transpir-ation rates (to a maximum of 1.9 mmol m^{-2} s^{-1} near 12h00) occurred, which would imply that about 25–32% replacement of leaf water loss per *hour* should occur. It is unclear as to where this is obtained, although it is suggested that the woody trunk, which is sponge-like, may serve as a water store.

2. *Ferocactus acanthodes* (Cactaceae)—as indicated by their common name of 'barrel cactus', they are roughly spherical in morphology (Fig. 3.21). These dicots use CAM photosynthesis. Succulent plants generally have a thick chlorenchyma, which in *F. acanthodes* extended more than 3 mm below the surface. This results in an extremely high ratio of chlorenchyma surface area per unit stem surface area of 137. An analogous ratio for C$_3$ plants is about 15–30 (Nobel *et al.* 1975). Thus, a large surface area is available for CO$_2$ diffusion into the chlorophyll-containing cells of this cactus.

The optimal temperature for nocturnal stomatal opening was about 12.6°C, which is quite similar to that recorded for other CAM plants (Patten and Dinger 1969). That the stomata open preferentially on cool nights means less water loss, because the stem:air water vapour concentra-tion differential tends to be lower than during warmer nights. Also, the biochemistry of CO$_2$ fixation by *F. acanthodes* is also well adapted to cool nocturnal temperatures. This species naturally occurs in regions that have winter rains and that are cool at night for a large part of the year (Shreve and Wiggins, 1964).

F. acanthodes swells up on encountering rain, and shrinks when there is drought. This is accompanied by changes in internal solutes, with higher values recorded during drought (approximately 2-fold changes during drought). As might be expected of such a succulent CAM plant, it can

Fig. 3.21   Barrel cactus (*Ferocactus acanthodes*), Arizona.

use up to 33% of its mass for nocturnal stomatal opening without any major uptake of water from the soil and a further 17% during a sustained 4 month drought (Nobel 1977).

There is considerable water loss that accompanies flowering, corresponding to approximately 5.7% of the stem water content on a single day. Actually, relatively little is known about the water relations of flowering for cacti. MacDougal and Spalding (1910) noted that each flower of the giant saguaro cactus (*Carnegiea gigantea*) may contain 33 g of water, and may transpire 11 g during its single day of opening (they also note that considerable water was lost during the bud stage). Although a large saguaro may weigh over 1,000 kg and have several hundred flowers, the fractional decrease in water during flowering is actually quite small. Cacti flowers tend to be greater in number during wet years and also for plants well supplied with water, indicating some dependency of flowering on the overall water relations of the plant.

3. *Agave deserti* (Agavaceae)—this monocot plant also has CAM. Similar to *F. acanthodes*, it has a very shallow root system (mean root depth = 8 cm), which allows it to respond to brief pulses of rain (Noble 1976; Jordan and Nobel 1984). Succulent plants often have very shallow root systems (see also Von Willert *et al.* (1992) for examples from the Namib desert) to exploit brief pulses of rain. For the summer, no stomatal opening occurs (and, hence, no photosynthesis) but it could be induced by watering (Hartsock and Nobel 1976). As was the case with *F. acanthodes*, this species could also use water storage, so that stomatal opening could occur even when the water potential of the soil was less than plant water potential. Full stomatal opening occurred just 48 h after rain. As is the case with several other CAM species, optimal temperatures for photosynthesis occurred at about 15°C.

(a)

(b)

Fig. 3.22   The genus *Lithops* (Mesembryanthemaceae; common name 'stone plants') consists of (a) leaf succulents that appear stone-like, submerged in the rocky surfaces that they live in. The only part of the plant that lies above the soil surface is about 0.5 cm, which (b) has a window of variable opacity (Fig. 3.22a from www.cactuslimon.com/ [Date accessed 23 June 2008].) (Fig. 3.22b from http://cacti.co.nz/cultivation.htm/ [Date accessed 23 June 2008].)

3.7.2   Leaf succulents

In leaf succulents, nearly the entire leaf is succulent (e.g. *Lithops, Aloe, Crassula,* and *Haworthia*). In many species, the stem is extremely short or even non-existent. In some species of *Crassula*, the stem is not succulent but the leaf is covered with a wax-like epidermis. Leaf succulents may include halophytic species of Chenopodiaceae, which have a strongly defined cuticle. In *Lithops* and *Conophytum* species, the leaf area is minimized and evaporative areas are small. Other species, such as those in the genera *Aloe* and *Haworthia*, form rosettes that minimize radiation from the sun and from the soil. In times of extreme drought, leaf succulents may also lose their leaves.

Turner and Picker (1993) examined two species in the genus *Lithops* (Mesembryanthemaceae; common name 'stone plants'), which consists of leaf succulents that appear stone-like, submerged in the rocky surfaces that they live in. The only part of the plant that lies above the soil surface is about 0.5 cm, which has a window of variable opacity (Fig. 3.22) (Turner and Picker 1993). Many of the common mechanisms for controlling leaf temperatures (e.g. radiation with the surroundings, convective cooling, and evaporation) are not available for these plants because they are submerged in the soil. Turner and Picker (1993) ran a mathematical model using standard models of a plant and field measurements of populations near Ceres in the succulent Karoo (Western Cape, South Africa; mean annual rainfall = 400–500 mm) and on the Hamiltonberg near Walvis Bay, Namibia (<100 mm mean annual rainfall), and showed that leaf temperatures are governed by the following: (1) leaf and soil temperatures are linked; (2) variations in surface energy budgets of the leaves have little effect on leaf temperature; and (3) variation in window clarity causes significant changes in leaf temperature. The effects of these are as follows: (1) thermally coupling the plant and soil combines the plant's thermal capacity with the soil's thermal capacity and reduces daily variation in leaf temperature; (2) the steep vertical variation in temperature that occurs in soils keeps the deeper parts of the plant cool relative to the hotter surface regions; (3) variation in leaf temperature is not related to variation in leaf colour (the leaves are cryptically coloured); and (4) variation in window clarity is probably the only thermal adaptation to hot conditions that embedded dwarf succulents employ.

3.8   Halophytes

Halophytes are plants that adapt in various ways to high salt regimes (Waisel 1972). The accumulation of saline and alkali salts in desert environments is due to high evaporation rates which exceed precipitation to the point that moisture in the soil is carried up to the soil surface, rather than leaching downwards (Day and Ludeke 1993). The salts are carried upwards with the rising moisture. Soil water in arid soils may contain between 2,000 and 20,000 ppm of salts (Fuller 1975).

There are two main types of halophytes (Waisel 1972):

1. Salt *accumulators* (usually NaCl) in vacuoles or specific organs, usually associated with succulence (e.g. Chenopodiaceae: *Salicornia, Suaeda, Chenopodium, Atriplex*). *Atriplex halimus* (Chenopodiaceae) is a large shrub (reaching up to 3 m) (Fig. 3.23). These shrubs are covered with vesiculated hairs, containing high concentrations of NaCl and oxalate.

Fig. 3.23   *Atriplex halimus.* (Copyright Bertrand Boeken.)

Under normal conditions, there is a positive response to the addition of NaCl and no inhibitory effect on growth up to 100 mM was observed (Waisel 1972). Kam and Degen (1989) have shown that the rodent *Psammomys obesus* (Gerbillidae) can remove the saline surface of the *Atriplex* leaf and consume the leaves. This is sufficient to maintain the animal, even in lactation.

Phragmites communis (Poaceae) occurs as halophytic and glycophytic (non-salt tolerant) forms and can germinate in a wide range of saline media (0–0.5 M NaCl). High germination percentages (>90%) were obtained in media with 0.4 M NaCl and slightly lower in 0.5 M NaCl. However, for the glycophytic ecotype, only 20% germinated at 0.4 M and 0% in the 0.5 M media (Waisel 1972).

Sarcobatus vermiculatus is a common halophyte north of 37°N in the Great Basin desert in places such as Mono Lake and Owens Lake. It is spinescent with succulent, winter-deciduous leaves, although in warmer areas such as in the Mojave desert, it may be evergreen (Danin 1996). Plants under water stress become more spiny. It may establish itself on habitats rich in salt. The sand of the *Sarcobatus* nebkas (phytogenic dunes) has a lighter colour than the surrounding ground (Danin 1996), probably because salts have been accumulated by recycling of salt-rich leaves deposited on the soil surface (Fireman and Hayward 1952). This species will not establish itself in non-saline soils in the presence of non-halophytic competitors.

2. Salt *excretors* (e.g. *Tamarix* and *Reaumuria* (Tamaricaceae)). *Tamarix aphylla* has growth that is inhibited by salinity at concentrations as low as 0.1 M NaCl but stops growing in a medium containing about 0.5 M NaCl (Waisel 1972). Ma *et al.* (2007) examined the stable carbon isotope ratios of the desert plant *Reaumuria soongorica* and the physicochemical properties of soil in the Gobi desert. Specifically, they examined the correlations between $\delta^{13}C$ values and the soil factors in the major distribution areas in northwestern China. They found correlations between $\delta^{13}C$ values in *R. soongorica* that significantly increased with decreasing soil water content (SWC) and increasing total dissolved solids (TDS) in soil. There were no significant correlations between the $\delta^{13}C$ values and pH, total nitrogen, soil organic matter (SOM), total phosphorus, and effective phosphorus in soil. Ma *et al.* (2007) concluded that the variation in $\delta^{13}C$ values of *R. soongorica* was probably caused by stomatal limitation rather than by nutrient-related changes in photosynthetic efficiency.

Desert halophytes tend to rely on the accumulation of inorganic cations (mostly Na^+ and K^+) for osmotic adjustment to drought and salinity (Flowers *et al.* 1977; Flowers and Yeo 1986; Smith *et al.* 1997). *Drought tolerance* relies heavily on K^+ uptake and accumulation for osmotic adjustment, and *salinity tolerance* relies on Na^+ for osmotic adjustment. As a result, high sodium phenotypes (e.g. Chenopodiaceae) and low sodium phenotypes (e.g. Poaceae) (Flowers and Yeo 1986), or even subspecies of *Atriplex canescens* (Glenn *et al.* 1992), can be distinguished from one another on the basis of the evolution of ion accumulation in response to either drought stress or salinity.

3.9   Phreatophytes

A phreatophyte is a deep-rooted plant that obtains its water from the water table or from another deepwater source such as an aquifer. Some plants are obligate phreatophytes in that there is a strong positive association with the water table while in others the relationship is facultative. In *A. raddiana*, roots may be shallow to capture rain from floodwater in ephemeral rivers (wadis) and they have deep roots to maximize uptake from aquifers (Sher *et al.* submitted) (Fig. 3.24). Similar situations exist for *Acacia mellifera* in southern Africa.

The mean maximum rooting depth worldwide was 4.6 ± 0.5 m, and the individual maximum rooting depth was 68 m for *A. erioloba* and *B. albitrunca*, the roots of which were found during well drilling in deep sandy soils in the central Kalahari desert in Botswana (Jennings 1974).

Fig. 3.24   Deep root of an *Acacia raddiana* in the Arabian desert, Jordan.

The 10 deepest rooting species are, in decreasing order, as follows: *B. albi-trunca* (68 m), *A. erioloba* (60 m), *Prosopis juliflora* (53 m), *Eucalyptus marginata* (40 m), *Retama raetam* (20 m), *Tamarix aphylla* (20 m), *Andira humilis* (18 m), *Alhagi maurorum* (now *A. graecorum*) (15 m), *Prosopis farcta* (15 m), and *Prosopis glandulosa* (15 m). Unsurprisingly, all but two of these species (*E. marginata* and *A. humilis*) are desert dwellers. Two additional plant species, *P. euphratica* and *Tamarix ramosissima* from the Taklamakan desert, have roots that are 22.7 m and 23.7 m from ground-water. However, this is not because they grew down but rather because the dunes have grown up around the stem of the trees (Gries *et al.* 2003).

3.9.1 Hydraulic lift

Studies by Nobel and Sanderson (1984) showed that the rate of water loss from attached roots of *A. deserti* plants dried in air at 20°C and a 1.2 kPa saturation deficit (50% relative humidity) decreased about 200-fold in 72 h, which would greatly limit water loss from the plant to a drying soil. At 96 h after rewetting roots of *A. deserti* that had been exposed to air at the same temperature and relative humidity, rehydration of existing roots, and development of new roots contributed about equally to water uptake by the whole plant. Nobel and Sanderson (1984) concluded that roots of these desert succulents readily take up water from a wet soil but lose little water to a dry soil, thus effectively acting like rectifiers with respect to plant–soil water movement. However, Richards and Caldwell (1987) have shown that hydraulic lift can occur, whereby water is lifted by the roots from moist areas to drier areas. Water that is released from the roots when transpira-tion ends (usually at night) usually passes into the upper soil layers where it is absorbed and then re-absorbed by the plant the following day and then transpired. Part of the process involves reverse flow, where the water passes by osmosis out of the xylem of the upper roots (when transpira-tion ceases) into the dry neighbouring soil (*contra* the observations of Nobel and Sanderson (1984)—Fig. 3.25). Hydraulic lift has been shown in many trees and shrubs, mostly in arid and semi-arid regions (23 species of grasses, herbs, shrubs, and trees) (although not exclusively so, see Dawson (1993) for examples in the mesic sugar maple *Acer saccharum*). A number of different plant species may benefit from hydraulic lift (Fig. 3.26; e.g. *A. erioloba* benefitting *Grewia flava*, *Ziziphus mucronata*, and *Tarchonanthus camphoratus*).

The first field evidence of hydraulic lift was shown in the desert shrub *Artemisia tridentata*. When the shrubs were covered with opaque plastic bags, water potential rose continuously for more than 2 days until the shrubs were again exposed to daylight. When the shrubs were illuminated at night, the increase of water potential was suppressed (Richards and Caldwell 1987). Using isotopes of deuterium, Richards and Caldwell (1987) showed that water taken up by the roots of *A. tridentata* was subsequently

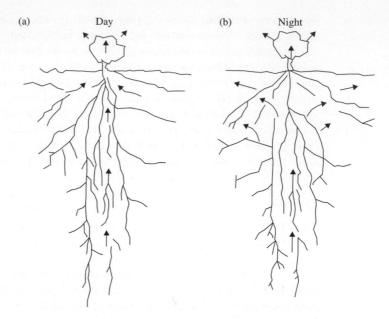

Fig. 3.25   Pattern of water flow through the root system during day and night periods according to the hydraulic lift hypothesis. (a) During the day, water is absorbed from all depths in which soil moisture is available and passes into the transpiration stream. (b) At night, when transpiration is reduced and plant water potential rises, the primary pathway for water movement is from moist soil through the root system to drier soil layers. (From Caldwell *et al.* 1998.)

Fig. 3.26   Facilitation of a number of plant species under the canopy of *Acacia erioloba* in the arid Northern Cape province (South Africa) probably occurs as a result of hydraulic lift and, perhaps, increased nitrogen levels because *A. erioloba* is known to fix nitrogen.

detected in the adjacent roots of grass plants. In this species, up to 33% of the daily evapotranspiration may be returned to the upper soil layers.

In the desert succulent, *Yucca schidigera*, which has some deeper roots (most succulents have shallow roots, e.g. upper 10 cm—Young and Nobel (1986); von Willert *et al.* (1992)), there is diel cycling of hydraulic lift in the opposite direction to C_3 plants. Being a CAM plant, they open their stomata during the night and close them during the day. Consequently, as one might anticipate, hydraulic lift occurs during the day (Yoder and Nowak 1999). These authors contend that this might be more beneficial to the neighbouring C_3 and C_4 plants because they transpire at this time. Yoder and Nowak (1999) also showed that there was a strong negative correlation ($r = -0.92$) between the frequency of plants displaying hydraulic lift at 0.35 m depth (where there are many roots) and the coarseness of the sand, probably because there is less root-soil contact in coarse-structured soils than in finer soils (Passioura 1991). It is also possible for the reverse process to occur. That is, inverse hydraulic lift occurs when roots move water down into the deeper soils and allow the water to flow into the dry sand there (Schulze *et al.* 1998). It is claimed that this may allow roots to grow easily in dry soil so that the roots can get down into these deep soils (Schulze *et al.* 1998).

4 Morphological, physiological, and behavioural adaptations of desert animals to the abiotic environment

Animals must be able to withstand the lack of water and the high and low temperatures in deserts to survive there. Many animals show unique morphological adaptations to desert extremes, while others are able to avoid these by behavioural means. This chapter will focus on patterns of convergent evolution of traits to assess which features represent unique desert adaptations.

Willmer *et al.* (2000) consider there to be two major strategies to deal with extremes of temperature: evaders and endurers. As the names imply, evaders avoid the heat such as by using burrows and endurers tolerate it. According to Willmer *et al.* (2000), a third group inhabits warm desert habitats, namely, evaporators. The latter group uses evaporative cooling to endure the heat. Roughly speaking, small organisms (<20 g) are evaders, intermediate-sized organisms are evaporators and large organisms (mostly mammals and very large birds) are endurers. The main reason that these categories are linked in this way is that there is a simple relationship between surface area and volume. A small organism, if it had cubic dimensions, may have a surface area of, say, 1 cm × 1 cm × 6 sides = 6 cm^2. Its volume will be 1 cm × 1 cm × 1 cm = 1 cm^3. A slightly larger organism will be, say, 2 cm × 2 cm × 6 sides = 24 cm^2. Its volume will be 2 cm × 2 cm × 2 cm = 8 cm^3. An even larger organism may be 3 cm × 3 cm × 6 sides = 54 cm^2. Its volume will be 3 cm × 3 cm × 3 cm = 27 cm^3. Thus, the small organism will have a surface area:volume ratio of 6:1, an intermediate-sized organism will have a ratio of 24:8 = 3:1, and a large organism will have a ratio of 54:27 = 2:1. This means that a small organism will be able to gain heat and lose it again quite quickly through its large surface area, whereas a large organism will find it considerably more difficult to do so.

Small organisms tend to be convectively coupled, meaning that wind affects their body temperatures greatly because of their relatively large surface areas. On the other hand, large organisms tend to be radiation coupled (heat, either directly from the sun or reflected from the ground (albedo)), affects their body temperatures greatly because of their relatively small surface areas (Gates 2003). Furthermore, most invertebrates, amphibians and reptiles are ectothermic because they have external heat sources only and, consequently, the body temperature they have is affected by the convection and radiation around them. Conversely, birds and mammals are considered endothermic because they have an internal heat source and, consequently, their body temperatures are less variable. Another set of terms for these are heterotherms (also known as *poikilotherms*) and homeotherms (also known as *homoiotherms*), respectively. However, some animals do not fit into this generalization very well. For example, the Namib desert golden mole, *Eremitalpa granti namibensis* (Chrysochloridae; Insectivora), is a 15–40 g mammal yet allows T_b to fluctuate considerably while under the soft dune sand where it lives (Fielden *et al.* 1990a, b; Seymour and Seely 1996) (Fig. 4.1). In a counterexample, in the Negev desert, Prange and Pinshow (1994) showed that female 5.5 g grasshoppers, *Poekilocerus bufonius*, could maintain relatively constant body temperatures up to an air temperature of about 48°C (Fig. 4.2) by evaporative cooling. Desert cicadas (Toolson 1987; Sanborn *et al.* 1990) and large beetles (Bartholomew and Casey 1977) are also endothermic insects. Nonetheless, in general, 'evader', 'evaporator', and 'endurer' are useful categories, although there is a lot of overlap between the categories of 'evaders' and 'evaporators' and they will be condensed into a single category here.

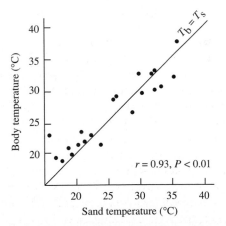

Fig. 4.1   Body temperature (T_b) fluctuations closely match those of sand temperature (T_s) fluctuations in the Namib golden mole. (From Fielden *et al.* 1990. With kind permission of Elsevier.)

4.1 Evaders and evaporators

Small animals, generally classified as 'evaders', include invertebrates (with the notable exceptions listed above), desert amphibians and reptiles, and also smaller mammals, rodents, and insectivores. The term 'evader' refers to the animals' behaviour, which helps to prevent overheating of the body on hot sunny days, and avoids the need for cooling by evaporative water loss, which is not feasible for small animals living in an arid habitat. Evaders make use of microenvironments such as shady rock crevices, underground burrows and shade cast by plants, for behavioural thermoregulation (Fig. 4.3). Evaders also use behaviour to prevent excessive cooling of the body, retreating to shelter when T_a declines at night. Willmer *et al.* (2000) define 'evaporators' as animals that depend on sufficient water intake to enable them to cool T_b by evaporation. Few of these species can survive in deserts, and those that do either live on the edges of deserts where they can access water or have behavioural and physiological adaptations that reduce reliance on evaporative cooling. So for evaporators, evasion may be an important part of their thermoregulatory strategy. 'Evaporators' include medium-sized mammals such as jack rabbits, dogs, foxes and also desert birds such as larks. There is a lot of overlap here in the evaporator classification, both for 'evaders' and 'endurers' so one must be aware that some species could fit into either. For example, both 'evaders' and 'endurers' will cool themselves evaporatively.

Insects possess some of the most effective desert features. For example, they have a very small body size, which means that they have a large surface area:volume ratio, and, consequently, they can offload heat quickly and

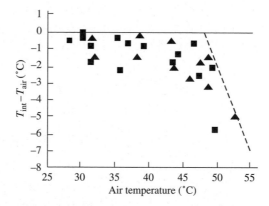

Fig. 4.2   Depression of internal temperature relative to air temperature in grasshoppers *Poekilocerus bufonius*. Female grasshoppers could maintain relatively constant body temperatures up to an air temperature of about 48°C. (From Prange and Pinshow 1994. Copyright Elsevier.)

gain it quickly when the day is cool. Many species, particularly tenebrionid beetles, have a waxy cuticle to reduce water loss across the body surface. The most extreme form of this is the wax bloom in Namib desert and North American tenebrionid beetles (Hadley 1979; McClain *et al.* 1985) (Fig. 4.4). Hadley (1979) has shown that there is a slight decrease in cuticular water loss of blue (i.e. light) coloured beetles compared with black beetles of the tenebrionid species, *Cryptoglossa verrucosa* in the Sonoran desert (0.11 mg cm^{-2} h^{-1} vs. 0.13 mg cm^{-2} h^{-1}). Another important feature is a discontinuous ventilation cycle. Insects and solifugids (Solifugidae: Arachnidae; also known as sun or wind spiders) use this system (Lighton and Fielden 1996), as do ixodid ticks (family Acari) (Fielden *et al.* 1993). However, the 'sit-and-wait' strategy employed by ticks, where they are inactive for long periods while waiting for a blood meal, might predispose them to a discontinuous ventilation strategy (Fielden *et al.* 1993). Spiracles are kept closed for >10 min to minimize respiratory water loss (Lighton and Fielden 1996). Spiracles must then be opened for gas exchange. This is an effective way of limiting water loss. In solifugids, there are three phases similar to those in insects comprising (1) a closed-spiracle phase, followed by (2) a diffusive phase characterized by tissue-level O_2 uptake but very low CO_2 emission (functionally equivalent to the insect fluttering-spiracle phase) and, finally, (3) an open-spiracle phase during which accumulated CO_2 escapes. In solifugids, the open-spiracle phase CO_2 emission volume was independent of temperature and metabolic rate, comprising 20 µl g^{-1} body mass (Lighton and Fielden 1996).

Fig. 4.3   Behavioural thermoregulation: *Platysaurus broadleyi* sunning itself on a rock, Namaqualand, South Africa.

Fig. 4.4   Wax blooms in Namib tenebrionid beetles. Lighter areas on the beetles indicate wax bloom. (From McClain *et al.* 1985. With the kind permission of the Ecological Society of America.)

Insects, land snails and many reptiles and birds excrete uric acid as a major nitrogenous waste while mammals excrete urea. Uric acid is largely insoluble in water and is excreted as paste, resulting in very little water loss. Most excretory systems (regardless of whether they are invertebrates or vertebrates, exotherms or endotherms) produce urine by refining a filtrate derived from body fluids. These systems are generally developed from a system of complex tubules. In the case of insects and other terrestrial arthropods, they use Malpighian tubules to excrete nitrogenous wastes and function in osmoregulation. Phillips (1964) has shown that insects such as the desert locust, *Schistocerca gregaria*, produce a relatively dry waste which is important for desert life to avoid excessive water loss. He showed that the maximum osmotic gradient of locusts fed a hypertonic saline solution was 2–3 times higher than locusts fed tap water, indicating considerable ability to regulate water absorption in relation to their requirements (Fig. 4.5). They are able to produce a re-usable rectal fluid that is about 20 μl as opposed to locusts fed tap water that do not produce any re-usable fluid. Mammals from very dry environments have very long loops of Henle to concentrate the ions and remove water for re-use (Fig. 4.6). They also use countercurrent multipliers within the loops of Henle to effectively concentrate their nitrogenous wastes (Fig. 4.7).

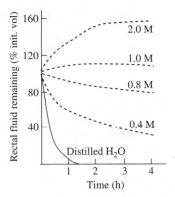

Fig. 4.5   Phillips (1964) showed that the maximum osmotic gradient of locusts fed a hypertonic saline solution was 2–3 times higher than locusts fed tap water, indicating considerable ability to regulate water absorption in relation to their requirements. (From Phillips 1964. With the kind permission of Oxford University Press.)

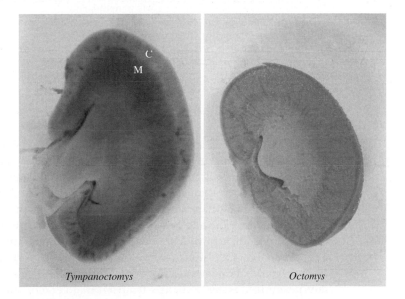

Fig. 4.6   Longitudinal sections of kidneys from *Tympanoctomys* and its close relative *Octomys*. Note the difference in the thickness of the cortex (C) and medulla (M) area. The medulla contains the loops of Henle, which extract salts and water. *Tympanoctomys* feeds on saltbush (hence, the thick medulla and long renal papilla) whereas *Octomys* feeds on cacti (and other plants) and does not need a specialized kidney like that of *Tympanoctomys*. (Photograph courtesy of Ricardo Ojeda.)

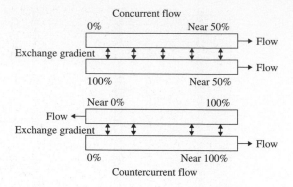

Fig. 4.7   Countercurrent multipliers within the loops of Henle effectively remove water from urine so that the body can retain water used to move the nitrogenous waste products. The diagram presents a generic representation of a concurrent and a countercurrent exchange system, with tubes containing fluid separated by a semipermeable membrane. Fluid is transferred across the barrier in the direction from greater to lesser according to the second law of thermodynamics. In the concurrent exchange system, the liquid flows in the same direction. A concurrent exchange system has a variable gradient over the length of the exchanger. With equal flows in the two vessels, this exchange method is capable of moving half of the property from one flow to the other, no matter how long the exchanger is. However, with the two flows moving in opposite directions, the countercurrent exchange system can maintain a nearly constant gradient between the two flows over their entire length. (From www.answers.com/topic/countercurrent-exchange. This modified figure is licenced to OpenLearn under the Creative Commons Attribution ShareAlike 2.5 License [Date accessed: 24 June 2008].)

4.1.1   Snails

One might think that snails would be rare animals in deserts, especially in limestone deserts such as the Negev desert of Israel. They occur, to varying degrees, in all deserts. They have unique adaptations for desert life. In the Negev desert, these snails can be found in a dormant state on the barren soil surface fully exposed to the sun in summer. Although some species develop calcareous epiphragms to reduce water loss from their shell openings, some use a mucous covering (Ward and Slotow 1992; Arad 1993) (Fig. 4.8). In winter, they become active during rainy periods, when they feed and reproduce. In the southern Namib desert, Dallas *et al.* (1991) examined water exchange, temperature tolerance and oxygen consumption of the snail, *Trigonephrus* sp., and related this to activity. Body temperature tracked sand temperature. Snails tolerated sand temperatures as high as 45°C. Mean oxygen consumption rates were 32.0 μl O_2 g^{-1} total body mass^{-1} h^{-1} at 15°C, when the snails were active, and 11.27 μl O_2 g^{-1} total body mass^{-1} h^{-1} at 25°C, when the snails were inactive. These values are 2–6 times lower than those recorded for the similarly sized mesic snail, *Helix aspersa*. At 25°C and 15% RH, mean water loss was 5.95 mg day^{-1}. Activity experiments indicated that low ambient temperatures and high

Fig. 4.8   *Trochoidea seetzenii* snails move to the tops of plants in the heat of summer, in the Negev desert.

humidities were favoured by the snails. This, together with the burying behaviour of these snails during high temperatures, suggests that they limit stress by restricting activity to physiologically favourable periods, even though more extreme conditions may be tolerated.

In the Negev desert, Schmidt-Nielsen *et al.* (1971) found that lethal temperatures of *Sphincterochila boisseri* lie between 50 C and 55 C, depending on the time of exposure. The temperature of the dormant animal within the shell, exposed to the sun on the soil surface in summer, does not reach a lethal level, although the temperature of the surrounding soil surface far exceeds this temperature. The oxygen consumption of dormant *S. boisseri* snails varies with temperature (Q_{10} = 2–4) (Schmidt-Nielsen *et al.* 1971). It is so low that the tissues could support this metabolic rate for several years, thus permitting continued dormancy even during periods of drought extending over more than 1 year.

The rate of water loss from dormant *S. boisseri*, exposed in their natural habitat in summer, is about 0–5 mg day^{-1} per snail (Schmidt-Nielsen *et al.* 1971). This rate, if continued unchanged, would give an annual loss <200 mg. A 4-g specimen contains about 1,400 mg water, and because the water loss during the cooler part of the year is lower, several years should elapse before critical levels of water loss would be reached. In snails collected in summer, the water content was not reduced, indicating no measurable depletion of water reserves during the hot season. However, Arad *et al.* (1990, 1993) showed that other Negev desert snails such as *Sphincterochila zonata* lost 4% of their body mass over 3 weeks, while mass loss for *Trochoidea simulata* was 5–7%. In another study, Arad (1993) found that *Eremina desertorum* lost 0.31% day^{-1}, *Euchondrus desertorum* lost 0.42% day^{-1} (= 9% mass loss over 21 days), and *Euchondrus albulus*

Fig. 4.9   *Eremina desertorum* snails are about 10–12 mm long yet they play an important role in the cycling of nitrogen in the Negev desert ecosystem. (From www.anbg.gov.au [Date accessed: 18 June 2008].)

lost 0.63% day^{-1} as adults (= 13.2% over 21 days) and almost double that (1.04% day^{-1}) as juveniles. Arad (1993) ascribes the higher values to the more mesic distribution of this last-mentioned species. The mean body mass of *E. desertorum* was 3.3 g, and for *E. desertorum* was 0.19 g and for *E. albulus* was 0.07 g. The small size of the last two species allows them to hide under rocks for most of the day and emerge at night (Fig. 4.9). They do not need to close off the shell entrances to moisture because the entrance to the shell is very contorted.

The ultimate vertebrate evaders are desert frogs such as *Cyclorana platycephala* (Fig. 4.10), *Limnodynastes spenceri* and *Neobatrachus pictus* from Australia, which spend most of the year in aestivation, inside a burrow (Lee and Mercer 1967). The North American desert spadefoot toad *Scaphiopus couchi* also aestivates (Mayhew 1965). Lee and Mercer (1967) found that the cocoon that envelopes the Australian frog *N. pictus* is identical to the *stratum corneum* of the epidermis and is derived by sloughing this layer as a single unit (see also Mayhew (1965) for *S. couchi*), as occurs in snakes. Aestivation is a form of dormancy, which enables animals to survive lack of water and high T_a during a hot, dry season. During the short rainy season, desert frogs accumulate water in the bladder, where it remains during aestivation. Thereafter, the frogs use it to osmoregulate.

Kangaroo rats (*Dipodomys* spp.) depend on metabolic water because there is little or no water available in their diet of seeds (MacMillen 1972). Kangaroo rats appear to be ill-adapted for life in a desert because, similar to other rodents, they neither sweat nor pant. Nevertheless, inside the burrow, they could lose water by evaporation from the lungs, which would be enhanced by T_b being higher than burrow T_a. As the water-carrying capacity of air increases with temperature, warm expired air contains more water than the cooler inhaled air (see under *Meriones crassus* below).

Fig. 4.10   Australian desert frog, *Cyclorana platycephala*. During aestivation, the frogs are protected from losing water to the dry soil in the burrow by a cocoon. At the end of the rainy season, the frogs burrow into the soil, and the skin undergoes a type of moulting process in which layers of epidermis are separated from the body but not shed, forming a protective cocoon, covering all parts of the body apart from the nostril openings. The cocoon thickens, becoming heavily keratinized, and prevents loss of water from the frog's body during the 9–10 months of aestivation. (This photograph is licensed to OpenLearn under a Creative Commons Attribution-NonCommercial-ShareAlike 2.0 Licence, and is copied from Robinson, M. (1999). *A Field Guide to Frogs of Australia*. p. 76. New Holland Publishers, Sydney, Australia.)

However, the temperature of the exhaled air in kangaroo rats is lower than that of T_b, and often close to T_a (Fig. 4.11). This is because the nasal passages (turbinates) of kangaroo rats are extremely narrow and convoluted and provide a temporal countercurrent cooling system, which operates as a heat exchanger (MacMillen 1972).

Shenbrot *et al.* (2002) have shown that jirds *Meriones crassus* (Gerbillidae, Rodentia; body mass range = 50–110 g, mean for non-lactating females = 80 g) have remarkably stable burrow temperatures. Although there are large differences between seasons (14°C in winter and 31°C in summer in sand and about 10°C in winter and 28°C in summer in loess), there is almost no variability in these temperatures (Fig. 4.12). Similarly, relative humidity is remarkably constant. Thus, although mean air temperatures may be lower than burrow temperatures, it is the escape from high air temperatures in the middle of the day, especially in summer, that make the burrow such a suitable place to rest. Conversely, the red vizcacha rat *Tympanoctomys barrerae* (Octodontidae, Rodentia) of the Monte desert in Argentina has non-random orientation of its burrow openings to face away from the cold winds in winter and into direct sunlight (Torres *et al.* 2003). It is apparent that burrows are very effective places to avoid either heat or cold.

Two special types of burrows are the tubular structures used by burrowing spiders and termite mounds:

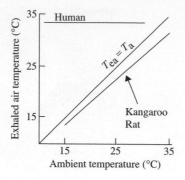

Fig. 4.11 Kangaroo rats *Dipodomys* spp. depend on metabolic water because there is virtually no water available in their diet of seeds. Inside the burrow, they could lose water by evaporation from the lungs, which would be enhanced by T_b being higher than burrow T_a. As the water-carrying capacity of air increases with temperature, warm expired air contains more water than the cooler inhaled air. However, the temperature of the exhaled air in kangaroo rats (T_{ea}) is lower than that of T_b, and often close to T_a, because the nasal passages (turbinates) of kangaroo rats are extremely narrow and convoluted and provide a temporal countercurrent cooling system, which operates as a heat exchanger. (This modified figure is licensed to OpenLearn under a Creative Commons Attribution-NonCommercial-ShareAlike 2.0 Licence.)

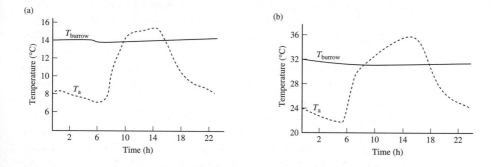

Fig. 4.12 There was no variability in burrow temperatures of *Meriones crassus* in (a) winter and (b) summer, indicating the stability of sand temperatures. Note that burrow temperatures differ considerably between winter and summer. (From Shenbrot *et al.* 2002. Copyright Elsevier.)

1. *Burrowing spiders*—Lubin and Henschel (1990) studied the spider *Seothyra henscheli* (Eresidae) that burrows beneath the Namib dunes. Burrows are web-lined and about 10–15 cm in depth, with a web capture surface. When a prey item (often an ant) becomes entangled in the capture web, the spider rushes to the surface to strike at and subsequently disentangle the prey. Thereafter, the spider removes the

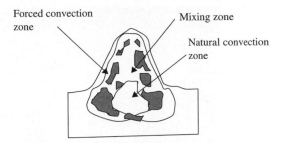

Fig. 4.13   Lüscher (1961) considered the closed macrotermite mound to work as an effect of the high metabolic rate of the termite colony. Specifically, the heat and humidity of the mound created by this high metabolic rate lowers the density of the air. The resulting buoyant forces drive the heat towards the chimney and exit channels. Homeostasis of the mound is achieved when there is a link between circulation rate and colony metabolism. (From Turner 2001. Copyright University of Chicago Press.)

prey from the capture web and withdraws with it to the bottom of the burrow. This spider, in the heat of the day, 'shuttles' with the prey item, taking it down to the depths of the burrow, because the temperature at the surface can be as much as 70°C. Although the critical thermal maximum (CTMax) temperature of these spiders is high (about 49°C), if a burrow was only 5 cm deep or less, it would get too hot for these spiders. The most important part of 'shuttling' is the post-strike retreat, which occurs when it gets too hot for the spider to spend time on the surface (Turner *et al.* 1993).

2. *Termite mounds*—Darlington (1987) considered there to be two basic types of macrotermite mound, open and closed. Darlington (1987) found that open mounds should function like a Venturi effect, where wind passing over the open colony forces air out of the colony as external air is drawn into the colony through termite entrance holes in the base of the mound. For a Venturi effect (better known as induced flow (Vogel 1994)) to work, there must be ventilation via holes in the ground and ventilation above the ground. A negative hydrostatic pressure gradient will result, so that air is drawn into the lower openings and out of the upper opening. Turner (1994) found just such an effect in a termite species of arid southern Africa, *Odontotermes transvaalensis*. On average, just 80 min of air circulation is needed for 95% of colony air to be exchanged with the surroundings.

Lüscher (1961) considered the closed macrotermite mound to work as an effect of the high metabolic rate of the termite colony. Specifically, the heat and humidity of the mound created by this high metabolic rate (estimated by Darlington *et al.* (1997) to be hundreds of watts) lowers the density of the air. The resulting buoyant forces drive the heat towards the chimney and exit channels (Fig. 4.13). Homeostasis of the mound is achieved when

Fig. 4.14   Unique bushy tail of *Xerus inauris*. (Photograph courtesy of Jane Waterman.)

there is a link between circulation rate and colony metabolism. This is known as a 'thermosiphon effect' (Lüscher 1961). However, Turner (2001) studied the closed mound of *Macrotermes michaelseni* and found that it is a bit more complicated than Lüscher (1961) assumed. Turner (2001) found that wind is the primary factor determining nest ventilation and that tidal effects are driven by local variation in wind speed and direction. However, consistent with Lüscher's hypothesis, Turner (2001) found that metabolism-induced variation in buoyant forces may function with tidal forces to create homeostasis within the mound.

One of the unique morphological characteristics of an evader/evaporator is the bushy tail of the Cape ground squirrel *Xerus inauris* (mean ± SE body mass of females = 655 ± 10 g, mean ± SE of males = 730 ± 10 g), which lives in the Kalahari, Karoo and Namib deserts of southern Africa. This tail acts as a parasol (umbrella), reducing the high body temperatures of these small mammals (Bennett *et al.* 1984). By using taxidermic models covered with the pelt of the animal, Bennett *et al.* (1984) measured the operative environmental temperatures (T_e) of models with raised tails (Fig. 4.14) and in a prone position. T_e is an effective way to measure the integrated radiant and convective thermal heat of an organism, and is the equilibrium temperature the organism would attain if it lacked metabolic heat and evaporative water loss (Bakken 1980). Between 09h15 and 11h30, squirrels usually raised their tails and faced their backs into the sun. After 11h30, most squirrels started disappearing from the surface, shuttling into and out of their burrows, and emerging only for brief periods on to the soil surface to forage (Fig. 4.15) (Bennett *et al.* 1984). At this time, T_e exceeded 40°C (burrow temperature was only 27°C). The ground squirrel started to forage more consistently on the surface in the late afternoon (after about 17h30). Mean difference in

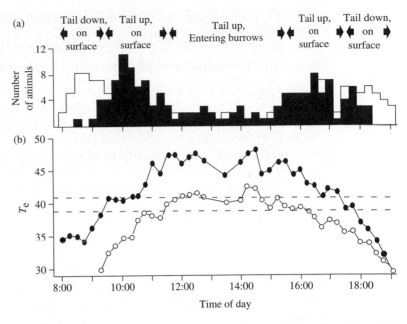

Fig. 4.15 (a and b) Between 09h15 and 11h30, squirrels usually raised their tails and faced their backs into the sun. After 11h30, most squirrels started disappearing from the surface, shuttling into and out of their burrows, emerging only for brief periods on to the soil surface to forage. Black columns = individuals with tails up over their backs; white columns = animals with tailsdown; black circles = model with the tail down; white circles = model with the tail up; dashed lines = approximate range of ambient temperatures that begins to elicit a rise in body temperature and salivation. (From Bennett *et al.* 1984. Copyright University of Chicago Press.)

T_e between parasol tails and prone tails between 09h15 and 17h30 was 5.6 °C (maximum = 8.3°C).

In Australia, rates of tritiated water turnover and pulmocutaneous evaporation were compared by Haines *et al.* (1974) in three species of desert-dwelling dasyurid marsupials and five species of murid rodents. Water turnover in the dasyurids, *Dasycercus cristicauda* and *Dasyuroides byrnei*, and in the murids, *Notomys alexis, N. cervinus, Pseudomys australis,* and *P. desertor,* was <120 ml kg$^{-0.82}$ per 24 h (note that turnover is raised to the power of −0.82, which is considered to be the allometric equation for body mass) (Calder 1984) and, thus, was similar to that of other small desert mammals. In contrast, the dasyurid *Sminthopsis crassicaudata* and the murid *Leporillus conditor* expended water at rates comparable to that of other non-desert-dwelling species. When forced to minimize water intake, *N. alexis, N. cervinus, P. australis,* and *P. desertor* reduced water turnover by 70% and evaporation by 30%. Without drinking water, *D. byrnei* did not reduce evaporative loss, although total water turnover fell by about 40%. The granivorous murids obtain only small quantities of water with food and minimize water loss, whereas the carnivorous dasyurids ingest about five times more water with each unit of metabolizable energy than rodents and have less need for water conservation.

4.1.2 Physiological mechanisms of controlling heat gain

Birds and larger desert mammals that use evaporative cooling risk dehydrating because of the difficulty of finding sufficient drinking water. For mammals, evaporative heat loss includes panting and sweating.

In small mammals and birds, the temperature of exhaled air is often lower than T_b, resulting in condensation of water on the nasal mucosa. While resting in their cool burrows during the heat of the day, small desert mammals rely on this mechanism for water conservation. However, for mammals and birds exposed to high T_a, the nasal countercurrent heat exchanger minimizes water loss, and so works against the need to increase heat loss by evaporation of water. The most important of these characteristics is the carotid *rete mirabile*, a maze of blood vessels that works similar to the radiator of a vehicle. Warm blood flowing from the heart to the brain passes through a network of vessels surrounded by veins carrying blood already cooled through evaporation (in the nasal area). Heat is exchanged in this process and thus lowers the temperature of the blood to the brain. It is a very efficient way to protect the body and simultaneously avoid too much sweating, which has the result of fluid loss. In desert-dwelling pigeons, Pinshow *et al.* (1982) have shown that the *rete mirabile ophthalmicum* works by shunting warm blood to the curved outer surface of the eye, where it is cooled convectively and is then shunted back to the brain.

In the Namib desert, Downs and Perrin (1990) studied the thermal mechanisms employed by four gerbil (*Gerbillurus*) species. In spite of the fact that all four species are nocturnal, and thus adaptations to cold temperatures should be needed when they are active, their basal metabolic rates (BMR) were lower than expected based on body mass. In other words, they too had xeric characteristics. Their thermoneutral zones (where there is no relationship between ambient temperature and metabolic rate) were narrow and exceeded their burrow temperatures. At high ambient temperatures, they did use evaporative cooling (Fig. 4.16), although it is probably unlikely that this would be needed in the Namib desert.

Some small organisms enter torpor (a lowering of T_b below T_a), either on a daily or on a seasonal basis. Torpor can be advantageous to mammals and birds because they reduce their requirements for energy and decrease cutaneous, respiratory and excretory water loss (Lovegrove *et al.* 1999). Torpor can be separated into hibernation (in winter cold periods), aestivation (to avoid heat) and short-term torpor. An interesting example of torpor occurs in the round-eared elephant shrew *Macroscelides proboscideus* (Macroscelidea, Mammalia), which occurs in the arid parts of South Africa, Botswana and Namibia. Lovegrove *et al.* (1999) showed that torpor,

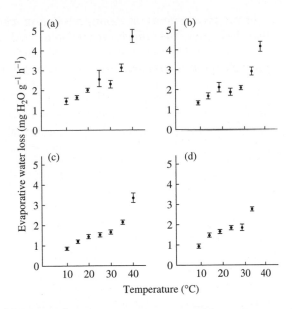

Fig. 4.16 At high ambient temperatures, nocturnally-active gerbils used evaporative cooling, although it is probably unlikely that this would be needed in the Namib desert. (From Downs and Perrin 1990. Copyright Elsevier.)

which varied in duration from <1 h to about 18 h, was induced by food deprivation and not by low T_a. Mzilikazi and Lovegrove (2003) have shown that arousal from torpor can be achieved by passive thermoregulation when the sun rises. In an Australian study, Tomlinson *et al.* (2007) investigated whether the endemic desert mouse *Pseudomys hermannsburgensis* entered torpor. They found that this species became hypothermic at low ambient temperatures (T_b was about 17°C at $T_a = 15$°C) but they did not spontaneously arouse themselves. However, they did survive and became normothermic ($T_b = 33$°C) if returned to room temperature (23°C). They concluded that this species, similar to other Australian mammals (see Stafford Smith and Morton 1990), does not enter torpor but can survive hypothermia.

In the red-headed finch *Amadina erythrocephalus* found in arid parts of South Africa and Namibia (Passeriformes, Aves), McKechnie and Lovegrove (2003) have shown that a shallow rest-phase hypothermia exists. As was the case with elephant shrews, there was about a 5°C decrease in body temperature associated with lower availability of food (but not low T_a). Here too, this species was considered to have a metabolic rate consistent with that of desert birds but significantly lower than for mesic birds. Lane *et al.* (2004) has shown that torpor may exist in the nightjars and poor wills (Caprimulgiformes, Aves) but there is neither evidence that this is related to desert life nor evidence that a passerine such as the red-headed finch can enter torpor (McKechnie and Lovegrove 2003).

Panting is an important cooling mechanism for foxes and other animals that chase prey. The fennec fox (*Fennecus zerda*), a species found in the Sahara desert, is reputed to pant at 690 times per minute after chasing prey (Maloiy *et al.* 1982). Rüppell's foxes (*Vulpes rueppellii*) live in the Rub' al-Khali (the so-called Empty Quarter) of Arabia, the largest existing sand sea, which is an extremely arid desert with no permanent sources of drinking water. These foxes obtain all their water from food, supplemented by metabolic water production. As a result of their nocturnality, Rüppell's foxes might be expected to have a reduced total evaporative water loss (TEWL) in comparison to fox species living in mesic habitats. Resting in a den during the day would reduce TEWL, but Rüppell's foxes would have to travel long distances at night while hunting their prey, mainly rodents, birds and arthropods, thereby increasing the need for evaporative cooling. Williams *et al.* (2002) measured TEWL of individual foxes at 35°C and found it to be about 50 g water day^{-1}, which is about 55% lower than allometric (body mass) expectations for other mammalian species. This was achieved by reducing either cutaneous or respiratory water loss (Williams *et al.* 2002).

Because birds of all sizes tolerate hot arid conditions, physiologists considered that desert birds, being diurnal animals exposed to extremes of ambient temperature and aridity in deserts, are successful because they have higher T_b (41–42°C) than mammals, reducing their relative need for evaporative cooling. Also, because birds are uricotelic (they excrete uric acid rather than urea), relatively little water is required for the excretion of nitrogenous waste (see above).

Chukars (*Alectoris chukar*) and Sand Partridges (*Ammoperdix heyi*), two ground-dwelling phasianids (Phasianidae, Galliformes, Aves), are permanent residents of the Negev desert and sympatric over much of their ranges. Chukars (body mass = 350–600 g) are widely distributed and inhabit deserts only at the margins of their ranges. On the other hand, Sand Partridges (body mass = 150–250 g) inhabit only arid and very arid areas (Alkon *et al.* 1982; Pinshow *et al.* 1983; Degen *et al.* 1984). Both species are adapted to arid habitats because of their low-energy metabolism, which ranges from 43% to 81% of that expected for birds of similar body mass. During summer, Sand Partridges have lower energy expenditures (5.5 kJ g$^{-0.61}$ d^{-1}) and water influxes (72.3 ml kg$^{-0.75}$ d^{-1}) than Chukars (6.42 kJ g$^{-0.61}$ d^{-1} and 93.5 ml kg$^{-0.75}$ d^{-1}, respectively) (Kam *et al.* 1987), demonstrating that the desert specialist is better adapted to arid conditions (here energy expenditure is raised to the power of -0.61 and water influx to -0.75, the allometric equations for body mass)(Calder 1984). However, both species obtain more than half of their water influx in summer by drinking because their summer diet is relatively dry, consisting of seeds (80%), some green vegetation (1–8%) and, in Chukars, occasional arthropods. This situation changes abruptly after winter rains, which induces germination and reduces the availability of seeds. Chukars are unable to maintain energy balance in the face of low ambient temperatures and a diet (90% green vegetation) that contains high water but comparatively little energy (Alkon *et al.* 1982), and they mobilize fat reserves to meet energy requirements. Most sand partridges leave the Negev after winter rains, migrating to the lower elevation, warmer and drier Arava (part of the Syrian-African Rift Valley). In contrast to expectation, the winter rainy season appears to be the most stressful time of the year for both species. The adaptations to hot, dry conditions possessed by sand partridges may be accompanied by constraints on their abilities to cope with cool, wet conditions, and this may restrict them to arid and very arid habitats.

Many desert birds, particularly ground-nesting species, use panting for cooling, thereby incurring increased evaporative water loss. Female dune larks, *Certhilauda erythrochlamys*, incubating their eggs pant during midday to regulate their own body temperature and hence their eggs (Williams 2001). Crowned plovers *Vanellus coronatus* (Charadriiformes) are also ground nesters, as are desert sandgrouse (*Pterocles* spp., Pteroclidiformes) and, in addition to panting, they may also use gular fluttering, a rapid vibration of the floor of the mouth that provides rapid evaporative heat loss with up to 2°C cooling in the mouth (Hinsley *et al.* 1993; Downs and Ward 1997). *Pterocles* spp. can afford to lose water in this way, as these birds fly long distances every day to drink water from pools (Cade and Maclean 1967; Hinsley *et al.* 1993). Other birds such as desert larks do not show this behaviour as they rely entirely on water obtained from their food, so they cannot afford to lose so much water by evaporation (Williams 2001). Crowned plovers do not drink but will pant or use gular fluttering on extreme occasions when forced to cool their eggs. A problem with panting and gular fluttering is that, while it achieves cooling by evaporative water loss, it can also result in an increase in CO_2 in the lungs, which leads to respiratory alkalosis (i.e. a change in acid–base balance) (Calder and Schmidt-Nielsen 1966). Larks do not usually nest in the open where they are exposed to direct sunlight and albedo (reflection of sunlight off ground surfaces), while plovers and sandgrouse do. Downs and Ward (1997) considered whether Crowned plovers raised themselves above their eggs to cool themselves or their eggs. Maclean (1967) had speculated that this was done in Double-banded coursers, *Rhinoptilus cursorius*, in the Kalahari desert because the wind passing over the eggs would convectively cool them. However, Downs and Ward (1997) found that there was a greater cooling effect on the adults. Adult plovers cooled themselves and then sat back on their eggs, cooling the eggs in turn.

An additional unique adaptation of sandgrouse is the evolution of curled belly feathers. When they have young in their nests, males sometimes fly as much as 40 km to reach water. They stand in the water, and the feathers expand and collect water in the curls (Cade and Maclean 1967; Rijke

Fig. 4.17   Namaqua sandgrouse. (Photograph courtesy of Alastair Rae.)

1972; Joubert and Maclean 1973) (Fig. 4.17). Thereafter, they drink water themselves and fly back to their chicks, who drink the water by stripping it from the belly feathers of the parent.

4.2   Adaptations to handle unique situations

4.2.1   Salt glands in birds and reptiles

There are many species of marine birds that need to deal with the problem of excess seawater. This is done by using unique nasal glands called salt glands, which are effective transport epithelia for removing excess salt. Similar to the kidney, they work by using osmosis to remove salts through special glands in the nares. The same salt glands are possessed by a few taxa of desert birds. The desert orders with salt glands include Struthioniformes (ostriches), Gruiformes (including bustards), Charadriiformes (including lapwings, coursers and plovers), Galliformes (recorded in the sand partridge *A. heyi* only), Anseriformes (geese), Cuculiformes (roadrunner), Phoenicopteriformes (flamingos) and Falconiformes (raptors) (Maclean 1996). The production of excess salt mostly occurs as a result of attempting to reduce NaCl loads when extremely high T_a is experienced, such as the production of salt in the Australian Pratincole *Stiltia isabella* (Jesson and Maclean 1976) and Inland Dotterel *Peltohyas australis* (Maclean 1976). High NaCl loads near saline lakes may also lead to the production of salt in these glands (Mahoney and Jehl 1985a, b). In raptors and the roadrunner, *Geococcyx californianus*, the birds incur a salt load from their (mostly) mammalian prey. This has been recorded in 16 Accipitridae species and 5 species of Falconidae (Maclean 1996). In the case of the Gabar Goshawk

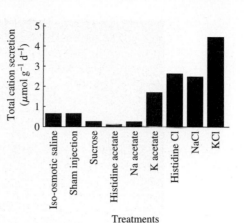

Fig. 4.18   Hazard (2001) examined the extrinsic factors (salts and other loads) and intrinsic factors (hormones and neurotransmitters) controlling rate and composition of secretion by the desert iguana (*Dipsosaurus dorsalis*), an herbivorous desert lizard. Desert iguanas normally secrete potassium chloride to help eliminate the high amounts of potassium found in the desert plants they eat. Other vertebrate salt glands secrete in response to any osmotic challenge (e.g. NaCl, sucrose). Desert iguana salt glands respond specifically to increases in plasma potassium or chloride. They do not respond to sodium alone or other osmotic challenges (sucrose, histidine acetate). Effects of potassium and chloride appear to be additive. (From Hazard 2001. With kind permission of University of Chicago Press.)

Micronisus gabar, which lives in the arid areas of the Kalahari, Namib, and Karoo, a bird was observed to start secreting fluid from its external nares about 9 min after starting to eat a mouse (Cade and Greenwald 1966).

In addition to occurring in desert birds, some reptiles secrete salt through salt glands. This is known from several species in the Iguanidae, Agamidae (two species of large herbivorous *Uromastyx*), Scincidae (skinks), Xantusidae, Lacertidae, Teiidae, and Varanidae. In addition to secreting NaCl, some of these reptiles may also secrete K and the accompanying anion may either be Cl or bicarbonate. For example, Hazard (2001) found that *Dipsosaurus dorsalis*, an herbivorous desert lizard, only secreted increased levels of K and Cl; there was no response to increased levels of Na or bicarbonate. She concluded that this was due to the specificity of dietary K or Cl for these herbivorous lizards (Fig. 4.18).

4.2.2   Mammals that consume halophytes

Although salty areas are found in all deserts, there are relatively few mammal species that can tolerate these plants. A number of insect species, especially the leafhoppers (Cicadellidae, Insecta), have taken advantage of this niche. Nonetheless, halophytic plants have very negative water potentials, which mean that they take up large amounts of water and,

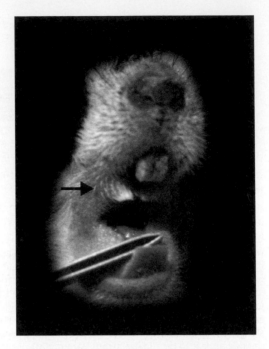

Fig. 4.19   South American vizcacha rat *Tympanoctomys barrerae* uses bristle-like hairs (see arrow) on either side of the mouth to remove the salt from *Atriplex* salt glands (From Mares *et al.* 1997. Copyright: American Institute of Biological Sciences.)

in doing so, also take up large amounts of salts. In some plant species (e.g. *Atriplex* (Chenopodiaceae)) that are green and succulent (West 1983; Mares *et al.* 1997), there are specialized salt glands on the leaves where this salt is deposited. A small number of small mammal species have developed ways to avoiding the salts. In the Negev desert, the fat sand rat *Psammomys obesus* removes the salt from the leaves using their teeth (Degen 1988). Similar devices have been employed by the North American chisel-toothed kangaroo rat, *Dipodomys microps* and the South American vizcacha rat, *T. barrerae*. In this latter species, a native of the Monte desert, an additional feature is the use of bristle-like hairs on either side of the mouth that occlude with the lower incisors and act to remove the salt from *Atriplex* salt glands (Fig. 4.19). The kidney of *T. barrerae* is similar to that of *P. obesus*, in that it has a long renal papilla, which is a structural adaptation that permits it to act as a countercurrent filter to more effectively remove salts (Abdallah and Tawfik 1969). An additional problem encountered by *P. obesus* is that *Atriplex halimus* also contains very high levels of calcium oxalate. The way that *P. obesus* deals with this problem is by bacterial degradation of oxalates. The intake ratio of oxalate:calcium is 4.5:1 while the excreta of *P. obesus* is 1.25:1, and is probably mostly digested by intestinal bacteria (Palgi *et al.* 2005).

4.2.3   Animals in temporary pools

A number of different animals live in unique communities in the small, ephemeral water pools that collect in deserts after rains. They may be divided into three groups, based on their responses to droughts. The *drought escapers* are winged insects, amphibians and some invertebrates that use these water bodies when present, but escape by migration or other means when the water dries up. In the cases of crustacean larvae, such as tadpole, fairy and clam shrimps, adults must lay drought-tolerant eggs before the pool dries up. The adults then die. *Drought resistors* include snails and mites and have a dormant stage that is resistant to desiccation. They have a waterproof layer such as an exoskeleton or shell that prevents the body tissues from losing too much water. They are also capable of burrowing into the fine mud that seals the bottoms of many pools. *Drought tolerators* such as rotifers can tolerate very high levels of desiccation. This is known as cryptobiosis (Jönsson and Järemo 2005). These animals can rehydrate themselves very quickly and can be fully functional in as little as 30 min (Williams 1985). Water is not the only cue, because these organisms can also respond to other factors such as salinity, oxygen content, temperature, and other physical and chemical factors in the water (Scholnick 1994).

4.3   Endurers

The best-known examples of desert endurers include the camel, the oryx, and desert sheep. In fact, most desert endurers are large mammals. Their relatively low surface area:volume ratio means that they have more difficulty than small animals in losing heat from the body at high T_a. Mammalian and avian endurers (such as ostriches, which are also large and often live in deserts) are too large to shelter in burrows and, if no shade is available, they may be forced to remain exposed to solar radiation during the day. The hair and feathers of large desert mammals can play an important role in insulation, both from solar heat and nocturnal cold.

Large mammals tend to be inactive during the hottest part of the day, thereby reducing metabolic heat production. Hartmann's mountain zebras *Equus zebra hartmannae* (Namib desert) (Fig. 4.20) and oryx (also known as gemsbok), *Oryx gazella* (Namib, Kalahari, and Karoo deserts), orient their bodies with the sun during the day. Hartmann's mountain zebras will climb eastward-facing slopes to absorb the sun's morning warmth. As the day progresses they find shade. The oryx of the southern African deserts commonly stands on the top of open dunes in the heat of the day

Fig. 4.20   Hartmann's mountain zebra in the Namib desert.

Fig. 4.21   Oryx in the Namib crossing sands.

to catch the cool winds passing over them. Nonetheless, this species is also known to cover great distances, even at noon (Fig. 4.21). In Africa's Namib desert, Hartmann's mountain zebras have been observed to sniff out water on the surface of dry river beds. They paw at the ground with their hooves to get to water that is sometimes 3 feet below the surface. By doing so, these zebras benefit other desert-dwelling animals. It has also been mentioned that Hartmann's mountain zebras can go without water for 4 days. In contrast, the Asiatic wild ass *Equus hemionus* in the Negev desert (Israel) must drink daily (Saltz *et al.* 2000).

The Arabian oryx, *Oryx leucoryx*, lives in the Arabian desert (Fig. 4.22), which includes areas where free-standing water is rarely, if ever, available. Where possible, the Arabian oryx spends time sitting in the shade of evergreen trees during the hottest part of the day. On hot days, these

Fig. 4.22   Arabian oryx (right) and another (Sahara-dwelling) desert antelope, the addax *Addax nasomaculatus* (left).

oryx also dig into the sand, exposing cool sand below the surface and sit in the depressions. Body heat is lost to the cooler sand by conduction (Williams *et al.* 2001; Ostrowski *et al.* 2003). Arabian oryx forage at night during the summer, avoiding exposure to high T_a and intense solar radiation (Williams *et al.* 2001). They feed on grasses and rely on the water content of the plants for their intake of water (Ostrowski *et al.* 2003). BMR and TEWL at 30°C were measured in Arabian oryx living in the Arabian desert, as were field metabolic rates (FMR) and field water influx rates (a measure of water intake) were measured using the doubly labelled water technique (Williams *et al.* 2001). In the summer, when grasses were parched, field metabolic rates of free-ranging oryx were 11,076 kJ day^{-1} in contrast to 22,081 kJ day^{-1} in spring, after rains. Williams *et al.* (2001) suggest that Arabian oryx cut their energy expenditure in summer by changing both behaviour and physiology. In summer, oryx forage at night and rest during the day. After spring rains, increased energy expenditure may occur because these animals must walk longer distances to forage, and also these animals have higher costs of thermoregulation because of reduced T_a (Williams *et al.* 2001).

At rest, the body temperature of normal healthy camels, *Camelus dromedarius* (Fig. 4.23), can vary from about 34°C to >40°C (Schmidt-Nielsen *et al.* 1956). This means that, in contrast to popular expectation, these animals are essentially heterotherms. However, temperature regulation in this species depends heavily on the availability of water. In summer, the diurnal variations in a camel deprived of drinking water may exceed 6°C, but in animals with free access to water the variations are similar to those

Fig. 4.23   Camel eating a spiny shrub, *Alhagi graecorum.*

found in the winter (about 2°C). Variation in T_b has important consequences for water conservation because:

1. An increase in T_b means that heat is stored in the body instead of being
    dissipated by evaporation of water. At night the excess heat can be given
    off without expenditure of water.
2. The high T_b means that heat gain from the hot environment is reduced
    because the temperature gradient is reduced. According to the Stefan-
    Boltzmann law, a body under constant conditions changes temperature
    to match that of its surroundings at a rate that is equal to the fourth
    power of the difference between them.

Heat regulation in camels occurs by evaporation from the skin surface
(sweating), with no apparent increase in respiratory rate or panting.
Evaporation from isolated skin areas increases linearly with increased
heat load at a critical temperature of around 35°C. The fur of the camel
is an efficient barrier against heat gain from the environment and water

expenditure is about 50% higher in camels that have been shorn (Schmidt-Nielsen *et al.* 1956).

Schmidt-Nielsen *et al.* (1971, 1981) showed that a 17% weight loss due to dehydration in a camel was accompanied by a 9% reduction in plasma volume and a 38% fluid loss from the gut. A camel has up to 75 litres of fluid in its rumen (85% of which is water) and another 8 litres in the intestine. The 38% of water loss in the gut is therefore about 30 litres, which minimizes strain on the blood circulation during dehydration. The camel can cope with up to 30% water loss, meaning that camel tissues are more resistant to high osmotic pressures than those of many animals. When provided with water after such a high level of dehydration, the camel can drink rapidly taking in up to 200 litres of water in just a few minutes. Much of the water taken in is stored temporarily in the gut, preventing excessive dilution of the blood, which would be harmful.

Schmidt-Nielsen *et al.*'s (1981) study improved our understanding of the common perceptions that camels store free water in the rumen and utilize water derived from metabolism of the lipids released from adipose tissue in the hump. Although camels have a great deal of water in the rumen and intestine, it is proportionately no more than is present in other ruminants. The oxidation of 1 g fat yields 1.07 g water; thus, a 40-kg hump could yield 43 litres of water that can be drawn on during a long journey. However, because this mechanism requires oxygen that can only be obtained by ventilating the lungs, there must be a net loss of water from the respiratory tract when the camel breathes dry air. Whether the fat reserves make a positive or negative contribution to the animal's overall water balance therefore depends on conditions in the upper respiratory tract.

In general, long limbs, tails or necks provide large surface areas from which heat can be dissipated, and behaviour patterns may maximize loss of heat from these areas (Crawford and Schmidt-Nielsen 1967). The ostrich, *Struthio camelus*, is the largest living bird, weighing 70–100 kg, with some males weighing up to 150 kg. Ostriches forage during the day, selecting plants with high water content during times of water shortage (Williams *et al.* 1993). The long, naked neck and legs of the ostrich provide a large surface area for convective and radiative cooling (Crawford and Schmidt-Nielsen 1967). The ostrich uses behaviour to enhance the cooling effects of feather erection at a high ambient temperature and incident solar radiation (Sauer and Sauer 1967; Louw *et al.* 1969). Sparsely distributed long feathers on the dorsal surface of the bird erect in response to warming of the skin, thereby increasing the thickness of the insulation between solar radiation and skin. The gaps between the feathers allow through air movements, which cool the skin by convection (Sauer and Sauer 1967; Louw *et al.* 1969). The birds supplement the physiological response during the hottest part of the day by orientating themselves towards the sun and bowing their wings away from the thorax, forming an 'umbrella' which shades the exposed thorax. The naked skin of the thorax acts as a surface for heat loss by both radiation and convection (Crawford and Schmidt-Nielsen 1967). At night when ambient temperatures decline, ostriches conserve heat by folding their wings close to the thorax and tucking their legs under the body while they sit on the ground (Sauer and Sauer 1967). The dorsal feathers respond to low T_a by flattening and interlocking, which traps an insulating layer of air next to the skin, and keeps most of the skin at 34.5°C (Louw *et al.* 1969).

Certain large lizard species behave similar to endurers, but they are evaders and evaporators too, showing that we should not apply this classification too strictly. One of the more interesting adaptations, which also occurs in aquatic amphibians and turtles, occurs in the Sonoran desert-dwelling Gila monsters, *Heloderma suspectum* (Davis and DeNardo 2007). These lizards use their urinary bladders to store dilute urine, drawing on it to buffer plasma osmolality when they are dehydrated or food limited. Plasma osmolality increased 2.5 times faster when their urinary bladders were empty. These large lizards (mass = 350–600 g) could draw on either drinking (which provides a more immediate osmotic benefit) or use water stored in their urinary bladders within 24 h.

4.4   Removing the effects of phylogeny

There are several animal taxa for which suitable, phylogenetically controlled analyses have been conducted. This means that the effects of phylogeny, which may be considerable, have been removed (Felsenstein 1985; Garland *et al.* 1992). Removing the effects of phylogeny allows one to test whether an adaptation has occurred. Otherwise, it is possible that lack of statistical independence (pseudoreplication) could occur because characters may evolve by chance alone or because of phylogenetic inertia (Felsenstein 1985; Pagel 1994). For example, one might find that a trait is considered a desert adaptation because many desert-dwelling species possess it and non-desert-dwelling species do not. However, if there are many desert-dwelling species in a particular part of a clade, then this character may have evolved by chance alone. Adaptations require that one demonstrate that new evolutionary features are acquired *de novo* (Coddington 1988). An additional study, on small mammals of the genus *Peromyscus*, uses a 'common garden' approach, where all animals were raised in the laboratory under standard conditions (Mueller and Diamond 2001). Here we will consider phylogenetically controlled studies on ectothermic invertebrates, ectothermic vertebrates, endothermic birds, and endothermic mammals.

4.4.1   Insects (tenebrionid beetles)

In the Namib desert, tenebrionid beetle species (also known as dark-ling beetles) are particularly common. There are 13 species in the genus *Onymacris* that are very abundant. Ward and Seely (1996b) tested a number of hypotheses that relate to the physiology and associated behaviour of these species:

1. Preferred body temperatures (the body temperature that a beetle prefers to be active at; determined in a circular thermal gradient) closely match the body temperatures (T_b) actually attained in the field. It has been shown by Roberts *et al.* (1991) that there is a correlation between preferred and field T_b ($r^2 = 0.8$), without removing the effects of phylogeny. Preferred T_bs should have evolved to match the temperatures at which an animal is most energetically efficient (Huey and Bennett 1987). Furthermore, Heinrich (1977, 1993) predicted that the extremes of temperature, the critical thermal maxima (CTMax) and minima (CTMin), are key adaptations because it is the extremes of temperature that exert the strongest selection pressures. Thus, Ward and Seely (1996a) also examined relationships between CTMax, CTMin and preferred and attained field T_b.

2. Desert beetles have evolved longer legs (relative to their body lengths) to enable them to 'stilt' (Penrith 1984) (see Fig. 4.24 for an example of this in *Stenocara gracilipes*). This means that extending their legs gets them out of the hot boundary layer of air that usually envelopes the ground. For example, Medvedev (1965) found that tenebrionid beetles could lower their body temperatures between 3°C and 21°C in the Kara Kum desert of Turkmenistan, and Edney (1971) showed that reductions

Fig. 4.24   Long legs of *Stenocara gracilipes* at Epupa Falls, Namibia. This feature makes it easy for this species to engage in stilting behaviour. (Photograph courtesy of Hans Hillewaert. This file is licensed under the Creative Commons Attribution ShareAlike 2.5 License.)

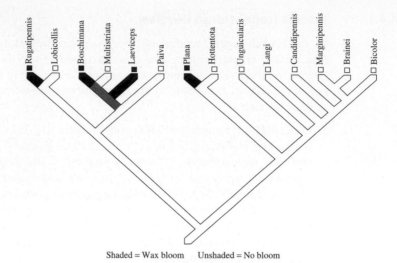

Shaded = Wax bloom   Unshaded = No bloom

Fig. 4.25   Phylogeny of *Onymacris* with wax blooms. Grey = uncertain origin of wax bloom. (From Ward and Seely 1996b. With kind permission of Blackwell Publishing.)

Fig. 4.26   Fog basking by the Namib tenebrionid beetle *Onymacris unguicularis*. (Kind permission of the Desert Research Foundation of Namibia.)

of T_b in tenebrionid beetles could be as much as 4°C in the Namib desert.

3. Wax blooms are more likely to occur in desert than in coastal populations or species (McClain *et al.* 1985) (Figs. 4.4 and 4.25). The wax bloom is an effective cuticular barrier to limit evaporative water loss (Hadley 1970; McClain *et al.* 1985).

4. Fog basking allows some species to take advantage of the thick advective fogs that carpet the Namib from the sea (Fig. 4.26). Hamilton and Seely (1976) and Seely *et al.* (1983) found that two beetle species,

Fig. 4.27   Photo of white *Onymacris bicolor* and black *O. unguicularis.*

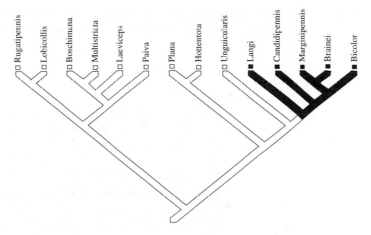

Fig. 4.28   Phylogeny of *Onymacris* with white abdomen. Black = white abdomen. From Ward and Seely 1996b. With kind permission of Blackwell Publishing.)

Onymacris unguicularis and *Onymacris bicolor,* climbed to the top of a dune and allowed the fog to condense on their abdomens and drip down into their mouths. Thus, one would expect that coastal species would be more likely to possess this behaviour.

5. Some species have a white abdomen (Fig. 4.27). Ward and Seely (1996a) tested whether these species were more likely to have evolved in desert than in coastal regions (Fig. 4.28).

After removing the effects of phylogeny, Ward and Seely (1996a) found that preferred T_b and actual T_b attained in the field were well matched

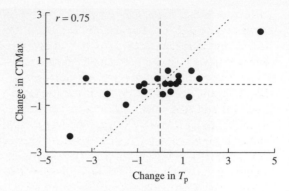

Fig. 4.29
After removing the effects of phylogeny, Ward and Seely (1996b) found that preferred T_b and actual T_b attained in the field were highly positively correlated. (From Ward and Seely 1996b. With kind permission of Blackwell Publishing.)

(Fig. 4.29), indicating perfect coadaptation. However, *contra* Heinrich (1977, 1993), they found no correlation between CTMax, CTMin and preferred and attained T_b. In another study, Ward (1991) tested whether there was any support for Hamilton's (1975) 'maxithermy' hypothesis. Hamilton (1975) had suggested that desert beetles were mostly black to maximize thermal gain, which would allow them maximize efficiency of food intake over a short time period. Ward (1991) surmised that, if this were to be correct, starving the beetles (of three species) should lead to their preference for progressively lower temperatures. However, the beetles preferred the same (high) temperatures, regardless of the degree of starvation. This is inconsistent with both Hamilton's (1975) and Heinrich's (1977, 1993) hypotheses. A possible reason why these beetles do not show strong selection for critical thermal extremes is that they only emerge from beneath the sand when CTMin is exceeded (Seely and Mitchell 1987) and descend beneath it before CTMax is exceeded or climb bushes to avoid the heat, moving off the hot sand (Ward and Seely 1996c). Their preferences for high T_b are still poorly understood.

In the case of fog basking, Ward and Seely (1996b) showed that it had evolved on two separate occasions and, thus, constitutes an adaptation to desert conditions. Similarly, they found that the wax bloom was indeed an adaptive characteristic, as had been claimed by McClain *et al.* (1985). However, the loss of the wax bloom in *O. multistriata* and in one subspecies of *Onymacris*, *O. rugatipennis rugatipennis* (it does occur in another desert subspecies, *O. r. albotessalata*), both of which occur in the desert interior, is perplexing.

Ward and Seely (1996b) found no support for stilting as an adaptive characteristic in this genus. This may occur because thermal mixing of the boundary layer occurs. Also, small organisms such as beetles are known to be convectively coupled and not radiation coupled (Gates 2003). This means that wind speed affects their T_b more than radiation. A study by Turner and Lombard (1991) showed that beetle colour had no effect on T_b. Interestingly, Ward and Seely (1996b) found that desert interior species had longer legs and coastal species had shorter legs than expected by chance. They suggested that a possible explanation for this was that long legs were ancestral and that there was little selection against them. However, tenebrionid beetles living on a sand substrate other than their own, often had broken leg segments, suggesting that there was some selection against long legs (Koch 1962). A more parsimonious explanation could simply be that, if long legs were not needed, they would lose this characteristic.

Ward and Seely (1996b) showed that all white species had evolved from a single node (Fig. 4.28) and, thus, no claim could be made about unique, independent events. Moreover, white abdomens occurred in the coastal and not the desert interior species, contrary to the prediction.

In summary, Ward and Seely (1996b) showed that there were some characteristics that could be considered to be adaptive, others that were unlikely to be, and a few that showed some interesting trends that bear further investigation. Most importantly, perhaps, not all such patterns would have been apparent had a conventional analysis been attempted.

4.4.2   Lizards

Huey and Bennett (1987) examined the effects of phylogeny on Australian skinks (Lygosominae, Lacertidae, Reptilia). Geographical associations fall into two regions, the peripheral areas of southeastern Australia (so-called Bassian region), which has mostly warm, dry summers and cold, wet winters, and the interior areas (so-called Eyrean region), which are hotter and have lower and less predictable rainfall. Research had shown that skinks in peripheral areas of Australia had lower thermal preferences (see explanation under tenebrionid beetles above) and critical thermal limits (especially with regard to righting themselves after they had fallen over) than species in the desert interior areas. Huey and Bennett (1987) also wished to ascertain whether these species also had lower optimal sprint temperatures because escape speeds are vital for lizards.

Thermal preferences (T_p) differ considerably among genera (range 24–35°C), but critical thermal maxima (CTMax) (38–45°C) and optimal temperatures for sprinting (T_o) vary less (32–35°C), presumably because these have more important effects on fitness (Huey and Stevenson 1979; Huey 1982; Huey and Bennett 1987). Diurnal genera have relatively high T_p, T_o, and CTMax while nocturnal genera have low T_p but moderate to high T_o and CTMax. However, there is considerable conservatism in T_p among Australian skinks; for example, about 91% of the variation in preferred body temperatures is within genera (Bennett and John-Alder 1986). Consequently, treating species as independent data points appears

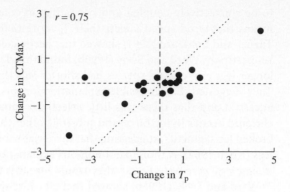

Fig. 4.30   In a re-analysis of Huey and Bennett's data, Garland et al. (1991) found that the only significant correlations were between the change in preferred temperature (T_p) and the change in critical thermal maximum temperature (CTMax). (Modified from Garland et al. 1991. With kind permission of Blackwell Publishing.)

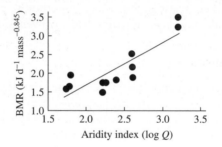

Fig. 4.31   Mass-adjusted basal metabolic rates (BMR) of 12 species of larks as a function of environmental aridity; log Q has low values when hot and dry and high values when it is wet and moist. (From Tieleman et al. 2003. With kind permission of the Royal Society of London.)

inappropriate (Huey and Bennett 1987). Crepuscular and nocturnal genera (*Eremiascincus* and *Hemiergus*) had very low T_p. Among the diurnal lizards, desert interior species (*Egernia* and *Ctenotus*) had higher T_p than their peripheral counterparts (*Leiolopisma* and *Sphenomorphus*). In a re-analysis of Huey and Bennett's data, Garland et al. (1991) found that the only significant correlations were between T_p and CTMax (Fig. 4.30).

4.4.3   Birds

Using a study based on independent phylogenetic contrasts, Tieleman et al. (2003a) compared 22 species of larks with regard to the BMR and TEWL of arid and mesic species. For 12 lark species, they found that differences in body mass explained more of the variance in BMR (53%) and

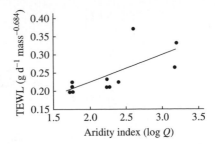

Fig. 4.32   Mass-adjusted total evaporative water loss (TEWL) of 12 species of larks as a function of environmental aridity; log Q has low values when it is hot and dry and high values when it is cool and moist. (From Tieleman *et al.* 2003. With kind permission of the Royal Society of London.)

TEWL (72%) than aridity alone (38% and 15%, respectively). Nonetheless, a decreasing value of BMR (Fig. 4.31) and TEWL (Fig. 4.32) with increasing aridity was found after the effects of body mass had been removed. Interspecific correlations between the phenotype and the environment can be explained by adaptation via the process of natural selection or they may be a consequence of phenotypic plasticity. Phenotypic plasticity in desert birds may occur as acclimation to the local environment in adults or through restricted access to food as juveniles (ontogeny effect). In other studies, Tieleman *et al.* (2002, 2003b) found that there was no effect of restricted access to food, acclimation or photoperiod and, therefore, Tieleman *et al.* (2003a) conclude that natural selection is the major selective force.

4.4.4   Small mammals

Two studies, by Murie (1961) and McNab and Morrison (1963), showed significant differences in the metabolism of arid and mesic populations of *Peromyscus* species. Furthermore, in a literature review of BMR of 487 mammal species of a wide range of body sizes, Lovegrove (2000) showed significant differences between xeric and mesic species.

Mueller and Diamond (2001) performed the equivalent of a common garden experiment on five species of the genus *Peromyscus*. Two of these species were from desert habitats, *P. eremicus* from the Lower Sonoran desert and *P. melanophrys* from Mexico from yucca/agave desert scrub. The other three species came from more mesic habitats, namely, *P. californicus* from chaparral/coastal sage scrub, *P. maniculatus* from deciduous woodland/meadow habitat and *P. leucopus* from mixed deciduous–coniferous forest. Net primary productivity (NPP) varied greatly, from 48 g C m^{-2} y^{-1} to 604 g C m^{-2} y^{-1}.The animals were bred for many generations in captivity. Thereafter, a study was performed, using identical diets and noting the origin of each species. Mueller and Diamond (2001) tested for relationships

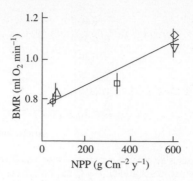

Fig. 4.33   Mueller and Diamond (2001) found a significant positive correlation between basal metabolic rate (BMR) measured as oxygen consumption (body-mass-adjusted) of five species of *Peromyscus* mice as a function of habitat net primary productivity (NPP), an index of the local productivity of the environment where the species was originally found. Each symbol represents a different species. (From Mueller and Diamond 2001. Copyright: National Academy of Sciences, USA.)

between standard metabolic characteristics and NPP, an index of the local productivity of the environment where the species was originally found. They found three measures of metabolic rate to be correlated with NPP, specifically BMR (Fig. 4.33), dry matter intake (DMI) and digestible dry matter intake (DDMI). Interspecific comparisons of BMR and field metabolic rate (FMR), which is about the same as daily metabolizable energy consumption, and which can be approximated by DDMI in steady state (Mueller and Diamond 2001), have shown a correlation between these two measures in rodents (Koteja 1991). Thus, Mueller and Diamond (2001) concluded that animals with little food have evolved to run more slowly (they had a low FMR and, consequently, DDMI) and are also able to have a low BMR and vice versa. There is a link between BMR and FMR because BMR is the maintenance cost of one's body parts (heart, intestine, muscles, etc.) that enables animals to maintain either low or high metabolic rates while active (Mueller and Diamond 2001). One might expect that an animal that consumes more food to have larger small intestines and higher glucose uptake rates, which is indeed what Mueller and Diamond (2001) found.

Mueller and Diamond (2001) also tested for a correlation between the above-mentioned metabolic measures and variability in NPP (since mean NPP and the coefficient of variation in NPP are closely correlated—Dobson and Crawley (1987) and Lovegrove (2000); see also Chapter 1). However, there was no significant correlation between the metabolic measures and the coefficient of variation in mean annual rainfall (no c.v. was available for NPP, but c.v. for mean annual rainfall and NPP are closely correlated). Because their sample size was merely five species, this lack of correlation was probably not surprising and could be explained as a Type II error.

Nonetheless, the correlations of metabolic rate with NPP were significant and strong (range of coefficient of determination was 82–90%, once
differences in body mass had been accounted for).

4.4.5 Medium-sized mammals

Results from xeric small desert carnivores are somewhat equivocal. Maloiy
et al. (1982) showed that TEWL was about 36% of the value expected from
an allometric curve. Afik and Pinshow (1993) argued that the values for
desert wolves did not differ from the expectation for TEWL for mesic
wolves. Williams *et al.* (2002) found that BMR of Rüppell's foxes was
similar to that of mesic species but found that TEWL was 50–65% that
of mesic species. Williams *et al.* (2004) used six species of foxes to test
for differences among desert and mesic species, removing the effects of
phylogeny. They found that, despite the fact that BMR did not differ from
their mesic relatives, TEWL and body mass were lower than those of mesic
species (Fig. 4.34). Most importantly, these results indicate that selection
has favoured smaller body sizes in xeric species, which results in smaller
litter sizes. Smaller body size as an adaptation to desert conditions is consistent with evidence in desert wolves (Afik and Pinshow 1993), other fox
species (Dayan *et al.* 1989) and the Nubian ibex *Capra ibex nubiana*, a
medium-sized herbivore of the Negev desert, which is considerably smaller
than its alpine relative, *Capra ibex ibex* (Gross *et al.* 1996).

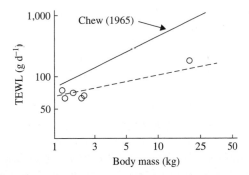

Fig. 4.34   Williams *et al.* (2004) found that, for six species of foxes, total evaporative water loss
(TEWL) values were lower than those of mesic species. Data from Chew (1965) indicate
the regression line for TEWL for all mammals. (From Williams *et al.* 2004. With kind
permission of Springer Science and Business Media.)

5 The role of competition and facilitation in structuring desert communities

It has long been considered that abiotic factors are far more important than biotic variables in controlling the structure of desert communities (Shreve 1942; Went 1955; Noy-Meir 1973; Grime 1977). In recent years, this perception has changed because some prime examples of species interactions have come from experimental studies in desert ecosystems. Few will doubt that desert rodents present some of the best evidence (as reviewed below) for competition (Abramsky *et al.* 1990; Kotler *et al.* 1993; Hughes *et al.* 1994). Reviews by Fowler (1986) and theoretical considerations of Newman (1973), Tilman (1982, 1988), and Chesson (2000) also indicate that competition among desert plants occurs. This chapter will focus on some of the key competitive interactions among desert organisms, drawn from a wide range of studies in several deserts.

5.1   Plant communities

Goldberg and Novoplansky (1997) have proposed a general schema for understanding the potential role of competition in plant communities. They call this the two-phase resource pulse hypothesis. Resources come in pulses, varying considerably in the duration of pulse availability (Chesson *et al.* 2004). Specifically, when a soil resource such as water and/or nutrients are limiting, the ability of individuals to monopolize resources by competitive ability (*sensu* Grime 1977) will occur during pulses of resource availability—either of water itself (the most limiting factor) or nutrients (which are linked to water availability)—depending on their abilities to suppress growth (termed competitive effect; *sensu* Goldberg (1990)) or to avoid suppression themselves (termed competitive response; *sensu* Goldberg (1990)). Interpulse periods are important, too, as the ability of plants to survive and, therefore, to persist during these periods (termed stress tolerance by Grime (1977)) depends on how much resource is available. If the low level of resources is affected by plant density or abundance, then competition will still be important. If not, for example, if there are other causes of resource loss unrelated to competition such as evaporation, leaching, volatilization, and drainage, then competition will be unimportant. These are key issues of what Goldberg and Novoplansky (1997) term the Grime–Tilman debate. Grime (1977) considered stress tolerance to be the most important factor (i.e. abiotic factors are more important) whereas Tilman (1982, 1988) considered competition to be important regardless of (or even particularly because of) low levels of water and/or nutrients. The magnitude of interactions will depend on the level of resources available between pulses that affect survival and the amount of resources available during resource pulses that facilitate growth. The most probable relationship is a positive correlation, so that competition would result in fewer resources during pulse periods, thereby reducing growth, and would also reduce survival during interpulse periods. Under these circumstances, competition is likely to be important (as Tilman (1988) would predict). If, however, there is no relationship or a negative correlation between competition during resource pulses and during interpulse periods, and there is little or no relationship between resource availability and vegetation presence or abundance, then stress tolerance (*sensu* Grime 1977) is more likely to be important.

5.1.1   Annual plant communities

An interesting approach to the study of desert annuals was undertaken by Goldberg *et al.* (2001). Instead of focusing on the density of a single species at a time, Goldberg *et al.* (2001) noticed that density-dependent regulation should occur at the level of the whole community, especially where these plants occur in mixed-species groups as is so commonly the case. They examined the effects on different life history stages, to determine whether similar responses were detected. Goldberg *et al.* (2001) constructed semi-natural communities of desert annuals in the Negev desert of Israel, which were composed of all the constituent species in the same relative proportions as found in the natural habitat. These experimental communities were planted at a range of densities that were both far less than and far greater than natural field densities. Goldberg *et al.* (2001) demonstrated evidence of community-level density dependence. Exploitation competition should be the most common form of competition in plants because plants remove resources such as nutrients by exploiting the resource (Tilman 1982, 1988). Interference competition could occur, but it is a little harder to understand because it could only really occur by allelopathy (e.g. negative effects of some toxin in the soil) or by other non-uptake mechanisms (*sensu* Goldberg 1990) such as attraction of natural herbivores. Exploitation competition was shown most clearly with regard to the growth phase of the experiment. At the survival stage, the effects were highly variable, but negative effects of density were quite rare. Rather, there were either positive (facilitation) or no significant effects of increasing density. They could not ascribe this to nurse plant effects (see below) because the plants were too similar in size, but could conclude that exploitation competition was unimportant at the survival stage. In their study, Goldberg *et al.* (2001) found that annual graminoids were superior competitors to dicots at the emergence and survival stages. However, the two growth forms did not differ in competitive ability for growth or final size. Nonetheless, dicots were, on average, larger in biomass. Consistent with the former result, grasses are always the numerical dominants, but they are also biomass dominants in the source communities. How the latter might occur in nature was not determined.

Chesson (2000) has considered there to be a temporal mechanism by which a number of species can coexist. Specifically, he estimated the contribution of temporal niches based on both among-year and within-year temporal niches in persistence and coexistence. For this mechanism to work, plants must increase when rare (Fig. 5.1), countering tendencies to local extinction and promoting species diversity. In the Sonoran desert of North America, Pantastico-Caldas and Venable (1993), Pake and Venable (1995, 1996), and Adondakis and Venable (2004), as well as Facelli *et al.* (2005) in chenopod shrublands of south Australia, have shown that there is sufficient variation within years in the fraction of seedlings that germinate and that there is little correlation within years in terms of the species' germination responses (see also Chesson and Huntly 1989). This provides the species with slightly different temporal windows combined with the buffering effect of delayed germination. Chesson (2000) termed this the storage effect, because some storage mechanism must exist so that species can persist from one year to the next. Adondakis and Venable (2004)

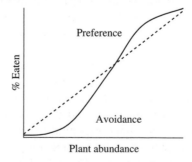

Fig. 5.1   Mechanism of lottery model of coexistence. Following this model, there should be avoidance of species when rare and they should be preferred when common.

found that under a particular set of field conditions, one species may produce more seedlings in a given year than another and vice versa. Moreover, species differ in the environmental conditions under which each does best, which is also affected in some cases by the environmental conditions in the previous summer.

5.1.2 Interactions among desert shrubs

Many studies have inferred the presence of interspecific shrub–shrub competition by means of nearest-neighbour distances. That is, if shrubs are considered to be competing with one another they should be very evenly dispersed, while if they are not competing they may have a random or contagious (clumped) distribution. In the latter case, facilitation may occur where there is a positive effect of one species' presence on that of another.

For example, the nearest-neighbour technique was used by Carrick (2003) to infer the nature of interactions between the three most abundant species in the succulent Karoo, an arid area of western South Africa. Carrick (2003) studied the relationships among two species of Mesembryanthema (Aizoaceae) (*Ruschia robusta* and *Leipoldtia schultzei*) and an asteraceous plant (*Hirpicium alienatum*). He found that both intraspecific and interspecific competitions were important. Neither of the two Mesembryanthema dominated *Hirpicium* although *Leipoldtia* was dominant over *Ruschia*. The two Mesembryanthema species had most of their roots in the top 5 cm of soil, whereas the asteraceous shrub had most of its roots at greater depths. This rooting niche separation may have led to the lack of effect on *Hirpicium* and the strong negative effect of *Leipoldtia* on *Ruschia*. Both of the mesembryanthemaceous plants can use small-pulsed rain events but presumably, where the species grow in close proximity, *Ruschia* must suffer the negative effects of competition with *Leipoldtia*. This could be explained by using Tilman's (1982, 1988) model, which indicates that *Ruschia* has a higher R^* value than *Leipoldtia* (i.e. it is less efficient than *Leipoldtia*) either because of lower growth and/or because of greater costs associated with growth.

An experimental study was used by Fonteyn and Mahall (1978) to determine whether the two shrub species *Larrea tridentata* (Zygophyllaceae) and *Ambrosia dumosa* (Asteraceae) compete in the Mojave desert of North America. *Larrea* is tall and evergreen and *Ambrosia* is short and drought-deciduous. The two species are dominant over wide areas and may constitute up to 70% of the plants of the Mojave desert. Locally, *Larrea* made up about 40% of individuals and *Ambrosia* about 50% of individuals. The two species appeared to be independently distributed of one another. The following treatments were applied: control (no removal), removal of all *Larrea* except for the central one in 100 m^2 plots, removal of all *Ambrosia* except the central one, and all of both species removed, leaving a single *Larrea* present. The assumption was that water would be the limiting factor. They found that interspecific competition was more important than intraspecific competition and that there was indeed competition for water. Similar results were obtained in the Negev desert of Israel (Friedman 1971). Friedman found that *Artemisia herba-alba* (Asteraceae) seedlings were severely inhibited by the presence of adult *Zygophyllum dumosum* (Zygophyllaceae) growing within 2 m of them.

5.1.3 Facilitation and nurse plant effects

A great number of shrubs have been shown to have nurse plant effects on annual plants in particular, although other shrubs and geophytes (see Fig. 5.2) may also benefit from this (see review by Callaway 1995). Essentially, this means that the annual plants grow up under the shrub and benefit from a number of factors. These factors include increased water availability (including from hydraulic lift—see Chapter 3), lower soil temperatures created by shading, and higher resource availability, particularly higher nitrogen availability. For example, Franco and Nobel (1989) found that complete shading from direct sunlight decreases maximum soil surface temperatures in summer by 11°C, which also had strong effects on the internal temperatures of the cacti *Carnegiea gigantea* and *Stenocereus thurberi*. Desert legumes, in particular, can alter the availability of soil nitrogen (Franco-Pizaña *et al.* 1995). Columnar cacti established beneath trees or shrubs may ultimately outcompete the nurse plants, leading to a cyclical succession process (Yeaton 1978; McAuliffe 1988), where sun-tolerant shrubs colonize open spaces, providing shade (and other factors listed above) to another set of colonists and, in the end, are outcompeted by these other plants (Suzán *et al.* 1996; Tielborger and Kadmon 2000). Miriti (2006) has shown that *Ambrosia dumosa* (Asteraceae) in the Mojave

Fig. 5.2 *Sternbergia clusiana* (Amaryllidaceae) benefiting from facilitation by the thorny *Sarcopoterium spinosum*.

desert (North America) can shift ontogenetically from being facilitated by growing close to adult *Ambrosia* early in life to competition with the adults as they age (Fig. 5.3). Osem *et al.* (2004, 2007) found that the spiny shrub *Sarcopoterium spinosum* (Rosaceae) in the northern Negev desert (Israel) has significant facilitative effects on annual plants growing under them that depend on the presence of grazing and topography. On north-facing slopes, where there is grazing, facilitative effects occur (Osem *et al.* 2007), especially for large annuals. There was no effect on south-facing slopes (Osem *et al.* 2007).

5.2 Competition between animals

MacArthur and Pianka (1966), Rosenzweig (1985) and Brown (1988) have developed some theories regarding the role of competition in arid areas that work at different scales, specifically the patch scale (Brown 1988) and the habitat scale (MacArthur and Pianka 1966; Rosenzweig 1985).

5.2.1 Patch scale

Brown's (1988) model considers how animals make decisions regarding which patch to stay in and for how long. Animals must make decisions to stay in a patch based on the combined effects of competition, predation risk and the missed opportunity costs of not foraging elsewhere. Predation risk also affects patch selection because the perceived risk of being eaten is probably as important (or even more so) as actually being consumed. For example, predators that are prevented from killing their prey can separate non-lethal predation behaviour from direct mortality effects. Werner and

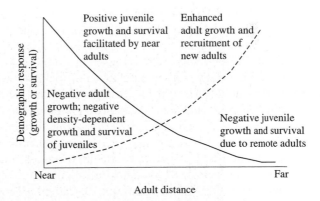

Fig. 5.3   Miriti (2006) has shown that *Ambrosia dumosa* (Asteraceae) in the Mojave desert can shift ontogenetically from being facilitated by growing close to adult *Ambrosia* early in life to competition with the adults as they age. (From Miriti 2006. With kind permission of Blackwell Publishing.)

Anholt (1996) have shown that non-lethal behavioural predation effects (predation risk) can be a significant component of competitive effects (see Chapter 6). Missed opportunity costs (MOC) is a term borrowed from microeconomic theory and considers that, when one makes a decision to do something, one is not only considering the value of that alone but also its value relative to something else one is not doing at the time—this is MOC. For example, one buys an item with the limited money one has, there is a missed opportunity to buy something else. Brown (1988) developed the concept of giving-up density (GUD) to consider when an animal should leave a patch (habitat). An animal should leave a patch when the benefits of foraging there equal the costs thereof. This is when the patch harvest rate (H) is no longer greater than the sum of the energetic (C), predation (P) and MOC of not foraging elsewhere. Thus, an animal forages in a patch or habitat until

$$H = C + P + MOC$$

Brown (1988) also developed the practical technique of assessing GUDs to demonstrate this (although *per capita* activity can show it just as easily—see example from Mitchell *et al.* (1990) below). Basically, an amount of seed is placed in a tray with a large amount of the substrate to mimic the natural foraging conditions experienced by an animal. In many cases, a constant amount of millet is placed in sand to mimic the natural foraging conditions for desert rodents (Mitchell *et al.* 1990; Hughes and Ward 1993; Ziv *et al.* 1993, 1995; Hughes *et al.* 1994). The more seed removed from the tray, the greater the perceived value of the tray and vice versa. Conversely, if a tray has low perceived value (i.e. the harvest rate (H) is low relative to C (energetic costs of foraging), or P (predation risk) or MOC (missed opportunity costs of not foraging elsewhere)), then it should have a high GUD and the animal moves on to the next patch.

It has been widely shown that animals forage less on moonlit nights than on dark nights because predation risk is higher (Kotler 1984; Brown 1988). Thus, GUDs should be higher on moonlit nights (i.e. they will move to another patch earlier, such as one with more available food still left in the habitat) than on a dark night (see Chapter 6). In a similar vein, Mitchell *et al.* (1990) considered two foraging models for two gerbil species foraging in the Negev desert (Israel). One model considered a time-minimizer satisfying an energy requirement. Under this model, an animal should increase its foraging effort with increased competition. The second model considers an animal maximizing fitness as a function of multiple inputs subject to a time constraint. The latter model may also predict that foraging effort should increase with increased competition because of the MOC that results when different inputs are complementary. However, if the fitness-maximizer with multiple inputs incurs an energy cost of foraging (in addition to MOC), then it should often reduce foraging effort in response to an increase in competition. The effect of increased competition was tested using two species of gerbils, *Gerbillus andersoni allenbyi* and *Gerbillus pyramidum* in the Negev Desert (Israel). Mitchell *et al.*'s (1990) results showed that *per capita* activity (as measured by tracking densities) declined as a function of intraspecific density for each species and as a function of interspecific density for G. *a. allenbyi* (Fig. 5.4). No interspecific effect was found for G. *pyramidum*.

5.2.2   Habitat selection models

When competitors have distinct preferences, MacArthur and Pianka (1966) predicted that habitat selectivity should increase in the presence of an interspecific competitor (Fig. 5.5). When the competitor is removed, habitat selectivity should decrease, resulting in the expansion of a rival species into the niche formerly occupied by its competitor. When species B is removed, species A expands into the other habitat.

Rosenzweig's theories of habitat selection (summarized in his 1981 paper and in Rosenzweig and Abramsky (1986) on centrifugal community organization) are based on Ideal Free Distribution ideas derived from Fretwell and Lucas (1970). He uses the term *isoleg* to indicate the point at which a species switches from using one habitat to another. The word 'isoleg' comes from the Greek 'iso' and 'lego', meaning 'equal choice'. An isoleg is a line in state space such that some aspect of a species' habitat selection is constant at every point along the line (Figs. 5.6a, b and 5.7).

Rosenzweig and Abramsky (1986) also found that a common type of community organization occurred where many species preferred

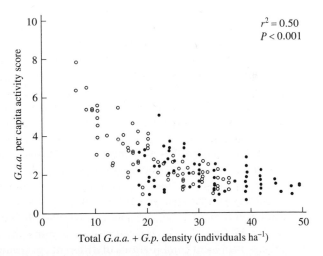

Fig. 5.4   Mitchell *et al.*'s (1990) results showed that *per capita* activity (as measured by tracking densities) declined as a function of intraspecific density for each species and as a function of interspecific density for G. *andersoni allenbyi*. (From Mitchell *et al.* 1990. With kind permission of the Ecological Society of America.)

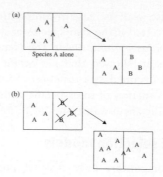

Fig. 5.5   Schematic diagrams of MacArthur and Pianka (1966) predicted that habitat selectivity should increase in the presence of an interspecific competitor. (a) When species A occurs alone, it occupies both habitats. When it occurs with species B, species A occupies one habitat and species B the other habitat. This is called niche compression. (b) When species B is removed, species A expands into the other habitat. (Modified from MacArthur and Pianka 1966. With kind permission of University of Chicago Press.)

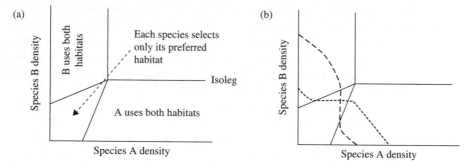

Fig. 5.6   (a) Isolegs of two species with distinct preferences. (b) Isolegs of two species with distinct preferences plus isoclines. Isoclines (dotted line: species A; dashed line: species B) are parallel to the axis in region of distinct preference because the species occur in different habitats and do not affect one another. (Modified from Rosenzweig 1981. With kind permission of Academic Press.)

the same habitat. This they termed centrifugal community organization (Fig. 5.8). At low population densities, all species occurred in this favoured habitat. At high population densities, one species outcompeted the others in this favoured habitat. Centrifugal communities can reach equilibrium if each species has a secondary habitat that they do best in. The biological basis for centrifugal community organization is that habitats represent combinations of different environmental variables, and although the ideal combination is the same for many species in the guild (in the primary shared habitat), each species is adapted to tolerate relative deprivation of a different combination of the mixture of variables in each

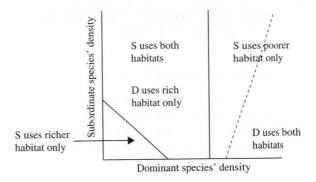

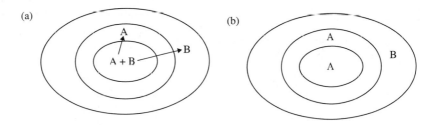

Fig. 5.7   Isolegs of a dominant and a subordinate species with shared preferences. Dashed line represents the isoleg where dominant species (D) changes habitat. Solid line represents the isoleg where subordinate species (S) changes habitats. (Modified from Rosenzweig 1985. With kind permission of Academic Press.)

Fig. 5.8   Rosenzweig and Abramsky (1986) also found that a common type of community organization occurred where many species preferred the same habitat. This they termed centrifugal community organization. (a) Equilibrium is reached when the two species have different alternative habitats in which they occur. (b) If someone were to assess habitat selection of two species on the basis of presence/absence, they might appear to have different habitat preferences if they occur at sufficiently high densities. (Modified from Rosenzweig and Abramsky 1986. With kind permission of Blackwell Publishing.)

species' secondary habitat (Fig. 5.8). Note that centrifugal community organization predicts the opposite of MacArthur and Pianka's (1966) niche compression hypothesis; that is, following niche compression a species reduces its niche under competition, while a species expands its niche under centrifugal theory.

Note that there is no contradiction between Brown's (1988) paper on a patch scale and Rosenzweig's (1985) and Rosenzweig and Abramsky's (1986) papers on habitat selection. Brown (1988) uses individual behaviour to assess the likelihood for different factors promoting coexistence between species, and Rosenzweig (1985) and Rosenzweig and Abramsky (1986) use habitat selection theory (calculating isoclines and isolegs) for assessing factors promoting species coexistence. Both approaches assume that optimal behaviour will occur.

5.2.3   Interactions among macroarthropod detritivores

Ward and Seely (1996a) tested some of Rosenzweig's habitat selection theories and compared them to MacArthur and Pianka's (1966) theory. They examined the factors affecting habitat selection by two abundant tenebrionid beetle species in the Namib desert, Namibia. Both species occupy the Kuiseb riverbed. The spatial distributions of these beetles at the microhabitat scale were negatively correlated. The most abundant species, *Physadesmia globosa*, occurs mostly under the trees, while the other species, *Onymacris rugatipennis*, occurs mostly in the open areas between trees. There was far more detritus present under the trees than in the open habitat (mostly flowers of the dominant *Acacia erioloba* trees). Ward and Seely (1996a) assumed that *P. globosa* occupied the areas under the trees because they were more efficient there. In contrast, they assumed that *O. rugatipennis* occupied the open areas between the trees because they were less efficient than *P. globosa* under the trees. They did a removal experiment, where they removed 25% of *P. globosa* each week and observed the numerical response of *O. rugatipennis*. They then replaced the *P. globosa* beetles. No matter how many *P. globosa* they removed from under the trees, *O. rugatipennis* did not move under the trees. Most *O. rugatipennis* beetles were found in the open, barely vege-tated habitat, the number of this species caught in pitfall traps increased following both removals and decreased following *P. globosa* replacement under the trees (Figs. 5.9 and 5.10).

It appears that intraspecific competition forces some *P. globosa* to occupy the open habitat. Interspecific competition between *P. globosa* and *O. rug-atipennis* in the open habitat reduces the number of *O. rugatipennis* that can coexist with *P. globosa* there. Removal of *P. globosa* under the trees

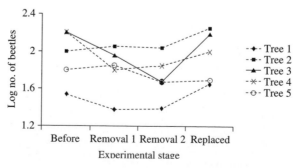

Fig. 5.9   Number of *Physadesmia globosa* under trees. (Modified from Ward and Seely 1996a.)

allows conspecifics in the open habitat to move under the trees, releasing *O. rugatipennis* into the open habitat from competition (Fig. 5.11). This then results in an increase in the numbers of *O. rugatipennis* in the open habitat as a result of immigration from neighbouring areas (i.e. from outside the experimental arena). *P. globosa* beetles were more efficient under the trees (as predicted) but, contrary to their prediction, *O. rugatipennis* beetles were more efficient in the open areas and less efficient under the trees (Fig. 5.12).

Ward and Seely (1996a) found that differences in foraging efficiency, measured as giving-up times in artificial food patches (similar to Brown's (1988) GUDs), created a possible mechanism of coexistence that explains the distinct preferences of these two species for tree and open habitats. Note that the longer a species occupies a habitat, i.e. the greater the giving-up times (GUTs), the greater the preference of that species for the habitat (see also Brown 1988).

One might expect that this would fit the centrifugal community organization model (*sensu* Rosenzweig and Abramsky 1986) because *P. globosa* should occupy its own habitat when its density is low (i.e. under the trees) and move into a secondary habitat (in the open areas). Where

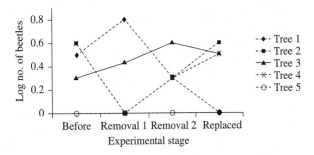

Fig. 5.10   Number of *Onymacris rugatipennis* under trees. (Modified from Ward and Seely 1996a.)

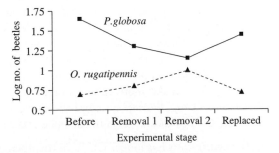

Fig. 5.11   Number of beetles in the open. (Modified from Ward and Seely 1996a.)

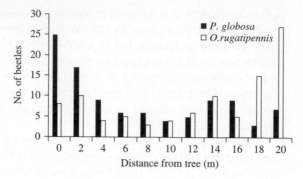

Fig. 5.12   Number of beetles vs. distance from trees. (Modified from Ward and Seely 1996a.)

would *O. rugatipennis* move into a secondary habitat? Remember, equilibrium can only be achieved when each species has a secondary habitat (Rosenzweig and Abramsky 1986).

Does it match MacArthur and Pianka's (1966) niche compression model? Following this model, habitat selectivity should increase in the presence of an interspecific competitor. When the competitor is removed, habitat selectivity should decrease, resulting in expansion of a rival species into the niche formerly occupied by its competitor. With respect to the community of tenebrionid beetles in the Kuiseb riverbed, the niche compression and centrifugal organization models make slightly different predictions.

Under the centrifugal model, most *O. rugatipennis* should move under the trees once *P. globosa* is removed because they have a shared preference for this habitat. The niche compression model makes the prediction that *O. rugatipennis* should expand its niche by moving into the tree habitat when *P. globosa* is removed. However, because *O. rugatipennis* must have a distinct preference for the open habitat under this model, most individuals should remain in the latter habitat.

The simple answer is that neither model explains the situation particularly well. Brown and Rosenzweig (1986) developed a distinct preference model that, unlike the niche compression and centrifugal models, considers the resources that vary spatially and temporally in resource density. They found that niche shifts predicted by this model can behave 'perversely'—an increase in a competitor's density may increase or decrease niche breadth. The effect of a competitor depends on the particular system and that no general conclusion is possible. Study of the isolegs of optimal behaviour is necessary to make more robust predictions about niche shifts in the *P. globosa—O. rugatipennis* system. Indeed, there may actually be three reasons why *O. rugatipennis* stays in the open and *P. globosa* under the trees:

1. *O. rugatipennis* has longer GUTs in the open and *P. globosa* has longer GUTs under the trees.

2. *O. rugatipennis* has longer legs than *P. globosa* and is more capable of rapid movement on smooth surfaces such as the open sand habitat they inhabit than *P. globosa*, but may be impeded when moving under the dense sticks in the litter under the trees.
3. *O. rugatipennis* has greater tolerance of the high ambient temperatures experienced in the open habitat than *P. globosa* (Roberts *et al.* 1991).

5.2.4 The granivore guild

In the Namib desert (Namibia), Hughes *et al.* (1994) tested whether generalist striped field mice *Rhabdomys pumilio* were outcompeting specialist gerbils *Gerbillurus tytonis* in the interdune valleys. They removed all the *R. pumilio* and tested to see whether the gerbil would lower its GUD (i.e. have a stronger preference for that habitat). When *R. pumilio* was removed from nara and grass habitats, the gerbil indeed lowered its GUD, and raised it again when *R. pumilio* was replaced again (Fig. 5.13). Does this match the niche compression hypothesis of MacArthur and Pianka (1966)? Removal of *R. pumilio* from the nara microhabitat resulted in an increase in gerbil activity in the grass microhabitat, i.e. niche expansion occurred after competitor removal. This is consistent with the niche compression hypothesis, but the niche compression hypothesis applies to distinct preference systems, yet here they have a shared-preference system (both the gerbil and the striped field mice *R. pumilio* preferred nara). Thus, a shared-preference model such as one mooted by Rosenzweig (1985) may be more appropriate.

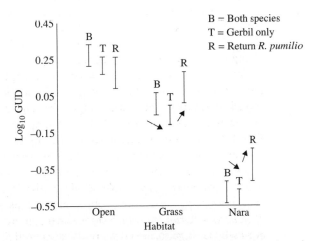

Fig. 5.13 *Rhabdomys pumilio* lowering and raising its giving-up density (GUD) in the grass and nara habitats. No change was detected in the open habitat. (Modified from Hughes *et al.* 1994. With kind permission of the Ecological Society of America.)

In the Negev desert (Israel), Ziv *et al.* (1993) have examined the factors that affect competition between two gerbil species. The larger species, *G. pyramidum* (mean mass = 40 g), dominates in the semistabilized dunes of the western Negev while the smaller species *Gerbillus andersoni allenbyi* (mean mass = 26 g) prefers the same habitat but is often forced to occupy a secondary habitat of stabilized dunes. This system was shown to be one of shared-preference habitat selection by Abramsky *et al.* (1990). Ziv *et al.* (1995) showed that the higher sand content of the semistabilized sands made it more efficient for both species to forage there. Ziv *et al.* (1993) found that *G. pyramidum* was active in the early evening (until about 22h00) and *G. a. allenbyi* in the later part of the night. Ziv *et al.* (1993) suspected that interference competition was responsible, that is, *G. pyramidum* was competitively excluding *G. a. allenbyi* by interference. They demonstrated, by the exclusion of *G. pyramidum* from some plots, that this was indeed the case (Fig. 5.14). Kotler *et al.* (1993) showed that seeds need to be replaced within the same evening for this mechanism to work so that sufficient seeds could be available for *G. a. allenbyi* to use in the second part of the night, which was later shown by Ben-Natan *et al.* (2004) to be the case (Fig. 5.15).

Other studies have also documented competition between rodents and ants and between rodents and birds. It appears that competition between rodents and ants are mostly indirect interactions (see below). Competition between granivorous bird species may be less common, or even non-existent (Rotenberry 1980; Wiens and Rotenberry 1981). Dunning (1986) claimed

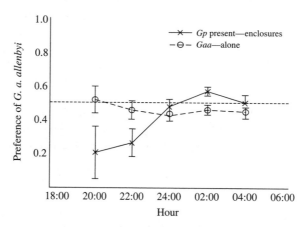

Fig. 5.14   Ziv *et al.* (1993) excluded *Gerbillus pyramidum* from plots also containing *G. andersoni allenbyi.* They found that *G. pyramidum* was engaged in interference competition with *G. a. allenbyi.* Where *G. pyramidum* occurred with *G. a. allenbyi,* the latter species avoided these areas in the early evening and preferred the plots later in the night. This indicated that *G. pyramidum* was temporally excluding *G. a. allenbyi* from being active in the early evening. (From Ziv *et al.* 1993. With kind permission of Blackwell Publishing.)

that the reason that Wiens and Rotenberry (1981) did not find any evidence for competition among bird species in shrub-steppe habitats in the Great Basin desert (North America) may be due to differences in morphology caused by differences resulting from interspecific competition during the non-breeding season. However, Repasky and Schluter (1996) found that there was no evidence for interspecific competition between granivorous bird species in their wintering habitats in the Sonoran desert.

Brown *et al.* (1997) tested for competitive effects between gerbils and a species of desert bird, the crested lark *Galerida cristata* in the Negev desert using the GUD technique described above. The two gerbils are nocturnal and the lark is diurnal. They found that the gerbils had lower GUDs (indicating that they were competitively superior there) in the bush microhabitat and larks had lower GUDs in the open microhabitat. As indicated above, the gerbils had shared habitat preferences for the semistabilized habitat and, consequently, lower GUDs there, while the larks had lower GUDs in the stabilized habitat. However, gerbils had lower GUDs in all months in both microhabitats and in stabilized habitats (i.e. gerbils were competitively superior in all habitats and microhabitats). Brown *et al.* (1997) proposed that larks may be 'cream skimmers' in space and time, taking only the best food in all places, leaving the gerbils to 'pick the crumbs' remaining. Alternative (non-mutually exclusive) explanations not examined by Brown *et al.* (1997) may include foraging by larks on non-grain items such as insects and/or larks may specialize on adjacent rocky habitats.

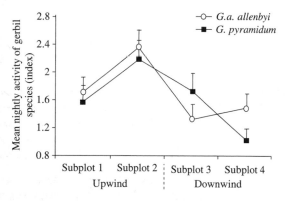

Fig. 5.15   Ben-Natan *et al.* (2004) found that seeds need to be replaced within the same evening for temporal partitioning to work as a mechanism of coexistence so that sufficient seeds could be available for *Gerbillus andersoni allenbyi* to use in the second part of the night. They used fences placed in a semicircle on semistabilized dunes. Subplot 1 was 1.6 m upwind of the fence, subplot 2 was immediately upwind (and against) the fence, subplot 3 was immediately downwind (and against) the fence and subplot 4 was 1.6 m downwind of the fence. The results show that the activity (range = 0.4) of *G. pyramidum* was lower than *G. a. allenbyi* on the downwind side of the fence only. (From Ben-Natan *et al.* 2004. With kind permission of Blackwell Publishing.)

5.3 Indirect interactions: keystone species, apparent competition, and priority effects

What is an indirect effect? A useful example to demonstrate the difference between indirect and direct effects comes from the Chihuahuan desert of North America, which occurs via the indirect effects of rodents on ants that are mediated via effects on annual plants. Davidson *et al.* (1985) found that ants increased in density and then decreased after rodent removal (Fig. 5.16). For the first two years, densities of ant colonies were twice as high on rodent removal plots as on control plots. By the third year, ant colonies were nearly equally dense on control and removal plots. From the fourth year on, ant colony densities declined, nearing extinction by the 11th year. The ant response to rodent removal was an indirect and not a direct increase because rodents eat larger seeds than ants, and large-seeded plants compete with smaller-seeded plants. Any initial advantage to the ants of rodent removal was lost when the large-seeded plants out-competed the smaller-seeded plants. Rodents indirectly benefited ants by controlling the increase of competitively superior large-seeded plants.

Menge (1995) has considered the different types of indirect interactions that might occur among species. It might appear that these interactions could make community ecology difficult to study because these effects might not appear as obvious as direct effects. Even exploitation competition (see under *Annual Plants* above) can be considered to be an indirect interaction because two species may never directly observe one another (e.g. in the case of animals, one forages diurnally and the other nocturnally or, in the case of plants, it is the expected means of competition because plants remove resources from the soil) yet they have a joint negative effect on their food source, which is depleted. Menge (1995) found, albeit for rocky intertidal systems, that indirect effects actually acted rather quickly and that the most important types of indirect interactions were keystone species effects and apparent competition. We consider here

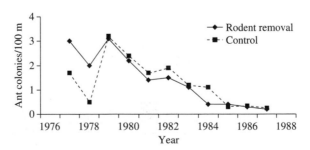

Fig. 5.16   Davidson *et al.* (1985) found that ants increased in density and then decreased after rodent removal. (From Davidson *et al.* 1985. With kind permission of the Ecological Society of America.)

whether the same is true for desert species, and also consider the role of priority effects.

5.3.1   Keystone species

In keystone species, the effects of a particular species on its interactions with others are far greater than that of simple dominance (Paine 1966; Power *et al.* 1996). In the latter case, a species has effects that depend on biomass or numbers and are proportional to those effects. Key to demonstrating that a species is a keystone species is to remove the species to test whether its removal causes the loss of these effects (Power *et al.* 1996).

Munzbergova and Ward (2002) showed that *Acacia raddiana* trees (Fabaceae) are keystone species in the Negev desert (Israel) (Fig. 5.17). In populations with high *Acacia* mortality, an average of five other plant species disappear. They also showed that plant species diversity is higher under trees than in the open spaces between trees. In this sense, *Acacia* trees act like nurse plants, increasing diversity (Fig. 5.17). However, they differ from nurse plants in that it is the species itself that is important. Once that species disappears from the ecosystem, it is not replaced by other species with similar effects. One of the most important effects of *Acacia* species on the soils was through increased nitrogen, which in turn benefited the plants growing under the trees. This *Acacia* species, similar to many others, fixes nitrogen. Similar keystone effects have been demonstrated for *A. erioloba* (Milton and Dean 1995) and by Suzán *et al.* (1996) for *Olneya tesota* (both Fabaceae).

Kangaroo rats *Dipodomys* species (Rodentia) also have interesting keystone effects, as shown in a number of studies (Brown and Davidson 1977; Brown and Heske 1990a, b; Heske *et al.* 1993; Valone *et al.* 1994; Guo 1996; Brock and Kelt 2004) in the Sonoran and Chihuahuan deserts of North America. These effects occur because the kangaroo rats affect plant community structure, especially through preferential consumption of large seeds (Brown and Heske 1990a, b; Heske *et al.* 1993; Valone *et al.* 1994; Guo 1996) and by their effects on soil disturbance (Heske *et al.* 1993). In

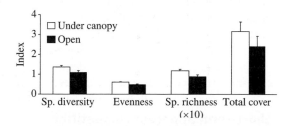

Fig. 5.17   Munzbergova and Ward (2002) showed that plant species diversity is higher under *Acacia raddiana* trees than in the open spaces between trees. (From Munzbergova and Ward 2002. With kind permission of Opulus Press.)

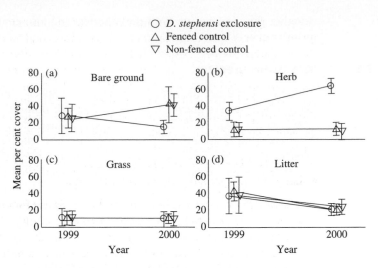

Fig. 5.18   Brock and Kelt (2004) removed *D. stephensi* from the Sonoran desert of southern California, which resulted in large changes in the abundance of herbs. However, most of these species were exotic *Erodium cicutarium, E. botrys, Bromus madritensis,* and *Vulpia myuros* plants. The biggest changes were in the abundance of *E. cicutarium*. (From Brock and Kelt 2004. Copyright Elsevier.)

the banner-tailed kangaroo rat (*D. spectabilis*), Guo (1996) has shown in the Chihuahuan desert that kangaroo rat burrows have strong effects on plant community structure. Valone *et al.* (1994) recognize that the inter-actions between rodents and ants in the Chihuahuan desert (summer rainfall) may be more complex than in the Sonoran desert (summer- and winter-rainfall)(Brown and Davidson 1977). Nonetheless, after 15 years of maintaining the Chihuahuan desert experiment, Valone *et al.* (1994) recognize that the major interactions between rodents and ants are indi-rectly mediated through vegetation (see also Samson *et al.* 1992) rather than through direct competition for seed resources. The removal of three species of kangaroo rats (*D. ordii, D. merriami, D. spectabilis*) by Brown and Heske (1990b) led to large changes in the abundance of grasses in particular. Brock and Kelt (2004) removed *D. stephensi* from the Sonoran desert of southern California, which resulted in large changes in the abun-dance of exotic *Erodium cicutarium, E. botrys, Bromus madritensis,* and *Vulpia myuros* plants. The biggest changes were in the abundance of *E. cic-utarium* (Fig. 5.18). These findings demonstrate that indirect effects can be extremely important in structuring desert communities (Strauss 1991).

5.3.2   Short-term apparent competition

Holt and Kotler (1987) considered the situation where two prey species are consumed by a third predator species. If one assumes that neither of the prey species competes with the other, but that more predators persist when both prey species are present because more total food is available for the predator. The net result is that there should be more predation when both are present. Thus, each prey species has a negative indirect effect on the other through its direct positive effect on the abundance of the predator. Holt and Kotler (1987) considered interspecific interactions to reflect the cumulative consequences of individual behavioural acts. The foraging decisions by predators influence the way in which predation shapes the structure of prey communities. Alternative prey species co-occurring in a patch embedded in a matrix of many similar patches may interact through a shared mobile predator in two distinct ways:

1. The functional response by an individual predator foraging in the patch on one prey species may be affected by the density of a second prey species in the patch because any time spent handling one prey reduces the time available for capturing other prey (this is part of what Brown (1988) considered the MOC).
2. The presence of a second prey species may alter the likelihood of predators to aggregate or remain in a given patch.

Holt and Kotler (1987) argue that this aggregative numerical response can in many circumstances generate negative–negative interactions, which they termed apparent competition between prey species that otherwise would not interact (Fig. 5.19).

Veech (2001) tested for apparent competition by examining the foraging behaviour of two heteromyid rodent species (Heteromyidae, Rodentia), Merriam's kangaroo rats (*D. merriami*) and little pocket mice (*Perognathus longimembris*). Veech (2001) tested the preferences of both rodent species for the seeds of eight plant species. Both rodent species exhibited distinct but variable preferences for some seeds and avoidance of others. However, the differences in preference appeared to have only an occasional effect on the strength of the short-term apparent competition detected in a field experiment. Veech (2001) found that captive individuals of both rodent species had approximately equal foraging effort (i.e. time spent foraging) in patches that contained a highly preferred seed type (*Oryzopsis hymenoides*) regardless of seed density and the presence of a less preferred seed

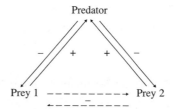

Fig. 5.19   Short-term apparent competition. Solid line: direct effect; dashed line: indirect effect.

type (*Astragalus cicer*) in the patches. The rodents also harvested a large proportion of *O. hymenoides* seeds regardless of initial seed density; this precluded a negative indirect effect of *A. cicer* on *O. hymenoides*. However, there was a negative indirect effect of *O. hymenoides* on *A. cicer* caused by rodents having a lower foraging effort in patches that only contained *A. cicer* seeds than in patches that contained *A. cicer* and *O. hymenoides* seeds. The indirect interaction between *O. hymenoides* and *A. cicer* represented a case of short-term apparent competition that was non-reciprocal. Most importantly, this indirect interaction was caused by the foraging behaviour of the rodents.

5.3.3   Priority effects

A number of studies have shown that priority effects can be very important in ecosystems. A priority effect indicates that the order in which a species

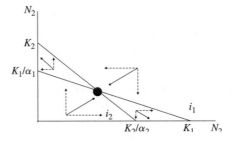

Fig. 5.20   Lotka-Volterra models can predict priority effects when $\alpha > 1$ (where α is the competition coefficient). The species that is excluded depends on the initial numbers of both species. An equilibrium is only achieved if both species are either below or above carrying capacity (K). N: number of individuals in species; i: isocline. Dashed lines indicate the direction of change for each species separately; solid line indicates the overall change that occurs in both species.

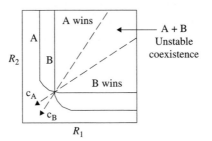

Fig. 5.21   A priority effect was also predicted by Tilman's (1988) resource allocation models when consumption vectors were reversed (i.e. stable coexistence occurs only when consumption vectors are closest to the resource vector where they are most limiting). R_1 and R_2 are resources 1 and 2; c: consumption vectors for species A and B. (From Tilman 1988. Copyright Princeton University Press.)

enters a system affects the outcome of the interactions. This can apply to either competition or predation. For example, Blaustein and Margalit (1996) found that the 'winner' of the interaction between a tadpole or a larval mosquito in ephemeral desert pools depended on the species that arrived there first. If the tadpole *Bufo viridis* arrived in a pool first, it would consume the mosquito larvae that arrived there subsequently. Conversely, if the mosquito larvae *Culiseta longiareolata* arrived there first, they would consume the tadpoles. This is a classic example of the interaction between theory and experiment as it was previously predicted by both Lotka-Volterra models (Fig. 5.20) when $\alpha > 1$ (where α is the competition coefficient) and by Tilman's (1988) resource allocation models (Fig. 5.21) when consumption vectors were reversed. Priority effects can be thought of as a form of temporal resource partitioning. However, there is a problem in assigning causation. Does a priority effect occur because of competition or in spite of it?

6 The importance of predation and parasitism

A number of excellent experimental studies have demonstrated the importance of predation in structuring desert ecosystems, and how predation and competition interact to structure desert communities. There are two ways that predation can be effective: (1) by direct mortality (Abramsky *et al*. 1990, 1992; Hermony *et al*. 1992); and (2) the predation risk experienced by the animal (Kotler *et al*. 2004).

6.1   Direct mortality

As an example of direct mortality, Abramsky *et al*. (1990, 1992) and Hermony *et al*. (1992) considered the effects of direct predation on desert snails by two species of desert rodents, *Gerbillus dasyurus* and *Acomys cahirinus*. In the central Negev desert highlands of Israel, rodents forage on the rocky hillsides of the wadi–hillslope ecosystem (see Fig. 2.7). The rodents are primarily found on the upper slopes where there are burrows available. They consume their snail prey (mostly *Trochoidea seetzenii*) and deposit them in piles, colloquially known as 'feeding tables'. Abramsky *et al*. (1990) made use of artificial shelters for rodents because they found that natural shelters were a limiting factor for the rodents. They found that rodent densities increased in areas with artificial shelters and that snail densities decreased. They found that there was a direct negative effect of predation by the rodents on snail numbers and that there was an indirect effect induced by the movement of the snails from the wadis to the hillsides. Hermony *et al*. (1992) showed that snails primarily bred in wadis during the winter rains (as found by Ward and Slotow 1992) and moved on to the lower slopes in the summer months. The rodents are restricted in their movements by their own predators (such as owls and foxes) to the upper hillslopes. Thus, the rodent–snail interaction is maintained by spatial heterogeneity in the distributions of both snails and rodents, and by the sensitivity of rodents to predation risk by their own predators.

Groner and Ayal (2001) examined the effects of direct mortality of darkling or tenebrionid beetles (Tenebrionidae) by migratory birds on the size distributions of these beetles in the Negev desert. Tenebrionid beetles in the Negev Desert exhibit size-related habitat segregation, with larger species found in denser cover and medium- and small-sized beetles found on the hillsides. Birds are purported to be the cause of size dependence in that plant cover reduces the predation efficiency of birds upon large tenebrionids, and birds prefer larger tenebrionids (especially *Adesmia dilatata* (spring active), *Trachyderma philistina* and *Pimelia grandis* (the last two species both summer active)). Groner and Ayal (2001) found that plant cover reduced predation rate by the most common spring and summer predatory birds, which were white storks (*Ciconia ciconia*) and stone curlews (*Burhinus oedicnemus*). Large tenebrionids are the most profitable size for a bird to consume, medium-sized species (e.g. *Adesmia metallica syriaca*) are less so (albeit still acceptable) and small species (e.g. *Opatroides punctulatus*, *Zophosis punctata*, *Adelostoma grande*) are unprofitable and are generally ignored. The well-vegetated wadi habitats are dominated by large and small species of beetles whereas medium-sized tenebrionids are under-represented in this habitat. The results of cage experiments indicated possible apparent competition (see Chapter 5) between the large and the medium/small tenebrionids in the wadis. Groner and Ayal (2001) found that large (and profitable) species are refuge-dependent, as they need to hide under the bushes in the wadis. Storks had 79% lower predation rates when foraging in the highly vegetated wadis and stone curlews had 54% lower predation rates when foraging there. Medium-sized (acceptable) species use enemy-free space on the hillslopes (where there are no predators), and the distribution of the small species is essentially independent of avian predator activity.

6.2   Predation risk

The effects of predation risk can have large consequences for patch use and habitat selection. For example, Kotler *et al.* (2004) consider apprehension, which is the behavioural change related to the risk of predation experienced by the animal, that takes away from time available for foraging. Predation risk, which includes the time taken away from foraging and from direct observation of predators, should increase with energetic state of the animal (an animal that is in a higher energetic state should be able to spend more time in non-energy gaining activities). They tested the responses of Allenby's gerbil, *Gerbillus andersoni allenbyi* (Rodentia), in the Negev desert (Israel) to predation risk while altering the energetic state of the animal. They also altered the risk to the gerbils by introducing barn owls, *Tyto alba*. The gerbils took about 4.5 times more seeds when they were in a higher energetic state, and took about 17% fewer seeds when barn owls were present. Seeds were presented when owls were present in either bush (sheltered) or in the open (i.e. unprotected) microhabitats; they took about 26% fewer seeds from the open microhabitats that were accessible to owls. Regarding time allocation, gerbils had higher GUDs (i.e. allocated less time foraging—see Chapter 5 for the explanation of GUDs) when the risk of owl predation was higher (i.e. in the open and when owls were present). When more seeds were added, the gerbils became more risk averse (i.e. they devoted more time to predation avoidance and less time foraging).

6.3   Isodars

Another term was added to the lexicon of Rosenzweig of density-dependent habitat selection (see Chapter 5) by Morris (1988) and named *isodars*. Rosenzweig's theories of habitat selection are based on the assumption of an Ideal Free Distribution (Fretwell and Lucas 1970). Initially, all species occupy the best habitat and then are forced to occupy successively poorer habitats as good habitats become filled. The term *isodar* indicates lines of equal fitness in a phase–plane diagram, where the density of the species in habitat 1 (chosen as the habitat with higher fitness) is plotted against the density of the same species in habitat 2 (Morris 1988) (Fig. 6.1). Isodars are calculated by regressing density in one habitat against density in another habitat (Morris 1988). Unfortunately, this limits one to assessments of two habitats only and assumes that habitat selection is cost-free (Shenbrot 2004). The regression slope of an isodar regression shows differences in habitat quality (e.g. in predation risk or resource acquisition) while regression intercepts indicate quantitative differences in resource availability. Non-significant regression lines indicate density-independent habitat selection. Shenbrot (2004) tested the isodar theory of habitat selection in the Negev desert (Israel) using the fat sand rat *Psammomys obesus* (Rodentia) (Fig. 6.2), which occurs in well-protected loessal wadi habitats (dominated by dense stands of the halophytic plant *Atriplex halimus* (Fig. 3.6)) and in the adjacent less-protected alluvial terraces, dominated by *Anabasis articulata* (Fig. 3.2). The efficiency of energy utilization by the rodents of these two plant species is similar (Degen *et al.* 2000) but the rodents perceive *A. halimus* in the wadi habitat to provide more reliable cover from predation, as they spend less time above-ground and move more quickly (presumably to escape predation) in the alluvial terraces than in the wadis (Tchabovsky *et al.* 2001). The habitat shifts of *P. obesus* were associated with different phenologies of the main foraging plants in the two microhabitats: well-protected, winter vegetation of *A. halimus* in habitat 1 (wadi) and less-protected summer vegetation of *A. articulata* in habitat 2 (alluvial terraces).

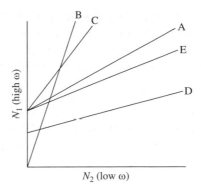

Fig. 6.1   Various types of isodars. A = parallel regulation; B = divergent regulation (quantitatively identical habitats); C = divergent regulation (quantitatively different habitats); D = crossover regulation; E = convergent regulation. All forms can be differentiated by linear regression. (From Morris 1988.)

Fig. 6.2   *Psammomys obesus.* (Photograph courtesy of Georgy Shenbrot.)

Based on isodars, there are five different models of density-dependent habitat selection (*sensu* Morris 1988) that differ in qualitative and quantitative features. In the parallel regulation model, habitats differ only quantitatively and have a slope equal to 1 and a positive intercept (Fig. 6.1). Two models of divergent regulation occur when the isodars have a slope >1. The intercept should be 0 in quantitatively equal habitats. It should be >0 if the qualitatively better habitat is also quantitatively better (e.g. if there is lower predation risk and greater foraging opportunity in that habitat). Models of convergent and crossover regulation reveal differences in habitat 1 that are due to quantitative differences between the two habitats but where habitat 2 is qualitatively better (e.g. better foraging opportunities in habitat 1 but lower predation risk in habitat 2). This results in isodars with a positive intercept but with a slope <0. The last two models differ in the values of the carrying capacity (K) and are distinguishable by the value of the point of equal densities on the isodar line, that are within (crossover) or outside of the values (convergent) of the observed population densities (Fig. 6.1).

Shenbrot (2004) found that winter distribution patterns of *P. obesus* depended on the rainfall of the preceding autumn (Fig. 6.3). Habitat distributions for winters preceded by dry autumns showed that isodars corresponding to divergent regulation occurred, where wadi habitat was both quantitatively and qualitatively better than the terrace. The data on habitat distribution for winters preceded by wet autumns fitted the divergent model of population regulation for quantitatively identical habitats. The isodars indicate that in winter after a wet autumn, the wadi habitat was qualitatively better than terrace habitat but quantitatively the two habitats were identical.

The summer distribution of fat sand rats *P. obesus* in the two-habitat system supported Shenbrot's (2004) hypothesis that wadis are quantitatively

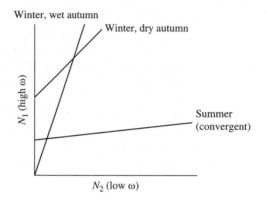

Fig. 6.3 *Psammomys obesus* isodars. The analysis of long-term data supported the predictions for summers and for winters following dry autumn conditions but supported the divergent model of population regulation for winters following autumn seasons with high precipitation. ω = fitness. (From Shenbrot 2004. With kind permission of Blackwell Publishing.)

Table 6.1 Estimation of the isodar parameters for the *Psammomys obesus* long-term data (1993–2001) (Shenbrot 2004).

Season	n	Slope	Intercept	r^2
Summer	27	0.339 ± 0.08	0.639 ± 0.11	0.78
Winter (all together)	24	3.429 ± 2.61	0.409 ± 0.85	0.25
Winter after dry autumn	12	4.629 ± 0.59	1.299 ± 0.23	0.97
Winter after wet autumn	12	4.809 ± 2.79	−0.05 ± 0.58	0.59

better but qualitatively poorer than the alluvial terrace habitat. The pattern fits the crossover model of population regulation, i.e. sand rats perceive the terrace as a superior habitat at low density but switch to the wadi at high density (Fig. 6.3 and Table 6.1). This crossover regulation can be explained by interactions between higher food availability and higher risk of predation in the terrace habitat if predation is density-dependent. At low densities, the combination of better foraging conditions with relatively low predation pressure favours the selection of the terrace habitat, while at higher densities increased predation pressure shifts preference to the wadi. Shenbrot's field observations confirmed that the major predators of *P. obesus* were red fox *Vulpes vulpes*, caracal *Felis caracal,* and several species of diurnal birds of prey. Mammalian predators should be equally effective in both habitats, whereas the risk of visual detection by birds of prey seems to be higher in the more exposed terrace habitat. The birds of prey are non-specialized rodent predators and, thus, cumulative predation risk is likely to increase with prey density (Norrdahl and Korpimäki 2002).

6.4   Spiders

In a single wadi system in the Negev desert (Israel), Lubin *et al.* (1993) and Ward and Lubin (1993) examined the effects of web relocation (a form of habitat selection) on fitness of two spiders, *Latrodectus revivensis* (Theridiidae) (Fig. 6.4), a widow spider that feeds on cursorial prey such as darkling beetles, and *Stegodyphus lineatus* (Eresidae) (Fig. 6.5), which traps flying insects. They found that both spider species moved nests relatively frequently as juveniles, always moving to nests that could accommodate their progressively larger bodies. Ward and Lubin (1993) found that food-supplemented *Stegodyphus* spiders bred earlier and had more

Fig. 6.4   Web of *Latrodectus revivensis*. (Photograph courtesy of Yael Lubin.)

Fig. 6.5   Web of *Stegodyphus lineatus*. (Photograph courtesy of Trine Bilde.)

young than non-supplemented spiders. Also, these spiders moved more frequently if close to areas with greater annual plant densities—which attracted aerial insects to their webs. In contrast, there was a negative effect of dispersal on *Latrodectus* spiders; mortality increased to about 40% (Lubin *et al.* 1993) from an overall level of about 2.5% in the nest. Nonetheless, *Latrodectus* spiders had better body condition and had greater reproductive success when they relocated their nests. Thus, both studies, albeit on spiders with different types of prey, showed the pivotal role of food availability on activity and reproductive output. Similar results were obtained in North American deserts by Riechert (1981) and Riechert and Harp (1987) for the sheetweb-building spider *Agelenopsis aperta* (Agelenidae) and in the Australian desert spider *Geolycosa godeffroyi* (Lycosidae) (Humphreys 1973).

Shadow competition for food may occur when sedentary foragers closer to a source of food reduce the prey's availability to those further away (Lubin *et al.* 2001). This process should increase with the size and density of a group of predators. Lubin *et al.* (2001) tested for shadow competition in a burrowing spider *Seothyra henscheli* (Eresidae), which forages mainly on ants, in the Namib Desert (see Chapter 4 for further reference to the thermal niche of this spider). Individual spiders occurring inside or on the periphery of clusters were compared to solitary spiders in a natural population. Spiders in the population grew more slowly in clusters than did solitary spiders. The greatest effect was at highest densities, where nearly all spiders maintained active webs, indicating a state of hunger. Ants reach spider webs at different locations within the patches of different densities. Simulation modelling confirmed that shadow competition adequately explained the patterns of foraging and growth of sedentary foragers such as these spiders (Lubin *et al.* 2001). What causes spiders to keep to the centre of a cluster? There are two reasons, which may not be mutually exclusive:

1. These spiders occur in dune sand and tend to keep close to the maternal burrow because of uncertainty over dune stability further away (Henschel and Lubin 1992, 1997). Peripheral webs would be more susceptible to dune instability than those in the centre.
2. Predation on spiders, especially by another spider, *Palpimanus stridulator* (Palpimanidae) (Henschel and Lubin 1992), should be higher on the periphery than in the centre because of a 'selfish herd' effect (Hamilton 1971); that is, it will always be better for a spider to occur in the centre of a group to avoid being eaten on the outside. Indeed, survival was lower for peripherally located spiders, in spite of the higher growth rate (Lubin *et al.* 2001).

6.5   Scorpions

A few desert arachnids may specialize on certain prey types. For example, in the Kara Kum desert in central Asia, *Minosiella intermedia* (Gnaphosidae), which is the most common spider in rodent burrows, specialized and accepted only fleas and small scarab beetles (Krivokhatsky and Fet 1982). Two scorpions are specialists. The Australian species *Isometroides vescus* focuses on trapdoor spiders (Ctenizidae)(Main 1956) and the Saharo-Arabian desert species *Scorpio maurus* takes up to 77% of its food from the terrestrial isopod *Hemilepistus reaumuri*, although the values for the last-mentioned species may be as low as 20% (Shachak 1980). Indeed, the latter species may often place their burrows as close as 10 cm from the nearest isopod burrows (Shachak 1980). However, Polis and McCormick (1986) found that scorpions more often took prey of different sizes depending on their own body sizes. This is known as intraguild predation, and is consistent with the gape-limitation hypothesis (Zaret 1980); that is, the mouth size of an organism necessarily limits the size of the prey that they can ingest. Although this is not universally true (e.g. the spider *Latrodectus hesperus* can catch scorpions and sun spiders (also known as wind spiders; order Solifugae) that are several times bigger than themselves) (Polis and Yamashita 1991), many scorpions often change size dramatically during development. For example, growing *Paruroctonus mesaensis* increase 40–60 times in mass. Instar 2 scorpions eat prey that average 5 mm in length, whereas adults consume prey that are about three times larger, 66% of which are different scorpion species (Polis and Yamashita 1991). Indeed, the effects of age structure, trophic opportunism, cannibalism and intraguild predation on other predatory arthropods are the norm rather than the exception.

Polis and McCormick (1986) removed about 6,000 scorpions from $300 \times 100 \text{ m}^2$ plots over 29 months in the Coachella valley, Mojave desert

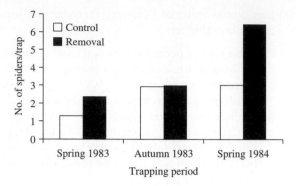

Fig. 6.6   Polis and McCormick (1986) removed about 6,000 scorpions from 300 × 100 m² plots over 29 months. They found that the number of spiders increased in the removal plots in the spring of 1983 and 1984. (Modified from Polis and McCormick 1986.)

(North America). They found that the number of spiders increased in the removal plots (Fig. 6.6). This could be explained either by exploitation competition (i.e. with no scorpions present there was more prey remaining for spiders to consume) or direct intraguild predation. They found no effect of exploitation competition as prey did not increase in the removal plots and spiders did not grow bigger in these plots. Rather, scorpion predation on spiders (intraguild predation) explained the difference in spider numbers. Polis and McCormick (1986) record 'looping mutual predation', where one species eats another and vice versa, as rather common in the Coachella valley in the Mojave desert (North America). Scorpions eat spiders and solifuges, spiders eat scorpions and solifuges, etc. A similar result to the Coachella valley study was recorded in the Namib desert on *Acacia erioloba* trees in the Kuiseb river. In that study, *Gandanimeno eresus* (Eresidae) spider populations were reduced by 42% when the scorpion *Uroplectes otjimbinguensis* was added and increased by 2.9 times when the same scorpion was removed (no statement of numbers of scorpions added or removed was given; reported by Polis and Yamashita (1991)).

6.6   Visually hunting predators

Kotler (1984) showed that moonlight was important for visually hunting predators. By adding lanterns to a site in the Great Basin desert (North America), he showed that rodents had lower foraging activity than near control (i.e. unlit) sites (see also Price *et al.* 1984). This effectively demonstrated that there should be a difference between full moon and new moon nights, as he also found (Fig. 6.7). This has subsequently been shown

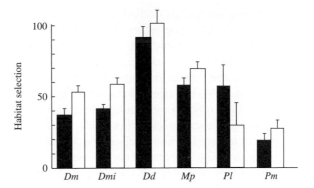

Fig. 6.7   Kotler (1984) showed that illumination was important for visually hunting predators. By adding lanterns to a site in the Great Basin desert (North America), he showed that rodents had lower activity (i.e. showed greater predation risk) than near control sites. Dm = *Dipodomys merriami*; Dmi = *Dipodomys microps*; Dd = *Dipodomys deserti*; Mp = *Microdipodops pallidus*; Pl = *Perognathus longimembris*; and Pm = *Peromyscus maniculatus*. (From Kotler 1984. With kind permission of the Ecological Society of America.)

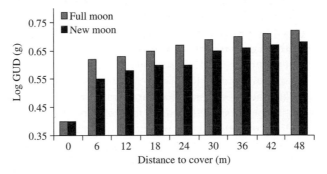

Fig. 6.8   Gerbils in the Namib desert have lower GUDs on new moon (dark) nights and close to cover—that is, the patch is more valuable when predation risk is low, so they stay there longer and eat more. (From Hughes and Ward 1993. With kind permission of Elsevier.)

on a number of occasions (e.g. Hughes and Ward (1993) in the Namib desert (Africa), Kotler *et al.* (1994, 2004) in the Negev desert (Israel)). For example, Hughes and Ward (1993) showed that gerbils in the Namib desert have lower GUDs on new moon (dark) nights and close to cover—that is, the patch is more valuable when predation risk is low, so they stay there longer and eat more (Fig. 6.8).

6.7   Snakes, scent-hunting predators

Many members of the Reptilia are able to use vision to hunt for their predators. These include chameleons, geckos, iguanas, and agamas. It is only the autarchoglossans (also called the 'independent tongued' reptiles) that are capable of picking up heavy, non-airborne chemicals from surfaces with their tongues (Vitt and Pianka 1994). The tongue deposits these chemicals on the vomeronasal organ, from where the information is obtained to enable the animal to assess the suitability of the prey item for capture. Bouskila (1995) has stressed that there is an important difference between snakes (and other scent-hunting vertebrate predators) and visually hunting vertebrate predators such as owls, foxes, coyotes, and jackals (see also the Hughes *et al.* (1994) study in the Namib, where owls and jackals were the main predators). One of the consequences of this difference in hunting mode is that snakes are sit-and-wait predators that predominantly hide in bushes, while owls and other visually hunting predators hunt primarily in the open. Bouskila (1995) found that, when sidewinder snakes (*Crotalus cerastes*) in the Mojave desert (North America) were the main predators, the kangaroo rats, *Dipodomys deserti* and *D. merriami*, preferred to forage in the open and avoided the bush (Fig. 6.9). This microhabitat choice is the opposite of the microhabitat preferred by the sidewinder snake in this habitat, which prefers the bush over open microhabitats. Moreover, this is also the opposite behaviour of the gerbils (mentioned above) studied by Kotler *et al.* (2004) in the Negev desert (Israel), and the gerbils in the Namib desert studied by Hughes *et al.* (1994) (see Chapter 5) because they prefer open microhabitats. Interestingly, the dominant kangaroo rat species (*D. deserti*) foraged more in the microhabitat avoided by the snake but the subordinate kangaroo rat species, *D. merriami*, chose the same microhabitat as the snake to avoid competition. This is yet another way that competition and predation interact.

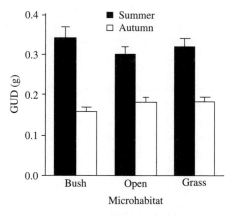

Fig. 6.9   Bouskila (1995) found that when sidewinder snakes (*Crotalus cerastes*) in the Mojave desert (North America) were the main predators, the kangaroo rats, *Dipodomys deserti*, and *D. merriami*, preferred to forage in the open and avoided the bush. (From Bouskila 1995. With kind permission of the Ecological Society of America.)

Another interesting feature of Bouskila's (1995) study is that there was no effect of moonlight on foraging activity when snakes were the main predators; that is, kangaroo rats did not forage more on dark nights than on moonlit nights. This is *contra* examples provided by Kotler (1984) and Price *et al.* (1984) in North American deserts and Hughes and Ward (1993) in the Namib desert, among others. All these latter cases involved visually hunting predators such as owls, foxes, and jackals. Bouskila (1995) observed that if the snakes were inactive (in autumn, on account of low temperatures), then there was a preference for foraging on dark nights. This means that desert rodents do not have many places to hide in the summer months because visually hunting predators occupy the open microhabitats and scent-hunting predators occupy the bush microhabitats. In contrast, in the winter months, rodents become averse to using moonlit nights, because snakes are ectotherms and hibernate during the winter, but visually hunting predators such as owls and large mammals are still active because they are endotherms.

6.8   Keystone predation

Although keystone species can easily be described for competitive scenarios, it is actually for predation that Paine (1966) first described it. Keystone predators are defined as having a greater effect than that explained by density or dominance alone (Paine 1966). He described a simple system with relatively few species. Once systems become more complex, there are many potential keystone predators (Paine 1980). In species-rich communities, dominance by a single predator or a few predators may be sufficient to explain predation (i.e. it is based on density rather than unique species with stronger effects). In North America, Henke and Bryant (1999) reduced the densities of coyotes *Canis latrans* from 0.12 km^{-2} to 0.06 km^{-2} in two treatment plots and kept two plots constant at about 0.14 km^{-2} in the Chihuahuan desert (350 mm mean annual rainfall). Each plot was 5,000 ha in size. They found that the treatment plots had lower species richness and lower diversity of rodent species. Without coyote predation, Ord's kangaroo rat (*Dipodomys ordii*) became the most abundant rodent in shrubland and was the only rodent species caught in grassland after 12 months of coyote removal. Rodent density and biomass, black-tailed jackrabbit *Lepus californicus* density, and the relative abundance of badgers *Taxidea taxus*, bobcats *Felis rufus*, and gray foxes *Urocyon cineroargenteus* increased on treatment sites. Thus, there is strong evidence for a mesopredator-controlled coexistence of species and, consequently, evidence for keystone predation.

Similarly, Johnson *et al.* (2007) have shown that 18 mammal species have gone extinct since European settlement began in Australia. The causes of these extinctions are not entirely clear, although many sources have blamed the introduction of red foxes *V. vulpes* and cats *Felis catus*. Cats are widespread throughout Australia and red foxes occur everywhere except in the northern tropics. Overkill is claimed to be the main threat for small mammals in Australia. Australia's largest extant predator is the dingo *Canis lupus dingo*, which was introduced to Australia by native Australians (Glen *et al.* 2007). Where dingoes are locally abundant, cats and red foxes are rare (Newsome 2001; Glen and Dickman 2005). Dingoes may limit the populations of these two smaller introduced predators and indeed may directly cause their mortality (O'Neill 2002; Mitchell and Banks 2005). European settlers have killed dingoes, especially in sheep-farming areas. Johnson *et al.* (2007) tested whether, in areas where dingoes have remained abundant, native marsupial species have remained more common than in areas where dingoes have been eliminated. They showed that the dingo, the top predator, is indeed limiting the presence of intro-duced mesopredators (red foxes and cats). The dingo, itself introduced some 3,500–4,000 y ago from southcentral Asia, could have eliminated the thylacine *Thylacinus cynocephalus* and the devil *Sarcophilus harrisii* (formerly known as the 'Tasmanian devil'), although this is debatable (Johnson and Wroe 2003). Nonetheless, dingoes appear to limit the popu-lations of large macropods and emus (Pople *et al.* 2000) and, therefore, is considered the top predator in Australia (Glen *et al.* 2007). This, too, constitutes evidence for keystone predation.

Lloyd (2007) studied the effects of removal of two mesopredators, the black-backed jackal *Canis mesomelas* and caracal *F. caracal*, in the

Table 6.2 Daily nest predation rates (% ±SE) on nine bird species did not differ signifi-cantly between the Kalahari National Park (no predator control) and rangeland (inten-sive control) (paired *t*-test: $t_8 = 0.014$, $P = 0.9$). Sample size of nests in parentheses. 1 = *Rhinoptilus africanus*; 2 = *Pterocles namaqua*; 3 = *Chersomanes albofasciata*; 4 = *Eremopterix verticalis*; 5 = *Eremopterix australis*; 6 = *Malcorus pectoralis*; 7 = *Melaenornis infuscatus*; 8 = *Passer melanurus*; 9 = *Emberiza impetuani*. (From Lloyd 2007.)

Bird species	National park	Rangeland
Double-banded courser[1]	0.85 ± 0.42 (45)	0.50 ± 0.50 (12)
Namaqua sandgrouse[2]	4.70 ± 1.73 (32)	9.19 ± 0.65 (278)
Spike-heeled lark[3]	4.39 ± 1.29 (28)	5.79 ± 0.96 (55)
Grey-backed sparrow lark[4]	8.96 ± 1.05 (129)	6.70 ± 0.48 (368)
Black-eared sparrow lark[5]	6.89 ± 1.39 (47)	5.06 ± 0.59 (159)
Rufous-eared warbler[6]	4.38 ± 1.29 (21)	2.60 ± 1.15 (13)
Chat flycatcher[7]	4.03 ± 1.49 (22)	3.69 ± 1.22 (26)
Cape sparrow[8]	8.54 ± 1.74 (27)	4.48 ± 1.17 (27)
Lark-like bunting[9]	6.39 ± 1.42 (33)	10.98 ± 1.92 (35)
Mean predation	5.46 ± 1.96	5.43 ± 2.80

Kalahari desert and in the Karoo (South Africa) because they kill sheep, and tested the effects on nine bird species. He found no significant effect of removal of these medium-sized predators on these birds (Table 6.2). A possible reason for this is that the jackal and caracal are not the largest predators in southern African deserts. Indeed, lions *Panthera leo*, leopards *Panthera pardus*, cheetah *Acinonyx jubatus*, spotted hyaenas *Crocuta crocuta*, brown hyaenas *Hyaena brunnea,* and African wild dog *Lycaon pictus* are considerably larger desert carnivores. Lloyd (2007) also considered a further complication due to multispecies interactions. For example, the effects of the removal of jackals and caracals could have been masked by higher levels of predation by the rhombic egg-eater *Dasypeltis scabra*, an egg-eating snake, which can account for 13–70% of predation on bird nests at the egg stage (Lloyd 2004). Either or both of these reasons may explain why the removal of mesopredators (jackals and caracals) does not constitute evidence for keystone predation.

6.9   Animal parasites and parasitoids

Parasitism has been little studied in deserts, largely because many researchers have believed that the harsh environment has limited the ability of parasites to invade these habitats. Recent work suggests that this may be a misconception and that parasite–host interactions may be as important in deserts as they are elsewhere. I will consider some fascinating examples of parasitism, such as parasitoids controlling the body temperatures of their hosts to ensure the survival of their offspring and host choice in fleas being controlled by the off-host environment (*contra* conventional wisdom that it is the host's physiology that limits the success of the parasite).

What is the difference among parasites, parasitoids and brood parasites? Parasites typically do not kill their hosts but can suppress their metabolism severely, parasitoids do ultimately kill the host, while brood parasites usually have a strong negative impact on host eggs, sometimes killing them, to the benefit of their own eggs and young. The host to the brood parasite raises the parasite's young once they have hatched.

6.9.1   Parasites

Parasites may be divided into endoparasites, which occur inside the body of the host and that are typically small (although tapeworms, for example, can be extremely large) and ectoparasites, which are external (Lafferty and Kuris 2002; Stiling 2002). Parasites can be extremely abundant and may be as much as four times more common than other organisms in an ecosystem (Lafferty and Kuris 2002; Stiling 2002). Krasnov *et al.* (1997) have studied the effects of ectoparasites, specifically fleas (Siphonaptera; Fig. 6.10) on rodents in the Negev desert of Israel. Fleas are not as specific in their

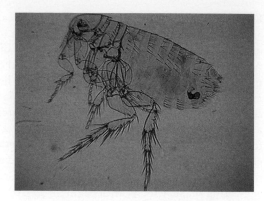

Fig. 6.10   A flea (*Xenopsylla dipodilla*) from the Negev desert, Israel (photograph courtesy of Boris Krasnov).

host preferences as one might expect. A single flea species may parasitize several rodent host species. In the fleas studied by Krasnov *et al.* (1997), they have also shown that it is not only the host and its immediate environment (e.g. the burrow of the host) that limits the numbers or presence of fleas but also the general environment of the desert that is important. For example, there was complete replacement of one flea species (*Xenopsylla conformis*) with another (*Xenopsylla ramesis*) on the same rodent hosts (*Meriones crassus* and *G. dasyurus*) at either end of a steep precipitation gradient in the Negev desert (Krasnov *et al.* 1998). This replacement was due, partly, to abiotic features of the habitats such as ambient temperature, humidity and substrate type. Yet other flea species in this desert depend on the host identity–habitat identity interplay (B. Krasnov, pers. comm.). Krasnov *et al.* (2006) have found that temperate and desert habitats may differ in host–parasite relationships, particularly for pre-imago fleas where the burrow is the ultimate habitat, because of the more extreme nature of the desert environment. Most desert rodents and insectivores dig deep burrows to avoid environmental extremes while temperate rodents and insectivores occupy above-ground or shallow burrows. Between-habitat differences in the desert environment are likely to be more extreme than in temperate environments. An alternative explanation is that interspecific visits are more frequent in temperate habitats than in desert habitats because of the higher densities of small mammals in temperate habitats, resulting in greater host-switching (Krasnov *et al.* 2006).

Krasnov *et al.* (2003) have also used isodars to study the relationships between the abundance of fleas on specific hosts. They examined the choices of five flea species for two rodent species, where rodents represented different 'habitats'. They studied the fleas *X. conformis*, *X. ramesis*, *Nosopsyllus iranus* and *Stenoponia tripectinata* which parasitize two rodents, *G. dasyurus* and *M. crassus* in the compact soils of the Makhtesh

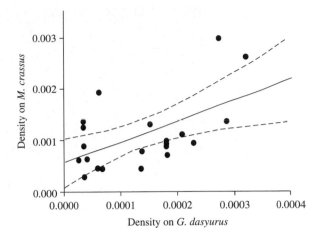

Fig. 6.11   *Xenopsylla conformis* was a density-dependent host selector that showed sharp selectivity at low density. (From Krasnov *et al.* 2003.)

Ramon erosion cirque. They also studied the effects of the flea *Synosternus cleopatrae* on the rodents *Gerbillus andersoni allenbyi* and *Gerbillus pyramidum* in the western Negev desert, where semistabilized sands are occupied by these two species. Two flea species, *N. iranus* and *S. tripectinata*, were non-selectors with no relationship between density and host quality. Three flea species, *X. conformis*, *X. ramesis*, and *S. cleopatrae*, perceived either quantitative differences between the two hosts or qualitative differences. Quantitative differences pertain to the amount of the resource, which in the case of fleas is likely to be the organic matter in the nest for flea larvae. Qualitative differences pertain to the pattern of resource acquisition such as in host defensiveness between hosts. *X. conformis* was a density-dependent host selector that showed sharp selectivity at low density (Fig. 6.11). *X. ramesis* and *S. cleopatrae* were density-independent host selectors with a direct correspondence between density with habitat quality (Fig. 6.12). Thus, fleas, similar to many other organisms, can make choices about their environments, in this case, their hosts and the host's environment, in a way that maximizes their reproductive output.

An interesting case of an endoparasite parasitizing a toad occurs in ephemeral Arizona (United States) pools in the Sonoran desert. The parasite is a polystomatid flatworm *Pseudodiplorchis americanus* (Monogenea, Platyhelminthes) which parasitizes a desert toad *Scaphiopus couchii* (Tinsley 1999; Tinsley *et al.* 2002). The toad hibernates for 9–10 months and only enters the water for a few hours to a few days a year to breed. The parasite lays eggs at the time that the toads are spawning, allowing the larvae only that short period to infect other mature adult hosts while they too are spawning. It is too risky for the parasites to infect the tadpoles

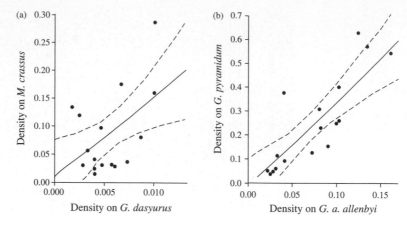

Fig. 6.12   Density-independent host selection occurs when there is a positive correlation between density and habitat quality. (a) *Xenopsylla ramesis* and (b) *Synosternus cleopatrae*. (From Krasnov *et al.* 2003.)

instead of the adults because of the high probability that the pond may dry out before the tadpoles mature.

6.9.2   Parasitoids

Ward and Henschel (1992) have shown that there is a unique interaction that occurs between the parasitoid *Pseudopompilus humboldti* (Pompilidae, Hymenoptera) and its spider prey *Stegodyphus lineatus* in the Negev desert of Israel. The pompilid wasp typically alights on the capture web of the spider and gently shakes it, giving the appearance that there is a prey item attached to the web. The spider, which hides in its dense silk nest, runs down to investigate. The pompilid attacks the spider and anaesthetizes it. It then positions the spider in the entrance of the nest allowing the egg it has just laid on the spider to develop there, rather than pushing it back into the nest, where it would be invisible to predators or scavengers. Ward and Henschel (1992) performed a simple experiment to test whether positioning at the nest entrance was because of the high ambient temperatures that the spider would reach inside the nest in the heat of the day. They pushed some of the spiders that were anaesthetized, back up into the nest and the rest they manipulated but left on the nest entrance. The mean ambient temperature of spiders inside the nest was on average 6°C higher than that of spiders left on the nest entrance during the heat of the day. More importantly, all spiders left on the nest entrance survived and all the spiders in the nest died, presumably from overheating. Thus, this is an effective way that pompilid wasps can protect their offspring by controlling temperature indirectly via host manipulation. This also demonstrates an adaptive trade-off between thermoregulatory requirements and predation risk.

Fig. 6.13   *Carparachne aureoflava* spiders (Heteropodidae) have a unique mechanism to avoid parasitism by pompilid wasps, wheeling down the dune face to escape parasitism, relying on gravity for momentum. (Photograph courtesy of Joh Henschel.)

Henschel (1990) showed in the Namib desert that pompilid wasps can attack spiders that burrow in shifting dunes. These spiders (*Carparachne aureoflava*, Heteropodidae) have a unique mechanism to avoid this parasitism, namely, when exposed by the wasp they wheel down the dune face to escape parasitism, relying on gravity for momentum (Fig. 6.13). They may rotate between 600 rpm and 2,650 rpm and achieve speeds that can be as much as 0.5–1.5 m s^{-1}, depending on the body size and steepness of the dune slope. This strategy appears successful; spiders that wheeled to escape avoided parasitism while those that did not, failed to escape from parasitism by the pompilid spider.

6.9.3   Brood parasites

Brood parasites and their hosts may be involved in an 'arms race' (Dawkins and Krebs 1979) where each adaptation of the parasite is met by a counter-adaptation of the host, which in turn is met by another adaptation of the parasite, etc. Alternatively, there may be an 'evolutionary equilibrium' (Lotem *et al.* 1995) where there is a form of matching of adaptations of the brood parasite with limitations on counter-adaptations by the host. For example, the effect of experience can be important so that it does not pay the naïve host to be overcautious in ejecting eggs when the eggs of the brood parasite are remarkably similar to their own. This usually leaves some percentage of eggs of the brood parasite in the nest (Lotem *et al.* 1995). Another form of interaction is 'evolutionary lag' (Ward *et al.* 1996) where adaptations of the brood parasite are not yet matched by those of the host. Although there are a few examples of birds that act as brood parasites in deserts (e.g. brown-headed cowbirds *Molothrus ater* in North America; Ward and Smith (2000)), many of the best-known brood parasites are insects. Typically, brood parasites parasitize social insects and do so by mimicking the odour spectrum of their hosts (Rasa and Heg 2004).

A pertinent desert example comes from darkling or tenebrionid beetles (Tenebrionidae). *Parastizopus armaticeps* is parasitized by the brood-parasitic tenebrionid *Eremostibes opacus* in the Kalahari desert of southern Africa (Rasa and Heg 2004). The host species, *P. armaticeps*, has continuous provisioning of its young. The burrow entrance must remain open to allow food provisioning to occur because they do not store food items. This also, inevitably, allows the brood parasite *E. opacus*, whose odour mimics that of the host, access to the burrow; nearly 90% of burrows contained at least one brood parasite. Similar to the situation with avian brood parasites (Ward *et al.* 1996), the duration that the brood parasite's eggs take to hatch is slightly shorter than that of the host, ensuring that the host raises the eggs of the brood parasite as well as its own. In spite of good odour matching, Rasa and Heg (2004) found that about 7% of brood parasites were evicted from the burrow. Rasa and Heg (2004) found a very strong effect of guarding duration (Fig. 6.14) and the number of offspring on the presence of the brood parasite *E. opacus* in the burrow. This indicates that

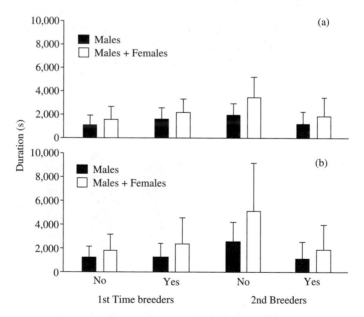

Fig. 6.14   Rasa and Heg (2004) found a very strong effect of guarding duration on the presence of the brood parasite *Eremostibes opacus*. (a) total breeding period. (b) early reproductive period. Values are total guarding duration ± S.D. No = no parasite contact; Yes = raised with parasite in the parental burrow. (From Rasa and Heg 2004.)

variation in guarding behaviour by the host pair might be an important source of variation in brood parasitism. There are trade-offs between time spent by the host female in guarding and collecting food and by the host male in guarding and lengthening the burrow to achieve optimal burrow moisture conditions for larval development. Thus, when pairs face food scarcity, or rapid desiccation of the burrow or have a large brood (or all or some of the above), they may need more time for the above activities at the expense of guarding the burrow from parasites. Surprisingly, there was no effect of prior experience with the brood parasite (Fig. 6.14). Attack frequency was actually lower for pairs with prior breeding experience. There was no effect on the number of brood parasites in the burrow. Interestingly, males guarded more when they had no prior experience with the brood parasite. This indicates that, in general, *P. armaticeps* does not learn to recognize the parasite.

In arid Spain, annual rainfall occurs mainly during the winter months (250–300 mm rain). Potential evapotranspiration is about three times higher than mean annual rainfall (Sierra *et al.* 1990), which defines it as a desert area. González-Megías and Sánchez-Piñero (2004) showed that brood parasitism occurs in dung beetles (Scarabeidae) in the arid Guadix-Basa basin; the host species *Onthophagus merdarius* is parasitized by *Aphodius tersus*. Offspring mortality is high (about 95%). Surprisingly, they found that there were neither differences in nesting rates nor in nesting traits (number of brood masses, depth of brood masses, size of brood masses) when brood parasites were excluded (i.e. brood parasite present or absent) (Fig. 6.15). Thus, González-Megías and Sánchez-Piñero (2004) found it difficult to determine whether an 'evolutionary equilibrium' (which they call

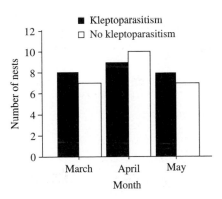

Fig. 6.15   In the arid Guadix-Basa basin of Spain, the host species *Onthophagus merdarius* is parasitized by *Aphodius tersus*. They found that there were neither differences in nesting rates nor in nesting traits (number of brood masses, depth of brood masses, size of brood masses) in which the presence of the brood parasite was manipulated (i.e. brood parasite present or absent). (From Gonzalez-Megias and Sanchez-Pinero 2004. With kind permission of Blackwell Publishing.)

the 'best of the bad') or an 'evolutionary lag' occurred. In the case of the dung beetles in Spain, the adult hosts seal up the burrow and the brood parasite enters thereafter, in contrast to the previous example of the tenebrionid beetles of the Kalahari desert. This leaves the dung beetles with few behavioural opportunities to respond to brood parasitism (González-Megías and Sánchez-Piñero 2004). Thus, in both cases of brood parasitism shown here, it would appear that there is an evolutionary lag (*sensu* Ward *et al.* 1996) that may be a consequence of either lack of prior experience or lack of time to respond to brood parasites.

7 Plant–animal interactions in deserts

It is widely believed that abiotic factors have greater influence than biotic factors in determining the biodiversity of arid ecosystems. Nonetheless, desert animals and plants interact in ways which have strongly influenced their respective evolutionary trajectories. This chapter begins with herbivory because of its widespread impacts, many of which are presumed to be negative. It then moves on to some other important aspects of desert plant–animal interactions, with a focus on pollination and seed dispersal. Of the various forms of pollination, the chapter will explore the yucca moth–yucca and senita moth–senita cactus mutualisms. With regard to the role of animals in seed predation and seed dispersal, it will consider effects of small mammals and ants on seed abundance, and the role of large mammals in dispersing the seeds of keystone *Acacia* species (Milton *et al.* 1999; Munzbergova and Ward 2002). This selection of examples illustrates how the relatively simple nature of the desert environment has given biologists unique insights into the importance of plant–animal interactions for ecosystem function.

7.1   Herbivory

It has been argued that herbivory by mammals does not contribute significantly to arid ecosystem functioning and biodiversity maintenance (reviewed by Noy-Meir 1973). Instead, abiotic factors such as high temporal and spatial variation in rainfall are suggested to be the most important factors for the ecology of arid ecosystems. There is a strong negative correlation between the coefficient of variation in mean annual rainfall among years and median annual rainfall of arid regions, which results in high variability in the germination of annual plants and high variability in the growth of perennial plants (Ward 2001, 2005a). Similarly, spatial variation in rainfall is high and is not correlated with distance among sampling points (Ward *et al*. 2000a, 2004). This variability in rainfall results in high spatio-temporal variability in plant abundance and availability to herbivores. Ward *et al*. (2000a) showed that, in the Negev Desert of Israel, only 1% of plant species were present in permanent plots in all years and approximately half the plant species were found only once in 10 years (Fig. 7.1).

Temporal variation in plant species richness can also be quite large; note the relationship between the coefficient of variation in plant species richness and total plant species richness (Fig. 7.2). This relationship is an envelope effect in that there is more variability when the total number of species is small (because there may be various reasons (such as edaphic variability) why total species numbers are limited) and it decreases as species richness increases, probably being limited by precipitation (Fig. 7.2).

Further contributing to spatial variation, in some arid regions, is the pattern of 'contracted vegetation' (*sensu* Whittaker 1975) (Fig. 9.1), whereby plants are almost entirely restricted to ephemeral watercourses. Another confounding factor is that geological substrates vary considerably

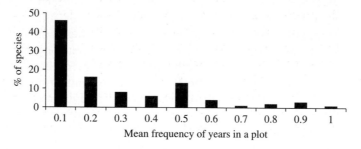

Fig. 7.1   Histogram of frequency of occurrence of plant species over time in Makhtesh Ramon, Israel. Most species rarely occur in any single plot. (From Ward *et al*. 2000a.)

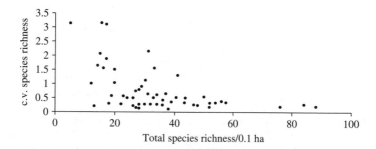

Fig. 7.2   Temporal variation in 0.1 ha vegetation plots in Makhtesh Ramon, Israel. c.v. = coefficient of variation (From Ward *et al*. 2000a.)

among arid regions, particularly in their nutrient status and water retention capacities (Landsberg *et al.* 1999a; Ward 2005a). Patchy nutrients and
water availability lead to considerable differences in plant composition
and nutritional quality among habitats (Stafford Smith and Morton 1990;
Ward and Olsvig-Whittaker 1993; Ward *et al.* 1993; Ward 2005a). The high
spatio-temporal variability in the availability of plants to herbivores necessarily limits the numbers of herbivores that can be sustained in arid ecosystems, which is considered to limit their impacts on plant resources.

Milchunas *et al.* (1988) predicted that a long evolutionary history of
grazing results in the selection for regrowth following herbivory and for
prostrate growth forms. In such communities, grazing causes rapid shifts
between suites of species adapted to either grazing avoidance/tolerance
or competition. In their global review, Milchunas and Lauenroth (1993)
showed convincingly that evolutionary history of grazing had an effect on
grazing responses inside and outside herbivore exclosures in North and
South America (Fig. 7.3). What does this mean? Milchunas and Lauenroth
(1993) infer that species that are highly palatable have been removed from
the vegetation in areas with a long evolutionary history of grazing and
only non-palatable species remain. Thus, there is no clear effect of grazing on changes in plant species composition. A possible reason for this is
the *Narcissus effect* (*sensu* Colwell and Winkler 1984), which means that
selection in the past has resulted in the extinction of all non-resistant/
tolerant genotypes. Thus, all extant species are similarly resistant to herbivores, resulting in an absence of an effect of current herbivory on plant
diversity (Ward and Olsvig-Whittaker 1993; Perevolotsky and Seligman
1998). Presumably, in such ecosystems, conditions seldom favour growth-
dominated genotypes. Thus, only one (resistant/tolerant) genotype exists
in these populations. Interestingly, re-examination of the same data for

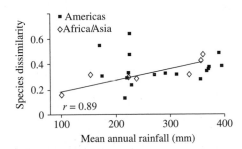

Fig. 7.3   Differences in species composition between grazed and ungrazed lands in arid ecosystems of the Americas and Africa and Asia (data limited to <400 mm rainfall from
Milchunas and Lauenroth (1993)). There was no significant relationship between species dissimilarity and mean annual rainfall for the American comparison, while there
was a significant relationship ($P < 0.001$) for the Africa and Asia comparison. (Modified
from Milchunas and Lauenroth 1993.)

Africa and Asia (Ward 2005a) shows no such effect, and indicates that grazing responses are positively correlated with mean annual rainfall in those studies (Fig. 7.3).

7.1.1 Grazing effects on species composition

Major differences between the effects of herbivores and carnivores on their food items are that herbivores seldom eat the entire food item and plants differ considerably in their quality. Plants can be of low quality because they contain low levels of energy and protein, have high levels of fibre, have high levels of defence compounds and may have lots of mechanical defences (thorns). Herbivores can alter plant community composition by selecting dominant species, causing rare species to become more common or by selecting rare species, increasing degree of dominance. However, this process usually does not affect diversity. Chesson (2000) developed a lottery model to explain how herbivores might affect plant diversity. In plant communities, spaces periodically become available when an inhabitant dies. Any species that has propagules ready at that time and place can occupy the space. This model makes the assumption that all plant species can increase when rare. Herbivores can increase the number of coexisting species by eliminating individuals of certain species, thereby freeing up space for other species that take their place opportunistically. If plants are avoided when rare, then the lottery model can explain coexistence of more species under herbivory (Fig. 5.1).

7.1.2 Long-term studies of the effects of large mammals on arid vegetation

What do field-based studies of the effects of herbivory by large mammals tell us about the effects of large mammals on vegetation of arid zones? Longer-term studies need to be considered when assessing the impact of herbivory in arid-zone vegetation because short-term studies might only show us the relatively trivial effects of differences in biomass consumption and show little in terms of changes in species composition. Although the list below is not intended to be exhaustive, such studies show inconsistent patterns in the response of arid vegetation to mammalian herbivory:

1. Goldberg and Turner (1986) analysed vegetation changes in nine permanent 100 m² plots first established in 1906 near Tucson, Arizona, USA (mean annual rainfall = 250 mm). These plots were fenced to exclude large herbivores in 1906 and were examined periodically until 1978. There were no consistent, directional changes in vegetation composition between 1906 and 1978, despite large fluctuations in absolute cover and density of the species. For most species, and in most plots, the changes in absolute cover and density appear to have been a response to sequences of either exceptionally wet years or exceptionally dry years. Only two species, *Krameria grayi* and *Janusia gracilis*, appeared

to increase over the study period—the former species is reported to be very palatable to livestock. A study comparing vegetation inside and outside the above-mentioned fenced areas following 50 years of protection showed that the total plant density was significantly higher within the fenced areas but there were no large differences in the composition of the vegetation (Blydenstein *et al.* 1957). As indicated above by Chesson (2000), it is changes in vegetation composition that are required to demonstrate changes in effects of herbivory rather than changes in biomass alone.

2. Ward *et al.* (1998, 2000a) and Saltz *et al.* (1999) examined the effects of reintroduced Asiatic wild asses, *Equus hemionus onager* (also called onagers or kulans), in 11 pairs of permanent plots in the central Negev desert of Israel (mean annual rainfall = 56 mm) from 1992 to 1997. There has been considerable concern that the reintroduction of such a large equid (~200 kg) would cause habitat degradation through heavy grazing because large, hindgut fermenters are dependent on processing large quantities of low-quality forage. They found that fenced plots (i.e. wild asses excluded) had significantly higher plant cover than unfenced plots when differences in rainfall among plots were accounted for, although there were no significant differences in plant species richness, diversity or dominance between fenced and unfenced plots. Three plant species showed significant increases in percentage cover in the fenced plots, and one species significantly increased in cover in the unfenced plots. Eight plant species invaded the fenced plots, three species invaded the unfenced plots, and one species disappeared from the unfenced plots during the study. Unfenced plots showed a directional change away from their original species composition (although plant species richness and diversity remained the same) while vegetation in fenced plots did not change over the period (Fig. 7.4a–c) (Ward *et al.* 2000a). These results indicate that herbivory by wild asses is causing a change in the relative abundance of certain species (unfenced plots) and that competitive effects in the protected plots have occurred when plants are protected from grazing.

3. Ward and Saltz (1994), Ward *et al.* (1997, 2000a), Saltz and Ward (2000), and Ruiz *et al.* (2001, 2002) studied the interactions between the dorcas gazelle, *Gazella dorcas*, and the desert lily, *Pancratium sickenbergeri*, in sand dunes in the central Negev desert from 1990 to 2002. Gazelles dig in the sand to remove all or part of the bulbs of the lilies during the dry summer months, while in the winter months they consume the leaves. There are no leaves on the sand surface during the summer. From October–December they consume virtually all flowers when available— flowers have a 1:30,000 chance of surviving (Saltz and Ward 2000). They found that the gazelles entirely consume about 5% of the plants per annum, but may eat part of up to 60% of plants each year. Lily populations enclosed in 1994 (15 m × 15 m enclosures) now have about twice as many plants as populations outside the enclosures (478 vs. 255 plants per plot), indicating a significant negative impact of herbivory.

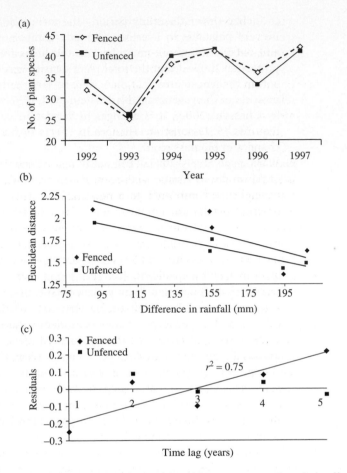

Fig. 7.4   Onager plots and plant species richness. (a) Herbivores appear to have little effect on plant species richness in the Negev desert. (From Ward *et al.* 2000a.) (b) The change in Euclidean distance (overall changes among plots) over time is largely explained by differences in annual rainfall ($r^2 = 0.80$ (Fenced) and $r^2 = 0.94$ (Unfenced)). (c) When the effects of differences in rainfall were removed, fenced plots deviated from their original composition ($r^2 = 0.75$) whereas unfenced plots stayed the same.

7.1.3   Effects of herbivory on relationships among plant functional types

Some of the most interesting effects of herbivory on plant diversity are through the effects of selective herbivory on the relationships among plant functional types (Noy-Meir *et al.* 1989; Westoby 1989, 1999). Arid regions that experience summer rainfall are usually grass-dominated (e.g. Namib and Kalahari deserts, southern Sahara, Australia), while deserts with winter rainfall (e.g. Negev, Sonoran, and central Asian deserts) are usually dominated by asteraceous and other dicotyledonous annual plants (Louw and Seely 1982; Shmida and Darom 1986). More conventionally, the most important changes in vegetation in response to herbivory occur in the relative abundance of tall and short annual and perennial plants (Noy-Meir et al. 1989; Ward 2005a).

The 'classical' theory of Dyksterhuis (1949) postulates that the main effect of grazers is through differential removal of plant parts among plant species which shifts the balance of relative species abundances. This is established in the ungrazed ('climax') state, mainly by competition for water, light, and nutrients, to a new stable balance, which depends on differential defoliation and regrowth. The relative abundance of some plants in a community decreases consistently in response to increased grazing intensity ('decreasers'), while that of others increases consistently ('increasers'), and some species only appear above a certain threshold of grazing intensity ('invaders'). Decreasers are plants with attributes that favour them in competition for space and other resources but disadvantage them under differential defoliation. Such attributes include erect tall shoots with elevated renewal buds, long growing season, and perennial life cycles, and readily palatable and available to grazers (especially grasses and legumes) (Noy-Meir et al. 1989; Westoby 1989). Increasers (and invaders) are plants with at least some of the converse attributes: low or prostrate shoots with renewal buds close to or below ground, short growing season, annual or short perennial life cycle, and lower palatability to grazers due to chemical or morphological 'defensive' characters (especially forbs (non-legume dicots)).

The responses of many species in arid zones appear to be consistent with a modified version of the 'classical' theory of grazing response, with its basic mechanism being a balance between competition and differential defoliation. Noy-Meir et al. (1989) and others (Diaz et al. 2001; Vesk et al. 2004; Ward 2006) have shown that height decreases under increased grazing pressure because tall species receive most grazing pressure, perennials decrease because they are more available to herbivores, leaf size decreases because larger leaves provide larger bites for grazers, and high specific leaf area (SLA) species (which have thin, soft leaves) may be favoured by selective grazers (Vesk et al. 2004). Westoby (1999) found that, under intense, non-selective grazing, all species are grazed and high-SLA species may have an advantage because they have faster regrowth, which is due to quicker leaf turnover and a greater rate of regrowth per unit of carbon invested in leaf tissue (see also Vesk et al. 2004).

In Australia, Landsberg et al. (1999a) have shown that 'large erect tussocks branching above-ground' and 'small, sprawling basal tussocks' may potentially be recognized as functional grass types that are reliable indicators of light and heavy grazing, respectively. Heavy grazing is associated with an increased abundance of herbaceous forbs, many of which are facultative annuals in Australia. This trend is consistent with other studies that have shown increases in annual plants with heavy grazing (Noy-Meir et al. 1989; Friedel et al. 1990). The tendency towards a decrease in the relative abundance of grasses at heavily grazed sites has also been seen in other studies (James et al. 1999; Landsberg et al. 1999b). However, Landsberg et al. (1999a) note the general absence of clear patterns and pointed to the complexity of grazing effects (such as strength of selection, degree of defoliation, and variance in recruitment opportunities) and lack of evolutionary history of grazing by large mammalian herbivores in Australia as reasons for weak selective pressure for grazing-related traits (Landsberg et al. 1999a).

Contrary to the observations in Australia mentioned above, in arid Tunisian rangelands (mean annual rainfall = 100–200 mm), Jauffret and Lavorel (2003) found no decrease in the abundance of perennial grasses. This result is also in contrast with the observations in more mesic systems (Noy-Meir et al. 1989; Skarpe 1990; McIntyre and Lavorel 2001). Jauffret and Lavorel (2003) account for this due to the near or complete elimination of perennial grasses (e.g. *Pennisetum elatum* and *Hyparrhenia hirta*) and ascribed this to thousands of years of heavy grazing. This heavy grazing has left Tunisian ecosystems with a homogenized flora consisting only of species that are highly tolerant of herbivory and other forms of disturbance. Very similar results were obtained by Milchunas and Lauenroth (1993), as mentioned above.

A relative increase in woody shrubs has often been recorded in semi-arid rangelands, especially when these have a short- or light-grazing history (Archer et al. 1988; Pickup and Stafford Smith 1993; Skarpe 2000; Ward et al. 2004; Ward 2005b; Kraaij and Ward 2006). Chamaephytes (shrubs with below-ground growth structures) can resist intense or frequent disturbances by growing less tall and resprouting, and they tend to be less palatable than most grasses. The Tunisian system has apparently reached the stage where chamaephytes are the only life form remaining at abundances high enough to observe a significant response in terms of abundance and quality (also true in the Negev desert in Israel; Ward and Olsvig-Whittaker (1993)).

It has been reported in many arid ecosystems that annual species replace perennials following heavy grazing, owing to their ability to quickly invade open spaces and utilize soil resources (Kelly and Walker 1977; Cheal 1993; Freeman and Emlen 1995). Perennials are always present and thus are permanently available to browsers. The transient nature of the annual lifestyle means that herbivores are less likely to encounter them and, thus, they increase in abundance while perennials decrease with grazing. However, in a study of permanent plots from 1989 to 1996 in Namaqualand, South Africa (mean annual rainfall = 76 mm), Milton and Dean (2000) found that the reduction of perennial grasses by cattle grazing favoured annual plants in wet years only. Dry conditions prohibited the establishment of annual plants regardless of whether perennial grasses were present or not. This pattern has also been reported by Van Rooyen *et al.* (1991) and Jeltsch *et al.* (1997) in the Kalahari desert, South Africa. Similarly, in a long-term study in a Chihuahuan desert site in southeastern Arizona (North America), Kelt and Valone (1995) found that the removal of herbivores (cattle) had little impact on the abundance and diversity of annual plants. Historical effects of herbivory may cloud our ability to detect differences in the effects of herbivory on perennial and annual plants.

Palatability was a major factor for determining the plant selection by herbivores in arid rangelands, according to the observations of Jauffret and Lavorel (2003) in Tunisia, Ward *et al.* (2000a) in Israel and Landsberg *et al.* (1999a) in Australia. Spiny plants were more frequent among grazing increasers in Tunisia. However, other studies have shown that spiny species such as *Echinops polyceras* and *Acacia raddiana* are favoured food plants of wild asses and camels, respectively (Rohner and Ward 1997; Ward *et al.* 1998). Some examples of reduced palatability are pertinent here:

1. Milton (1991) has shown that spinescence in plants increases with arid-ity, soil fertility, and mammalian herbivory at regional and local scales in the arid Karoo of southern Africa. Vegetation of moist, nutrient-rich habitats within arid areas was more spinescent than that of the sur-rounding dry plains. Spinescence in plants of drainage lines and pans in arid southern Africa occurs in a wide range of genera and appears to have been selected by the effect of large mammals which concentrate on these moist patches. Milton (1991) concluded that, in arid areas, mois-ture may be important in mediating mammalian selection of spines-cence.

2. Rohner and Ward (1997) have shown that there are inducible defences in *A. raddiana* trees in the Negev desert of Israel because they only invest in a change of strategy when there is herbivory. In plants that are eaten, there are higher levels of condensed tannins in plants, leaves are smaller, and thorns longer (Fig. 7.5). Essentially, the thorns are hid-ing small leaves. Having small leaves is not a constraint because light levels are very high in deserts. However, in the absence of herbivory, larger leaves are the default condition because plants can grow faster when their light-capturing surfaces are larger. Ward *et al.* (2000a) and Jauffret and Lavorel (2003), among others, have shown that palatability (or lack thereof) may play an important role in determining the effects of mammalian herbivory on arid ecosystems. Jauffret and Lavorel (2003) consider the fact that long-spined species such as *Astragalus armatus* and *toxic* and *highly fibrous* species (such as *Thymelaea hirsuta*) are dominant in arid Tunisian rangelands a consequence of the long grazing history. Similarly, unpalatable shrubs such as *Hammada sco-paria, T. hirsuta,* and *Anabasis articulata* are often dominant in heavily

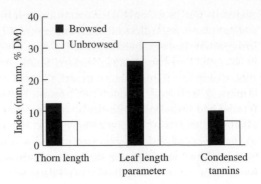

Fig. 7.5 *Acacia raddiana* leaves, tannins, and thorns. This species invests in higher tannin concentrations, and hides its small leaves among long thorns. (Modified from Rohner and Ward 1997. With kind permission of Opulus Press.)

grazed arid regions of the Middle East (Ward *et al.* 2000b; Ward 2005a). Geophytes, such as *Urginea maritima*, are also widespread and abundant in the Middle East, particularly where there is heavy grazing and trampling (Hadar *et al.* 1999). Similar to prostrate and rosette plants, they are close to or under the ground and unavailable to grazers for much of the year. When they produce leaves in the winter months, they are largely untouched by grazers because of the defensive chemicals in the leaves (Ward *et al.* 1997). Furthermore, the short reproductive period of geophytes enables early flowering, seed setting, and dispersal despite heavy grazing (Hadar *et al.* 1999).

7.1.4 Is Australia a special case?—a meta-analysis

Vesk *et al.* (2004) performed a meta-analysis of 11 lists of grazing responses from five published Australian semi-arid and arid shrubland and woodland studies in an attempt to assess the generality of the results of the Diaz *et al.* (2001) study mentioned above. They found that the traits shown to predict grazing responses in the Argentinian and Israeli studies did not adequately explain responses in Australian semi-arid and arid rangelands. They found no effects of plant height or leaf size on grazing. Annuals were no less likely than perennials to decrease with increased grazing pressure (see also Milton and Dean 2000). Analyses of traits within growth forms provided little evidence for relationships between traits and responses other than that annual grasses, which have high specific leaf area, tend to be increasers. Vesk *et al.* (2004) believe that because the Australian rangelands have lower productivity, less continuous sward, higher growth form diversity, and more bare ground than ecosystems in the Diaz *et al.* (2001) study, grazers can move through vegetation and taller species do not necessarily receive more grazing pressure because grazers can access short species from the side rather than by grazing the sward down to them. In contrast with Vesk *et al.*'s (2004) general conclusions, an earlier study of two arid Australian shrublands (which was included in the meta-analysis of Vesk *et al.* (2004)) found associations between increased grazing pressure and small plant size, small leaves, high fecundity and plasticity of growth form (Landsberg *et al.* 1999a). However, many attributes of plants recorded in the Landsberg *et al.* (1999a) study varied independently of each other and grazing-related attributes were only convincingly demonstrated in grasses. Vesk *et al.* (2004) recognized that they could not discount evolutionary history of grazing or the 'Australia is a "special case" argument' for the differences between their results and those of Diaz *et al.* (2001).

7.1.5   Effects of insect herbivory on desert plants

It has been claimed by Crawley (1989) that plants have more impact on the population dynamics of insects than insects have on the population dynamics of plants. In general, it is probably true that monophagous desert insects have little impact on equilibrium plant abundance even when the insects are food-limited (Crawley 1983). However, several studies have suggested that herbivorous insects have a great impact on the evolution and population dynamics of desert plants (Ayal and Izhaki 1993; Ayal 1994; Becerra 1994; Wilby *et al.* 2005). Herbivorous insects may reduce the reproductive success of their host plants either by directly feeding on their flowers (Ayal and Izhaki 1993; Ayal 1994) and seeds (Wilby *et al.* 2001; Or and Ward 2003) or by indirectly feeding on other plant parts such as foliage and roots (Becerra and Venable 1990; Becerra 1994).

Two examples where insects have notable interactions (one direct and one indirect) with desert plants are as follows:

1. Ayal and Izhaki (1993) and Ayal (1994) have studied the mirid bug, *Capsodes infuscatus* (Hemiptera: Miridae), in a central Negev desert habitat in Israel. This bug deposits eggs inside the inflorescence stalk of its host plant *Asphodelus ramosus* (Fig. 7.6) in spring. Developing nymphs as well as adults feed on this plant. Different structures of *A. ramosus* are consumed by the bugs, including leaves, flower stalks, buds, flowers, and fruits (Ayal and Izhaki 1993). *C. infuscatus* nymph feeding may kill young inflorescences, or suppress the development of the inflorescence branches and kill all its flowers while adult feeding may also kill green fruits (Ayal 1994). All stages of *C. infuscatus* feed upon *A. ramosus*. Nymphs consume leaves early in the season, but as they develop, they feed on inflorescence stalks, flowers, and fruits (Ayal and Izhaki 1993). A positive correlation between the number of young nymphs of *C. infuscatus* per clone (*A. ramosus* also reproduces vegetatively) early in the season, long before fruit appearance, and consequent damage to fruit production in *A. ramosus* has been shown (Ayal and Izhaki 1993).

Fig. 7.6   *Asphodelus ramosus* from the Negev desert.

2. One example of an interesting chemical interaction in desert ecosystems is between a tree (Family: Burseraceae) and a leaf beetle (Family:
Chrysomelidae). A desert tree from Tehuacan desert near Zapotitlan,
Mexico, *Bursera schlechtendalii*, has resinous ducts in its leaves that
eject an unpleasant syringe-like squirt of terpene resins, from 5 to
150 cm and may persist for a few seconds (Fig. 7.7). Some leaves do not
actually squirt liquid into the air but still release large amounts of ter-
penes that cover the surface of the leaf (called the 'rapid bath response'
by Becerra and Venable (1990)). The leaf beetle *Blepharida* sp. nov. is
capable of severing the resin canals by biting the midvein of the leaf
(Becerra 1994). Becerra (1994) determined the reaction of larvae to
Bursera resins by allowing them to incise the leaf midveins and then
moving them to intact leaves. Canals were intact in the new leaves,
leaving the beetle larvae with a squirt of resins. They attempted to clean
themselves and then abandoned the leaf. The larvae may even remain
inactive for several hours before starting to incise another leaf. Thus,
resin flow can deter this beetle if canals are not deactivated (Becerra
and Venable 1990). Larvae living on plants with a higher frequency
of leaf response had greater mortality or, in some cases, were smaller.
Early instar larvae are incapable of severing leaf veins because of their
smaller mandibles. They feed by mining the surfaces of the leaves but
sometimes die when they rupture the resin canals (Becerra 1994).

Interestingly, larvae from low-response plants increased their vein-cutting
time when transplanted to high-response plants. When placed on high-response plants, some larvae fed without cutting the veins and were covered
with resins. After getting squirted by several leaves, they started to sever
the leaves. Larvae from high-response plants continued cutting veins after

Fig. 7.7   Forceful squirt from *Bursera* sp. (From Becerra 1994. With kind permission of the Ecological Society of America.)

being deposited on less responsive plants although they did so for a shorter time. These differences in behaviour based on their experiences on previous plants indicate that the behaviour is plastic and that *Blepharida* pays a handling-time cost. Becerra and Venable (1990) showed that *Blepharida* larvae can take up to 1.5 h to deactivate the resin canals of a single leaf of a high-response plant yet consuming the leaf thereafter can take 10–20 min only.

3. Interspecific facultative mutualisms typically involve guilds of interacting species. Within such a guild, species may differ in their abilities to reciprocate with a particular host. For plants that secrete extrafloral nectar, visitation by a single ant species may optimize the anti-herbivore benefits that the plant may derive; ants can be very effective in biting other animals, especially mammals, that attack a plant. Ants, for their part, gain from the extrafloral nectar provided by the host plant. Multiple ant species that vary in anti-herbivore abilities may result in reduced benefits, relative to an exclusive association with a high-quality mutualist.

How do facultative ant–plant mutualisms persist? Given that extrafloral nectar is costly to produce, how do plants avoid the problem of diminishing returns as partner diversity increases? Miller (2007) tested the prediction that association with two ant partners (*Crematogaster opuntiae* and *Liometopum apiculatum*) weakens benefits to the extrafloral nectar-producing tree cholla cactus (*Opuntia imbricata*). He found that only one ant (*L. apiculatum*) provided protection against herbivores and seed predators. However, this species is associated with cacti more frequently than *Crematogaster*. *Liometopum* showed greater constancy on plants they occupied, and they more frequently colonized vacant plants of the tree cholla cactus. Furthermore, *Liometopum* replaced but were never replaced by *Crematogaster*. *Liometopum* was more abundant on reproductive plants and showed greater overlap with cactus enemies. Nonetheless, Miller (2007) showed that simulations of cactus lifetime reproductive output indicated that the associations with high- and low-quality mutualists did not reduce plant benefits relative to an exclusive *L. apiculatum–O. imbricata* association.

7.2   Pollination

The most frequent type of mutualism is plant–pollinator interactions (Fig. 7.8). Facultative mutualisms allow for co-pollination, whereas obligate mutualisms involve the complete interdependency of both partners, the best-known example being the fig-fig wasp system (Bronstein 2001). The interactions between yuccas and yucca moths and senita cactus and senita moths are obligate mutualists that naturally occur in deserts.

Waser *et al.* (1996) expect plant generalization (i.e. more than one pollinator per plant species) to occur as long as temporal and spatial variance in pollinator quality is appreciable, different pollinator species do not fluctuate in unison, and they are similar in their pollination effectiveness. Further, they consider pollinator generalization likely to occur when floral rewards are similar across plant species, travel is costly, constraints of behaviour and morphology are minor, and/or pollinator lifespan is long relative to flowering of individual plant species. Nevertheless, plants with highly specialized pollination systems are not uncommon in the tropics and some temperate regions (review by Johnson and Steiner 2000).

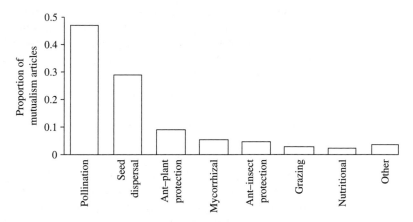

Fig. 7.8   Frequency of different types of plant–animal interactions listed as mutualisms, based on the number of articles published on a particular topic. (From Stiling 2002. With kind permission of Pearson Higher Education Company.)

One of the more interesting examples of pollinator specialization and diversification occurs in the guild of bees that pollinate the creosote bush *Larrea tridentata*. In this case, the historical biogeography (20,000 years BP to the present) of this desert plant is well understood (Minckley *et al.* 2000). This history, coupled with the distribution pattern of its bee fauna, suggests that the specialization for creosote bush pollen has evolved repeatedly among bees in the Lower Sonoran and Mojave deserts. In these highly xeric environments, species of specialist bees surpass generalist bees in diversity, biomass, and abundance (Minckley *et al.* 2000). These specialist bees can facultatively remain in diapause through resource-poor years and later emerge synchronously when their host plants bloom in resource-rich years. Repeated origins of pollen specialization to one host plant where flowering occurs least predictably is a counterexample to Waser *et al.*'s (1996) proposition. Host–plant synchronization, perhaps a paucity of alternative floral hosts, or even the flowering attributes of creosote bush or a combination of these factors may account for the diversity of bee specialists that depend on *L. tridentata*.

7.2.1   Yucca–yucca moth mutualism

Yucca plants (genus *Yucca*) and yucca moths (genera *Tegeticula* and *Parategeticula*; Lepidoptera, Family: Prodoxidae) are highly coevolved. Particular species of moth have evolved with particular species of yucca. The pollinator of the yucca is always female. While at the flower, the moth climbs halfway up the pistil and inserts her ovipositor into the ovary of the plant (Fig. 7.9). The moth's eggs are laid into the plant's ovary. She then climbs up to the top of the pistil and rubs some of her collected pollen onto the stigma of the plant, fertilizing the flower, and thereby ensuring the production of seeds (Miller 1995). As the larvae develop, they feed on the developing seeds of the yucca, but they only eat a portion of them. What is different about this relationship is that there is no immediate reward for the individual insect following the pollination process (Pellmyr 2003). In more conventional plant–pollinator interactions, the pollinator will be rewarded with nectar and pollen, which happens to fertilize the next plant visited. Here, the yucca moth collects pollen, although she does not eat it. Pellmyr's (2003) theory about the costs of seed production and the natural selection of *Tegeticula* and *Parategeticula* moths holds that if the moths lay a greater number of eggs, then the plant would suffer because of the moth's reproductive success (i.e. the larvae would eat almost all the fertilized seeds of the plant). Evolutionarily speaking, moths that lay too many eggs and, thus, minimize the production of the developing seeds are disadvantaged because the flower in question aborts the developing fruit and the larvae relying on it starve. This keeps the moth/yucca equilibrium stable, so the fitness increases in one species do not affect those of the other.

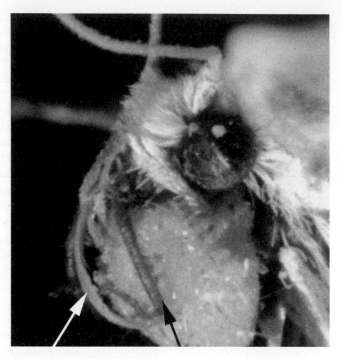

Fig. 7.9   Head of female yucca moth *Tegeticula carnerosanella* with yucca pollen load. Black arrow = left tentacle; white arrow = proboscis. (From Pellmyr and Krenn 2002. With kind permission of National Academy of Sciences, USA.)

When two organisms have evolved to a point where both benefit from the relationship and neither is harmed, mutualism occurs. Coevolution of stable mutualism occurs because both species have mechanisms to prevent excessive exploitation. For example, yucca flower abortion occurs if too many eggs are laid (Pellmyr and Huth 1994). A strong negative effect exists between moth egg number and probability of flower retention in yuccas. Furthermore, they showed a strong positive effect between the number of pollinations received and the probability of flower retention. Selective maturation of fruit with low egg loads and high pollen loads provides a mechanism to increase the quantity and possibly the quality of seeds produced, and simultaneously select against moths that lay many eggs per flower or provide low-quality pollinations. These results explain the stability of this type of interaction, and explain why selection for high-quality pollination also provides a mechanism to help explain the evolution of active pollination among yucca moths.

Is there also a genetic cost through selfish moth behaviour that may lead to high levels of self fertilization in the yuccas? Observations of a *Tegeticula yuccasella* yucca moth on *Yucca filamentosa* revealed that females remained on the plant and oviposited in 66% of all instances after observed pollen collections, and 51% of all moths were observed to pollinate the same plant as well (Pellmyr *et al.* 1997). Manual cross-pollination and self-pollination showed equal development and retention of fruits. Subsequent trials to assess inbreeding depression revealed significant negative effects on seed weight and germination frequency in selfed progeny arrays. Cumulative inbreeding depression was about 0.48 (i.e. the fitness of selfed seeds was less than half that of outcrossed seeds; Pellmyr (1996)). Estimates of outcrossing rates based on allozyme analyses of open-pollinated progeny arrays did not differ from 1.0; thus, outcrossing was the mode of reproduction. The discrepancy between high levels of behavioural self-pollination by the moths and nearly complete outcrossing in mature seeds can be explained through selective foreign pollen use by the females, or, more likely, pollen competition or selective abortion of self-pollinated flowers during early stages of fruit development. Thus, whenever the proportion of pollinated flowers exceeds the proportion that can be matured to ripe fruit based on resource availability, the potential detrimental genetic effects imposed through self-fertilized pollinations can be avoided in the plants. Because self-pollinated flowers have a lower probability of retention, selection should act on female moths to move among plants whenever moth density is high enough to trigger abortion.

Yucca moths are the only known pollinators of the yucca (O. Pellmyr, pers. comm.). Obviously, at the time of first colonization of the yuccas (yuccas are phylogenetically older than yucca moths), another pollination agent would have existed. The key is likely to be that pollination carries an unusually high fitness consequence in insects whose larvae are seed consumers. A female moth that can increase the probability of fruit production in flowers where she has laid eggs will have higher fitness than one who is less likely to do so, which can explain the origin and maintenance of active pollination in the moths. Can a moth stop pollinating if they select flowers that have already been pollinated? In at least some moth species, female moths can tell (by hormonal means) whether a flower has been visited before, and they are less likely to pollinate again (Pellmyr, pers. comm.). The drawback is that laying more eggs per flower (a consequence of coming second) reduces the probability of fruit retention quite dramatically, so there is a big fitness loss to investing only in previously visited flowers. Another important factor is that the fitness cost (in terms of structure and time allocation) of being a pollinator is trivial, so there is not a lot of selection against it (Pellmyr, pers. comm.).

Regarding cheating behaviour, Addicott and Tyre (1995) consider there to be partial support for the flower-dependent behaviour and probabilistic behaviour hypotheses for cheating in the yucca moth *T. yuccasella* and the yucca *Yucca kanabensis*. The flower-dependent hypothesis predicts that moths will respond to previous visits to a flower by modifying their oviposition and pollination behaviour. These flowers may have received sufficient pollen for complete fertilization of their ovules and, therefore, female yucca moths could conserve their pollen. This would allow them to have more pollen available to pollinate previously unvisited flowers without having to collect more pollen and move to another infloresence. This hypothesis depends on the assumption that yucca moths are able to detect the presence of previous ovipositions and that ovipositions are a good predictor of pollen in the stigma. Addicott and Tyre (1995) do not think that yucca moths detect pollen in the stigma because they only approach the stigma for the purpose of pollination. As predicted by this hypothesis, yucca moths modified their behaviour on previously visited flowers because bouts on such flowers involved fewer ovipositions and either a lower proportion of ovipositions followed by pollination or no pollination. However, the hypothesis does not explain why some moths failed to attempt to pollinate on flowers that had not been visited. Why would some moths not collect pollen or at least not collect pollen again once their initial supply is exhausted? According to Addicott and Tyre (1995), the most probable answer to this is that the moths are risk averse and the yuccas are self-incompatible. Moths that gather pollen from an inflorescence and then pollinate flowers on that inflorescence will experience very low reproductive success because the retention rate of self-pollinated flowers is basically zero (Pellmyr 1996). Moths that collect pollen should fly to another inflorescence but this may entail considerable risk, either due to predation by bats and night hawks (Aves: Caprimulgidae) or they may struggle to find another inflorescence.

The second hypothesis addressed by Addicott and Tyre (1995), the probabilistic behaviour hypothesis, follows a mixed strategy in an Evolutionarily Stable Strategy (ESS) model of game theory (Maynard Smith 1982), in that moths might respond to the probability that a particular flower had been pollinated previously or would be visited subsequently and pollinated by at least one other moth. The probability of visitation would be a function of the density of moths relative to flowers, which could vary between years, study sites or even within seasons (James *et al.* 1994). Thus, there is some support for both of the above hypotheses. They are not mutually exclusive because conditional mixed strategies are possible. The probability of pollination could depend on the state of the flower (e.g. number of previous ovipositions) and the state of the moth (e.g. age), as well as the density of moths relative to flowers, which would affect the probability of future visits by other moths to a certain flower (Parker 1984).

Cheater yucca moth species have evolved at least twice. Underlying obligate mutualism is an intrinsic conflict between the parties, in that each is under selection for increased exploitation of the other. Theoretical models suggest that this conflict is a source of evolutionary instability, and that evolution of 'cheating' by one party may lead to reciprocal extinction. Pellmyr *et al.* (1996) present phylogenetic evidence for the reversal of an obligate mutualism: within the yucca moth complex, distinct cheater species derived from obligate pollinators inflict a heavy cost on their yucca hosts. Phylogenetic data show the cheaters to have existed for a long time. Coexisting pollinators and cheaters are not sister taxa, supporting predictions that the evolution of cheating within a single pollinator is evolutionarily unstable. Several lines of evidence support an hypothesis that host shifts preceded the reversal of obligate mutualism. Host or partner shifts are mechanisms that can provide a route of evolutionary escape among obligate mutualists in general.

In another study, Marr *et al.* (2001) have focused on interactions between a cheater moth *Tegeticula intermedia* and the pollinator *T. yuccasella* in fruits of the host plant *Y. filamentosa*. They examined the effects of larval competition on the two species of moth. They found it to be weak and asymmetric, affecting the cheater larvae to a greater extent. There were insufficient larvae to cause seed limitation because no effect of pollinator larvae on either mass or mortality of cheater larvae was detected in years with the highest larval densities per fruit (yuccas abort fruits with many yucca moth larvae). This result is consistent with the hypothesis that the recent rapid radiation of species in the *T. yuccasella* complex (there is more than one species in this group) may be explained by the ability of multiple pollinator species (some of whom have become cheaters) to use fruits without severe competition. Pellmyr (pers. comm.) considers this to have been preceded by host shifts that led to the coexistence of two pollinator species on a host. Under such circumstances, loss of pollination can occur whether there is a fitness cost or not and becoming a cheater may not be selected for at all. Rather, there is a temporal niche shift that permits the cheater species to exploit seed resources that cannot be accessed by pollinator larvae. Therefore, there is no evidence for the selection for cheating *per se*, but it occurs merely as a by-product of another driver, namely, lack of access to the yucca seeds by the pollinator larvae.

7.2.2   The senita cactus–senita moth obligate mutualism

The senita moth *Upiga virescens* (Pyralidae, Lepidoptera) and the senita cactus *Lophocereus schottii* occur in the Sonoran desert in the United States and Mexico and are mostly obligate mutualists (see below; Fig. 7.10). The senita moth, similar to the yucca moth, has specialized morphological features that allow for pollen loading. Similar to other Lepidoptera, female senita moths avoided ovipositing eggs in flowers that contained an egg. Eggs hatch within three days of flower closing and larvae crawl down the wilting corolla and bore into the top of the fruit, which they consume before entering the cactus branch to pupate. However, only a fraction of eggs produced larvae that survived to become seed consumers themselves. About 20% of fruits were destroyed by larvae. Benefits of senita moths to pollination and fruit set in the senita cactus were about three to four times the costs of seed mortality induced by the larvae, which is similar to the yucca mutualism (Addicott and Tyre 1995). Although copollinators are

Fig. 7.10   Senita moths on senita cactus (copyright of Greg and Mary Beth Dimijian).

absent in yucca mutualisms, Fleming and Holland (1998) have shown that
diurnal halictid bees may also pollinate senita flowers. However, tempera-
ture-dependent flower closing limits their effectiveness (flowers are only
open for a few hours in the day, usually when it is overcast). Nonetheless,
the senita cactus is not entirely dependent on the senita moth and, consequently, lies between the categories of obligate and facultative mutualist.
Reduction in and lack of nectar production in the senita cactus discourage
co-pollinators that visit flowers for nectar rewards only. Reduced nectar
production clearly conserves energy for use in fruit production where fruit
set is resource-limited.

For senita cactus and senita moth interactions, it is the great benefit to
plants from pollination by moths and the low survivorship of moth larvae
that maintain the high benefit-to-cost ratio of the plant. Selective abortion
of fruit in yucca appears to be a mechanism inhibiting overexploitation by
yucca moths (Pellmyr and Huth 1994) but senita fruits contain only one
larva each (no continuum occurs as in yucca fruit). Thus, the criterion for
abortion would have to be presence or absence of larva in a fruit. Holland
and Fleming (1999) assume that flowers with greater pollination quality
and quantity would be preferentially retained by plants where resources
limit fruit production, increasing progeny survival of moths that actively
pollinate.

There is a major cost associated with a mutualistic relationship, such
as the yucca moth and yucca or senita moth–senita cactus relationship. If
either of the species, for any reason, cannot be found at the right place at
the right time, each of the species suffers reproductive failure. Bronstein
(2001) found that, if yuccas bloomed late, they ended up out of synchrony
with the emergence of most yucca moths. As a result, the yucca fruits
which set seed were the very earliest ones; late-blooming plants failed

completely. This dependence on timing, which only spans approximately a month in the case of yucca, can easily contribute to reproductive failure in both species. In the case of senita cactus, prolonged flowering occurs, which reduces the possibility of reproductive failure for the senita moth.

Holland *et al.* (2002) have modelled the senita moth–senita cactus mutualism using an isocline-based phase-plane scenario. Lotka-Volterra type models have been used in this regard but lead to 'runaway' population densities, particularly for obligate mutualisms (Stiling 2002). In many mutualisms, the deciding factor that separates the mutualist from parasite and predator may simply be population density because increasing or decreasing population density of a species may increase or decrease the costs and benefits to its partner. Thus, net effects depend on how benefits or costs to a mutualist vary with population density of its partner species (Holland *et al.* 2004). Holland *et al.* (2002) take a population view and assume that gross benefits and costs to the cactus population are related to the rates at which moths pollinate flowers and larvae cause fruit loss. Thus, gross benefits and costs are functions of moth abundance (designated as M) relative to the rate of flower production by the plant population. Flower production is the product of the number of plants (P) and the mean number of flowers per plant per night (F). They derived a functional response for gross benefits of pollination by modelling the plant population as a fixed set of flowers over each night's production and by modelling the pollinator population as randomly searching for and pollinating these flowers. The visitation rate per flower should be proportional to the ratio of pollinators to flowers (M/FP). Thus, a ratio-dependent functional response is derived (see also Thompson 1939).

The dynamics of the cactus population can be derived as follows:

$$dP/dt = (1-a)\alpha FP\left[1-\exp\{-\gamma_1 M/FP\}\right]$$
$$\times\left[1-\{1-\exp(-\gamma_2 M/FP)\}\right]-d_1 P - gP^2$$

with the addition of two parameters, $(1-a)$ and α. Some fraction of flowers, even if pollinated, do not set fruit. This fraction of unpollinated flowers that abcise plus pollinated flowers that abort is represented by a, such that the total fraction of flowers that can potentially set fruit is $(1-a)$. The parameter α is the fraction of mature fruit that lead to new plants. The rates at which gross benefits and costs are accrued are represented by γ_1 and γ_2, respectively. This model ignores the short-term seasonal effects of flowering phenology and diapause and focuses on long-term dynamics (Holland *et al.* 2002).

The dynamics of the moth population is written as follows:

$$dM/dt = (1-a)\alpha FP\left[1-\exp(-\gamma_1 M/FP)\right]\times\left[1-\exp(-\gamma_2 M/FP)\right]-d_2 M$$

Gross benefits and costs to the moth population are expressed in terms of recruitment. d_2M represents mortality and the first section represents net effects of moth recruitment.

This phase-plane diagram results in two equilibrium points, one of which is locally stable and the other locally unstable. However, the functional response, $(1 - a)\alpha FP[1 - \exp(-\gamma_1 M/FP)] \times [1 - \exp(-\gamma_2 M/FP)]$, assumes that pollination and oviposition are independent random events. In nature, however, pollination and oviposition are correlated behaviourally because female moths pollinate flowers as a way of provisioning their offspring with food (Fleming and Holland 1998). When this is incorporated into the functional response, the first term of the cactus equation becomes

$$(1-a)\alpha FP\left[\exp\left(-\gamma_2 M/FP\right) - \exp\left(-\gamma_1 M/FP\right)\right]$$

The functional response in the first term of the moth equation becomes

$$(1-a)\alpha FP\left[1 - \exp\left(-\gamma_2 M/FP\right)\right]$$

Gross recruitment of new moths is the number of flowers on which effective oviposition occurs (survival from eggs to pupae). The main difference between the state plane for the functional response of this model and the original is that there is now only one line representing the moth's zero isocline and there is at most only one nonzero equilibrium point (Holland *et al.* 2002). It is likely that this alteration of the model is more biologically reasonable because pollination behaviour has likely evolved in association with oviposition to increase the likelihood of egg and larval

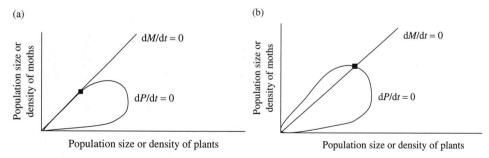

Fig. 7.11   Holland *et al.*'s (2002) benefit-cost model using population density as the parameter of interest. Diagram of the *P, M* state plane showing zero isoclines of plants and moths formed by plotting *M* vs. *P* for d*P*/d*t* = 0 and d*M*/d*t* = 0, respectively. There is only one stable equilibrium point (solid circle) in addition to the point at the origin (0,0). (a) There are no fruit abortions, *a* = 0. (b) There are fruit abortions, with *a* = 0.3. The other parameter values are *F* = 20, α = 0.13, γ_1 = 4.0, γ_2 = 2.0, d_1 = 0.1, d_2 = 1.0 and *g* = 0.001. (From Holland *et al.* 2002. With kind permission of University of Chicago Press.)

survival (Fig. 7.11a and b). This model would probably also work for the yucca moth–yucca system.

Note that Holland *et al.* (2004) have also used evolutionarily stable strategy (ESS) theory to show that plants can maximize fitness by allocating resources to the production of excess flowers at the expense of fruit. Fruit abortion resulting from excess flower production reduces pre-adult survival of the pollinating moths, and maintains its density beneath a threshold that would destabilize the mutualism. Such a strategy is evolutionarily stable against invasion by cheater plants that produce fewer flowers and abort few to no fruit. This mechanism may be a general process of preserving mutualistic interactions in nature.

7.3 Seed dispersal and seed predation

The effects of seed predators, such as desert rodents, finches, sparrows, and harvester ants, are less dramatic but may be equally effective at controlling plant populations. For example, Brown and Heske (1990) removed three species of kangaroo rats (*Dipodomys* spp.) from plots of Chihuahuan Desert shrub habitat from 1977 to 1990, and found that the density of tall perennial and annual grasses had increased approximately 3-fold and rodent species typical of arid grassland had colonized. In the same study, Heske *et al.* (1993) showed that significant increases in the abundance of a tall annual grass (*Aristida adscensionis*) and a perennial bunch grass (*Eragrostis lehmanniana*) occurred. This change in vegetative cover affected the use of these plots by several other rodent species and by foraging birds. The mechanism producing this change probably involved

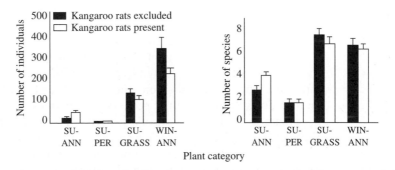

Fig. 7.12 There were significant increases in the abundance of a tall annual grass (*Aristida adscensionis*) and a perennial bunch grass (*Eragrostis lehmanniana*) as a result of kangaroo rat exclusion. Differences in plant species diversity were found for summer annual dicot species only. SU = summer, WIN = winter, ANN = annual, GRASS = grasses, and PER = perennial. Bars = S.E. (From Heske *et al.* 1993. With kind permission of Springer Science and Business Media.)

a combination of decreased soil disturbance and reduced predation on large-sized seeds when kangaroo rats were absent. Species diversity of summer annual dicotyledonous plants was greater on plots where kangaroo rats were present, as predicted by keystone predator models (Fig. 7.12; see also Fig. 5.18). However, Heske *et al.* (1993) were unclear whether this was caused directly by activities of the kangaroo rats or indirectly as a consequence of the increase in grass cover. Their study site was located in a natural transition between desert scrub and grassland, where abiotic conditions and the effects of organisms may be particularly influential in determining the structure and composition of vegetation. Under these conditions, kangaroo rats may have a dramatic effect on plant cover and species composition.

Seed dispersal by large mammalian herbivores is also important, particularly in cases where the seeds are hard (see Campos and Ojeda (1997) with regard to *Prosopis*, Rohner and Ward (1999) with regard to *Acacia*). In many cases, germination of seeds (such as of *Acacia* species) increases as mammal body size increases (see Fig. 11.5). This is because the mammals ingest the seeds and defaecate them later. This scarifies the seed and the greater the body mass of the animal, the longer it remains in the gut and the greater the mechanical effect of the gut's hydrochloric acid on inducing scarification (Rohner and Ward 1999; Bodmer and Ward 2006). In *Acacia* species, the seeds are very hard and can only germinate once scarification occurs. This may be done by water, requiring waiting until the rains in the following year, or it can be done by large mammals. In some cases, there can be negative effects on germination, such as in ostrich *Struthio camelus* (Aves, Family: Ratites) in Israel (Rohner and Ward 1999) and wild boar *Sus scrofa* in the Monte desert in Argentina (Campos and Ojeda 1997). In these cases, all seeds are damaged and cannot germinate.

In a 17-year study in the central Negev desert highlands of Israel, Indian Crested Porcupines, *Hystrix indica*, were found to focus their activities in midslope areas where plant biomass was maximal due to run-off water accumulation (Shachak *et al.* 1991; Boeken *et al.* 1995). In a 5-year study of a population of *Tulipa systola* in the same desert highlands, herbivory by porcupines was generally low although the effects on recruitment were consistently greater than on other parts of the plant (Boeken 1989), but they do not generally limit geophyte populations. However, pits dug by porcupines accumulate organic material, including seeds and water (Gutterman and Herr 1981; Boeken and Shachak 1998; Boeken *et al.* 1998). As a result of this accumulation of materials, plant density, biomass, and species richness were found to be much higher in porcupine diggings than in undisturbed areas (Boeken *et al.* 1995). These authors showed that plant density and diversity were limited by microsite availability due to a lack of water infiltration in undisturbed areas (Fig. 7.13). In contrast, diggings remained moist throughout the growing season and diggings were only limited by seed arrival.

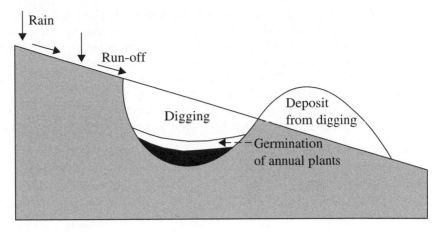

Fig. 7.13   Side view of a hill slope showing importance of porcupine diggings to plant diversity. (From Boeken *et al.* 1995.)

Granivory is an important interaction in ecological communities, especially in deserts where many plant populations exist as seeds for long periods (Davidson and Morton 1981; Morton 1985; Rissing 1986). Granivores can also be seed dispersers. Harvester ants have been shown, in a number of deserts (Australia, South Africa, and South America), to be the most important granivores and seed dispersers (Morton 1985; Kerley 1991) (Fig. 7.14), although rodents are more important in North American and Israeli deserts (Mares and Rosenzweig 1978; Abramsky 1983). Many seeds have appendages, known as elaiosomes, that are attractive to ants and encourage dispersal to 'safe sites' for germination and growth (Rissing 1981). Davidson and Morton (1981) have recorded myrmecochory (ant dispersal) in a wide range of Australian species, especially in diaspores of the family Chenopodiaceae. The widespread and dependable presence of ants in the Australian deserts, and the relative importance of ant species that are capable of carrying such large diaspores leads to the dependence of Australian plants on these dispersal strategies.

Rissing (1986) found that six plant species were significantly associated with nests of the desert seed-harvester ants, *Veromessor pergandei* and *Pogonomyrmex rugosus*, in the Mojave desert. Seeds of two common annuals, *Schismus arabicus* and *Plantago insularis*, have 15.6 and 6.5 times higher levels in terms of numbers of fruits or seeds growing on ant nest refuse piles compared with nearby controls. Interestingly, these two species do not have obvious appendages attractive to ants. Similar results have been recorded by Wilby *et al.* (2001) in the northern Negev desert, Israel, for *Messor ebeninus* and *M. arenarius*. A total of 55 plant species were found on the nest mounds as opposed to 25 in the undisturbed soil. The favoured food items of *M. ebeninus* are seeds of the grass *Stipa capensis*.

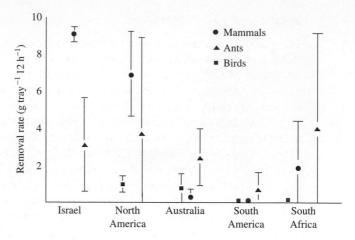

Fig. 7.14 Comparison of effects of ants, small mammals, and birds across several continents. (From Kerley 1991. With kind permission of Elsevier.)

In contrast with other plant species it occurred at much lower densities on the nest mounds, probably reflecting consumption. In contrast, another common species, *Reboudia pinnata*, increased from about 10% of samples on the undisturbed soil to 85% of mound samples. This last-mentioned plant species has a hardened fruit wall, which protects the seeds from predation (Gutterman 1993).

7.4 Are these coevolved systems?

All mutualistic interactions can be viewed in terms of the Red Queen hypothesis (Van Valen 1977) as each mutualist needs to evolve continually to avoid being exploited by its mutualist partner. Thus, such highly coevolved systems arose despite the needs of each conflicting!

1. To the plant, an ideal pollinator or seed disperser would move quickly among individuals but retain high fidelity to a plant species so that little pollen or seed is wasted.
2. To the pollinator or seed disperser, it would be best to be a generalist and obtain nectar and pollen from flowers or seeds in a small area, minimizing energy costs.

This casts doubt on whether there is true mutualism or whether both are trying to win an arms race. One way in which the plant can ensure the pollinator's/seed disperser's fidelity is to have sequential flowering among species within years and simultaneous flowering within a species. How is it generally done? Here are some examples.

7.4.1   **Senita and yucca systems**

There are a large number of similarities in the independently derived mutualisms in the senita cactus–senita moth and yucca–yucca moth systems, suggesting that they have evolved in response to similar selection pressures, including selection for reduced nectar production in the plants and specialized pollen-collecting structures and active pollination behaviour in the moths. Both systems feature pollinators whose life cycles are intimately associated with long-lived plants with seasonal flowering cycles. Fleming and Holland (1998) propose that three of their common features, namely, nocturnal flower opening, self-incompatibility, and resource-limited fruit set, have been important during the evolution of obligate mutualisms. Nocturnal flower opening is important for these mutualisms because it limits the number of potential flower visitors to moths only (Thompson and Pellmyr 1992) and excludes other co-pollinators. Self-incompatibility selects for pollinators that visit flowers on different plants and, thus, both yucca moths and senita moths are under strong natural selection to be effective outcrossers. Resource-limited fruit set and reduced nectar production characterize the yucca and senita systems. Reduced nectar production may be selected for, especially when unfertilized ovules rather than nectar or pollen is the primary reward attracting pollinators, which favours the evolution of specialized pollination. Pollen limitation does not appear to be important for fruit set in either the yucca or the senita cactus. Pellmyr *et al.* (1996) have suggested that differences among flower visitors in pollination quality (the genetic contribution to fruit set) can favour the evolution of obligate mutualisms through selective abortion of fruits of low genetic quality.

7.4.2   **Why Negev flowers are often red**

There are about 15 species of large, bowl-shaped flowers of six genera from three families in the Mediterranean region of Israel (Heinrich 1994). It is dominated by poppies (*Ranunculus* spp.) of two genera. Most species in this group have other colours in other parts of the world. *Ranunculus* has about 400 species worldwide, most of which are white or yellow (Heinrich 1994). Only three, all in the Mediterranean, are red. All of these species have cup-shaped flowers that are far broader than those in other countries. Wild tulips (*Tulipa* spp.) are mostly yellow, yet in Israel they are red. The species in this convergent guild do not flower simultaneously. Anemones usually flower first, followed by tulips, buttercups, and poppies (Heinrich 1994). These flowers are seldom pollinated by bees. Rather, they are mostly pollinated by scarab beetles (Family Scarabeidae) of the genus *Amphiocoma*. Dafni *et al.* (1990) distributed unscented, flower-shaped plastic cups of various colours in the field to act as beetle traps. Of the beetles trapped in the variously coloured flower models, 127 of 148 were caught in red flower models. *Amphiocoma* do most of the pollination of the red flowers, although the red colour also advertises sex. Once they detected a red flower, they stayed to mate. The antennae are microscopic in size. Their scent organs seem almost atrophied (Heinrich 1994) but their eyes are not. Their attraction to red flowers finds mates for them (Heinrich 1994). Dafni *et al.* (1990) showed that these *Amphiocoma* beetles could see the colour red. This resulted in enhanced mating for them. It is not known how the red flower guild evolved but a probable scenario is that the plants imitated one another, and that many species used the same red signal in their advertising campaigns that served to attract pollinators (Heinrich 1994). The pollinators in turn apparently preferred red over other colours (Heinrich 1994).

7.4.3 *Blepharida* chrysomelid beetles and *Bursera* tree systems

As it was first applied in plant–animal interactions by Ehrlich and Raven (1964), the hypothesis that rates of diversification in plants and plant-feeding insects is higher than in other taxa has been successfully applied (see also Thompson (1998) for more complex versions of this hypothesis). Several such studies have shown that plants and plant-feeding insects often have increased rates of diversification compared to sister groups with different life histories (Becerra 1997; Pellmyr 2003). Clearly, such claims are dependent on appropriate phylogenies. An exception to the lack of phylogenies is the study by Becerra (2003). Judy Becerra worked on 38 species of *Bursera* trees and their associated *Blepharida* leaf beetles (Family Chrysomelidae). Please note that not all species of *Blepharida* and *Bursera* occur in deserts or other arid systems; many occur in dry thickets and dry forests. Becerra (1997, 2003) reported evidence for convergent evolution of a combination of terpenoid defences and the force with which they are released upon attack. Species that produce simple chemical mixtures (one to a few monoterpenes) release the compounds with a forceful squirt upon damage (Fig. 7.7).

Species that use complex mixtures of monoterpenes and diterpenes (up to 12 compounds) do not have a forceful squirt. In Fig. 7.15, *Bursera* species (solid lines) are highly squirting species. *Blepharida* species (solid lines) have evolved the ability to counterattack their host's squirt defence by cutting the canals to stop the flow of resins. The *Bursera flavocostata* group (dashed lines) produce chemically similar complex mixtures that include between 7 and 12 terpene compounds. Beetles of the *Blepharida flavocostata* complex (dashed lines) are able to metabolize the complex mixtures of defensive chemicals present in these hosts.

Speciation events that appear synchronous among plants and herbivores lend further support to cospeciation owing to joint allopatry. Judy Becerra demonstrated that shared host plant defensive chemistry can be more important than phylogenetic association in host shifts of leaf beetles (Chrysomelidae). In other words, host shifts by the beetles on to distantly

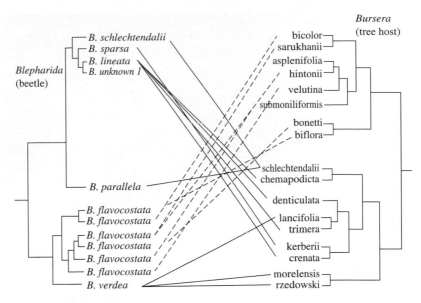

Fig. 7.15   Coevolution of *Blepharida* (beetle) (left) and *Bursera* (tree) (right) phylogenies. Solid and dashed lines indicate feeding associations of *Blepharida* on *Bursera* hosts. Solid lines indicate the highly squirting species of *Bursera* hosts (see Fig. 7.7). *Blepharida* species with solid lines indicate those species that have evolved the ability to counteract the host's squirt defence by cutting the canals to stop the flow of resins. Species with dashed lines produce produce chemically similar complex mixtures of 7–12 terpene compounds. Members of the *Blepharida flavocostata* complex (dashed lines) are capable of metabolizing the defensive chemicals of these host trees. Not all species are indicated in these phylogenies. (From Becerra 2003. Copyright of National Academy of Sciences, USA.)

related plant species were coincident with a shared chemistry with the former host plant species.

7.4.4   Dorcas gazelle—lily system

There is at least one case where coevolution can be claimed in a mammal system. Owing to the almost complete removal of all flowers of the lilies by dorcas gazelles (Fig. 7.16) (there is no vegetative reproduction in this species) mentioned above, the lily populations in the dunes can only be maintained by seed dispersal from source populations outside the dunes where gazelles are rare or absent (owing to low lily densities in the compact loess substrate).

There is strong selection on lilies to minimize the effects of gazelle herbivory: lilies that have their bulbs partially consumed in one year are less likely to produce flowers and produce fewer, smaller leaves in the following season. Ward and Saltz (1994) found that the gazelles select lilies

Fig. 7.16   Dorcas gazelle *Gazella dorcas*.

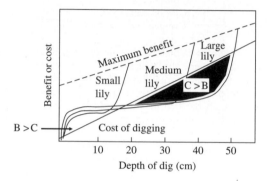

Fig. 7.17   Gazelle optimal foraging model. Gazelles should prefer small lilies because benefits exceed costs (*B* > *C*). (From Ward and Saltz 1994. With kind permission of the Ecological Society of America.)

according to their size in a manner consistent with an optimal foraging model (Fig. 7.17).

As predicted by this model, contrary to popular expectation that gazelles should prefer the largest plants, gazelles should prefer the smallest plants, and not completely consume large plants. This is indeed what they do because the cost of sand removal is high (Fig. 7.17). Furthermore, when searching for leaves (leaves are available on the surface for a few months only and gazelles do not bother to dig when there are leaves), gazelles do not follow a Markov model (which assumes that there is no effect of previous search history on the gazelles) in searching for plants, and instead, focus on high densities of lilies and eat the largest lily leaves once there.

Lilies also grow in ways that are consistent with coevolution. These lilies grow their bulbs down deeper into the sand (pulling them down with contractile roots) to minimize the effects of herbivory in populations where

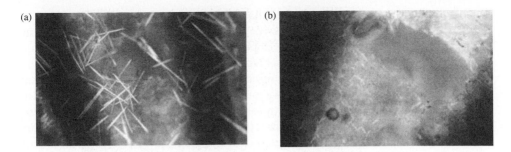

Fig. 7.18   Raphide photos, (a) with and (b) without raphides of calcium oxalate (from 1 cm near tip of leaf). (From Ward *et al.* 1997.)

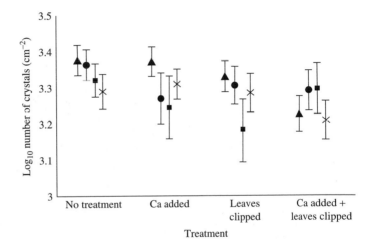

Fig. 7.19   Ruiz *et al.* (2001) showed that raphides were a constitutive defence because there was no effect of calcium supplementation or herbivory. (From Ruiz *et al.* 2001. With kind permission of Blackwell Publishing.)

gazelles are common but have bulbs under the surface in populations where gazelles are absent (Ward *et al.* 1997, 2000a). Lilies protect their leaves with calcium oxalate crystals (called 'raphides')—gazelles eat only the unprotected tips (Fig. 7.18a and b).

Lily populations where gazelles are common have more crystals in their leaves than where gazelles are absent (Ward *et al.* 1997; Ruiz *et al.* 2002). Ruiz *et al.* (2002) considered this to be a form of constitutive defence (i.e. unlike inducible defences, the strategy does not change when there is herbivory), because adding more calcium to the sand did not increase investment in defence (Fig. 7.19).

This study demonstrated that calcium oxalate is produced in leaves to protect them against herbivory—raphides in geophytes had previously been assumed to have developed as a consequence of excessive calcium uptake from the soil (Franchesci and Horner 1980). The close coevolution of the gazelle (optimal foraging behaviour both in terms of size of plant consumed and search behaviour, and avoidance of chemically defended parts of leaves) and the lily (evolution of deeper bulbs and chemical investment in leaves) indicates that strong biotic interactions between herbivore and plant can and do develop in arid regions in spite of the great impact of abiotic factors on plant populations.

8 Desert food webs and ecosystem ecology

8.1   Do deserts have simple food webs?

The answer to the question posed above is that it depends. For example, if the animal eating plants is relatively large (e.g. a dorcas gazelle (*Gazella dorcas*, which weighs about 15–20 kg)), it can only really be preyed upon by leopards *Panthera pardus* and perhaps striped hyaenas (*Hyaena hyaena*) in the Negev desert (Israel). In such a case there are only three links in the trophic chain or pyramid [plants–gazelles–leopards]. However, if the main consumers in the same desert system are macrodetritivores (as is often the case in desert ecosystems, where most annual plants end up as detritus), then they can be preyed upon by slightly bigger organisms (let us say a *Latrodectus revivensis* spider), which in turn can be preyed upon by a Great Grey Shrike *Lanius excubitor*, which can be preyed upon by a Rock Kestrel *Falco tinnunculus*. In this second case, there are six links in the trophic chain [plants–detritus–termites–spiders–shrikes–kestrels]. Ayal *et al.* (2005) found that if the animals at the bottom of the chain are small, then more steps can be incorporated as one moves up the chain.

8.1.1   Can we scale up from two-species interactions to desert ecosystems?

The simple answer is no. Ecological complexity can emerge from the existence of environmental heterogeneity and scaling effects (Kotliar and Wiens 1990; Ziv *et al.* 2005). The effects of scaling include the different changes in patterns produced by processes that occur at different temporal and spatial scales (Ziv *et al.* 2005). For example, the interspecific competition that has been recorded in various studies in the Negev with rodent species (Abramsky *et al.* 1998; Kotler *et al.* 2004) and in the Namib

(Hughes *et al.* 1994; Ward and Seely 1996a) may strongly influence species coexistence at the local (α) diversity scale but may be unimportant at the regional (γ) diversity scale because colonization and extinction dynamics may be more important than local diversity (Ziv *et al.* 2005). For example, Ziv *et al.* (2005) developed a model that examines rodent body sizes at a landscape scale, assuming that there is a strong interspecific density-dependent effect, with larger rodent species being competitively dominant (which is generally true, see Kotler and Brown (1988) and Brown (1989)). If one includes stochasticity in terms of demography and catastrophes and allows for the possibility of dispersal, then there are large discontinuities of body size and all of the largest species disappear (they occur in smaller numbers because of greater nutritional demands) (Fig. 8.1). This indicates that, in spite of the evidence of strong interspecific competition in some species (see Chapter 5 for further details), changes at a landscape scale may reverse some of the patterns at a patch or habitat scale.

Environmental heterogeneity may result from habitat diversity (the number of different habitats), habitat size and habitat patchiness (the continuity of a patch in a landscape) (Ziv *et al.* 2005). Each of these components may influence species diversity and degree of interaction by the ways in which they are affected by coexistence, colonization, and extinction effects. As indicated by Kotliar and Wiens (1990), different spatial and temporal scales may introduce different levels of heterogeneity of their own that may well influence the ways that organisms respond to their

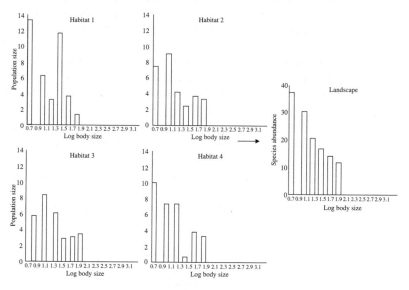

Fig. 8.1   In desert rodents, if one includes stochasticity in terms of demography and catastrophes and allows for the possibility of dispersal, Ziv *et al.* (2005) showed that there are large discontinuities of body size and all of the largest species disappear. The largest species occur in smaller numbers because of greater nutritional demands. (From Ziv *et al.* 2005. With kind permission of Oxford University Press.)

environments. This has led scientists to concur that scale itself (whether spatial or temporal) is an important subject for study (Addicott *et al.* 1987; Dunning *et al.* 1992; Wiens *et al.* 1993; Ziv *et al.* 2005).

For the reasons outlined above, I focus on trophic levels and, more closely, on food webs. Many ecologists have considered trophic levels to be somewhat redundant (see Cousins 1987 and references therein) and urge that we focus on food webs because of the far greater realism involved in them. Nonetheless, some (Ayal *et al.* 2005) have argued that trophic levels help to simplify our understanding of the interactions between parts of the ecological pyramid and have also indicated that even food webs have their problems because a food web quickly degenerates into a series of lines and arrows with little indication, if any, of the relative importance of some interactions.

8.2 The first supermodel—HSS

The first major model of trophic interactions was developed by Hairston, Smith and Slobodkin (1960), hence its acronym of HSS. Their model has been distilled into the single phrase 'why is the world green?'. Hairston *et al.* (1960) noticed that the terrestrial world is largely a green place, indicating the disproportionate productivity of green plants. They argued that fire was generally too unreliable and too stochastic to be considered a major factor in controlling plant biomass. Consumers clearly did not remove as much green material as was produced, presumably because predators ate too many of them to allow for high levels of herbivory. Hence, the world is green (Fig. 8.2). This means that there is 'top-down' control (i.e. that predators control the number of herbivores) and not 'bottom-up' control, where productivity is paramount (Hairston *et al.* 1960; Oksanen *et al.* 1981). However, the excess food supply for herbivores may only be apparent

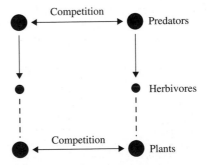

Fig. 8.2   Schematic diagram of Hairston, Smith and Slobodkin (1960) model of trophic dynamics. There is 'top-down' control, where predators control the number of herbivores. The size of the circle indicates the relative size of the populations. Double-headed arrows indicate competition and single-headed arrows indicate predation or herbivory.

rather than real—many plants contain toxic compounds that render them unsuitable as food. Thus, a large standing crop of plant biomass may not represent a surplus of available food (Murdoch 1966). Oksanen *et al.* (1981) have claimed that the interactions among trophic levels in a food chain changes as the productivity of the ecosystem increases (Fig. 8.3). However, deserts are ecosystems with low productivity, and yet predation may be very important (Polis 1991; Groner and Ayal 2001).

Hairston and Hairston (1993) found that aquatic communities differ from terrestrial ones in that lakes and freshwater systems tend to have four rather than three trophic levels. This difference leads to an absence of a large standing crop of producers in lakes. This may reflect the small size of producers (phytoplankton) relative to their consumers (zooplankton), and the presence of a microbial loop that redirects energy and nutrients back up into the food chain that would otherwise be lost to detritivores or decomposers. Both factors may contribute to an extra trophic level in aquatic systems. The end result is that terrestrial communities are green and aquatic communities are not (they are blue). This difference in the standing crop of primary producers can be attributed to the difference in the length of the food chains in the two habitats. However, Polis (1991, 1994) and Ayal *et al.* (2005) have indicated that, especially in invertebrate-dominated terrestrial food webs such as in deserts, scaling of organism size may be related to the size of the plants they occur under. For example, as noted in Chapter 6, Ayal *et al.* (2005) noted that tenebrionid beetles, which are some of the most abundant organisms in deserts, are small in plains with low plant cover, intermediate on slopes with intermediate plant cover, and high in ephemeral river systems where vegetation cover is generally higher.

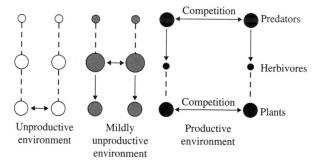

Fig. 8.3   Oksanen *et al.* (1981) consider the interactions among trophic levels to depend on the primary productivity of the environment. The size of the circle indicates the relative size of the populations. Double-headed arrows indicate competition and single-headed arrows indicate predation or herbivory. This model is probably inappropriate for deserts because predators can be very important in spite of the low productivity of the environment. (Modified from Oksanen *et al.* 1981. With kind permission of University of Chicago Press.)

Ayal *et al.* (2005) further observed that a critical distinction between herbivores and macrodetritivores is that the latter have no negative effect on plant dynamics or productivity (the plants are already dead in the case of detritivores). Ayal *et al.* (2005) argue that, in contrast to other studies that consider deserts to be largely one-link communities (Fretwell 1977; Oksanen *et al.* 1981; Oksanen and Oksanen 2000), desert communities may have as many as four links or more.

8.2.1   Cohen's laws about food webs

Based on a study of 113 food webs, Cohen (1989) developed five 'laws' about food webs:

1. Cycles (looping) (e.g. species A eats species B and species B eats species A) are rare (3 of 113 webs)).
2. Chains are short (4–5 links usually).
3. Scale invariance (lack of differences between webs of different sizes [nos. of spp.]) of proportion of top, intermediate and basal species.
4. Scale invariance of proportions of different kinds of links.
5. Ratio of links to number of species is scale invariant (slope ≃2; e.g. web of 25 spp. has about 50 links).

Cohen (1989) also found that, for a given number of species, food webs in constant environments have a higher level of connectivity than food webs in fluctuating environments. Also, food chains in two-dimensional habitats are shorter than those in three-dimensional habitats (e.g. lakes or forests with a well-developed canopy). Cohen (1989) developed his cascade model of food web structure based on these five 'laws'. However, Cohen's (1989) model considers 'trophic species' (i.e. those with the same function, not necessarily biological species). His model's predictions are consistent with the data from the 113 webs, but this is only correct if looping is rare, there is no cannibalism, and if there is a hierarchy of body size, that is, body size increases with trophic level.

8.2.2   Polis and Ayal's problems with these 'laws'

Polis (1991, 1994) and Ayal *et al.* (2005) note that the above assumptions are not true for many invertebrate-dominated webs. Polis (1991) found that actual food webs are much more complex than the ones described by previous workers. He found that:

1. Energetics is not necessarily the most appropriate way to view food webs (*contra* Hairston and Hairston 1993 above).
2. Interaction webs (describing population effects) and descriptive webs (quantifying energy and matter flow) are not necessarily congruent.
3. Another way of saying the above is that an apparently weak link (in terms of diet or energy transfer) can be a key link dynamically (e.g.

parasites can regulate predator populations but accumulate little
energy—see Fig. 8.4).
4. Consumer regulation of populations need involve little energy transfer
   and few feeding interactions.

Polis (1991) studied the Coachella Valley web (Mojave desert, North
America) and found that predators eat from all trophic levels. Polis (1991)
worked mostly on scorpions and emphasized the role of food webs rather
than trophic pyramids (Lindemann 1942) or detritus cascades (Cousins 1980).
Polis (1991) called the utility of the 'trophic level' concept into question, as did
Cousins (1987). Polis (1991) found that consumers may eat all trophic levels
of arthropods in addition to plant material and vertebrates. This creates a
problem of assigning a specific trophic level to a species that vary ontogenetically, seasonally or even opportunistically. Polis (1991) also found that:

1. Longer chain lengths may occur in deserts (6–11 links are common, in
   comparison with average lengths of 2.7–2.9 published elsewhere and
   4–5 of Cohen (1989)).
2. Omnivory and looping are not rare.
3. Absence of compartmentalization (i.e. *contra* 'trophic species' of
   Cohen).
4. Connectivity is greater (number of interactors per species is 1–2 orders
   of magnitude higher than average from published catalogues of webs).
5. Fewer top predators.
6. Prey:predator ratio is >1 (Cohen's (1989) models predict 1:1).

The theory of food webs is still in its infancy (Pimm 1991; Polis 1991;
Winemiller and Polis 1996). Many of these characteristics are hypothesized by food web theorists (Yodzis 1988; Cohen 1989) to cause complete
instability. Polis (1991) considers there to be four major problems with

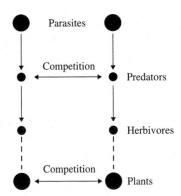

Fig. 8.4 An apparently weak link (in terms of diet or energy transfer) can be a key link dynamically
(e.g. parasites can regulate predator populations but accumulate little energy). Unlike
Figs. 8.2 and 8.3, sizes of circles indicate magnitudes of effects rather than population
sizes.

food web theories that make them inadequate for 'abstracting empirical regularities':

1. Inadequate representation of species diversity. What this means is that lumping biological species into trophic species results in depauperate webs by definition.
2. Inadequate dietary information. Most of the chains of length 1 in web catalogues (e.g. herbivores with no predators) are simply an artefact of inadequate sampling. For example, a scorpion's diet showed no asymptote after 200 nights of sampling and 2,000 person-hours; the 100th prey item was recorded on the 181st night. Differences in body size and resource use among age classes are often equivalent to or greater than differences among most biological species (see Ayal *et al.* 2005).
3. Food web theorists (Cohen 1989) dismiss loops as 'unreasonable structures', yet they are common. This can be especially true of cannibalism. Also, ontogenetic reversal of predation can occur. For example, gopher snakes (*Pituophis catenifer deserticola*) eat eggs and young of burrowing owls (*Athene cunicularia*), while adult burrowing owls eat young gopher snakes (Polis and Yamashita 1991). Normal mutual predation can also be important, for example, ants involved in territorial battles eat each other.

8.3 Interactions among habitats—donor–recipient habitat interactions

Spatial subsidies between webs can make food web theories more complicated. Often, consumers in one system are subsidized via consumption from another web in a different habitat. This is called a donor-controlled interaction because the consumers have no effect on the other web. Their populations are maintained at high levels, which may allow top-down effects in their 'home' web not possible solely with *in situ* productivity. As an example of a spatial subsidy, Polis and Hurd (1996) found in the Namib desert coastal system that black widow spiders (*Latrodectus indistinctus*, Theridiidae) suppress herbivores on dune plants, but high spider populations are actually maintained by feeding on detrital-algae-feeding flies from the marine system next door.

In North America, marine input supports abundant detritivore and scavenger populations on desert coasts. Some of these consumers fall prey to local and mobile terrestrial predators. In the Baja California desert system of North America, insects, spiders, scorpions, lizards, rodents, and coyotes are 3–24 times more abundant on the coast and small islands compared with inland areas and large islands (Polis and Hurd 1996; Rose and Polis 1997). In Baja, coastal spiders are six times more abundant than inland spiders. Their diets, as confirmed by ^{13}C and ^{15}N stable isotope analyses, are significantly more marine-based than is that of inland counterparts (Anderson and Polis 1998). In addition, on the Baja mainland, coastal coyotes eat ~50% mammals and ~50% marine prey and carcasses (Rose and Polis 1997). There, coastal rodent populations are significantly less dense than on islands lacking coyotes, suggesting that marine-subsidized coyotes depress local rodent populations. In the hyper-arid Peruvian section of the Atacama desert (mean annual rainfall = 2 mm), Catenazzi and Donnelly (2007) found that, in spite of the absence of an effect of El Niño currents (unlike the Baja California example where there is a strong effect of El Niño), the marine green alga *Ulva* had a strong effect via the invertebrates that forage on it. Large effects higher up the food chain were seen on geckos *Phyllodactylus angustidigitus* (Gekkonidae), solifuges *Chinchippus peruvianus* (Ammotrechidae), and scorpions *Brachistosternus ehrenbergii* (Bothriuridae).

Worldwide, nutrient budgets of many terrestrial ecosystems depend on aerial transfer of nutrients. For example, in much of the Amazon Basin, soils are nutrient-poor due to limited river deposition and extreme leaching (Swap *et al.* 1992). Phosphorus, which is an element that limits net primary productivity (after nitrogen, according to Liebig's law), may be transferred intercontinentally. About 13–190 kg ha^{-1} year^{-1} is carried by dust blown from the Sahara 5,000 km away (Swap *et al.* 1992). Such input doubles the standing stock of phosphorus over 4,700–22,000 years. Thus, the productivity of Amazon rainforests depends on fertilization from another large ecosystem, the Sahara. Clearly, these two ecosystems are separated by an ocean, yet they are still atmospherically coupled (Pye 1987; Swap *et al.* 1992).

8.4   Effects of precipitation, nutrients, disturbances and decomposition

I consider here the roles of precipitation (which can come as rainfall, fog or snow) and nutrients as well as disturbances (which can be as important as nutrient changes) on ecosystem ecology, and also relate this to decomposition processes, following a model of Whitford (2002) (see also Crawford and Gosz 1982).

8.4.1   Effects of precipitation

Noy-Meir (1973) listed three attributes of arid ecosystems:

1. Total precipitation is so low as to ensure that water is the dominant factor for biological processes.
2. Precipitation is highly variable throughout the year (and spatially) and occurs in infrequent and discrete events.
3. Variation in precipitation is unpredictable.

This led to the formation of the pulse-reserve paradigm (as elucidated by K. Bridges and M. Westoby and described by Noy-Meir (1973)), where a rain event triggers a *pulse* of activity. Some of this is lost either to consumption and/or mortality and the remainder is committed to a *reserve* such as seeds or storage (as in geophytes or succulents). The magnitude of the pulse depends on the season (e.g. rainfall in mid-summer in the Arabian desert will have little or no effect on growth and survival because rainfall mostly comes in spring) and size and duration of the precipitation event. In general, therefore, deserts are pulse-driven ecosystems; that is, precipitation occurs in pulses rather than continuously (Schwinning *et al.* 2004). It is also noteworthy that nitrogen may also place a limit on productivity (West and Skujins 1978), at least during periods of adequate moisture. Reynolds *et al.* (2004) have developed a modified model of the pulse-reserve system that they believe is more general in that it takes antecedent conditions in the soil (e.g. how much rain has previously fallen and how recently it fell and soil type) and plant functional type into consideration (Fig. 8.5). Reynolds *et al.* (2004) consider that productivity is not a response to individual-pulsed events *per se* but rather to soil water recharge and availability, which can be affected by soil type, topography, atmospheric conditions as well as current plant cover and biomass, all

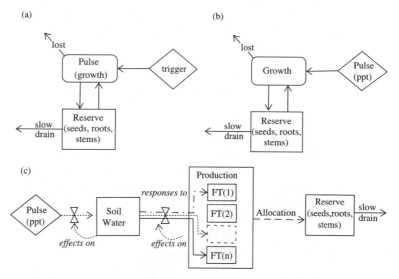

Fig. 8.5   Three types of pulse-reserve models. (a) Pulse-reserve model of Bridges and Westoby (unpubl. data, presented in Noy-Meir (1973)). (b) Common interpretation of pulse-reserve model in which 'pulse' events are equated with the triggering events of precipitation, rather than with a pulse of growth as envisioned in (a) above. (c) Reynolds *et al.* (2004) have developed a modified model of the pulse-reserve system that they believe is more general in that it takes antecedent conditions in the soil (e.g. how much rain has previously fallen and how recently it fell and soil type) and plant functional type into consideration. FT = plant functional type. (From Reynolds *et al.* 2004.)

of which can interact in a multitude of non-linear ways. Nonetheless, Reynolds *et al.* (2004) still support the pulse-reserve model but are a little contentious of its details.

Rainfall pulses mostly are less than 2 mm and few exceed 10 mm (Fig. 8.6). Biological soil crusts probably play the major role in carbon fluxes in hot deserts because most rainfall events are less than 2 mm (Cable and Huxman 2004). However, there are many other studies that have shown that responses to precipitation increase with the amount of precipitation (Ettershank *et al.* 1978; Le Houerou 1984; Gutierrez and Whitford 1987;

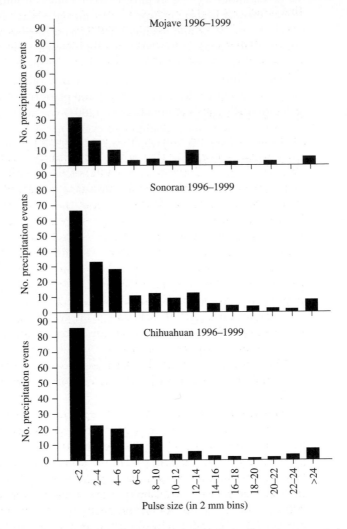

Fig. 8.6   Rainfall pulses for the Mojave, Sonoran, and Chihuahuan deserts are mostly less than 2 mm and few exceed 10 mm. (From Cable and Huxman 2004.)

Fisher *et al.* 1988; Gutierrez *et al.* 1988; Stephens and Whitford 1993). Sher *et al.* (2004) have also shown that interpulse interval (i.e. number of days between rain events) had important effects on the survival of annual plants in the Negev desert (Israel). They found that reduced interpulse intervals had a positive effect on survival (Fig. 8.7) and, in some cases, on growth.

Noy-Meir (1973) and Beatley (1974) noted the importance of precipitation thresholds for triggering germination events, and predicted that recruitment into populations for long-lived plants should be triggered by rare rainfall events of large magnitude. Wiegand *et al.* (2004) examined this with regard to *Acacia* trees germinating in Israeli deserts and found that large, rare events were important for germination and smaller, pulsed events could be important for population dynamics, especially because the maintenance of populations of long-lived trees such as these requires frequent post-recruitment rainfall to allow the trees to survive through the crucial first year.

8.4.2   Effects of nutrients

There is no question that rainfall (or snow in the case of cold deserts such as the Gobi and Great Basin deserts) limits productivity in deserts (Whitford 2002; Chesson *et al.* 2004). This has often resulted in the assumption that nutrients are unimportant. Whitford (2002) has shown that if the expected rainfall is very low, then nutrient effects may well be low (see also Floret *et al.* (1982) and Penning de Vries and Djiteye (1982) for perspectives from the Sahara). However, when rainfall is above average, even if only for short periods, then nutrients can indeed be important. The nutrient most often assumed to be important is nitrogen (Charley and Cowling 1968). In Australia, phosphorus is also an important nutrient (Orians and Milewski 2007, see below). Generally, nitrogen and phosphorus are most likely to be important. Phosphorus is a product of rock weathering while nitrogen comes from an atmospheric pool. Phosphorus is in lower concentration in ancient shield-platform deserts such as the Australian deserts than in more recent basin and range deserts such as the Great Basin desert in North America (Whitford 2002).

Ludwig and Flavill (1979) found that primary productivity was reduced in the Chihuahuan desert (North America) as a consequence of nitrogen limitation, while Floret *et al.* (1982) found that nitrogen limitation reduced productivity in the Tunisian part of the Sahara during wet periods. In the Sahel in the southern Sahara, Penning de Vries and Djiteye (1982) found that reduced nitrogen availability below a mean annual rainfall of about 200 mm was the source of low productivity. Charley and Cowling (1968) attributed lower productivity in Australian deserts to reduced availability of nitrogen in saltbush desert areas and showed that nitrogen and phosphorus

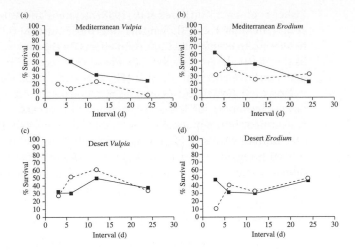

Fig. 8.7 (a–d) Sher *et al.* (2004) have also shown that interpulse interval (i.e. number of days between rain events) had important effects on the survival of annual plants in the Negev desert (Israel). They found that reduced interpulse intervals had a positive effect on survival and, in some cases, on growth. Black squares = high rainfall (500 mm/season); clear circles = low rainfall (100 mm/season). (From Sher *et al.* 2004.)

were limiting in central Australian deserts. Friedel *et al.* (1980) showed that sulphur could also be a limiting factor in some Australian desert habitats.

Stafford Smith and Morton (1990) and Orians and Milewski (2007) have stressed the importance of low nutrient availability (especially in phosphorus) in Australian arid systems and have coupled this to the effects of fire. Most Australian soils have 10–440 ppm total P. Samples from arid-zone soils in Australia yielded a mean of 240 ppm total P compared with 643 ppm total P in arid zones from other continents (Charley and Cowling 1968; Stafford Smith and Morton 1990). Orians and Milewski (2007) noted that Australia is particularly flat, which leads to leaching of available nutrients during flood events. Fire is also a prominent feature of the Australian landscape (Stafford Smith and Morton 1990; Creagh 1992; Orians and Milewski 2007). Orians and Milewski (2007) relate the poor nutrients to fire because few animals can consume plants with such poor nutrients, resulting in large amounts of 'expendable energy' to produce well-defended foliage and large amounts of lignified tissues, which leads to intense fires, especially in the spinifex grasslands and mulga (*Acacia*) shrublands. Stafford Smith and Morton (1990) emphasize that many of these features can also be found in other desert regions. However, it is the geographic size of arid Australia, covering 70% of the continent, that makes it so effective an arid region (see also Friedel *et al.* 1990). This seems somewhat overstated in that there are deserts that are even larger; for example, the Sahara and the Gobi desert. What might be more important is the proportion of the continent of Australia that is arid is greater than in the Sahara or the Gobi desert.

In a series of water supplementation–fertilization experiments in the Chihuahuan desert, a number of studies have shown that nitrogen availability limits biomass production in perennial and annual plants and has an effect on annual plant community composition (Ettershank *et al.* 1978; Gutierrez and Whitford 1987; Fisher *et al.* 1988; Gutierrez *et al.* 1988). However, nitrogen fertilization did not result in changes in productivity in perennial grasses. Irrigation, however, resulted in greater biomass production in the perennial grass, *Bouteloua eriopoda* (Stephens and Whitford 1993). In general, nitrogen fertilization and irrigation experiments showed that nitrogen availability affected plant productivity only if moisture availability is high for a complete plant growth cycle (James and Jurinak 1978; Romney *et al.* 1978).

8.4.3   Disturbances

A number of factors affect the spatial distribution of nutrients in desert ecosystems. Most importantly, perhaps, is the effect of so-called islands of fertility, where individual shrubs, or occasionally trees, create unique microhabitats for other plants to grow under (Franco and Nobel 1989; Parker 1989; Valiente-Banuet and Ezcurra 1991; Suzán *et al.* 1996; Munzbergova and Ward 2002). Note that facilitative effects do not always occur (McAuliffe 1984; Tielborger and Kadmon 2000). An interesting relationship occurs when there is a cyclical relationship between plant species, such as between *Larrea tridentata* and *Opuntia leptocaulis* in the Chihuahuan desert (Yeaton 1978) and between *Acacia reficiens* and various grass species in the Namib desert (Wiegand *et al.* 2005).

Other important effects come from a variety of animal species. The term now used for these physical effects of animals on ecosystems is known as *ecosystem engineering* (Jones *et al.* 1994). For example, in North American deserts, heteromyid rodents play an important role in controlling habitat structure (Davidson *et al.* 1985; Ernest *et al.* 2000). In deserts worldwide, termites play an important role, perhaps more than any other organism, largely because of their effects of decomposition (see Whitford 2002 below), but also because they produce macropores that allow the infiltration of water into the soil to depths of as much as 2 m (Whitford 2002). Harvester ants have large effects on ecosystems because they collect seeds from considerable distances and disperse them close to their mounds, where they later germinate. Wilby *et al.* (2001, 2005) have shown that the harvester ant *Messor ebeninus* (Fig. 8.8) has a particularly large effect on the crucifer *Reboudia pinnata*, which increased in abundance from about 10% of samples on undisturbed soil to about 85% of samples on mound samples (Fig. 8.9). The terminal seeds in each pod of *R. pinnata* are surrounded by a hardened fruit wall, which protects the seeds from predation (Gutterman 1993). A total of 55 species were found on the nest mounds of harvester ants compared with 25 on undisturbed soil (Wilby *et al.* 2001).

Fig. 8.8   Harvester ant *Messor ebeninus* mound near Sayeret Shaked, northern Negev desert, Israel. Harvester ants typically surround their nests with inedible material. (Copyright of Bertrand Boeken.)

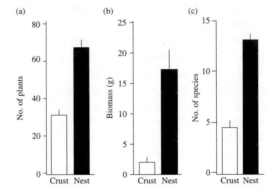

Fig. 8.9   (a–c) The crucifer *Reboudia pinnata* increased in abundance from about 10% of samples on undisturbed soil to about 85% of samples on mound samples. (From Wilby *et al.* 2005. With kind permission of Oxford University Press.)

In the Negev desert, the Indian crested porcupine *Hystrix indica* has large effects as a result of creating depressions in the loess habitat where they remove geophytes such as *Tulipa systola* and *Bellevalia* spp. and where many annual plants are subsequently able to germinate (Boeken *et al.* 1995; Alkon 1999). Boeken *et al.* (1995) found 49 species in 150 porcupine pits compared with 28 in matched samples from undisturbed soil. It appears that the altered abiotic conditions (pits have greater soil moisture accumulation and perhaps higher nitrogen) have increased seed capture. Many of the plant species occurring in these depressions are considered to be more mesic in origin (Boeken *et al.* 1995). Interestingly, in sand dunes where the dorcas gazelle *G. dorcas* removed the geophyte *Pancratium sickenbergeri*

(Ward *et al.* 2000a), no effect of increased plant diversity was noticed. Whitford (1999) has shown that goannas *Varanus gouldii* (Varaniidae) may have important roles in Australian deserts, leading to the formation of banded mulga (*Acacia*) landscapes.

8.4.4 Decomposition

Based on large numbers of empirical studies (Parker *et al.* 1984; Whitford *et al.* 1986; Stephens and Whitford 1993; Nash and Whitford 1995; Whitford 1996; Mun and Whitford 1998), Whitford (2002) proposed a conceptual model to account for decomposition processes in deserts. The model predicts that there is initially a high rate of mass loss from the litter on the surface, resulting from leaching of materials from leaf surfaces and from the breakdown of lignins by photochemical degradation, because of the high light intensities and albedo in deserts. If light intensities are low and/or sun angles are low, then decomposition is primarily through the action of microflora (Whitford *et al.* 1986). When light intensities are high, photo-oxidation occurs and results in further breakdown by water and/or wind.

A major component of decomposition of surface litter is by the action of termites. Termites may consume up to half the total surface litter and most animal faeces. Most materials consumed by termites are completely converted into CO_2 and water because of the action of the symbiotic gut microflora of termites. However, there is a strong *negative* (not *positive*) correlation between termite abundance and soil organic matter (and soil nutrients) ($r = -0.97$) in spite of the fact that soil organic matter and nitrogen are usually positively correlated. Thus, little of the litter is converted to soil organic matter, and minerals in litter are returned to the soil in a mineralized state through animal faeces of species that prey on termites, such as lizards and spiders (Whitford 2002).

The process of decomposition of buried litter and dead roots may be very different from that of surface litter (Whitford 2002). Buried litter accumulates moisture, even in relatively dry soils. This consequently lower temperatures, and higher moisture contents allow microflora and microfauna to grow. Increasing populations of microflora attract grazers such as protozoans, nematodes, and microarthropods, which attract predators such as predatory nematodes and nematophagous mites (Acari). Complex food webs may be established around moist roots and buried litter. The extracellular enzymes of the microflora rapidly decompose compounds such as sugars, fats, starches, celluloses, and waxes. More complex acid-soluble compounds are slowly attacked by a small subset of microbial heterotrophs (Whitford 2002), although Vishnevetsky and Steinberger (1997) note that relatively little microbial decomposition of either above-ground or below-ground litter occurs (see also Whitford *et al.* 1986).

9 Biodiversity and biogeography of deserts

Although there is a common perception that deserts support few species, some deserts have high local diversity, largely because organisms are capable of exploiting patches of high productivity. For example, Shmida (1985) and Ward and Olsvig-Whittaker (1993) noted that most desert vegetation is *contracted* vegetation (*sensu* Whittaker 1977) (Fig. 9.1) below about 70 mm of mean annual rainfall, while above this rainfall value, vegetation can be considered *diffuse* (or widespread). Edaphic conditions may affect the position of this boundary. The contracted vegetation exploits the more productive moisture resources close to wadis (*arroyos*). In good rainfall years, annual plants may also grow on the hillsides and on hammadas in contracted vegetation. Diffuse vegetation occurs widely and can exploit a number of different niches.

Here we differentiate between local species richness (also called α diversity), β diversity, which is also known as species turnover or the change

Fig. 9.1   Contracted vegetation is restricted to the wadis (arroyos). This usually occurs below a mean annual rainfall of about 70 mm.

in species among sites, and γ diversity, which is regional species diversity. A combination of β and γ diversity is also known as differentiation diversity (Cowling *et al.* 1999). The size of a region varies considerably, which affects the determination of regional species pools (i.e. γ or regional diversity), because the species–area curve is one of the few 'laws' in nature, which indicates that as area increases, the number of species increases (Arrhenius 1921; Schoener 1989; Pimm 1991; Rosenzweig 1995). Wherever possible, the size of the region being referred to will be indicated.

Productivity–diversity relationships have been well studied in some deserts and have helped us to understand the factors controlling ecosystem function at a large spatial scale. Studies of convergence of desert communities and consideration of the similarity of desert communities with neighbouring mesic communities are some of the best elucidated of this genre. This chapter will also consider the major differences and similarities among desert taxa in the various deserts of the world to draw inferences on the major biogeographic patterns.

9.1 Are deserts species-poor? α, β, and γ diversity patterns

9.1.1 Plants

At the 0.1 ha scale (which is considered α diversity or local diversity scale), some Middle Eastern desert communities in the steppe and true deserts (e.g. Negev desert) have some of the highest species richness values recorded. In some cases, α diversity can be in excess of 100 species per 0.1 ha (Aronson and Shmida 1992; Ward and Olsvig-Whittaker 1993; Ward *et al.* 1993). These are mostly annual plants, often belonging to the Poaceae, where there are many relatives of barley *Hordeum vulgarum*, oats *Avena sterilis*, and wheat *Triticum dicoccoides*, as one might expect from the birthplace of modern agriculture (Ward and Olsvig-Whittaker 1993; Ward *et al.* 1993). These are all winter rainfall deserts. In the Succulent Karoo communities of South Africa, species richness can also be very high (mean = 74 species, range = 32–115 species), where most species are dwarf, leaf succulent shrubs (mostly Aizoaceae). Cowling and Hilton-Taylor (1999) consider species presence in the Succulent Karoo to be largely determined by a lottery process (*sensu* Chesson and Warner 1981), where functionally equivalent shrubs coexist in highly dynamic communities. Predictable winter rain and fog-ameliorated summers may provide continuous recruitment whereas occasional droughts create stochastic conditions for coexistence (Von Willert *et al.* 1985; Jürgens *et al.* 1997). The Succulent Karoo has species richness values that are almost double that of the adjacent Nama Karoo (mean = 47 species, range = 22–76 species) (Cowling *et al.* 1989). The Nama Karoo has values slightly higher than those recorded for Sonoran desert communities, which were considered by Whittaker and Niering (1975) to be some of the most diverse vegetation in North America.

High β diversity (also called species turnover along habitat gradients, such as rainfall and edaphic gradients) is largely due to habitat specialization and geographic vicariance (Cody 1986; Cowling *et al.* 1992). In general, this aspect of floral diversity has been poorly studied in drylands (Cowling and Hilton-Taylor 1999). Based on the data from Jürgens (1986) from the Succulent Karoo (South Africa), Cowling *et al.* (1989) found that there was a compositional shift of 1.5 (using Wilson and Shmida's (1984) β values) for four sites along a gradient of increasing soil depth, spanning only 100 m in horizontal distance in the *knersvlakte* (quartz fields) in the Succulent Karoo. Ihlenfeldt (1994) found that there was considerable species turnover in the genus *Argyroderma* (Aizoaceae) in the same area. Thus, in an apparently homogeneous environment, there was exceptional species turnover, based largely on edaphic changes (Ihlenfeldt 1994). Similar patterns of species change have been recorded for other genera of Aizoaceae (Hammer 1993; Schmiedel and Jürgens 1999) as well as geophytes (Goldblatt and Manning 1996; Esler *et al.* 1999). Comparatively speaking, β diversity in the adjacent Nama Karoo of South Africa is low (Cowling and Hilton-Taylor 1999). Hoffman (1989) recorded a species turnover of 1.9 for four sites along a 250 km gradient of increasing aridity, from succulent thorn thickets (mean annual rainfall = 450 mm) to karroid shrubland (mean annual rainfall = 200 mm). Also in the Nama Karoo, Palmer and Cowling (1994) recorded β diversity values of 1.1 and 1.5 for five sites spanning topo-moisture gradients of 500 m and 300 mm year^{-1} on dolerite and sandstone substrates. Cowling and Hilton-Taylor (1999) consider species turnover in the Succulent Karoo to have occurred explosively within certain lineages (e.g. Aizoaceae), which has resulted in the coexistence of many related species separated by very short distances.

In terms of regional data for arid habitats, Cowling *et al.* (1998) found that winter rainfall arid lands have more plant species than summer rainfall areas, when measured globally (almost twice as species-rich as equivalent summer rainfall areas). When compared with winter rainfall areas, the Succulent Karoo (which is in a winter rainfall area) has the highest regional diversity (nearly four times as high as in similar-sized areas of North America). The Namib desert has between two and four times as many species as the Sahara in North Africa, in spite of the greater topographic complexity of the latter region (Cowling *et al.* 1998).

9.1.2 Animals

Because most deserts are recent in their distributions, many species are (convergently) derived from mesic faunas (Morton 1993). There are also some interesting patterns of certain species from the arid regions of northern and southern Africa that are the same species (or closely related species) yet

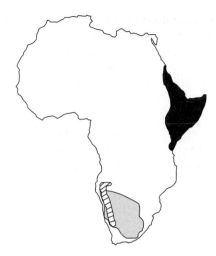

Fig. 9.2   Map of the distribution of the small mammal *Xerus*, which is a desert species found in deserts of northern and southern Africa (see Chapter 4), yet is not found in areas in between. The areas between these deserts are dominated by savanna, grassland and forest. (From Herron *et al.* 2005. With kind permission of University of Chicago Press.)

are separated by savanna, grassland and forest, which indicates that they were once contiguously distributed prior to the Pleistocene (Fig. 9.2).

9.1.2.1 Lizards

The regional lizard fauna (γ diversity) in the deserts of Australia is richer than the lizard fauna of North American deserts (170 vs. 57 species) (Schall and Pianka 1978), even though deserts are very similar in size on these continents (about 8 million km^2—Westoby 1993). Local diversity (α diversity) in Australia is also richer (mean of 30 species vs. 7 species) on average than in North American deserts. Pianka (1969) proposed a number of reasons for the greater diversity of Australian desert lizard species:

1. In Australian deserts, lizards replace the North American desert species of mammals.
2. Some Australian desert lizards are more narrowly specialized than their North American equivalents, for example, the skink genus *Ctenotus*.
3. As a consequence of the greater environmental stability of the Australian desert, lizards have been able to partition their niches both spatially and temporally. For example, there are virtually no nocturnal North American gecko species versus 32–44% in Australia.
4. There is greater environmental heterogeneity of the Australian deserts than their North American counterparts. However, the low topographical

variety of Australian deserts (Stafford Smith and Morton 1990; Orians and Milewski 2007) would militate against this argument.

Morton and James (1988) considered why subterranean lizards are absent from North American deserts, yet are quite common in Australian deserts. Subterranean lizard species are also common in the Kalahari desert (southern Africa)(Huey *et al.* 1974). Similar to Pianka (1986), Morton and James (1988) considered ecological factors to be of greater importance than other factors in explaining higher present-day diversity in Australia. Lizards are quite diverse in many parts of the world, probably because the costs of thermoregulation are lower in arid areas and they can become inactive during stress periods, which confers an advantage for them over endotherms (birds and mammals), which must feed on a daily basis. Among the most diverse habitats for lizards are the spinifex grasses (*Triodia* and *Plectrachne*) (Fig. 9.3). Pianka (1972) and Cogger (1992) consider that the spiny nature of these grasses makes predation on lizards very difficult, the microclimate is probably less harsh than the microhabitats at large and there is horizontal structural diversity within spinifex. Pianka (1981) also considered spinifex hummocks to provide a rich insect supply. Morton and James (1988) show that termites are particularly abundant in spinifex grasslands because spinifex is low in nutrients (as indicated by its sclerophylly). These insects are primarily subterranean, which may explain why there are so many subterranean lizard species.

James and Shine (2000) have more recently moved the focus away from local-scale explanations of lizard diversity and have attempted a regional analysis. They used the Australian comb-eared skinks of the genus *Ctenotus* and found that more species occur in the arid zone (9.3 species per site) than in other biomes (means = 2.4 to 7.6). Pianka (1969) found

Fig. 9.3   Spinifex grasslands in the Strzelecki desert, South Australia. (From online photograph, Encyclopaedia Britannica Junior. Date accessed: 12 February 2008.)

that as many as 11 species of *Ctenotus* occur sympatrically. Pianka (1969) considered ecological coexistence to occur on the basis of differences in body size, foraging time, microhabitats and habitats (see also Morton and James 1988). However, James and Shine (2000) found that the total number of species occurring in the arid zone is actually lower, not higher, per unit area of habitat than other biomes in Australia. Thus, although xeric *Ctenotus* have a higher α diversity than mesic species of Australia, they have a lower γ (regional) diversity. This occurs because most xeric species occur over enormous areas (average = 1,035,000 km^2) whereas their congeners have smaller geographic ranges (200–373,000 km^2). The enormous geographic distributions of xeric taxa probably reflect the spatial (especially topographic) homogeneity of desert regions of Australia (see Chapter 8). This means that the sizes of geographic zones of individual species are large, which leads to greater probabilities of evolutionary radiation (Schluter and Ricklefs 1993). Thus, contrary to the patterns of other taxa, significant radiation has occurred within the xeric regions, rather than radiation within the mesic regions with subsequent radiation into the massive desert zones. James and Shine (2000) recognized that biological attributes regarding interactions with other species or with other resources (e.g. shelter or prey) may still be important at microhabitat scales (Pianka 1986; Morton and James 1988).

9.1.2.2 Granivores

Presence/absence data for the small mammal species at sites in seven deserts were analysed for evidence of similarity in community structure (Kelt *et al.* 1996). The deserts studied by Kelt *et al.* (1996) were in North and South America, Australia, the Middle East and greater Eurasia (including the Thar, Turkestan, and Gobi deserts). They found that there was low α diversity (2–4 spp. per site), high β diversity (i.e. high species turnover or many changes across sites) and local coexistence of 20–30% of species in terms of γ (regional) diversity. Although there were some similarities across deserts, trophic structure differed considerably. Deserts in the northern hemisphere (especially in North America) had more granivores and the Turkestan desert had more folivores. Carnivorous small mammals were particularly abundant in Australia, and omnivores were common in Australia, the Thar desert of India, and South America. They found that the structure of the small mammal communities in deserts was strongly affected by historical factors. Different taxa with distinct trophic adaptations were common in different deserts.

Morton and Davidson (1988) considered the diversity of arid Australian and North American harvester ant faunas. Because there are fewer rodents in Australia than in North America, they predicted that harvester ants should be more diverse. They found that there was similar α diversity between the deserts but that there was higher β diversity in Australia. The species richness in North American deserts ranged from two at lower rainfall to a maximum of eight at higher rainfall, whereas in Australia, species richness ranged from 6 to 12 harvester ant species. Richness and diversity were significantly correlated with mean annual precipitation in North American deserts but there was no significant relationship in Australia. Consequently, Australian deserts had higher species richness at low rainfall than North American deserts (<300 mm rainfall). As mentioned in Chapter 7, granivory is an important interaction in ecological communities, especially in deserts where many plant populations exist as seeds for long periods (Davidson and Morton 1981; Morton 1985; Rissing 1986). Harvester ants have been shown, in a number of deserts (Australia, South Africa and South America), to be the most important granivores and seed dispersers (Morton 1985; Kerley 1991) (Fig. 7.20), although rodents are more important in North American and Israeli deserts (Mares and Rosenzweig 1977, 1978; Abramsky 1983).

9.1.2.3 Birds

Wiens (1991) found no evidence that local bird species diversity (α diversity) differed between Australian and North American desert shrublands, at a scale of about 10 ha. In both cases, there were about six species for any given shrubland. Pianka and Huey (1971) found the species richnesses of Australian and Kalahari (southern Africa) deserts to be similar, in spite of the great differences in size (Australian deserts are far larger). These similarities in species diversity may be a consequence of association of bird species diversity with vegetation structural diversity rather than productivity *per se* (MacArthur and MacArthur 1961; Recher 1969; Pianka and Huey 1971; Cody 1970, 1993). Pianka and Huey (1971) found that about 63% of the variance in bird species richness could be explained by variance in plant height diversity. Because structural diversity of the three deserts is relatively similar, there may be little opportunity for more species to occupy different niches.

Overall, regional species diversity (γ diversity) is quite similar between Australian deserts (140 species (excluding water birds)) and North American deserts (130 species) (Schall and Pianka 1978; Morton 1993). Pianka and Huey (1971) compared avian functional diversity in the Kalahari desert (southern Africa) with western Australian deserts. They found that there were proportionately more ground carnivores (including insectivores) in the Kalahari desert (34%) than in Australia (18%), that avian ground herbivores (mostly granivores) were similar on the two continents and that there were more arboreal Australian species (53%) than in the Kalahari desert (38%).

9.1.2.4 Animals in ephemeral pools

Ward and Blaustein (1994) studied arthropod diversity in ephemeral pools in the Negev desert (Israel) (Fig. 9.4). They found that, while species–area relationships could explain some of the variance in species richness, more

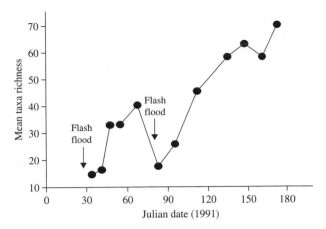

Fig. 9.4   Ward and Blaustein (1994) studied arthropod diversity in ephemeral pools in the Negev desert (Israel) and found that, while species:area relationships could explain some of the variance in species richness, flash floods caused pools to essentially return to their original state and for the colonization process to start afresh. (From Ward and Blaustein 1994. With kind permission of Blackwell Publishing.)

of the variance could be explained by the amount of vegetation in these pools. Overall, flash floods caused pools to return to their original state and for the colonization process to start afresh. In this case flash floods were by far the overriding factor determining arthropod diversity in ephemeral pools.

9.2   Productivity–diversity relationships in deserts

Ward and Olsvig-Whittaker (1993) and Ward *et al.* (1993) considered the Makhtesh Ramon as the junction of two major biogeographical zones, the Saharo-Arabian and the Irano-Turanian. They found that there was a single productivity curve based on rainfall that increased species richness with increasing rainfall. This was different from the result achieved by Ghazanfar (1991) in the desert of Oman, where a hump-shaped curve was obtained (Fig. 9.5). Rosenzweig and Abramsky (1993) would argue that Ward and Olsvig-Whittaker (1993) had sampled only a portion of the hump-shaped curve, that is, they had sampled the low productivity portion of the curve, which is correct. The declining portion of the curve would have been at higher productivity.

Abramsky and Rosenzweig (1984) found that there was a hump-shaped species diversity curve (Fig. 9.6), as predicted by Tilman (1982) and also by Newman (1973). Similar patterns were found in the Sonoran and Gobi deserts by Rosenzweig (1995). They considered the reason for the increase

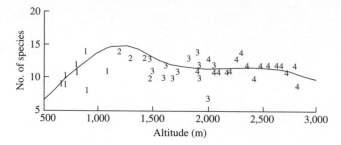

Fig. 9.5   Ghazanfar (1991), in the desert of Oman, obtained a hump-shaped species richness versus altitude curve for flowering plants. Numbers are the four ecological zones indicated by the clustering programme, TWINSPAN. (From Ghazanfar 1991. With kind permission of Blackwell Publishing.)

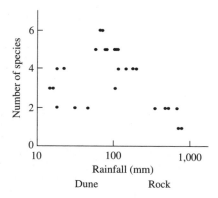

Fig. 9.6   Abramsky and Rosenzweig (1984) found that there was a hump-shaped species diversity curve for desert rodents. (From Abramsky and Rosenzweig 1984. With kind permission of Nature Publishing Group.)

in the hump-shaped diversity curve to be rather clear (Rosenzweig and Abramsky 1993). The curve increases initially because as productivity increases, more species can occupy a particular habitat. This is most probably a function of environmental heterogeneity. Rosenzweig and Abramsky (1993) find it more difficult to explain why the number of species declines after a certain point. It is commonly thought that this decline is a function of competition among species for resources (Newman 1973; Tilman 1982). However, Rosenzweig and Abramsky (1993) questioned whether this explanation for the decline phase is tautological. They argue that habitat and resource heterogeneity are *evolved* responses of organisms and find no *a priori* reason why more species can evolve into any particular variance rather than a smaller particular variance. That is, they wonder why species could not have evolved changes that might not develop in ecological time.

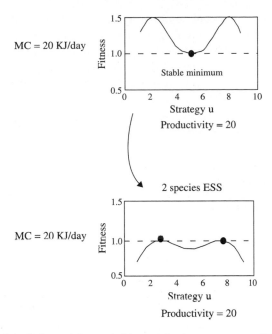

Fig. 9.7
Mitchell *et al.* (2005) showed that, as habitat overlap increases, competition favours the strategy with the lowest mean cost of foraging for all habitat types. The stable minimum is easily invaded by any strategy arbitrarily close to the resident. The arrow indicates that once the stable minimum is invaded, it can evolve to a two-species ESS. This allows environmental heterogeneity to be considered an example of evolutionary differences resulting in a decline in species diversity at high productivity. (Modified from Mitchell *et al.* (2005). With kind permission of Oxford University Press.)

More recently, Mitchell (2000) and Mitchell *et al.* (2005) have revived interest in this issue. Using an evolutionarily stable strategy (ESS) approach, they consider why two species cannot coexist at higher productivities. Mechanistically, Mitchell *et al.* (2005) consider that coexistence of two or more species can occur if the combination of maintenance cost and productivity allow the different species to use the heterogeneity in the resource with sufficient differences in their strategies. Maintenance costs and productivity determine the level of resources required by a given species to maintain a fitness of one (i.e. each individual replaces itself). When maintenance costs and productivity are low, a species can achieve a fitness of one even when competition keeps the resources at low levels. At low resource levels, habitat overlap among competitors is also low because the rate of energy harvest from secondary habitats is too close to the energy cost of using those habitats (see Brown (1988) and Chapter 5 for further explanation). When the maintenance cost is high, species need higher resource levels to achieve a fitness of one. If productivity is also high, then higher resource levels are needed to counteract increased density dependence of non-energetic components of fitness (e.g. finding burrows). In either case, the increased resource levels result in secondary habitats increasing in relative profitability (as predicted by Ideal Free Distribution (IFD) theory; Fretwell and Lucas (1970)), encouraging greater overlap among competitors. As habitat overlap increases, competition favours the strategy with the lowest mean cost of foraging for all habitat types (Fig. 9.7). This provides an evolutionary explanation for Rosenzweig and Abramsky's (1993) concerns about tautology, and allows environmental heterogeneity to be considered a *bona fide* example of evolutionary differences resulting in a decline in species diversity at high productivity.

9.3   Convergence and divergence of desert communities

One of the main differences between floras and faunas of the world, particularly in deserts, occurred because of the break-up of Pangaea (Wegener 1966) and the later split between the southern Gondwanan continent (which formed South America, Antarctica, Africa, Australia, and India) and the northern Laurasian continent (which formed North America and Eurasia). For example, the hemiparasites of the family Loranthaceae are mostly Gondwanan in origin, although some movement into adjacent areas has occurred (e.g. the invasion of the Negev desert (Israel) by the mistletoe *Plicosepalus acaciae* from Africa; Fig. 9.8). Similarly, there has been a divergence in the origin of desert birds, because the South African, South American, Indian, and Australian species are Gondwanan in origin whereas the North American and Eurasian species are Laurasian in origin (Cracraft 1973; Schodde 1982). This has led to a great interest in panbiogeography and vicariance biogeography (*sensu* Croizat 1962, 1982; Cracraft

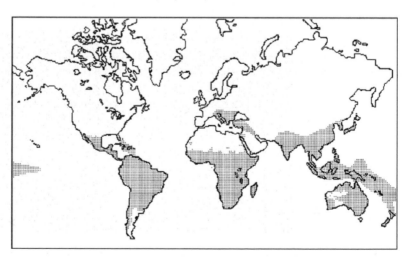

Fig. 9.8   Gondwanan distribution of Loranthaceae. (From www.parasiticplants.siu.edu [Date accessed: 27 June 2008].)

1973). However, a puzzling example is the absence of the Solifugae (sun spiders) from Australia (Fig. 9.9).

Perhaps more interesting are the cases of convergent evolution of desert forms, presumably because of the similarities in selection pressures placed on these organisms. The classic example of convergence is the succulent Cactaceae in the Americas and the Euphorbiaceae in Africa (Fig. 9.10). The Aizoaceae (Fig. 9.11) and Crassulaceae (in Africa) and Didiereaceae (arid regions of Madagascar) are also strongly succulent desert taxa.

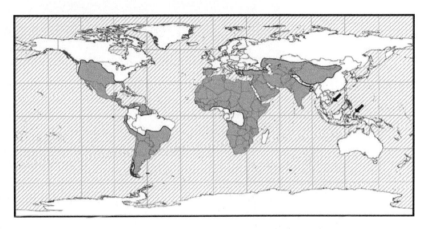

Fig. 9.9   The absence of the Solifugae (sun spiders) from Australia, which was also a part of Gondwana, is hard to explain.

(a)   (b)

Fig. 9.10   The classic example of convergence is the Cactaceae in the Americas and the Euphorbiaceae in Africa. Another pertinent example is the *Aloe* genus in South Africa (a) and *Yucca* genus (b) in North America.

Fig. 9.11   The Mesembryanthema (Aizoaceae) is also a strongly succulent desert taxon.

The deserts of North and South America are remarkably similar from a floristic point-of-view. Almost all of the large desert families (Asteraceae, Polygonaceae, Zygophyllaceae) and many genera are shared by the two continents (Raven 1963). Furthermore, the families Agavaceae, Cactaceae, Oenotheraceae, Garryaceae, Krameriaceae, Lennoaceae and Polemoniaceae are almost exclusively restricted to the Americas and have not dispersed to other arid regions (Turner 1977). Although some have claimed that this similarity was due to long-distance dispersal (Raven 1963; Solbrig 1973; Wells and Hunziker 1976) or the short distance that colonization needs to occur across the Isthmus of Panama, Turner (1977) has suggested that North and South America were geographically closer in the Early- to Mid-Tertiary (about 65 million years ago), resulting in the great similarity between their floras. However, the lack of similarity in their mammalian faunas is surprising (see below).

Whitford (2002) has indicated that many of the same genera of fresh-water pool (ephemeral) fauna inhabit ponds throughout the world. Many of the Anostraca, Conchostraca, Notostraca and Cladocera found in the Sahara desert are of the same genera as found in North American deserts (Rzóska 1984; Mackay *et al.* 1990; Maeda-Martinez 1991; Daniels *et al.* 2004). Daniels *et al.* (2004) have examined the phylogeny and distribution of the thermophilic genus *Streptocephalus* (Streptocephalidae, Anostraca) in North America, Africa, Eurasia, and Australia using molecular techniques. They found that there was considerable homoplasy in morphological characteristics (Maeda-Martinez 1991; Hamer *et al.* 1994a, b). Daniels *et al.* (2004) have found that the North American taxa are monophyletic and that none of these taxa has a close relationship with any of the other members of the genus. They believe that the distribution patterns of the genus *Streptocephalus* are best explained by vicariance during the break-up of the supercontinent of Gondwana. Only a single dispersal or vicariant event is needed to explain the monophyly of the North American species from Gondwana. Daniels *et al.* (2004) note that there is a faunistic link for a number of Gondwanan freshwater crustacean taxa between Africa and Australia and also with India (which was also a part of Gondwana) (Newman 1991).

There are also fascinating examples from desert rodents shown by Mares (1983), although more recently he has recognized that morphological similarity is not necessarily associated with trophic similarities. Kelt *et al.* (1996) found that the claims of convergent evolution in small mammal faunas (Mares 1983) to be spurious in that the mammals may look similar but occupied different niches. Mares (1983) has indicated that bipedal rodents are perceived to be granivorous. However, there is no link between bipedality and seed eating. In fact, bipedal rodents may also be herbivorous, omnivorous or insectivorous. Thus, morphological convergence is not necessarily linked with granivory.

9.3.1 Community-wide character displacement

Ecological character displacement may occur when any two or more species overlap in a crucial aspect of their niches. This may lead, in time, to morphological changes that differentiate the species (or genders—see Dayan *et al.* (1990) below) into different niche use. Ward (unpubl. obs.) considered the size distribution patterns of tenebrionid beetles (also called darkling beetles) in the Namib desert belonging to the genus *Onymacris* (see also Roberts *et al.* 1991; Ward and Seely 1996a–c). Although it may be difficult to assign competitors to any given pair of species, Ward (unpubl. obs.) assigned any pair of species that occurred either sympatrically (i.e. occurred together) or allopatrically (i.e. occurred separately), based on their presence or absence in quarter-degree square units. He found that that the differences in body lengths of beetles was greater for beetles that occurred sympatrically than allopatrically, inferring that interspecific competition could have occurred (Fig. 9.12).

Dayan *et al.* (1989) studied two foxes in the Saharo-Arabian desert, and included the data for a third species where it occurs. One species, the red fox *Vulpes vulpes*, is widespread in the Holarctic, whereas the smaller Rüppell's fox *V. ruepellii* is restricted to the deserts. The third species, Blanford's fox *V. cana*, is smaller than the other two species and is also restricted to deserts. They found that the carnassial teeth of these species were remarkably evenly spaced in size (Fig. 9.13) in the deserts where they are sympatric in spite of the general indication that the red fox follows Bergmann's rule (i.e. increases in size as one travels northwards). The only area where the red fox does not follow Bergmann's rule is where it is sympatric with

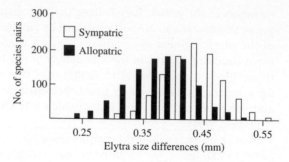

Fig. 9.12   Sympatric *Onymacris* beetle species were significantly more different in size than allopatric species.

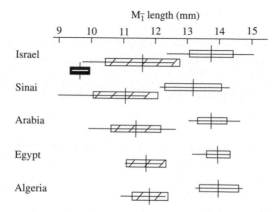

Fig. 9.13   Dayan *et al.* (1989) found that the lower carnassial tooth lengths of these foxes were remarkably evenly spaced in size in the deserts where they are sympatric. Vertical lines: means; bars: 2 standard deviations; and horizontal lines: range. Empty bars = red fox; dashed bars = Rüppell's fox; black bar = Blandford's fox. (From Dayan *et al.* 1989. With kind permission of Blackwell Publishing.)

Rüppell's fox. They understood this to indicate that ecological character displacement has occurred to limit the size similarity of these species.

In a similar study, Dayan *et al.* (1990) studied a group of felines (Felidae: Carnivora) in the Saharo-Arabian desert and Thar desert (India). They chose to include different sexes as different morphospecies because they differed considerably in their most crucial aspects, namely, tooth structure. They used the diameter of the upper canine tooth as an index of body size of the guild of three species in the Negev and Judean deserts of Israel (parts of the Saharo-Arabian desert complex) and four species in the Sind (Thar) desert. They found that the canine diameters were considerably more evenly spaced than expected by chance. They consider this to be consistent with

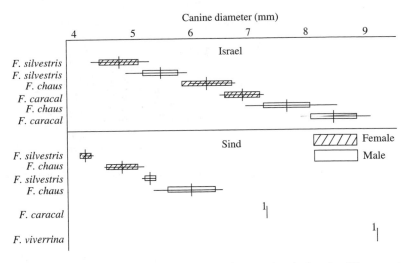

Fig. 9.14   Dayan et al. (1990) found that there were evenly spaced male–female differences in upper canine teeth of felines in Israel and in the Sind (Thar) desert of India. Vertical lines: means; bars: standard deviations; and horizontal lines: range. Numbers (sample sizes) indicate that only a single individual was measured. (From Dayan *et al.* 1990. With kind permission of University of Chicago Press.)

character displacement for prey items. The neck vertebrae of a prey animal would be sliced open and would more easily be sliced by teeth that are of an appropriate size. Teeth that are too large would be unable to penetrate the neck vertebrae and teeth that are too small would presumably be incapable of snapping the nerve chord. They also said that it may be possible that either sexual selection for tooth display (as in the classic lip-curling movement called 'flehmen'; Ewer (1973)) or interspecific displays (lumped as 'ethological displays') could explain this pattern (Ewer 1973). They find the ethological explanations less convincing because this should produce a relatively simple male–female, male–female, etc. difference based on overall body size, but there is no such pattern (Fig. 9.14).

   In both studies, Dayan *et al.* (1989, 1990) recognized that other possible reasons for differences might exist and are unaware of whether these species compete for food. Of course, if one measured enough features of an organism, one should find differences among completely random parameters. Indeed, Hutchinsonian differences in size (an expected ratio between competing species first described by Hutchinson (1959) of 1:1.3) have also been shown in a variety of inanimate objects (e.g. bicycles, cars, and kitchen knives) by Eadie *et al.* (1987). There may be good reasons for these differences (e.g. kitchen knives need not be too similar to one another otherwise one knife would do instead of two, etc.) or they may simply be an artefact of log-normal size distributions (Eadie *et al.* 1987). Nonetheless, Dayan *et al.* (1989, 1990) have given convincing reasons for

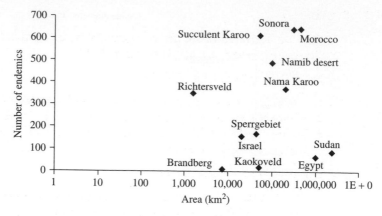

Fig. 9.15   Burke (2004) has shown that patterns of plant endemism in various parts of the world differ considerably. Sperrgebiet, Brandberg and Kaokoveld are in the Namib desert (Namibia), Richtersveld is part of the Karoo (South Africa). (From Burke 2004. With kind permission of Blackwell Publishing.)

the selection of the parameters they used, and thus ecological character displacement remains an interesting possibility.

9.4   Large-scale patterns in desert biogeography

Crisp *et al.* (2001) considered the factors that have led to endemism in the Australian flora. Crisp *et al.* (2001) found that, as is the case for other taxa (with the exception of the lizards; see Chapple and Keogh (2004) and below), the expansion of mesic species into the adjacent xeric areas has occurred, largely because the present position (and age) of deserts is relatively recent. Crisp *et al.* (2001) found that all centres of endemism are near-coastal, which they consider to be associated with Pleistocene expansions of the central deserts, which limited the viability of refugia for narrowly endemic species. Africa has also been well studied with regard to endemism (White 1993; Linder 2000). Linder (2000) found that climate stability rather than high rainfall was correlated with areas of endemism. He found that expansions of the desert during past arid cycles (Pleistocene, 10,000–20,000 years BP) have removed sources of endemism, even in apparently suitable areas such as mountain ranges. Indeed, the deserts were probably connected during the Pleistocene for different periods, leading to similarities in taxa and even shared species such as birds (Vernon 1999). Nonetheless, Burke (2004) has shown that patterns of plant endemism in various parts of the world differ considerably (Fig. 9.15).

9.4.1 Plants

One can derive 'rules' for desert vegetation, based on favourability, diversity and ecogeography, as follows (Shmida 1985):

Favourability (*sensu* Terborgh 1973):

1. Vegetation cover is positively correlated with rainfall (Shmida 1972).
2. Plant sizes are positively correlated with rainfall (Beatley 1974).
3. 'Rules' 1 and 2 combine to form the 'Walter correlation', which indicates that productivity is positively correlated with rainfall (Walter 1971).

Diversity (*sensu* Whittaker 1977):

1. The 'Whittaker law' indicates that local plant species diversity (α diversity) on a global scale is related to rainfall in a single-humped curve (Whittaker 1977). Maximum species richness is in the semi-desert zone (Whittaker 1977).
2. Edaphic heterogeneity, especially rockiness, enhances species diversity because rocks partition the habitat into more microniches (Shmida and Whittaker, unpubl. obs.; reported in Shmida (1985)). Rocky habitats at the arid end of the gradient have more species than comparable habitats and contain more humid elements (Shmida and Whittaker 1984).

Ecogeography:

1. Humid arboreal elements do not expand into deserts because they are physiologically constrained, whereas desert elements do not expand into more mesic habitats because they are outcompeted there (Evenari *et al.* 1982).
2. If elements of a mesic flora invade the desert, they will grow in more mesic habitats such as near oases, under rocks and in run-on areas (Boyko 1947).
3. Floristic similarity is negatively correlated with geographic distance between sites (Mares *et al.* 1985). This is probably one of the most important rules of phytogeography because deserts are generally spaced far apart from one another across the globe.

The various desert regions of the world have been divided by Shmida (1985) into nine phytogeographical regions (Fig. 9.16 and Table 9.1): (1) Australian; (2) Southern African; South American deserts, namely (3) Monte-Patagonian; (4) Atacama-Sechuran; (5) Sonoran; (6) Artemisian (Great Basin); (7) Irano-Turanian; (8) Sahelian; and (9) Saharo-Arabian.

In the Old World of the Northern Hemisphere, there is general agreement that there are three phytogeographical regions (Shmida 1985):

1. Irano-Turanian, including the Iranian and central Asian deserts (Walter 1973);

Table 9.1 The main plant families expressed as a percentage of species richness of some desert regions of the world. * = desert family. Exclusively desert families indicated in bold. (After Shmida 1985.)

Plant families	Australia	South Africa	Irano-Turanian	Arabian	Sahara	Thar	North America	World
Acanthaceae						2.7		
Agavaceae							1.0	
Aizoaceae	1.4	15.0		*2.1				*1.0
Amaranthaceae						2.4		
Asclepiadaceae		2.0						1.5
Asteraceae	23.2	20.2	11.6	14.0	11.0	6.4	19.3	11.1
Boraginaceae			4.3	3.8	2.3		4.6	
Brassicaceae	3.2		10.4	5.6	3.2		4.0	
Cactaceae							*2.8	*0.1
Capparidaceae					2.3	1.4		
Caryophyllaceae			4.6	5.4	2.6			
Chenopodiaceae	*11.6	2.7	*7.9	*7.4	*3.4	*1.0	*2.4	*0.7
Convolvulaceae						5.6		
Crassulaceae		*5.6	1.8					*0.7
Cucurbitaceae						3.2		
Cyperaceae								1.8
Epacridaceae	**1.8**							
Euphorbiaceae		2.3				3.4		2.6
Fabaceae	9.2	4.0	7.9	7.4	10.7	14.0	6.1	7.6
Fouquieriaceae							0.1	
Geraniaceae		2.9			1.4			
Goodeniaceae	**3.2**							
Hydrophyllaceae							3.1	
Iridaceae	3.3							
Lamiaceae			2.7	3.0	1.7			2.0
Liliaceae	2.2	8.3	2.4	4.8				
Loasaceae							2.2	
Malvaceae	1.9					4.6		
Melastomataceae								1.7
Myoporaceae	**1.6**							
Myrtaceae	**5.0**							
Onagraceae							2.2	
Orchidaceae								7.8
Oxalidaceae		1.5						
Poaceae	11.4	6.4	13.8	8.2	11.1	15.0	7.0	4.0
Polygonaceae			3.0				4.9	
Polemoniaceae							4.1	
Plumbaginaceae					1.8			
Proteaceae	1.8							
Rosaceae			2.4					
Rubiaceae								3.3
Scrophulariaceae		5.2	2.6			2.4	2.8	1.8
Solanaceae	2.4							
Zygophyllaceae	1.6	*2.3		*3.0	*2.8	*2.3		*0.1

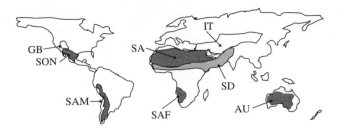

Fig. 9.16   Map of Shmida's (1985) desert phytogeographic regions of the world. AU: Australia; GB: Great Basin; IT: Irano-Turanian; SA: Saharo-Arabian; SAF: southern African; SAM: South American (includes Monte-Patagonian and Atacama-Sechuran); SON: Sonoran; SD: Sudano-Decanian. (From Shmida 1985. With kind permission of Elsevier.)

2. Saharo-Arabian, which includes the deserts of the Sahara and Arabia. Surprisingly, the deserts of the Irano-Turanian (cold) and Saharo-Arabian (hot) regions differ in temperatures but are highly similar floristically; and

3. Sahelian (also known as Sudano-Deccanian; Zohary (1973)), which includes the Thar (Great Indian) desert. This region also includes the arid savanna south of the Sahara. The last-mentioned is interesting, with taxa such as *Acacia* species, *Capparis decidua*, *Indigofera*, *Maerua*, *Moringa*, *Salvadora persica*, *Ziziphus*, and many members of the grasses (Poaceae) being shared with the arid savanna of Africa.

The environments of the Sahel and the Thar regions are similar but they are separated by the Indian Ocean. This suggests to Shmida (1985) that there was a connection of arid savanna via Saudi Arabia and southern Iran as long-distance dispersal and the Gondwana connection (India split off from Africa about 85 million years ago) seem unlikely because the similarity in genera and species is too great. Many Sahelian species occur in the mountains of Yemen and Oman (Zohary 1973). Long-distance dispersal may, of course, have caused the dispersal of species from Africa to India across the Red Sea and Gulf of Oman, which is a distance of 50–200 km.

An interesting example of dispersal of *Acacia raddiana* was considered by Shrestha *et al.* (2002) as an example of the similarities between Africa and Asia. Shrestha *et al.* (2002) have shown that mammalian dispersal significantly affects and, indeed, controls the biogeography of *Acacia* trees in the Middle East on a large geographic scale. Shrestha *et al.* (2002), using randomly amplified polymorphic DNA (RAPD) analyses, showed that there are two main genetic groups of *A. raddiana* trees in the Negev desert, one in the western Negev, extending to the northern shores of the Dead Sea and the other along the Syrian-African Rift valley from the Red Sea to the southern end of the Dead Sea (Fig. 9.17). As these trees have large, heavy seeds that need to be scarified prior to germination (which occurs

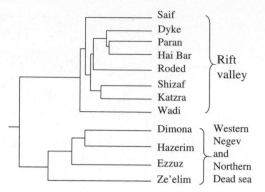

Fig. 9.17   Cluster analysis of *Acacia raddiana* populations in the Negev desert, Israel. (From Shrestha *et al.* 2002. With kind permission of Elsevier.)

easily in the guts of large herbivores; Rohner and Ward (1999)), they must have been dispersed from Africa (where the main populations of this species are found) by mammalian herbivores across the flat expanses of the western Negev desert to the northern Dead Sea. Independently, seeds must have been carried from south to north in the Syrian-African Rift valley from the Sinai (Egypt) and/or Saudi Arabia and up the wadis entering the valley by large mammals as water-borne transport of seeds in the west–east running wadis cannot account for the upward movement of seeds in the wadis or the north–south directionality in *A. raddiana* genetics.

Some perplexing differences between the Sahara and the southern African deserts occur. There are only eight true desert species shared between the Sahara and the Namib, for example (Werger 1978). The deserts differ considerably in their dominant taxa. The Chenopodiaceae (e.g. *Anabasis, Haloxylon, Artemisia, Calligonum, Ephedra,* and *Retama*) are dominants in the Sahara but are missing from southern African deserts, whereas the Aizoaceae, Amaryllidaceae, Crassulaceae, and Iridaceae (all of which are succulents or geophytes) are very poorly represented in the Sahara (Shmida 1985; Esler *et al.* 1999). This may be because the Namib in particular has been a desert for such a long time (ca. 55–80 million years; Ward *et al.* (1983)) whereas the Sahara has only been a desert for a maximum of about 7 million years (Schuster *et al.* 2006). Interestingly, the gymnosperm genera *Ephedra* (Sahara) and *Welwitschia* (Namib) are now considered to be members of the Ephedraceae in the tribe Gnetales (Price 1996; Jacobson and Lester 2003).

There are a number of geophytes with flattened leaves that lie prostrate on the soil surface in the Succulent Karoo of South Africa (Esler *et al.* 1999) (Fig. 9.18). At least eight families (Amaryllidaceae, Colchicaceae, Eriospermaceae, Geraniaceae, Hyacinthaceae, Iridaceae, Orchidaceae,

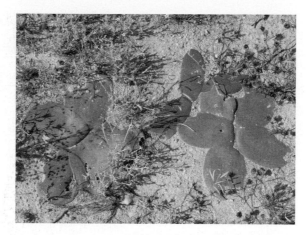

Fig. 9.18   Prostrate-leaved geophytes, *Brunsvigia* sp., from the Succulent Karoo (Namaqualand), South Africa.

Oxalidaceae) contain prostrate-leaved geophytes. Although this growth form occurs infrequently through the summer rainfall temperate regions of Africa, it is virtually absent in other regions in the rest of the world but is relatively common in many geophyte lineages in the Succulent Karoo biome and the Cape mediterranean zone (Fynbos biome) (Esler *et al.* 1999). One might argue that it has evolved from the adjacent fynbos, which is the world's most species-rich biome. However, this does not appear to be the case. A number of reasons have been postulated to explain this. Esler *et al.* (1999) believe that the mild winter temperatures and low variability in annual rainfall are key features for the presence of these geophytes in South Africa.

Schmiedel and Jürgens (1999) worked in the Knersvlakte, which is a quartz field region of the Succulent Karoo, South Africa. They also found very high local species diversity (52 quartz field specialist species), many of which were endemic species (39 species), with many belonging to the sub-family Mesembryanthema (Aizoaceae). Quartz fields supported many tiny, nearly globose, succulent chamaephytes, with convergent growth patterns being demonstrated in two genera *Argyroderma* and *Gibbaeum* (both Aizoaceae). Schmiedel and Jürgens (1999) believe that there is restricted competition from larger growth forms, which are incapable of growing in shallow soils of such low nutrient value and high soil salinity. Similar to Esler *et al.* (1999), Schmiedel and Jürgens (1999) believe that the mild winter temperatures and low variability in annual rainfall contribute to the success of these tiny chamaephytes. With regard to the biogeography of *Argyroderma* on the *knersvlakte*, Ellis and Weis (2006) and Ellis *et al.* (2006) used transplant experiments to demonstrate that there were survival

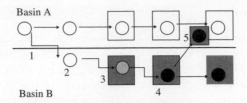

Fig. 9.19   Schematic diagram of radiation in genus *Argyroderma*. There are five stages proposed by Ellis *et al.* (2006): (1) Colonization of spatially isolated drainage basins. (2) Neutral genetic divergence as a result of restricted gene flow between basins. (3) Adaptive phenotypic divergence if the predominant edaphic environments differ between drainage basins. (4) Flowering time shifts associated with morphological changes in different habitats. (5) Range expansion on the same habitat resulting in coexistence of previously isolated taxa differentiated along habitat use and flowering time axes. Stages listed above are indicated by numbers on the diagram. (From Ellis *et al.* 2006. With kind permission of Blackwell Publishing.)

advantages for species that remained in their home sites relative to those that were switched between sparse and dense quartz habitats as well as between microenvironments within the dense quartz habitat. Ellis and Weis (2006) suggested that divergence between *Argyroderma* species occupying different edaphic microenvironments probably results from local adaptation (i.e. $G \times E$ interactions; see also Chapter 11), with coexistence facilitated by response to fine-scale habitat variation (Fig. 9.19).

The two most widespread families in deserts are the Chenopodiaceae and the Zygophyllaceae (Shmida 1985). Some genera, for example, *Artemisia* of the Asteraceae, are widespread in North America and in the Sahara and Arabian deserts, yet are absent from the southern African deserts. Among the 154 genera which Thorne (1973) listed as sub-cosmopolitan, about a quarter are halophytes (including the Chenopodiaceae and Tamaricaceae). Perhaps, once ecomorphological adaptation to extremely salty habitats occurred, there is a higher probability of long-distance dispersal over ocean barriers than salt adaptation occurring *de novo* on another continent (Shmida 1985). Interestingly, the four most important desert families (Aizoaceae, Chenopodiaceae, Portulacaceae, and Zygophyllaceae) are succulent or have members that are succulent (Shmida 1985; Cowling and Hilton-Taylor 1999).

Psammophilous (sand and dune) plants show a similar distribution to the halophytes. For example, in the Middle Eastern deserts, at least a few psammophilous genera (and species), such as *Artemisia monosperma* (Asteraceae), *Pancratium* (Amaryllidaceae), *Danthonia, Panicum,* and *Stipagrostis* (all Poaceae), grow both in deserts and in coastal sands (Danin 1996). A transitional group consists of halophilous–psammophilous taxa (e.g. *Tamarix nilotica* and *Zygophyllum album*) grow on salty sand in the Sahara and near the Mediterranean coast.

9.4.2 Animals

The situations with animals are more complex than with flowering plants (angiosperms) and gymnosperms (e.g. *Welwitschia* (Namib desert) and *Ephedra* (Saharo-Arabian deserts)). For example, the Solifugae (sun spiders) are found across the deserts of the world, with the exception of Australia. Conversely, the genera of invertebrates of ephemeral pools are largely shared across the world's deserts (Whitford 2002). This section will focus on a single taxon, the small mammals, which are rather well known.

There are distinct lineages of desert-dwelling small mammals. Most notable are the Australian taxa, which are mostly marsupials. The largest group of marsupial mammals is the Dasyuridae (e.g. *Antechinomys, Dasyuroides, Sminthopsis*). There are murid (Muridae) lineages in Australia, including two of the most species-rich genera, *Notomys* and *Pseudomys* (Kelt *et al.* 1996). Asian deserts are dominated by the Muridae and the Dipodidae, although there is no overlap of murid genera with those of Australian deserts. The Asian desert murids include the gerbils (Gerbillinae: e.g. *Dipodillus, Gerbillus, Meriones, Tatera*) and the dipodids (represented by *Allactaga, Jaculus,* and *Cardiocranus*). North America has the endemic family Heteromyidae, including the kangaroo rats *Dipodomys* and pocket mice *Perognathus*. The Heteromyidae are unique in that they have external fur-lined cheek pouches, which may be unique for specializing on seeds (Mares *et al.* 1997). North America also has a number of genera of cricetine rodents (Cricetinae). In South America, there are caviomorphs (e.g. *Octodon* and *Octodontomys*) and the more recent but more diverse cricetine group, including the genera *Akodon, Auliscomys, Eligmodontia,* and *Phyllotis*. Thus, each desert has relatively distinct lineages, with no overlap in genera (Kelt *et al.* 1996).

As indicated above, these taxa have evolved from mesic ancestors, on the periphery of the deserts. In North America, pluvial/interpluvial periods plus the presence of seed-specialized heteromyid rodents have led to the importance of granivory at both the local and regional scales (Heske *et al.* 1994). In contrast, the low relief and extensive area of the central Asian deserts (Gobi and Turkestan deserts) and the Australian deserts have not produced frequent isolation between populations, and so have not favoured extensive speciation (contrast this with the extensive radiations of Australian lizards; Morton and James (1988)). This topography has favoured small mammalian species with large geographic ranges and rather low β diversity (Shenbrot *et al.* 1994). The arid regions of Australia have produced mostly omnivores and carnivores, which may reflect phylogenetic conservatism because dasyurid marsupials are mostly carnivorous and conilurine rodents are mostly omnivorous (Kelt *et al.* 1996). However, the Thar desert (India) is relatively small and is bounded by forested areas and is largely anthropogenically derived (due to heavy human pressures) and is conspicuous for its absence of desert-adapted species (Prakash 1974).

The South American deserts show clear dominance by omnivores and folivores at both local and regional scales (Marquet 1994; Meserve *et al.* 1995). There are no water-independent species in South America, strict granivores are few, and carnivory is restricted mostly to the marsupial *Thylamys elegans* (Meserve 1981). The difference in species' diversities between the Sonoran desert (North America) and Monte deserts (South America) is remarkable, given their proximity (Mares *et al.* 1977). There are a number of major differences in the two mammalian faunas as a whole, based on analyses of a single site each:

1. Three orders (Artiodactyla, Lagomorpha, Insectivora) occur in the Sonoran desert and do not occur in the Monte desert.
2. The order Edentata (e.g. armadillo) is absent from the Sonoran desert.
3. Bat and rodent species in the Sonoran desert are about twice as common as in the Monte desert. There are 20 species of bats and 14 rodent species in the Sonoran desert versus nine species of bats and eight species of rodents in the Monte desert (Mares *et al.* 1977).

Mares *et al.* (1977) found that both α and β diversities (at a single site in the Sonoran and Monte deserts) are higher in the Sonoran desert of North America than in the Monte desert of South America. It is possible that the contraction and expansion of arid intermontane basins with each pluvial and interval phase (Schmidly *et al.* 1983) has resulted in greater opportunities for allopatric speciation in North America (especially of heteromyid rodents) than in South American deserts. Glacial cycles seem to have affected South America less strongly than in the northern hemisphere (Clapperton 1993). This is surprising in view of the relatively short distance that taxa would need to cross the Isthmus of Panama.

10 Human impacts and desertification

10.1   The sensitive desert ecosystem: myth or reality?

There is a common myth that deserts are extremely sensitive to perturbation. While it is true that tracks made decades ago can still be seen in certain desert areas (Belnap and Warren 2002; Kade and Warren 2002), there are also large regions of deserts that show little negative impact of heavy use by humans. This paradox can be explained by considering the interactions between the high spatial and temporal variability in rainfall and patterns of human disturbance.

Desertification is of great concern in many parts of the world, yet people struggle to define it. Historical patterns of climate indicate that there are cycles of drought and also cycles of higher rainfall (Nicholson 1978). However, drought alone cannot be responsible for desertification but can add to the problem. Clearly, losses of agricultural productivity are associated with the process of desertification, although these can have other causes such as declining returns from certain agricultural products (Milton et al. 1994). Indeed, it is the long-term decline in productivity and ecosystem function that are most closely tied to desertification. These are usually caused by direct human intervention. However, Emanuel et al. (1985) have predicted a 17% increase in the global desert lands because of climate changes expected with a doubling of atmospheric CO_2 concentrations, which may exacerbate the problem of desertification. The most important cause of desertification is pastoralism (Fig. 10.1), although North America is most negatively affected by agricultural use. Among the negative impacts of desertification, soil salinization, harvesting of woody plants for fuel (including use by non-desert communities), low agricultural productivity (especially in producing crops not ideally suited to the lands), and housing and related development are among the most obvious.

In South Africa, desirable forage species may be replaced by species that are inedible to livestock (Milton et al. 1994; Mbatha and Ward 2006),

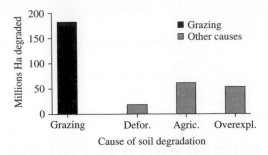

Fig. 10.1   Causes of soil degradation in Africa. Defor. = deforestation; Agric. = agricultural; Overexpl. = overexploitation from various sources. (From UNEP 2006.)

while in Australia, southern Africa, and North America, the replacement of grasslands by woody species are particularly negative effects of desert-ification. In South Africa, up to 20 million ha are affected by woody plant encroachment (Hoffman and Ashwell 2001; Ward 2005b). Desertification in some form is estimated to have occurred over about 42% of arid and semi-arid lands in Australia (Ludwig and Tongway 1995). The most common form of desertification in Australia is loss of perennial grasses from grasslands, savannas, and open woodlands, often with a replacement by inedible shrubs. This is especially a problem during droughts when grazing pressures reduce ground cover, making landscapes vulnerable to wind and water erosion (Ludwig and Tongway 1995). In the Atacama desert (Peru), desertification results from the replacement of perennial grasses with unpalatable native and exotic annuals and by an unpalatable tree *Acacia caven* (Fabaceae) (Ovalle *et al.* 1993), and in the Monte desert of Argentina, a woody tree *Geoffroea decorticans* (Fabaceae) invades the arid and semi-arid regions (Whitford 2002). In the Gobi and Taklamakan deserts of China, widespread dune formation has reduced agricultural productivity as has soil salinization caused by poor agricultural practices (Tang and Zhang 2001; Cui and Shao 2005).

A number of examples of desertification can help understand the diversity of processes that may lead to desertification:

1. Sinclair and Fryxell (1985) have considered the Sahel as a classical dis-aster zone. This area on the southern edge of the Sahara has a huge human and livestock population. Sinclair and Fryxell (1985) consider the following scenario as being integral to understanding the problem (Fig. 10.2): when herds of animals are kept in fixed places they tend to overgraze. This leads to raised albedo levels, which in turn leads to hotter soil, which in turn leads to reduced thermals and less rain. The situation perpetuates itself because less rain means that the live-stock are forced to eat the remaining vegetation. On the other hand, if livestock are allowed to be nomadic, albedo levels are ultimately lower,

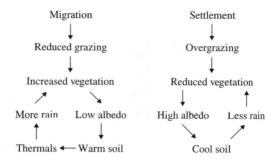

Fig. 10.2   Sinclair and Fryxell (1985) consider the absence of nomadism (migration) as being integral to understanding the problem of rangeland degradation. (From Sinclair and Fryxell 1985. With kind permission of National Research Council, Canada.)

which increases rainfall (Fig. 10.2). This is consistent with Hardin's (1968) *tragedy of the commons* model, which holds that in a communal system, each person stands to benefit by one animal for each one owned but the costs are shared by all, leading to the ultimate degradation of the lands. Schlesinger *et al.* (1990) have followed on from Sinclair and Fryxell's model to include more explicit incorporation of the positive feedback effects of moisture and the vegetation to include nutrients, especially nitrogen, which is the single most important limiting nutrient in deserts (Fig. 10.3). Schlesinger *et al.* (1990) consider the effects of increasing soil heterogeneity to be among the most important negative effects on arid regions, and one that can lead to the conversion of grasslands into shrublands (Schlesinger *et al.* (1996); see *bush encroachment* below). Greater soil heterogeneity can also be caused by off-road motor vehicles, which leads to the channelization of run-off and increased soil erosion (Webb 1982).

2. Erosion in Negev desert (Israel) wadis has been continuing since climatic changes during the Late Pleistocene–Early Holocene period, resulting in declines in dust deposition (Ward *et al.* 2001; Avni *et al.* 2006). Severe erosion causes the formation of gullies and channels, resulting in the formation of waterfalls during the winter floods in many wadi systems in the central Negev desert of Israel. These were caused by higher rain intensity at the end of the Pleistocene (Avni *et al.* 2006). In some areas, erosion of the original loess substrate has been complete, so that the underlying rock has been exposed (Fig. 10.4). Establishment of run-off harvesting farms in the 3rd century CE (mostly by Nabatean people) interrupted the Holocene natural erosion and gully incision, and led to the redeposition of up to 3.5 m of fine alluvial loess sediments originating from Late Pleistocene loess sections (Avni *et al.* 2006) as run-off from the hillslopes accumulated in the wadis. Ward *et al.* (2001) examined the effects of this erosion in four wadis in the central Negev desert on soil nutrients and

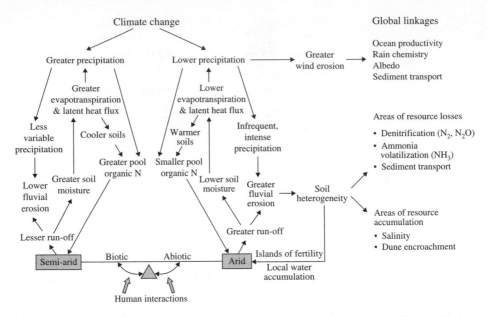

Fig. 10.3   The main effects of desertification on nutrients in arid ecosystems. (From Schlesinger *et al.* 1990.)

Fig. 10.4   Eroded waterfall in Nahal Zipporim, Negev desert, Israel.

plant community structure. They found significant negative effects of erosion on soil organic carbon, nitrate nitrogen, and water-holding capacity. Erosion resulted in an increase in plant species richness and significantly altered plant community structure in eroded areas of wadis. In addition to the loss of biodiversity that may result, this erosion may result in economic hardship for the Bedouin peoples whose herds depend on these resources (Ward *et al.* 2001). The establishment of run-off harvesting agriculture, which resulted in the accumulation of re-deposited loess

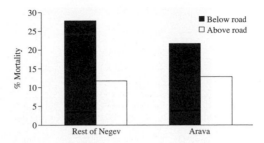

Fig. 10.5   *Acacia raddiana* mortality on the lower side of low-lying bridges is far higher than on the upper side. Similar values were recorded in the Syrian-African Rift valley (Arava) and in the rest of the Negev. (Modified from Ward and Rohner 1997.)

sediments from hillslopes, counteracted the natural trend of soil erosion (Avni *et al.* 2006).

3. Ward and Rohner (1997) studied the causes of large-scale mortality of *Acacia* trees in Negev desert wadis. In 75 wadis distributed across the Negev desert, they found that low-lying bridges were the cause of this problem. These bridges, pejoratively called 'Irish bridges' by the British soldiers during the Mandate period (1917–48) because they pass under rather than over the ephemeral waters, do not allow water to pass as easily to the lower parts of the rivers. Consequently, mortality of Acacias is far higher (as high as 61%) on the lower side of these bridges than on the upper side (Fig. 10.5).

4. High soil salinity occurs naturally in the desert environment. However, soil salinization is associated with irrigated areas that have poor water management, raising the natural salinity of the soil to the soil surface (Cui and Shao 2005). Another way in which arid areas can have raised levels of soil salinization occurs when native vegetation is removed, which alters water balance and evaporative flux (Amezketa 2006). Although climate, natural drainage patterns, topographic features, geological structure, parent material, and distance to the sea are natural factors influencing soil salinity, inappropriate irrigation methods, poor water quality, insufficient drainage, poor land management, overexploitation of groundwater, the clearing of trees, and the alteration of the natural water balance are important anthropogenic (agricultural) factors (Tang and Zhang 2001; Cui and Shao 2005; Amezketa 2006; Masoud and Koike 2006).

Soil salinization reduces soil quality, limits the growth of crops, constrains agricultural productivity, and in severe cases, leads to the abandonment of agricultural soils (Amezketa 2006) (Fig. 10.6). Thus, it is in desert margin areas that this type of desertification is most likely to occur. In China, about half of the land area has less than 200 mm year^{-1} of precipitation

Fig. 10.6   Sugar farms along the Nile River (desert in the distance).

(Tang and Zhang 2001). Soil salinization in northwestern China affects about 2 million ha, which makes up about one third of the saline area of China (Cui and Shao 2005). In the northwestern desert of Egypt (part of the Sahara), according to Misak *et al.* (1997), during 1962–77, the rate of the rise in the groundwater table in the Siwa oasis was 1.33 cm year^{-1}, while during 1977–90 it was 4.6 cm year^{-1}. Masoud and Koike (2006) found that soil salinization led to vegetation death in the Siwa oasis after the year 2000 largely as a result of improper soil drainage and a lack of an effective water resource management system. The water table has now reached the ground surface in some areas, causing an advanced stage of salinization. As a result, extensive patches have been gradually converted into salt marshes (Masoud and Koike 2006).

10.2   Pastoralism is the most important use of desert lands

The most important cause of desertification is grazing (Milton *et al.* 1994; UNEP 1996; Middleton and Thomas 1997) (Fig. 10.1). In general, where nomadic pastoralism can continue, these effects are less pronounced or even absent (Sinclair and Fryxell 1985). Similarly, where plants have sufficient time to recover from heavy grazing, these effects can be minimized. Some of the most obvious negative consequences of heavy grazing include

1. *Piosphere effects:* Osborn *et al.* (1932) were the first in Australia to recognize the radial symmetry in grazing intensity that develops around a water point. Osborn *et al.* (1932) used this radial symmetry to examine the effects of grazing on vegetation along transects radiating from water. Grazing impact is greatest close to a water point and decreases with distance from the water because livestock have to return regularly

(a)  (b)

Fig. 10.7   Fenceline contrast from (a) the Namib, Namibia. Mean annual rainfall = 150 mm, and (b) from the arid Northern Cape province, South Africa. Mean annual rainfall = 360 mm.

to drink. Lange (1969) coined the term *piosphere* for this water focused grazing pattern. Valentine (1947) also drew attention to the graduated use of forage away from an artificial water point in a black grama (*Bouteloua eriopoda*) grassland in the Chihuahuan Desert of North America. Valentine (1947) proposed that overstocking of lands in the southwestern desert areas of the United States had caused the failure to account for non-uniform use of forage in a paddock. As well as grazing effects, there are also effects from trampling and dust associated with the movement of animals close to the water point (Andrew and Lange 1986a, b). James *et al.* (1999) have described the piosphere effects in arid Australian ecosystems as follows:

a. The area near a watering point is usually bare, but supports short-lived, often unpalatable, trample-resistant species after rain. Trampling is most obvious within 100 m of the water point. This zone is often called the 'sacrifice zone'.
b. A dense zone of unpalatable woody shrubs usually occurs immediately beyond the denuded area.
c. Palatable perennial plants decline in abundance and species richness within zones a and b.
d. Species richness does not change consistently with increasing distance from water points.

An important effect can be seen in fenceline contrasts (e.g. Fig. 10.7a and b). Here, too, differences can be observed for the wrong reason because they may merely indicate short-term differences caused by grazing a paddock immediately prior to that observation. Nonetheless, Hendricks *et al.* (2005) in arid Namaqualand, South Africa, and Smet and Ward (2005, 2006) in the arid Northern Cape, South Africa, have shown that piosphere effects around water points can be significant. Similar techniques were used by Hanan *et al.* (1991) to examine piosphere effects around boreholes in Senegal, in the Sahel region of Africa. However, Hanan *et al.* (1991) found no consistent patterns in primary production with increasing distance from water points during the wet season and concluded that piosphere effects on vegetation, if present, were overridden by variation due to local topography, soil, and rainfall patterns. Jeltsch *et al.* (1997) measured differences in vegetation at two sites in the Kalahari desert (South Africa/Botswana). They then mathematically simulated a high rainfall site (385 mm) and a low rainfall site (220 mm). Jeltsch *et al.* (1997) have shown that distinct piospheres occur at the high rainfall site (as indicated by James *et al.* (1999) above) whereas at the low rainfall site, piosphere zone development is limited and influenced by rainfall alone.

2. Ward *et al.* (2000b) recorded that the communal ranching area of Otjimbingwe in Namibia (mean annual rainfall = 165 mm) had experienced a change in the people occupying these lands. During the time that Charles John Andersson (1856) occupied the lands as a trader, all of the people living there were otjiHerero speakers. The Damara peoples lived at least 60 km away (Fig. 10.8). The Herero people are very closely associated with their cattle, relying on them for meat and milk. In contrast, the Damara people were mostly vegetarian, although some of them consumed small stock such as goats and sheep. Today, there are approximately the same number of Herero and Damara people living in Otjimbingwe. This led Ward *et al.* (1998, 2000b) to believe that a possible reason for the change in population occupying Otjimbingwe had been land degradation, especially since Andersson (1856) and Lau (1989)

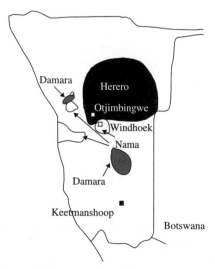

Fig. 10.8   Map of distribution of tribal groups of people around Otjimbingwe. The main tribal groups in this region are Herero, Damara, and Nama.

from Andersson's diaries had recorded as many as 14,000 cattle being present at certain water points in Otjimbingwe during Andersson's time there. Ward *et al.* (2000b) found that the numbers of people had increased dramatically since the mid-1950s. Fuller (1993) found that the number of people living in Otjimbingwe fluctuated considerably between 1920 and 1955, but that there were now some 8,500 people living there (Fig. 10.9). In addition, people had been able to produce as much as 95 tonnes of wheat in the Swakop river that runs ephemerally through Otjimbingwe.

Ward *et al.* (1998) compared the diversity of plants in the communal area of Otjimbingwe that has been heavily grazed for at least 150 years with that of several surrounding commercial cattle and sheep ranches where mean stocking density was about 10 times lower. No significant difference in diversity, plant species richness, or soil quality was found. However, within the 117,000 ha communal ranch, vegetation around water points that had been in use for 150 years (i.e. these were sites mentioned as having large stock numbers by Andersson (Lau 1989)) was more degraded than vegetation near water points that had only been in use for about 10 years (Fig. 10.10) (see *piosphere* effects above). This indicates that herbivores can have strong negative impacts on vegetation of deserts but that such impacts may take a very long time (at least 80 years in this case) to manifest themselves. Ward *et al.* (1998) also found that there were differences in the diversity of large mammals between communal and commercial ranches. Commercial ranches had a variety of species

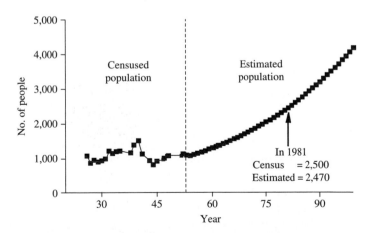

Fig. 10.9 Fuller (1993) found that the number of people living in Otjimbingwe fluctuated considerably between 1920 and 1955. There are currently (2008) some 8,500 people living there. A 3% increment in population growth (Namibia's national average population growth rate) was used post-1955 to predict population growth. Note the similarity in values between the last population census and the predicted value.

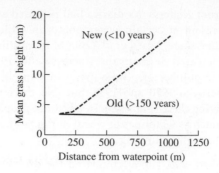

Fig. 10.10   Vegetation around water points that had been in use for 150 years (i.e. these were sites mentioned as having large stock numbers by Charles John Andersson) was more degraded than vegetation near water points that had only been in use for about 10 years. Lines are regression lines of sample means.

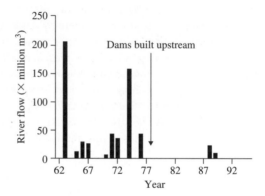

Fig. 10.11   Water flow in the Swakop river at Westfalenhof weir immediately upstream from Otjimbingwe. Water flowed through Otjimbingwe only a few times since the reservoirs were built in the mid-1970s to provide water to the capital city of Windhoek and to Okahandja, resulting in an absence of wheat production in the ephemeral Swakop river at Otjimbingwe.

such as kudu *Tragelaphus strepsiceros*, gemsbok *Oryx gazella*, Hartmann's mountain zebra *Equus zebra hartmannae*, and springbok *Antidorcas marsupialis*, while the only species that the communal ranch had was the steenbok *Raphicerus campestris*. The main reason for the lack of wheat production in the ephemeral Swakop river was that two reservoirs were built upstream to provide water to the capital city of Windhoek and to Okahandja (see water flow in the Swakop river—Fig. 10.11), causing water to flow through Otjimbingwe only a few times since the dams were built in the mid-1970s.

3. In a large-scale study in Namibia at 31 sites along a rainfall gradient from 100 to 450 mm per annum, there was no correlation between the

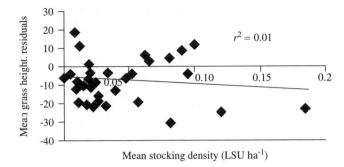

Fig. 10.12   There was no correlation between the residuals of grass production (regressed against mean annual rainfall to account for variation along the rainfall gradient) and stocking density (expressed as large stock units (LSU) per hectare) either in the current season or when averaged over the previous 11 years, as indicated in the figure. (From Ward and Ngairorue 2000.)

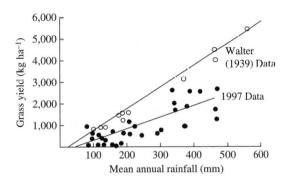

Fig. 10.13   Ward and Ngairorue (2000) compared data along the same gradient between 1939 and 1997, grass production in 1997 was approximately 50% lower than that in the earlier period. (From Ward and Ngairorue 2000.)

residuals of grass production (regressed against mean annual rainfall) and stocking density either in the current season or when averaged over the previous 11 years (Ward and Ngairorue 2000—Fig. 10.12). However, they compared data along the same gradient between 1939 and 1997, grass production in 1997 was approximately 50% lower than in the earlier period (Ward and Ngairorue 2000) (Fig. 10.13). This is yet another example of the longer-term impact of herbivory in such systems.

10.2.1   Oscillations of vegetation and herbivore populations

Researchers have become increasingly aware in recent years that arid grazing ecosystems are non-equilibrial, event-driven systems (Westoby 1980;

O'Connor 1985; Venter *et al.* 1989; Milchunas *et al.* 1988, 1989; Hoffman and Cowling 1990a). Ellis and Swift (1988) have contended that rainfall in arid regions is the major driving factor and has the ability to 'recharge' a system that suffers heavy grazing pressure. This can lead to oscillations of herbivore and plant populations, as envisaged for the arid Turkana region of Kenya by Ellis and Swift (1988) (Fig. 10.14).

Indeed, it has been claimed that where pastoralists are able to maintain their activities on a large spatial scale by migrating to areas where key rich resources can be exploited, allowing previously used resources time to recover, negative density-dependent effects of grazing on plant biodiversity do not develop (Sinclair and Fryxell 1985; Ellis and Swift 1988; Behnke and Abel 1996). Illius and O'Connor (2000) have suggested that herbivore populations use key preferred habitats or resources for much of the year and only move out of those habitats when resources are limiting. Consequently, one might not find any significant effects of mammalian herbivory in arid ecosystems at large, yet negative density-dependent effects of heavy grazing are likely to be found in key habitats. Where these habitats are provided with artificial water points, such problems might be particularly acute. Based on the field data from a Kalahari desert grazing system, spatially explicit modelling by Weber *et al.* (2000) indicates that the existence of long-term negative effects of herbivory depends on whether herbivores cause reductions in plant productivity (rather than short-term reductions in plant biomass) and local mortality of plant species during periods of reduced plant availability (see also O'Connor 1991). Such mortality may result in a change in plant species composition, and if the newly dominant species are less palatable to herbivores, then it will ultimately lead to rangeland degradation. Thus, Ellis and Swift's (1988) model mentioned above may be suitable for arid vegetation only if grazing does not differentially affect species and thereby alter species composition through changes in competitive interactions. Should there be any changes caused by, for example, changes in competitive

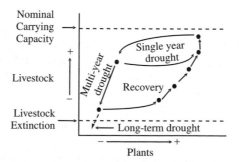

Fig. 10.14   Oscillations of herbivore and plant populations as envisaged for the arid Turkana region of Kenya by Ellis and Swift (1988). (From Ellis and Swift 1988.)

interactions or grazing-induced changes in dominance of particular species, the Ellis and Swift (1988) model will be inappropriate.

10.2.2 Bush or shrub encroachment

One of the most interesting, and enigmatic, purported effects of herbivory by large mammals is the initiation of bush encroachment (in North America, this phenomenon is known as shrub encroachment). In the past 50 years, evidence has accumulated suggesting that arid and semi-arid ecosystems throughout the world are being altered by bush encroachment (Hennessy *et al.* 1983; Idso 1992; reviewed by Archer *et al.* 1995; Scholes and Archer 1997). Bush encroachment is the suppression of palatable grasses and herbs by encroaching woody species (Fig. 10.15a and b). These woody species are often unpalatable to domestic livestock because they are thorny or have high fibre content (Lamprey 1983; Scholes and Walker 1993; Ward 2005b) (Fig. 10.16).

Factors causing bush encroachment are poorly understood. The first attempt at a general explanation for bush encroachment was Walter's (1939) two-layer hypothesis for tree–grass coexistence (Walter 1954; Noy-Meir 1982). Walter (1939, 1971) explained the coexistence of these two different life forms in terms of root separation. He assumed water to be the major limiting factor for both grassy and woody plants and hypothesized that grasses use only topsoil moisture, while woody plants mostly use subsoil moisture. Under this assumption, removal of grasses (e.g. by heavy grazing) allows more water to percolate into the sub-soil, where it is available for woody plant growth. This allows for mass recruitment of trees, leading to bush encroachment. Note that in arid and semi-arid ecosystems, cohorts of similarly aged trees have been widely reported, indicating

(a)   (b)

Fig. 10.15   Bush (shrub) encroachment in (a) the Namib desert, where mean annual rainfall is 150 mm, and (b) the Thar desert, near Bhuj, Gujarat, India, where mean annual rainfall is about 300 mm. In the Namib desert, the encroaching species is native (*Acacia reficiens*) while in Gujarat, the species is exotic (*Prosopis juliflora*).

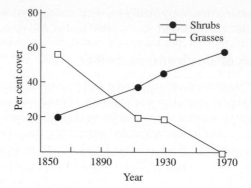

Fig. 10.16   Changes in % land area dominated by shrubs and grass on the Jornada experimental range from 1858 until 1962. Areas with >55% mesquite (*Prosopis*) increased from 2,500 ha to 27,000 ha, creosotebush (*Larrea*) from zero cover to 5,000 ha and tarbush (*Flourensia*) from no cover to 1,800 ha. (From Reynolds *et al.* 2000.)

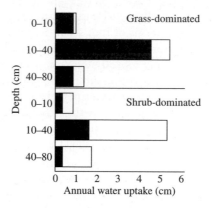

Fig. 10.17   Model predictions of the source of soil water transpired by various plant functional types in grass-dominated and shrub-dominated regions. The averages of 100-year simulations are shown as grouped by three major soil depths, indicating the depth that plants will place most of their roots. Black: annuals, forbs, and grasses; white: subshrubs and *Larrea tridentata*. (From Reynolds *et al.* 2000.)

repeated phases of mass recruitment (Reid and Ellis 1995; Wiegand *et al.* 2005, 2006). Hence, it is the initiation of bush encroachment that is considered the crucial stage in arid ecosystems and not the control of adult tree densities as may be the case in mesic regions (Higgins *et al.* 2000).

Reynolds *et al.* (2000) suggested that, because of the relatively shallow distribution of soil water, there is little opportunity for vertical partitioning of the soil water resource by differential rooting depths of the plant functional types, in contrast to the two-layer hypothesis of Walter (1971). However, functional types may avoid competition by keying on particular 'windows' of moisture availability via differences in phenologies (Fig. 10.17).

Although the two-layer theory is still widely accepted (Skarpe 1990a), field data and theoretical models have produced conflicting evidence. Several field studies have shown the increase of shrub or tree abundance under heavy grazing (van Vegten 1983; Skarpe 1990a, b; Perkins and Thomas 1993). However, the recruitment of honey mesquite, *Prosopis glandulosa*, a bush-encroaching tree in North America, is unrelated to herbaceous biomass or density, indicating that release from competition with grasses is not required for mass tree recruitment to occur (Brown and Archer 1989, 1999). Similarly, while some models have shown that the two-layer hypothesis may indeed lead to tree–grass coexistence (Walker *et al.* 1981; Walker and Noy-Meir 1982), a spatially explicit simulation model by Jeltsch *et al.* (1996) showed that rooting niche separation might not be sufficient to warrant coexistence under a range of climatic situations.

Field studies investigating root distribution and water uptake also produced mixed results. In these studies, great differences were observed in the degree of niche separation, depending on abiotic factors and the species involved (Hesla *et al.* 1985; Knoop and Walker 1985; Weltzin and McPherson 1997; see also Scholes and Archer (1997) and Higgins *et al.* (2000) for further references). Clearly, rooting niche separation cannot be an explanation for the *initiation* of bush encroachment because young trees use the same subsurface soil layer as grasses in the sensitive early stages of growth. Heavy grazing is not a sufficient cause of bush encroachment. For example, the trader and naturalist, Charles John Andersson (1856), reported heavy bush encroachment in areas in Namibia that were, according to his and other independent historical records, not heavily grazed. Andersson (1856) took three days to ride his horse 40 km along the length of the Waterberg in Namibia because of the high density of thorn bushes in that area! Subsequently, German troops stationed in the area recorded the region as being unencroached (and photographed it). Today, the region is again encroached, indicating some cyclicity to the pattern of encroachment. Heavy grazing in combination with rooting niche separation is not a prerequisite for bush encroachment because bush encroachment sometimes occurs on soils too shallow to allow for root separation (Wiegand *et al.* 2005). To date, mitigation protocols based on the two-layer theory (e.g. reducing livestock densities in years with below-average rainfall) have failed to reduce bush encroachment, indicating that the causes of the problem are poorly understood (Teague and Smit 1992; Smit *et al.* 1996).

As a consequence of the inadequacy of previous explanations for the occurrence of bush encroachment, several new hypotheses have been put forward to explain tree–grass coexistence. Disturbances have been mooted as major determinants of savanna structure, with savannas being portrayed as inherently unstable ecosystems that oscillate in an intermediate state between those of stable grasslands and forests because they are pushed back into the savanna state by frequent disturbances such as human impact (Scholes and Archer 1997; Jeltsch *et al*. 1998; Jeltsch *et al*. 2000), fire (Higgins *et al*. 2000), herbivory or drought (Scholes and Walker 1993), and spatial heterogeneities in water, nutrient, and seed distribution (Jeltsch *et al*. 1996). These disturbance-based hypotheses all suggest that bush encroachment occurs when disturbances shift savannas from open grassland towards the forest end of the environmental spectrum. All of these hypotheses may be valid for specific situations but may lack generality. None of these purported mechanisms of bush encroachment has been convincingly demonstrated under field conditions.

In an attempt to tease apart the various purported factors causing bush encroachment, Wiegand *et al*. (2006) used patch dynamic models, and showed that unique rainfall conditions led to mass recruitment of trees. Subsequently, trees started to compete with one another. This led to what they called a 'honeycomb rippling' model of competition, where trees were further apart and more evenly spaced as they grew. This model of competition was supported in a Namib desert study, where trees were situated at greater distances from one another as they grew (Wiegand *et al*. 2005) and the coefficient of variation in nearest-neighbour distances declined with increasing size (i.e. they became more evenly spaced; Ward (2005b)). To test these ideas, Kraaij and Ward (2006) ran multifactorial experiments in a semi-arid area north of Kimberley (Northern Cape, South Africa; mean annual rainfall = 360 mm) using encroaching *Acacia mellifera*. They found that rainfall addition to the maximum recorded in that area (about 800 mm) increased *A. mellifera* germination and survival, whereas nitrogen addition (30 g m^{-2}) decreased *A. mellifera* germination and survival by increasing the competitiveness of grasses (Fig. 10.18). Fire and grazing did not affect tree seedling germination and survival. They stressed that high rainfall *frequency* rather than rainfall *amount* resulted in germination and survival of *A. mellifera* trees. Doubling the annual mean rainfall (800 mm as opposed to 360 mm) did not lead to bush encroachment in the field when added twice per month over the growing season, while applying the same amount every two days for a month led to significant germination of tree seedlings.

These results may alter the way the problem of bush encroachment is approached, that is, as a problem initiated by unique rainfall conditions that may or may not be exacerbated by certain types of grazing, fire or, other disturbed conditions (Ward 2002, 2005b). One can model the management implications of rainfall effects on the initiation of bush encroachment as follows: without grazing or other disturbance, both grass and tree biomass increase with increasing rainfall. In an unwooded grazing system,

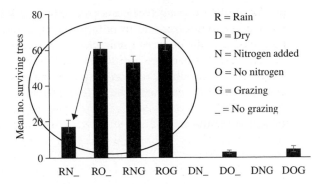

R = Rain
D = Dry
N = Nitrogen added
O = No nitrogen
G = Grazing
_ = No grazing

Fig. 10.18   Heavy rainfall is the most important factor affecting recruitment of tree seedlings. Nitrogen also has a significant effect (see arrow). Results are from a pot experiment. (From Kraaij and Ward 2006. Rain = received maximal rainfall; Dry = average rainfall; Nitrogen added = 30 g m^{-2} N once per month during summer, Grazing = clipped once per month during summer.)

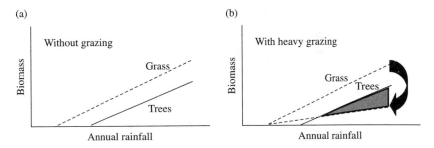

Fig. 10.19   Production of biomass vs. mean annual precipitation. (a) Grass production starts at lower mean annual precipitation (about 20 mm) whereas tree production starts at about 100 mm. (b) When there is disturbance, such as grazing, grass is removed. Note that the higher the rainfall, the greater the production of tree biomass.

grass biomass always exceeds tree biomass (Fig. 10.19a). When heavy grazing (or any form of disturbance) occurs, grass biomass per unit rainfall is reduced, reducing competition with trees (Fig. 10.19b). This releases water and nutrient resources for trees to germinate *en masse*. Because there is a greater probability that trees will recruit when rainfall is higher, the difference between tree and grass biomass increases with increasing rainfall. Therefore, the management consequence in areas prone to bush encroachment is that ranchers should limit stock in *wet* years and not in dry years (because trees cannot germinate).

Thus, the mitigation protocol for bush encroachment under this hypothesis differs considerably from those under the two-layer competition hypothesis. Under the conventional two-layer competition hypothesis, grazing during years with less than average precipitation should be reduced to a minimum so as not to give the trees a competitive advantage. In contrast, based on the results from the multifactorial experiments mentioned above, bush encroachment does not occur when water is limited and consequently such a management protocol would be futile. Thus, if tree–grass competition occurs, grazing should be reduced in years with greater than average rainfall, especially in open grazing lands (Fig. 10.19b).

10.2.3 Invasive species

The most reliable indicator of potential for a plant species to invade is weedy or invasive behaviour, such as taking over disturbed habitats, by that species or by congenerics (Scott and Panetta 1993). Repeated introductions over many years may further increase the probability that a species will become invasive (Scott and Panetta 1993). Plant invasions in Australian, North American, and the Karoo of South Africa habitats have been most severe along watercourses (Loope *et al.* 1988; Milton *et al.* 1999; Cronk and Fuller 2001). For example, invasions by *Tamarix* from Asia have followed the Colorado River and the Rio Grande in North America, and the Finke River in Australia. In the Karoo, the extent of invasion by exotic *Tamarix* species may be underestimated because they morphologically resemble a native species, *T. usneoides* (Milton *et al.* 1999). All *Tamarix* trees are reputed to increase soil salinity, lower water tables, and to reduce diversity of reptiles and birds (Griffin *et al.* 1989; Ellis 1995; Milton *et al.* 1999). *Nicotiana glauca* has invaded rivers in North America, Australia, and the Middle East (Milton *et al.* 1999; pers. obs.).

Milton *et al.* (1999) considers four families of plants in the arid Karoo (South Africa) to be particularly invasive, namely, Cactaceae (especially *Opuntia*), Fabaceae (especially *Prosopis*), Chenopodiaceae (especially *Atriplex* and *Salsola*), and Poaceae (especially perennial African C_4 species and annual C_3 species). *Opuntia ficus-indica* has been a major pest in the Karoo and *O. stricta* and *O. inermis* in Australian habitats. Feral livestock, especially pigs and donkeys, took refuge in these areas, making their control very difficult. Severe grazing took place in the remaining areas. In the Karoo, Du Toit (1942) estimated that this species infested as much as 900,000 ha. A phycitid moth *Cactoblastis cactorum* was introduced from Australia in 1932 and a cochineal bug *Dactylopius opuntiae* was brought in and proved to be effective biological control agents against *O. ficus-indica*. *D. opuntiae* was found to be more effective in South Africa, while *C. cactorum* was more effective in Australia (Milton *et al.* 1999). The African lovegrasses, *Eragrostis curvula* and *E. lehmanniana*, were introduced from Africa into North American deserts in the 1930s in an attempt to reclaim natural grasslands damaged by heavy grazing and cultivation (Bock *et al.* 1986, 2007) but are now spreading into undisturbed rangelands (McClaran and Anable 1992). Mediterranean annual grasses, particularly cheatgrass *Bromus tectorum*, also invaded

North American arid lands (Mack 1981). Milton *et al.* (1999) are concerned about the invasion of C₃ grasses into the Succulent Karoo, which is widely regarded as the most species-rich succulent flora.

10.2.4 Global climate changes

As indicated above, Emanuel *et al.* (1985) have predicted a dramatic increase in the global desert lands due to climate changes expected with a doubling of the atmospheric CO_2 concentrations, which may exacerbate the problem of desertification. Midgley and Thuiller (2007) have shown that some key Succulent Karoo plant lineages originated during cool Pleistocene times, and projected air temperatures under anthropogenic climate change are likely to exceed these significantly. Projected rainfall patterns are less certain, and projected values for coastal fog are unavailable, but if either of these two parameters also change together with rising temperatures, this seems certain to threaten the persistence of, at least, narrowly endemic plant species (see projected changes in the distribution of such narrowly endemic Namaqualand (South Africa) shrub species as *Ruschia caroli* and *R. robusta* (Fig. 10.20)).

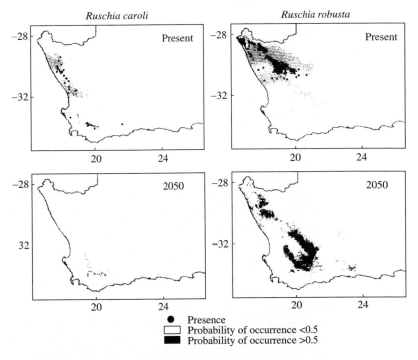

Fig. 10.20   Map of projected distributions of *Ruschia caroli* and *R. robusta* in Namaqualand under projected global climate change. (From Midgley and Thuiller 2007. With kind permission of Elsevier.)

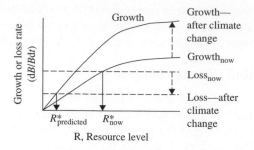

Fig. 10.21   Projected changes in R* under global CO_2 changes (adapted from Tilman 1988). R* is the point at which there is an equilibrium between growth and loss. Growth increases because C_3 trees grow faster than C_4 grasses under increased CO_2 and loss may decrease because trees are better defended than grasses through the presence of tannins.

Unlike the predicted situation with rising temperatures and/or changes in rainfall and coastal fog, bush or shrub encroachment may become particularly acute in many semi-arid habitats because of the effects of elevated CO_2. The net photosynthetic rates of C_3 plants relative to C_4 plants is likely to switch, so that higher photosynthetic rates will be recorded from C_3 plants such as encroaching trees rather than the current situation where C_4 grasses have higher photosynthetic rates. Consequently, C_3 trees are likely to grow faster under higher expected levels of CO_2 than grasses. If this is also associated with higher defence levels if these trees use tannins or other carbon-based polyphenols, then this problem will be exacerbated (see Fig. 10.21).

It is often thought that there may be an increase in the amount of carbon stored in ecosystems where encroachment of woody vegetation has occurred. For this reason, shrub or bush expansion could be considered to have a positive effect on carbon stores or sinks. This may be viewed as positive by researchers studying climate change effects because carbon storage benefits ecosystems by reducing the effects of CO_2 emissions from fossil fuels into the atmosphere (Pacala et al. 2001; Guo and Gifford 2002). Jackson et al. (2002) studied woody plant invasion along a precipitation gradient from 200 to 1,100 mm year[-1] by comparing carbon and nitrogen budgets and soil $\delta^{13}C$ profiles between six pairs of adjacent grasslands in the Chihuahuan desert (North America) in which one of each pair of grasslands was invaded by woody vegetation 30–100 years ago. They found that there was a negative correlation between changes in soil organic carbon (and nitrogen) content and precipitation, with drier sites gaining and wetter sites losing organic carbon and nitrogen (Jackson et al. 2002) (Fig. 10.22a and b). They concluded that assessments based on increased carbon storage from woody plant invasions to balance emissions were incorrect.

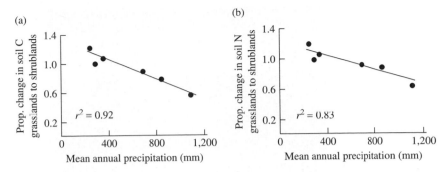

Fig. 10.22   Jackson *et al.* (2002) found a negative correlation in (a) soil organic carbon and (b) nitrogen budgets between six pairs of adjacent grasslands in the Chihuahuan desert (North America) in which one of each pair of grasslands was invaded by woody vegetation 30–100 years ago. (From Jackson *et al.* 2002. With kind permission of Nature Publishing Group.)

10.3   Military manoeuvres threaten some desert habitats and protect others

Military training areas hold great potential benefits for species and ecosystem conservation through the large areas under their control. However, military training exercises in desert areas have resulted in various disturbances through time (Belnap and Warren 2002; Kade and Warren 2002) (Fig. 10.23). For example, at the U.S. Army Yuma Proving Ground in southwestern Arizona, which served as a military base camp during World War II, there were a variety of disturbances, including vehicle traffic and foot traffic (tent rows, commons, and footpaths). Kade and Warren (2002) assessed the extent of soil and plant recovery in the period since abandonment by comparing sites with historic disturbance to an apparently undisturbed control site. The tented area, disturbed primarily by foot traffic, did not show full recovery of vegetation and biological soil crusts to pre-disturbance conditions. The slow recovery may be due to grading that removed topsoil and seed sources when the camp was established. In contrast, surprisingly perhaps, most plant species at the motor pool (i.e. vehicle use site) exhibited higher density and greater foliar cover than was found at the control site. This may be the result of a compacted soil layer that enhanced soil–water relations of the upper horizon of the sandy soil and provided fine plant roots with a greater amount of moisture, or it may be a consequence of the intermediate disturbance hypothesis, which suggests that there is a unimodal relationship between disturbance and plant cover (Horn 1975; Connell 1978).

Belnap and Warren (2002) found that tracks from military vehicles during the World War II period were still visible (as have Webb *et al.* (1978)

Fig. 10.23   Vehicle in the Namib.

and Webb (1982) for more recent tracks by off-road vehicles), particularly in areas of desert pavement, or *reg* (see Chapter 2). Compaction of desert soils is a major factor inducing accelerated soil erosion (Snyder *et al.* 1976; Iverson 1980) and decreased plant growth (Webb and Wilshire 1980). Wilshire and Nakata (1976) noted that some dry playa clays were minimally affected by off-road vehicle traffic, although these authors found significant compaction of coarser alluvial soils. Belnap *et al.* (2007) also found that wind erodibility of soils can be a serious problem after trampling, but recognized that there is a threshold of biomass below which cyanobacterial crusts are not the dominant factor in soil vulnerability to wind erosion. Livestock grazing in specific areas, such as near water points, can have similar negative effects caused by trampling (Sinclair and Fryxell 1985; Van de Koppel *et al.* 1997; Whitford and Kay 1999; Smet and Ward 2005). Although off-road vehicles can alter soil surface conditions in a number of ways that negatively affect soil erosion (Iverson 1980), decreased soil infiltration rates are often considered to be the major source of this problem. Reductions in infiltration rates are ascribed to decreases in soil porosity (Eckert *et al.* 1979), which is dependent on soil moisture content, soil texture, and compacting load (heavier vehicles such as tanks compact the soil surface more than lighter vehicles) (Archer and Smith 1972; Akram and Kemper 1979). Webb (1982) found that even off-road motorcycle traffic increased soil surface density and decreased soil infiltration rate. Webb (1982) found that the greatest effects on loamy soils in the Mojave desert occurred during the first few passes by an off-road vehicle.

According to a study by Belnap and Warren (2002) with regard to soils affected by military manoeuvres prior to and during World War II, soils in tracks had fewer rocks in the top 10 cm of the soil profile than adjacent untracked soils and penetrability was lower inside visible tracks. The cyanobacterial component of biological soil crusts had recovered its biomass by

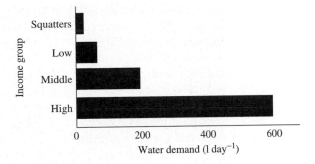

Fig. 10.24   Water use in neighbourhoods in Windhoek, capital city of Namibia. Squatters are people who live in temporary shelters. Mean annual rainfall in Windhoek is about 300 mm. (From Jacobson *et al.* 1995. With kind permission of the Desert Research Foundation of Namibia.)

about 50% in tracks relative to outside the tracks (Belnap and Warren 2002). Overall recovery of lichen cover has been much slower, especially in plant interspaces with less favourable moisture and temperature conditions, where *Collema tenax* had a 6% recovery and *Catapyrenium squamulosum* a 3% recovery. If recovery of the biological soil crust is linear, and complete only when the most sensitive species (in this case, *C. squamulosum*) has fully recovered in the most limiting microhabitats (plant interspaces), it may require as much as two millennia for full recovery of these areas (Belnap and Warren 2002).

10.4   Pumping aquifers: a problem of less water and more salinity

Some of the most obvious effects of aquifer pumping occur in desert golf courses. The negative effects are widespread, and include a more general problem of reduction in groundwater. For example, in San Antonio, Texas, a single golfer is calculated to use between 8,400 and 13,300 litres on a round (18 holes) of golf (Grigory 2007). In addition, high fertilization and insecticide levels are needed to keep the courses green. The use of the water from the Colorado River for urban purposes in southern California has resulted in the river no longer reaching the sea in the Baja peninsula, Mexico. The use of water in deserts by families differs tremendously, with greater use by high income families (Jacobson *et al.* 1995) (Fig. 10.24). Additional negative effects of groundwater depletion are found in many desert areas. For example, Lamoreaux *et al.* (1985) found that exploitation of groundwater for irrigation in the Kharga Oases of the Western desert of Egypt from springs as well as from shallow and deep artesian wells has caused severe declines and even termination of groundwater extraction from certain wells. By 1975, many deep wells had stopped flowing, and shallow wells were also being pumped. The major problem in Lamoreaux *et al.*'s (1985) view is that wells are placed too close to one another and are poorly managed. Dabous and Osmond (2001) found that, in the Western desert (Sahara), the observed lowering of groundwater is caused not only by pumping at a rate greater than inflow from the aquifer systems, but also by the withdrawal of pluvial water which is not being replaced.

One of the world's worst desertification areas is the Aral Sea region, which includes part of the Turkestan desert (Saiko and Zonn 2000). During the 1960s, a large-scale irrigation campaign attempted to improve cotton production in Soviet Central Asia. From 1960, ever-increasing water withdrawal from the two inflowing rivers, the Amudarya river and Syrdarya river, has resulted in the dramatic decline in the size of the sea. Desiccation was accompanied by the development and further acceleration of various desertification processes. Saiko and Zonn (2000) found that, for different reasons, the predominant direction and trends of desertification have been changing during each of the four identified periods from 1961 to 1995 (Fig. 10.25a–d). In 1950, the total irrigated area amounted to 5.4 million ha of Central Asia. Up to 1965, the rate of irrigation expansion slightly exceeded 0.5% per year. During the next five-year period, it increased at a rate of over 1% and from 1970 to 1975 it was 2% per annum (Zonn, 1993). However, expansion was particularly rapid during the next 13 years, when the area of irrigated land in Central Asia reached 9.4 million ha, showing an increase of 70% for the region as a whole. The area of irrigated land within the Aral Sea basin was estimated at close to 8 million ha (Saiko and Zonn 2000). The total area of the Aral Sea declined from 66,900 km^2 in 1960 to 32,000 km^2 in 1995 and the salinity of the sea changed from 11–14 g l^{-1} to 34 g l^{-1}. The commercial fish catch from the Aral Sea changed from 30–40,000 t $year^{-1}$ to no catch at all. The main causes of desertification of the Aral Sea were the decline in the groundwater level, increased mineralization and chemical pollution of watercourses, soil salinization, the spread of xerophytic and halophytic vegetation, and deflation and aeolian accumulation, with the development of salt storms (Saiko and Zonn 2000).

10.5   An embarrassment of riches: oil extraction in desert environments

Many desert substrates are negatively impacted by oil pollution (Malallah *et al.* 1998; Kwarteng 1999). Kuwait's desert environment was strongly affected during the 1990–91 first Arabian Gulf War by the formation of oil lakes and oil-contaminated surfaces when Iraq's army blew up oil fields. Currently, the affected areas consist of oil lakes, thick and disintegrated

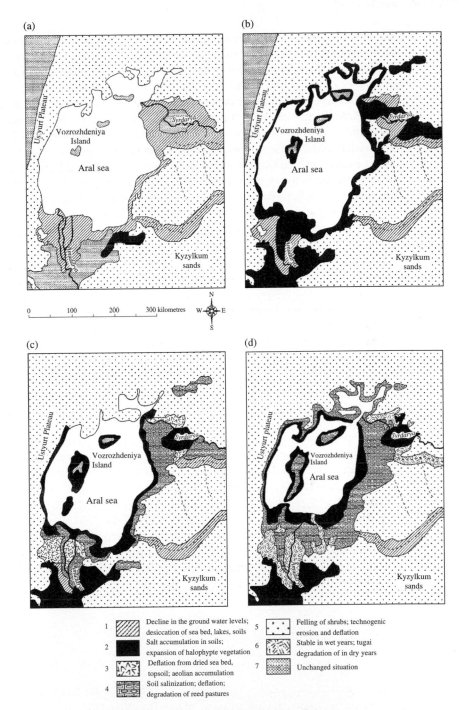

(a)

Us'yurt Plateau

Vozrozhdeniya
Island

Aral sea

Syrdarya

Kyzylkum
sands

0   100   200   300 kilometres

N
W ⊕ E
S

(b)

Ustyurt Plateau

Vozrozhdeniya
Island

Aral sea

Syrdarya

Kyzylkum
sands

(c)

Ustyurt Plateau

Vozrozhdeniya
Island

Aral sea

Syrdarya

Kyzylkum
sands

(d)

Ustyurt Plateau

Vozrozhdeniya
Island

Aral sea

Syrdarya

Kyzylkum
sands

1   Decline in the ground water levels;
desiccation of sea bed, lakes, soils

2   Salt accumulation in soils;
expansion of halophypte vegetation

3   Deflation from dried sea bed,
topsoil; aeolian accumulation

4   Soil salinization; deflation;
degradation of reed pastures

5   Felling of shrubs; technogenic
erosion and deflation

6   Stable in wet years; tugai
degradation of in dry years

7   Unchanged situation

Fig. 10.25   (a–d) In the Aral Sea region, the predominant direction and trends of desertification have changed during each of the four identified periods from 1961 to 1965. tugai (6) = riparian forests growing along the rivers in the continental desert regions of central Asia. (From Saiko and Zonn 2000. With kind permission of Elsevier.)

tarmats, black soil and vegetation. Kwarteng (1999) monitored the spatial and temporal changes of the oil lakes and polluted surfaces at the Greater Burgan oil field. Kwarteng (1999) documented the gradual disappearance of smaller oil lakes and soot/black soil from the surface with time. Even though some of the contaminants were obscured by sand and vegetation and not readily observed on the surface or from satellite images, the harmful chemicals remain in the soil. Some of the contaminated areas displayed a remarkable ability to support vegetation growth during the higher than average rainfall that occurred between 1992 and 1998, although Malallah *et al.* (1998) detected evidence of negative effects of oil pollution on four Kuwaiti annual flowering plants. In *Picris babylonica* (Asteraceae), the clearest effects were detected. These were apparently dependent on photosynthetic pigment degradation, indicating damage caused by environmental pollution (β-carotene protects chlorophylls against environmental damage). In this study, carotene levels were lower in polluted areas.

10.6   When is it desertification? The importance of reversibility

Many causes of desertification have obvious solutions. For example, in California, the baseline for comparison of water use on golf courses is the amount of growth that a crop would have multiplied by 0.80 (Green 2007). Now, it is well known that monocultures have a far higher water use than desert ecosystems. Thus, comparing water use in a crop plant to the amount of water a golf course may use is not a valid comparison. The real comparison in desert regions should be with a natural desert ecosystem,

Fig. 10.26   Lehavim housing development in the northern Negev desert, Israel.

where shrubs are 'islands of fertility' surrounded by areas with few or no plants. Similarly, effects of soil salinization, agricultural development in marginal desert lands and housing developments (e.g. Fig. 10.26) can be directly assessed in terms of their negative effects on the environment.

Another example comes from rangeland studies, which are largely based on changes in vegetation recorded by fixed-point, aerial, and/or satellite photographs of large geographic regions (Hoffman and Cowling 1990b; Pickup and Chewings 1994; Hoffman *et al.* 1995; Britz and Ward 2007). See, for example, Fig. 10.27a and b from the 2nd Anglo–Boer War battle site of Magersfontein (South Africa). In Fig. 10.27a, taken on or just before the date

(a)

(b)

Fig. 10.27   Magersfontein battle site in (a) the days before the battle (11 December 1899) and (b) in 2001.

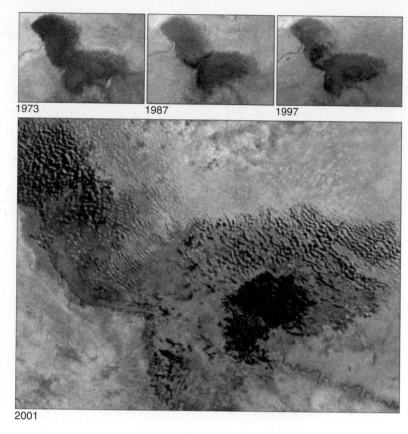

Fig. 10.28 Satellite photographs of changes in NDVI values for Lake Chad.

Fig. 10.29 Satellite photograph of Pniel Estates in the arid Northern Cape Province, South Africa. The bare area in the photograph (square) is the only area that is communally owned.

of the battle (11 December 1899), it is clear that the Boer soldiers had to have been able to detect the vaunted Black Watch soldiers of the British army (note open ground beyond the trenches). The photograph in Fig. 10.27b was taken at the same site in 2001. Clearly, the bush encroachment that occurs there today would have prevented the Boer soldiers from detecting the British soldiers. In another study, Hoffman *et al.* (1995) have considered conflicting evidence for the expansion of the eastern Karoo of South Africa from changes in $\delta^{13}C$ isotopes and fixed-point photographs. Studies suggested a greater per cent cover by grasses in the past, but researchers disagreed on the timing of the switch to a greater per cent cover by shrubs in the eastern Karoo (Acocks 1954). Hoffman *et al.* (1995) found that the expanding Karoo hypothesis of Acocks (1954) as well as the argument that the Karoo's carrying capacity has decreased in recent years was remiss. Indeed, Hoffman *et al.* (1995) found that higher rainfall in recent decades had led to an increase in grass cover over the same period, as shown by the long-term photographic record used by Hoffman *et al.* (1995).

Studies using satellite photographs have been criticized because they focus heavily on biomass removal (as indicated by changes in Normalized Difference Vegetation Indices (NDVI)) rather than on changes in diversity, species composition, and nutritional quality of vegetation (e.g. Fig. 10.28 (large scale) and Fig. 10.29 (small scale)). Changes in vegetation density may be confounded with the effects of natural climatic variation (or even anthropogenic global climatic change) on vegetation density. Pickup and Chewings (1994) have quite sensibly stressed that remote-sensing studies need to focus on vegetation recovery by the end of the wet season because dry season estimates may indicate short-term and trivial effects of consumption but may have little or nothing to do with long-term vegetation change and/or degradation. In addition, Saltz *et al.* (1999) have demonstrated that the reliability of NDVI is low in arid ecosystems where reflectance from the large bare soil surfaces (albedo) creates considerable vegetation density artefacts. These differences are dependent on soil type; for example, in Makhtesh Ramon in the central Negev desert of Israel, basalt shows very high NDVI values in spite of the fact that it is almost unvegetated with the exception of a few *Stipa capensis* (Poaceae) plants and a few scattered plants of various species (Saltz *et al.* 1999; Ward *et al.* 1998, 2000a). One would still have to ascertain whether there have been changes in vegetation species composition by ground-truthing (i.e. measurement of vegetation cover on the ground) because differences in biomass between wet seasons do not necessarily indicate whether there have been changes in the species that make up the index. For example, an index may have a value of 12 for a particular pixel, which may be made up of five species having values of $2 + 3 + 1 + 4 + 2 = 12$ or it may be a monospecific stand with a value of 12. Thus, while such studies have great potential benefits, unless they are well ground-truthed, they have little value of their own accord.

11 Conservation of deserts

11.1 Are deserts worth conserving?

Hopefully this book has managed to convince you that deserts are superb evolutionary laboratories of nature. For that alone, they merit conservation. Deserts are particularly well suited for the study of evolutionary changes in species. There are many additional reasons for why it is important to conserve deserts, for example:

1. Unique features of desert species and habitats.
2. Ecological benefits provided by these habitats.
3. Since many desert areas have historically been perceived as wastelands, many are in relatively pristine condition (but see Chapter 10 for negative human impacts on desert habitats).

Conservation can be carried out using many different approaches. Here we consider the following:

1. Focusing on the conservation of individual desert species versus a habitat-level approach.
2. Reintroductions and recolonizations of endangered species and revegetation of desert habitats.
3. In areas where there are strong genotype by environment ($G \times E$) interactions—that is, where evolution of new species starts to occur—it may be important to conserve each population separately.
4. Lastly, this chapter considers the institutional means of controlling desert habitats and whether we can afford such habitat conservation.

11.2 Conservation of desert species or habitats

Conservation can focus on a single species, with an emphasis on umbrella species, keystone species, focal species or indicator species. The term umbrella species infers that by saving a single species, one saves a lot of other species that are 'under the umbrella'. These are usually large species with low reproductive rates and large home ranges (Mills *et al.* 1993; Berger 1997). Keystone species are those species that play a disproportionately important role in the ecosystem and therefore saving them may save many other species that depend on them (see Chapters 5 and 6 for examples of such species). Focal species are those that have a high perceived value for conservation because they are aesthetically pleasing and conserving them will usually serve to conserve a lot of habitat, and consequently lead to the conservation of other species. Indicator species are considered to be useful for conservation because they are indicators of particular conservation priorities. In all four cases, it is clear that saving any of these species necessarily leads to saving a number of other species that either depend on them (e.g. keystone species) or happen to occupy the same habitats (e.g. umbrella, focal, and indicator species).

11.2.1   Umbrella species

Berger (1997) considered the value of the Namib desert-dwelling black rhinoceros, *Diceros bicornis* (Fig. 11.1), as an umbrella species. This is the only unfenced population of this species with more than 100 individuals (Berger 1997). He examined the value of conserving this species relative to the conservation of six large herbivores ranging in size from the giraffe, *Giraffa camelopardis*, to springbok, *Antidorcas marsupialis*, and the ostrich, *Struthio camelus*. He found that all species, with the exception of the black rhino, moved according to rainfall variation. Such large changes in population sizes meant that, at best, only populations of about 250 animals would be conserved in the area (about 7,000 km²) of the Kaokoveld of the Namib desert where the black rhinos occurred (Fig. 11.2). One third

Fig. 11.1   Black rhino. (Photograph courtesy of Alastair Rae.)

of the species never exceeded populations >50 individuals. One of the assumptions regarding suitability as an umbrella species is that black rhinos must be a viable population. Berger (1997) was most concerned that desert-dwelling black rhinos are not necessarily viable, largely because of poaching. Indeed, Berger and Cunningham (1994) considered the fact that black rhinos are dehorned by the wildlife authorities in Namibia, Zimbabwe, and Swaziland in an attempt to reduce poaching because these large animals are poached for their horns. They found that female black rhinos lose all their infants when there are dangerous carnivores such as spotted hyaenas, *Crocuta crocuta*, and lions, *Panthera leo*, in the area and lose none of their infants when there are no dangerous carnivores. However, Berger and Cunningham (1994) recognized that dehorning resulted in lower mortalities (33%) for inter-female rivalries. They concluded that dehorning could be a valid conservation strategy only where dangerous carnivores were excluded.

11.2.2   Keystone species

I discussed a number of examples of keystone species in Chapters 5 and 6. They have an importance that is in excess of their abundance. Examples include the African and Middle Eastern *Acacia* species. Another example of a keystone species is the camel, which because of its large size has a key role in the germination of *Acacia* species. Another keystone species is the elephant (Fig. 11.3), which plays a major role by pulling down large trees, making them available to shorter herbivores, particularly in the Namib desert. Other keystone species include lions, spotted hyaenas, dingoes,

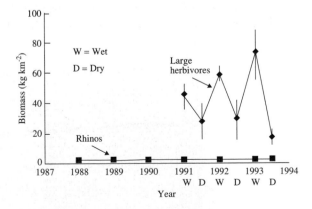

Fig. 11.2   In the Kaokoveld region of the Namib desert where the black rhinos occurred, about 33% of the large herbivore species never exceeded populations of more than 50 individuals. Black rhino populations were also too small to be useful indicator species. (From Berger 1997. With kind permission of Blackwell Publishing.)

and coyotes (Chapter 6) because of their important roles as keystone predators.

11.2.3   Focal species

Cohn (2001) considered the role of the cactus ferruginous owl as a focal species. This bird is an endangered subspecies in an area of the Sonoran desert near Tucson, Arizona. The owl was once found in wooded riparian areas from Baja California to central Arizona. However, the range of this owl has dwindled as rivers and washes dried up due to ground water pumping and expansion of cities in the region. Only about a dozen owls remained in the Tucson area in 1977. More recently, surveys have shown that there are about 70 owls (and 13 nests) around Tucson and the Organ Pipes Cactus National Monument. The discovery of the owl forced Pima County to abandon plans to develop a school, shopping mall, and other buildings in the northwestern parts of Tucson, which has grown from a mere 250 people in 1865 to about 485,000 people in 2000. This owl, together with the identification of 56 plants and animals in Pima County that were considered endangered, threatened or vulnerable, has been an effective focal species. Up to almost 1 million ha is now considered for some form of preservation.

11.2.4   Single populations

Another conservation issue deals with conserving single populations or metapopulations. One of the most common ways of assessing the viability of single populations is via the use of matrix models (Stearns 1992; Caswell 2001). Another more complex approach is to use spatially explicit models (Jeltsch *et al.* 2000; Wiegand *et al.* 1999, 2000). An example of the use of matrix models comes from Jimenez-Sierra *et al.* (2007), who studied the candy barrel cactus, *Echinocactus platyacanthus*, in the Tehuacán

Fig. 11.3   Desert elephant.

desert (part of the Chihuahuan desert) in Mexico. This species is endemic to Mexico. Tissue from inside the stem is used to prepare a traditional sweet or candy called acitrón, although it is mainly used for forage for goats and donkeys that feed on the flowers and fruits and on those stems that do not have spines. The species is not cultivated in Mexico and so the removal of these plants is entirely from native populations. Jimenez-Sierra *et al.* (2007) conducted three censuses in six populations during 1997, 1998, and 1999. They found that fruits contained many seeds (about 170 seeds/fruit) and that fecundity increased as plant size increased but that seedling establishment and recruitment were low (2×10^{-6}). The rates of population growth (λ) were close to 1, which indicates that the population is neither declining nor increasing in size, but that some populations were declining ($\lambda \ll 1$). Elasticity values, which are a measure of the sensitivity of the population to changes in individual fecundity, growth, and stasis (some individuals do not change size from one year to the next), indicated that the stasis of the adults contributed most to demography ($S = 0.98$), followed by growth ($G = 0.017$) and fecundity ($F = 0.001$). It had been proposed that barrel and globose cacti (or other species with short lifespans) would have higher elasticity values for growth and fecundity. However, they found that populations of this species behave similarly to the far larger columnar cactus species such as the saguaro *Carnegiea gigantea* (Steenbergh and Lowe 1977), *Neobuxbaumia tetetzo* (Godínez-Alvarez *et al.* 1999), and *Neobuxbaumia macrocephala* (Esparza-Olguín *et al.* 2002), in that stasis was the most important feature of population demography. Jimenez-Sierra *et al.* (2007) concluded from these studies that the protection of adult *E. platyacanthus* plants was most important for the conservation and management of this species. The conservation of these plants can only be maintained if the removal and destruction of large adults is stopped, especially because larger individuals produce more seeds. Among the methods that Jimenez-Sierra *et al.* (2007) consider will be useful for this species' conservation include (1) the establishment of grazing-free areas where competition with other shrubby species is minimized, (2) the collection and storage of seeds from areas that have deteriorated or have been subjected to heavy grazing pressure, and (3) the cultivation of the cactus in greenhouses by local inhabitants.

In spatially explicit models, Wiegand *et al.* (1999) studied the factors affecting the distribution of *Acacia raddiana* in the Negev desert of Israel because of the concerns expressed for their conservation by Ward and Rohner (1997) (see Chapter 10). They evaluated the relative importance of different processes such as seed production, seed infestation by bruchid beetles, germination, mortality, and infestation by the hemiparasitic mistletoe *Plicosepalus acaciae* for the survival and recruitment of *Acacia* trees in the Negev desert. The most important factors affecting mortality rates at different life stages were the production of uninfested seeds and the weather regime. The infection of trees by hemiparasitic mistletoes proved to be of

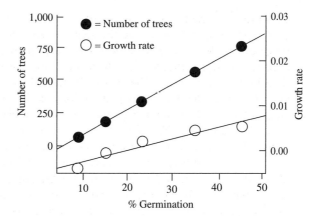

Fig. 11.4   An increase in the germination rate of *Acacia* seeds could counteract the detrimental effect of unfavourable climatic conditions. (From Wiegand *et al.* 1999. With kind permission of Elsevier.)

minor importance. The most important result Wiegand *et al.* (1999) found was that an increase in the germination rate of *Acacia* seeds is capable of counteracting the detrimental effect of unfavourable climatic conditions and the negative effects of seed infestation by bruchid beetles (Bruchidae) (Fig. 11.4). This may result from passage through the digestive tract of large mammalian herbivores, because of scarification by the hydrochloric acid in the digestive tract. Consequently, they recommended the use of increased large mammalian herbivore densities as a possible management option for enhancing the survival of *Acacia* populations in the Negev (see Rohner and Ward 1999). Rohner and Ward (1999) showed that the larger the herbivore, the greater the probability of germination (Fig. 11.5; see also Chapter 7) and recommended that camels be brought in to maximize germination probability. Camels also consume young seedlings, so they would need to be removed before the plants reached the seedling stage (Rohner and Ward 1999).

11.2.5   SLOSS or metapopulations

The debate over SLOSS (Single Large Or Several Small) habitats has long been an issue for discussion in the field of conservation. The debate deals with fragmented habitats and whether it is better to conserve one large habitat of a given size or to split it into several small habitats of the same size. This follows on from the dynamical theory of island biogeography of MacArthur and Wilson (1964). Primack (2006) considers the best reasons for conserving a *Single Large* habitat to be the fact that the number of species conserved increases (usually) with area ($S = cA^z$, where S = species richness, A = area conserved; c and z are positive fitted

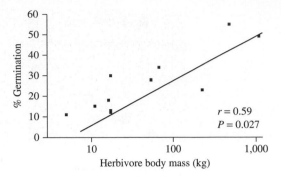

Fig. 11.5   Positive relationship between % germination and mammalian body size. The mechanism is that seeds remain in the gut of large mammals for longer than in small mammals. (From Bodmer and Ward 2006. With kind permission of Cambridge University Press.)

constraints where z lies between 0 and 1), there are fewer negative consequences of edge effects and it will preserve more species that happen to have large habitat requirements (e.g. elephants or lions). On the other hand, the benefits of conserving *Several Small* habitats of the same size may be that it could be easier to increase the diversity of habitats protected because they are spread out over a considerable distance, there would be a lower probability that any population might be eliminated by stochastic events such as disease or a similar catastrophe and it may be easier to convince people with competing interests to implement conservation efforts (e.g. for housing or agricultural developments). Primack (2006) proposes that the best of both worlds would be to have a group of large and small habitats that are connected by corridors or stepping stones because this would create metapopulations of protected species. Metapopulations, which are multiple populations of the same species that are connected through immigration and emigration (Pulliam 1988), are clearly important to conserve because sometimes a single population may go extinct for reasons that are unclear or because the population happens to be a 'sink' population. For example, the desert lily *Pancratium sickenbergeri* in the Negev desert (Israel) occurs in high densities in sand dunes but occurs at low densities in associated dense loess-sand habitats (Ward *et al*. 2000a). One might conserve the high density population because this should be where they stand the best chance of survival and reproduction. However, the sand dune populations are 'sink' populations as they have very high mortality of flowers (1:30,000) and no vegetative reproduction, while the loess-sand populations are 'source' populations where there is some reproduction and dispersal occurs to the 'sink' populations (*sensu* Pulliam 1988; Ward *et al*. 2000a). Without the 'source' populations, 'sink' populations would go extinct in a few years (Ward *et al*. 2000a).

Fig. 11.6   Nubian ibex.

Shkedy and Saltz (2000) considered the metapopulation dynamics of the Nubian ibex, *Capra ibex nubiana* (Fig. 11.6), a species of rocky cliffs in the Middle Eastern deserts. They used data over 20 years from the Israeli Nature Reserves Authority records, with some 1,650 observations. They found that there were three core zones in the Judean and Negev deserts (Israel) and that these were joined by corridors linking them. There were core areas in the Judean desert (about 1,000 animals on the west coast of the Dead Sea), the Negev highlands (about 500 animals), and the Eilat mountains region in the south (about 150 animals) (Fig. 11.7). Corridors were more likely to be flatter than core areas, presumably because ibex must move rapidly and directionally between core zones. Shkedy and Saltz (2000) considered that the extensive fencing of the international borders between Israel and Jordan and Israel and Egypt may curb the passage of ibex between the southern Eilat mountains and the central Negev highlands populations. They considered this species to be a potential umbrella species and that conserving metapopulations of this species could also aid in the conservation of other rock-dwelling species such as the Syrian hyrax, *Procavia syriaca*, Afghan fox, *Vulpes cana*, and leopard, *Panthera pardus*.

11.2.6   Conserving the whole habitat

There are problems associated with conserving large areas. For example, there is the SLOSS debate (*Single Large* or *Several Small* habitats) described above and the issue of global warming. Global warming may lead to increases in the sizes of desert habitats or may lead to decreases in the habitats suitable for particular species (Saltz *et al.* 2006; Foden *et al.* 2007; Midgley and Thuiller 2007).

One of the most important desert biomes to conserve is the Succulent Karoo of southern Africa (South Africa and Namibia), which occurs on the arid fringes of the Cape Floristic Province. The Succulent Karoo is the only arid habitat that is considered a hot spot of biodiversity. It includes 4,850 plant species of which about 40% (1,940 species) are endemic (Ihlenfeldt 1994; Hilton-Taylor 1996). This is particularly due to the rapid diversification of the Mesembryanthema (part of the family Aizoaceae, also known as ice plants). Both local (α) and regional (γ) diversity are high. On average, about 70 species have been recorded in a single 0.1 ha plot, with a maximum α diversity of 113 species, a diversity that is exceeded only in the Negev desert (Ward and Olsvig-Whittaker 1993; Ward *et al.* 1993). However, regional diversity is extraordinary, and is about four times higher than any other winter-rainfall desert in the world (Cowling *et al.* 1998). For example, in the mountainous Gariep section of this habitat, 331 plant species have been recorded in 1.3 km^2 in an area where annual rainfall is less than 70 mm (Von Willert *et al.* 1992). This high regional species richness of plants is caused by great compositional change in environmental and geographic gradients, especially with regard to edaphic specialists with limited distributions. Endemism is particularly acute among succulents (especially Mesembryanthema (Aizoaceae)) and bulbous plants and is focused on hard substrates such as quartzites,

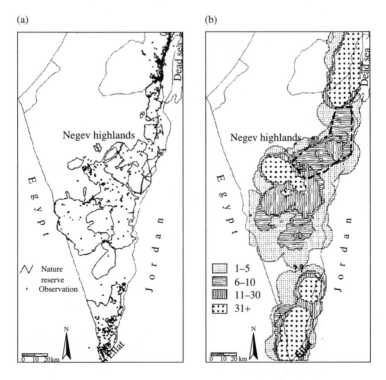

Fig. 11.7   Map of the core areas in the Judean desert (north, near Dead Sea), the Negev highlands and the Eilat mountains region in the south. Numbers in figure indicate numbers of animals seen. (From Shkedy and Saltz 2000. With kind permission of Blackwell Publishing.)

quartz-gravel plains, and shale ridges (Schmiedel and Jürgens 1999). There are 851 Red Data Book species in this biome (indicating threatened, vulnerable, and endangered species—Hilton-Taylor (1996)).

Cowling *et al.* (1999) have proposed a spatial scheme for the preservation of this region's biodiversity that maximizes the retention of species and allows for their persistence. By substituting space as surrogates for ecological and evolutionary processes, they consider it possible to achieve a system that combines retention and persistence of biodiversity. They compared the representation of species in the Red Data Book of plant species with their similar-sized system designed for both retention and persistence. The system designed for retention and persistence conserves considerably fewer Red Data Book plant species (37%), which indicates that including a design for persistence (e.g. to adjust for predicted changes in species' distributions caused by global climate changes as mentioned above and in Chapter 10) incurs a cost in terms of representation. However, this conservation system is predicted to persist in the face of global climatic changes by, for example, preserving altitudinal gradients of plant diversity (many species change rapidly along edaphic gradients—Cowling *et al.* (1999); Fig. 11.8) that allow for the maximization of plant diversity across

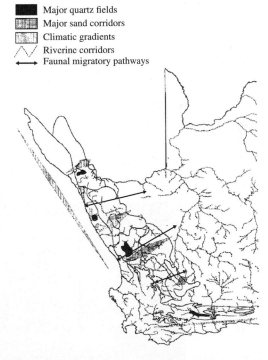

Fig. 11.8   Preserving altitudinal gradients of plant diversity in the Succulent Karoo. (From Cowling *et al.* 1999. With kind permission of Blackwell Publishing.)

very short distances and should protect many plant species even if global climate changes would change their distributions.

11.3 The 3 Rs: reintroduction, recolonization, and revegetation

Reintroductions of species occur where they have previously been eliminated from the wild or have declined to very low numbers. This section will cover the issue of reintroductions of two herbivore species in the Arabian desert. The first, the Asiatic wild ass *Equus hemionus* was reintroduced into the Makhtesh Ramon erosion cirque in the Negev desert in Israel in the 1950s (Saltz and Rubenstein 1995; Saltz *et al.* 2000, 2006). The second, the Arabian oryx *Oryx leucoryx* was introduced into Oman (Stanley-Price 1989; Spalton *et al.* 1999), Saudi Arabia (Treydte *et al.* 2001), and Israel (Gilad *et al.* 2008). The American black bear *Ursus americanus* has naturally recolonized the desert southwest of the United States and Mexico (Onorato *et al.* 2007). Finally, we consider the issue of revegetation of desert habitats.

11.3.1 Asiatic wild ass

The Asiatic wild ass *Equus hemionus* (Fig. 11.9) is a medium-sized (200 kg), polygynous species (Saltz and Rubenstein 1995; Saltz *et al.* 2000; Saltz *et al.* 2006). In some populations, these animals are considered harem breeders, which involves a single male mating with many females (Feh *et al.* 1994), although this was not the case in the study by Saltz *et al.* (2000). This species was once common throughout western Asia but was eliminated throughout most of its range with the introduction of modern firearms. The subspecies endemic to the Middle East (*E. h. hemipus*) became extinct at the beginning of the 20th century (Groves 1986).

Fig. 11.9   Asiatic wild ass.

In 1982, the Israel Nature Reserves Authority began to reintroduce Asiatic wild asses from a permanent breeding core founded in 1968 from six animals from the Persian subspecies (*E. h. onager*) and five animals from the Turkmen subspecies (*E. h. kulan*) (Saltz *et al.* 2000). Between 1982 and 1987, 28 animals were reintroduced into the Makhtesh Ramon erosion cirque. The animals were prime-age animals, which was considered to be vital for a successful reintroduction. Initially, there was a single dominant male that took up a territory of almost 20,000 ha of the cirque. Until 1989, reproductive success was low and population growth was slow (Saltz and Rubenstein 1995). Thereafter, reproductive success increased and more than 100 animals were recorded in 1997. As time passed, more and more males took up territories, and territories got progressively smaller (Fig. 11.10). Territories were focused around natural permanent and ephemeral watering points.

Saltz *et al.* (2000) found that in reintroduced, territorial polygynous species, effective population size (N_e) may be critically small. Their data indicate that N_e may stay very small for several years until population sizes increase, and ultimately depends on the numbers of males because effective population size depends on the number of breeding individuals. Where a population is a harem species, few males reproduce (most males are bachelor males that do not reproduce). Consequently, the number of breeding individuals is far less than the total number of individuals capable of reproducing. In the case mentioned above of a single territorial male reproducing and non-overlapping generations, then N_e is 4 because N_e is calculated as $4r(1 - r)N$, where r is the proportion of males and N is the total population size (Nunney 1993). Doubling the number of females from 11 to 22 would have increased N_e to 6.3 only. By 1995, with 40 breeding animals and five territorial males, and sex ratio at birth of 1:1 and more conventional age structure, N_e was 19.0 for a male survival rate of 0.8 year^{-1} and 25.0 for a male survival rate of 0.3 year^{-1} (note that if male survival is low there is a higher turnover in dominant, territorial males or harem holders, thus increasing N_e—D. Saltz, pers. comm.). Thus, the key feature for conservation strategies regarding this species is to maximize the numbers of male territories. Interestingly, the numbers of males born into this population were strongly male biased in the first years (until 1993) of reintroduction (>2:1).

Consistent with the Trivers and Willard (1973) maternal allocation hypothesis, females that are in good condition (as these females were) should produce mostly male offspring. The reason for this is that a female maximizes her own genetic output by producing a high-quality male offspring that will mate with many females, thereby increasing her own reproductive output in generations to come. Conversely, young (primiparous) or older females will do best if they produce female offspring because a female offspring (which will not necessarily be of high quality) will produce at least one offspring per annum during her reproductive period (Saltz and Rubenstein 1995). In future reintroductions of this species to other areas,

(a)   (d)

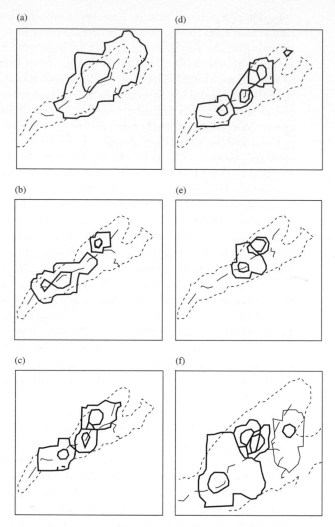

(b)   (e)

(c)   (f)

Fig. 11.10   Until 1989, reproductive success of Asiatic wild asses in Makhtesh Ramon erosion cirque was low and population growth was slow. Thereafter, reproductive success increased and more than 100 animals were recorded in 1997. As time passed, more and more males took up territories, and territories got progressively smaller. Dotted line represents perimeter of Makhtesh Ramon. Dashed line represents ephemeral river. (From Saltz *et al.* 2000. With kind permission of Blackwell Publishing.)

Saltz *et al.* (2000) recommend introducing prime-age females (as was done in the first reintroduction) to maximize the probability of survival and reproduction but to supplement these introductions with younger (primiparous) females so that the primary sex ratio remains as close to 1:1 as possible.

11.3.2   Arabian oryx

Spalton *et al.* (1999) recorded the successes and setbacks in the return of the Arabian oryx, *O. leucoryx* (80–100 kg), to Oman, which symbolized the success of a new approach to species conservation and established reintroduction as a conservation tool (Stanley-Price 1989). Ten years after the species had been exterminated in the wild by poaching, the first 10 founder oryx, descendants of the 'World Herd' based in a zoological garden in Phoenix, Arizona, USA, were reintroduced to the desert in central Oman in January 1982. A second release followed in 1984 and the population grew slowly through a 3-year drought that was broken by rain in June 1986. Further years of good rainfall and more founders meant that by April 1990 there were over 100 oryx in the wild, independent of supplementary feed and water, and using a range of over 11,000 km^2. The population continued to grow and by October 1995 numbered approximately 280 in the wild and used over 16,000 km^2 of the Arabian Oryx Sanctuary. However, in February 1996, there was further poaching and oryx were captured for sale as live animals outside the country. Despite the poaching, the population continued to increase and by October 1996 was estimated to be just over 400. However, poaching intensified and continued through late 1996 and 1997. By September 1998 it had reduced the wild population to an estimated 138 animals, of which just 28 were females. The wild population was no longer considered viable and action was taken to rescue some of the remaining animals from the wild to form a captive herd.

In Saudi Arabia, Treydte *et al.* (2001) found that the reintroduction of Arabian oryx has been considerably more successful. There were 17 Arabian oryx reintroduced into the wild in 1990. With a few subsequent additions from a captive herd, by 2000, the population had increased to 346 animals. The animals were reintroduced in Mahazat as-Sayd, a fenced reserve about 2,250 km^2 in area in west-central Arabia, which lies at the periphery of their historical home range (Treydte *et al.* 2001). The herd managers wished to assess how best to manage the herd, given the constraints that the reserve was fenced, the herd did not have predators and that there are large inter-annual fluctuations in primary productivity due to the high coefficient of variation in rainfall. The first two factors meant that the population would reach carrying capacity (K) because there was no predation and because the oryx herds could not move outside the reserve. The last-mentioned source of variability can be a considerable problem because variance in reproductive output has a stronger negative effect on reproductive success than changes in the mean value. Indeed, even if the mean value increases, it is possible for a population to go extinct for random demographic reasons such as founder effects and genetic drift (Ewens *et al.* 1996). Treydte *et al.* (2001) modelled strategies of no intervention, constant offtake of 15% per annum, and reducing the herd to 70% of K. They found that the last-mentioned strategy of reducing the herd to 70% of K would be the optimal strategy because it resulted in the least alteration of variance in reproductive success, as predicted by Lande *et al.* (1995) (see also Saltz *et al.* (2004) for a similar prediction for desert-dwelling Hartmann's mountain zebra, *Equus zebra hartmannae*, in Namibia). However, Treydte *et al.* (2001) recognized that keeping a population at a specific value of K would be difficult for managers to implement and suggested that a constant percentage offtake would be possible, albeit at a considerable cost in terms of increased variance in reproductive success, but nonetheless preferable to a strategy of no intervention.

11.3.3 Recolonization by the American black bear

An interesting case of recolonization involves the American black bear, *U. americanus*. American black bears, *U. americanus*, have naturally recolonized parts of their former range in the arid Trans-Pecos region of Texas and Mexico after more than 40 years of absence (Onorato *et al.* 2007). Using microsatellite loci, Onorato *et al.* (2007) found that these metapopulations were generally panmictic and that there is only moderate genetic structuring of these populations. Onorato *et al.* (2007) recommended that close contacts need to be made between Mexico and the United States to ensure that black bears can easily move between the two countries, thereby maintaining genetic homogeneity.

11.3.4 Revegetation

Some of the most effective revegetation schemes have been developed in the People's Republic of China. It is not always clear whether these schemes are involved in vegetating lands that are naturally dune sands and thus do not warrant revegetating because they could be maintained in their natural state or whether revegetation is needed to restore the lands to their original states. In some cases, where key installations such as railways occur, revegetation is needed even though the natural state of the vegetation is indeed desert (see also Whitford 2002). These revegetation techniques involve the creation of windbreaks made from willow or bamboo, followed by the formation of straw checkerboards, allowing time for native xerophytic shrubs to establish (Li *et al.* 2004). Among these, *Caragana korshinskii*, *Artemisia ordosica*, and *Hedysarum scoparium* are often planted in the Tengger desert of northern China (Li *et al.* 2004). From 1956 to 2001, the development of revegetated areas along the Baotou-Lanzhou railway line was monitored (Li *et al.* 2004). They monitored β diversity as a measure of species change over time (Fig. 11.11). These researchers found that 40 years after revegetation was started, the probability of new species arriving has declined and has tended towards 12–14 species. Importantly, there has been a change from inorganic soil crusts to a biological soil crust consisting of algae and lichens. However, Li *et al.* (2004) recognized that there were fewer moss species occurring in the revegetated lands than in naturally fixed dune surfaces.

11.4 The coalface of evolution—genotype by environment interactions

A number of studies have examined intraspecific variability to determine whether subspecies or variants occur. This can be termed the coalface of evolution and is particularly important for conservation because where there are genotype by environment ($G \times E$) interactions, populations should be separately managed (Rödl and Ward 2002; Ruiz *et al.* 2006b). Most frequently, this occurs in plant species, but it has also been described in reintroduced Arabian oryx, *O. leucoryx* (Marshall and Spalton 2000).

Shrestha *et al.* (2002) used random amplified polymorphic DNA to investigate the relationships among different populations of *A. raddiana* trees in the Negev desert (Israel)(see Chapters 7 and 9). They found that there was virtually no overlap among the different populations of desert *Acacia* populations (Fig. 11.12). Rödl and Ward (2002) studied the relationships among mistletoe *P. acaciae* populations parasitizing *A. raddiana* populations. They reciprocally switched mistletoe seedlings (Fig. 11.13) within the same wadi (control) and also moved mistletoe seedlings among adjacent wadis. They found that mistletoes moved between wadis (with as little as 1–2 km between them) had far lower survival values than those

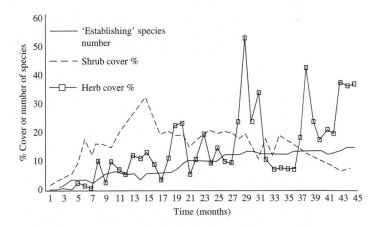

Fig. 11.11 The development of revegetated areas along the Baotou-Lanzhou railway line was monitored (β diversity) as an index of species change over time. (From Li *et al.* 2004. With kind permission of Blackwell Publishing.)

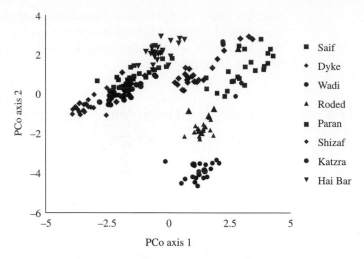

Fig. 11.12 PCoA analysis of *Acacia raddiana* populations. Each data point is a single individual in two-dimensional space. Note that there is very little overlap of individuals among populations. (From Shrestha *et al.* 2002. With kind permission of Elsevier.)

Fig. 11.13 Seedlings of the mistletoe *Plicosepalus acaciae*.

moved within the same wadi. This indicated that there was a strong geno-type by environment ($G \times E$) interaction (Fig. 11.14) and therefore different populations of mistletoes of the same species should be kept within the same wadi to avoid mixing of genes. A similar interaction occurs with the VAM (vesicular arbuscular mycorrhizae) communities and their obligate host, *Vangueria infausta* (Rubiaceae) in Botswana. Obligate VAM species gain phosphorus (and, in some circumstances, also water and some nutrients such as N, Ca, Mg, and Fe) from the VAM and the VAM species gain carbon from their hosts (Bohrer *et al.* 2001). When the host was transferred between areas, Bohrer *et al.* (2003) found that there was a significant

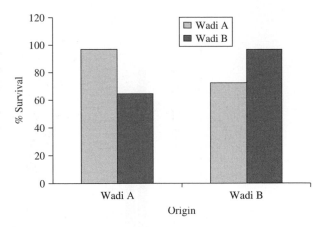

Fig. 11.14   Survival values of the mistletoe *Plicosepalus acaciae* in different wadi systems. (From Rödl and Ward 2002. With kind permission of Blackwell Publishing.)

$G \times E$ interaction in terms of Ca and N concentration in the shoots of these plants, indicating that there was local adaptation of the VAM species.

Nevo (1998) considered the importance of maintaining agricultural biodiversity of cereal species that originated in the Middle East's Fertile Crescent. These species included wild barley *Hordeum spontaneum*, emmer wheat *Triticum dicoccoides* (the progenitor of all wheats), and wild oats *Avena barbatus*. Nevo (1998) showed that allozyme variation of emmer wheat and wild barley was extremely high, and was significantly greater in Israel than in Turkey and in Iran. Most of the unique alleles were common or localized in distribution; 51 out of 65 alleles (79%) were unique, yet localized and not widespread (Fig. 11.15).

Volis *et al.* (1998) studied $G \times E$ interactions in wild barley, *H. spontaneum*, from 12 sites in the central parts of the range in Turkmenistan and from six peripheral sites in the Judean and Negev deserts in Israel. They found that, based on 16 morphological and phenological characteristics measured in a common garden experiment, peripheral populations in Israel were phenotypically more variable (as did Nevo (1998) above) and were more resistant to water stress. The researchers concluded that peripheral populations were more genetically variable and were better adapted (or pre-adapted; = *exaptation*) to environmental changes and were thus valuable for conservation. Later, Volis *et al.* (2000, 2001) studied the same species at four sites along an environmental gradient from the central Negev desert highlands to the mountains in northern Israel. Rainfall varied from about 100 mm in the desert to 1,100 mm in the northern Israeli mountains. Here too they found significant $G \times E$ interactions, again indicating the value of separate conservation of each of these populations.

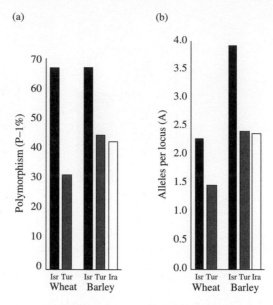

Fig. 11.15   Nevo (1998) showed that most of the unique alleles were common or localized in distribution; 51 out of 65 alleles (79%) were unique, yet localized and not widespread. Isr = Israel; Tur = Turkey; Ira = Iran. (From Nevo 1998.)

11.5   Who gets to pay for this conservation and how is it controlled?

There are major differences in the ways that people can control land. For example, in Israel there is no private land ownership, whereas in the United States private land ownership is very common. Consequently, the ways in which people perceive their abilities to control land access vary enormously. For example, Richer (1995) estimated the benefits of restricting the uses of 2.8 million ha of desert land and creating three new national parks and 76 new wilderness areas in the high and low deserts of eastern California (United States). In a 'willingness to pay' survey, California residents indicated that they would be willing to pay $177 million to $448 million year^{-1} to enact desert protection legislation. This estimate assumed that (1) the residents who did not complete and return the survey questionnaire ('nonrespondents') would receive no benefits from desert protection and (2) the estimate of willingness to pay for the 'respondents' is unbiased (Richer 1995). From this study, it is clear that people are willing to pay large amounts of money to protect desert habitats.

At the other end of the scale, different levels of institution control the communal land ownership of people inhabiting the Thar desert of

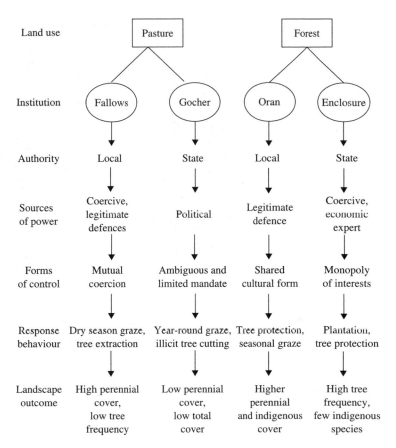

Fig. 11.16   Robbins (1998) studied 28 villages and included pastoral *sindhi* and *raika* castes, land-holding *rajputs*, and marginalized *bhil* and *meghwal* castes. Responses to authorities varied considerably. Gocher = sacred forest; Oran = controlled by village elites. (From Robbins 1998. With kind permission of Blackwell Publishing.)

Rajasthan (India) (Robbins 1998; see also Ward *et al.* (2000b) and Katjiua and Ward (2007) for another example of communal land tenure in the Namib and Kalahari deserts of Namibia, respectively). Four institutions govern the communal lands in Marwar, Rajasthan: Gram Panchayat *gochers*, semiprivate community fallows, forest department enclosures and traditional sacred forests or *oran*. *Gochers* and community fallows are pasture lands and forest department enclosures and *orans* are forest lands. Robbins (1998) studied 28 villages and included pastoral *sindhi* and *raika* castes, land-holding *rajputs*, and marginalized *bhil* and *meghwal* castes. Responses to authorities varied considerably (Fig. 11.16):

1. Gram Panchayat *gochers* are controlled by village committees (Gram Panchayat) and dominated by village elites (all of whom are men), under

266 THE BIOLOGY OF DESERTS

authority of the Rajasthan state. Restrictions are placed on tree cutting. Marginal community members and village women often ignore their authority and, consequently, compliance with regulations is irregular. Surveys indicated that opinions about control of the resources were ambiguous: 41% of the respondents believed that there was state control of *gochers* and about 45% believed that there was village control.

2. Community fallows are privately owned and are available as pasture for the entire community. This includes 'long-fallow' lands that may be set aside from production for as long as 10 years or more. Restrictions are placed on tree cutting and on wet season grazing (lands are closed during the rainy season to allow for growth of perennial grasses). Violators risk reprisals from private owners. Owners, on the other hand, must allow for open use of their resources by the community or risk punishment from tribal authorities or elders. Thus, the land is opened under a socially enforced obligation.

3. Forest department enclosures are fenced and guarded against cutting and grazing. The control by the forest department employees is limited, especially where local communities are wealthy (corruption of the employees occurs). However, as a major employer, especially for women interested in wages for planting exotic trees and tending nurseries, the forest department can reward villagers with jobs and access to steady wages. Robbins (1998) also found that many villagers defer to forest department officials for environmental knowledge. Here, there was little ambiguity with regard to the responses of the community: over 90% believed that there was state control of resources.

4. *Orans* have strong regulations against tree cutting. Grasses may be grazed but are generally not cut and/or removed. Browsing animals such as goats and camels may also remove leaves from lower branches of trees. Compliance to rules is complex as divine retribution is threatened (such as claims of blinding and paralysis) (Gadgil and Vartak 1975, 1994; Gold and Gujar 1989). These lands also fall under the secular authority of traditional village councils, elders, and the community itself (Robbins 1998). Most people (68%) believed that the village controlled these resources and only 19% thought that they were under state control. Consequently, divine and secular authorities ensured that trees were not cut (Robbins 1998).

Robbins (1998) found that there were essentially three criteria that determined whether rules would be followed:

1. The perception by the user of the legitimacy of the enforcing authority, for example, women tended to ignore the role of village elders regarding *gocher* management.
2. The stakes held by resource users in the protection of the resource, that is, if people stood to gain from maintaining a resource, then

they were more likely to do so (*contra* Hardin's (1968) 'tragedy of the commons').

3. The expectation of equal enforcement of rules.

All three of these could be affected by social caste and gender. Women in Rajasthan maintain and protect many of the traditional rules for resource preservation but disregard others where they either believe that men are making decisions on their behalf (Robbins 1998). In contrast, Ward *et al.* (2000b) found that women controlled more of the resources (especially with regard to livestock) than men in Otjimbingwe in the Namib desert and did not need to seek their permission for use of resources.

11.6   Conclusions

Deserts are often perceived as wastelands, and consequently, they are frequently underutilized. Thus, they may be conserved for this reason alone. Although we need to be wary of the potential for desertification, conserving these ecosystems should remain a priority. I believe that deserts make some of the most interesting and compelling places to study evolution in progress. They are also important because of the unique species that occur there and they provide an opportunity to understand biotic interactions because of the relative simplicity of the ecosystems.

References

Abdallah, A. and Tawfik, J. (1969). The anatomy and histology of the kidney of sand rats (*Psammomys obesus*). *Zeitschrift für Versuchstierkunde*, 11, 261–75.

Abrahams, A.D., Parsons, A.J., and Wainwright, J. (1995). Effects of vegetation change on interrill runoff and erosion, Walnut Gulch, southern Arizona. *Geomorphology*, 13, 37–48.

Abramsky, Z. (1983). Experiments on seed predation by rodents and ants in the Israeli desert. *Oecologia*, 57, 328–32.

Abramsky, Z. and Rosenzweig, M.L. (1984). Tilman's predicted productivity-diversity relationship shown by desert rodents. *Nature*, 309, 150–1.

Abramsky, Z., Rosenzweig, M.L., Pinshow, B., Brown, J.S., Kotler, B.P., and Mitchell, W.A. (1990). Habitat selection: an experimental field test with two gerbil species. *Ecology*, 71, 2358–69.

Abramsky, Z., Shachak, M., Subach, A., Brand, S., and Alfia, H. (1992). Predator-prey relationships: rodent–snail interactions in the central-Negev Desert of Israel. *Oikos*, 65, 128–33.

Abramsky, Z., Rosenzweig, M.L., and Subach, A. (1998). Do gerbils care more about competition or predation? *Oikos*, 83, 75–84.

Acocks, J.P.H. (1953). Veld types of South Afirca. *Memoirs of the Botanical Survey of South Africa*, 28, 1–192.

Addicott, J.F. and Tyre, A.J. (1995). Cheating in an obligate mutualism: how often do yucca moths benefit yuccas? *Oikos*, 72, 382–94.

Addicott, J.F., Aho, J.M., Antolin, M.F., Padilla, D.K., Richardson, J.S., and Soluk, D.A. (1987). Ecological neighbourhoods: scaling environmental patterns. *Oikos*, 49, 340–6.

Adondakis, S. and Venable, D.L. (2004). Dormancy and germination in a guild of Sonoran Desert annuals. *Ecology*, 85, 2582–90.

Afik, D. and Pinshow, B. (1993). Temperature regulation and water economy in desert wolves. *Journal of Arid Environments*, 24, 197–209.

Akram, M. and Kemper, W.D. (1979). Infiltration of soils as affected by the pressure and water content at the time of compaction. *Soil Science Society of America Journal*, 43, 1080–6.

Alkon, P.U. (1999). Microhabitat to landscape impacts: crested porcupine digs in the Negev Desert highlands. *Journal of Arid Environments*, 41, 183–202.

Alkon, P.U., Pinshow, B., and Degen, A.A. (1982). Seasonal water turnover rates and total body water volumes in desert chukar partridges. *Condor*, 82, 332–7.

Alpers, C.N. and Brimhall, G.H. (1988). Middle Miocene climate change in the Atacama Desert, northern Chile: evidence from supergene mineralization at La Escondida. *Geological Society of America Bulletin*, 100, 1640–56.

Amezketa, E. (2006). An integrated methology for assessing soil salinisation, a precondition for land desertification. *Journal of Arid Environments*, 67, 594–606.

Anderson, D.A. and Szarek, S.R. (1981). Ecophysiological studies on Sonoran Desert plants. VI. Seasonal photosynthesis and production in *Machaeranthera gracilis*, a winter ephemeral. *Plant, Cell and Environment*, 4, 243–50.

Anderson, W.B. and Polis, G.A. (1998). Marine subsidies of island communities in the Gulf of California: evidence from stable carbon and nitrogen isotopes. *Oikos*, 81, 75–80.

Andersson, C.J. (1856). *Lake Ngami; or explorations and discoveries, during four years' wanderings in the wilds of South Western Africa.* Hurst and Blackett, London.

Andrew, M.H. and Lange, R.T. (1986a). Development of a new piosphere in arid chenopod shrubland grazed by sheep. 1. Changes to the soil surface. *Australian Journal of Ecology*, 11, 395–409.

Andrew, M.H. and Lange, R.T. (1986b). Development of a new piosphere in arid chenopod shrubland grazed by sheep. 2. Changes to the vegetation. *Australian Journal of Ecology*, 11, 411–24.

Angiosperm Phylogeny Group (2003). An update of the Angiosperm Phylogeny Group classification for the orders and families of flowering plants: APG II. *Botanical Journal of the Linnean Society*, 141, 399–436.

Arad, Z. (1993). Water relations and resistance to desiccation in three Israeli desert snails, *Eremina desertorum*, *Euchondrus desertorum* and *Euchondrus albulus*. *Journal of Arid Environments*, 24, 387–95.

Arad, Z., Goldenberg, S. and Heller, J. (1990). Resistance to desiccation and distribution patterns in the land snail *Sphincterochila*. *Journal of Zoology, London*, 218, 353–64.

Arad, Z., Goldenberg, S. and Heller, J. (1993). Intraspecific variation in resistance to desiccation and climatic gradients in the distribution of the bush-dwelling land snail *Trochoidea simulata*. *Journal of Zoology, London*, 229, 249–65.

Aranibar, J.N., Otter, L., Macko, S.A., Feral, C.J.W., Epstein, H.E., Dowty, P.R., Eckardt, F.D., Shugart, H.H., and Swap, R.J. (2004). Nitrogen cycling in the soil–plant system along a precipitation gradient in the Kalahari sands. *Global Change Biology*, 10, 359–73.

Archer, J.R. and Smith, P.D. (1972). The relation between bulk density, available water capacity, and air capacity of soils. *Journal of Soil Science*, 23, 475–80.

Archer, S., Scifres, C.J., Bassham, C., and Maggio, R. (1988). Autogenic succession in a subtropical savanna: rates, dynamics and processes in the conversion of grassland to thorn woodland. *Ecological Monographs*, 58, 111–27.

Archer, S., Schimel, D.S., and Holland, E.A. (1995). Mechanisms of shrubland expansion: land-use, climate or CO_2? *Climatic Change*, 29, 91–9.

Armstrong, S. (1990). Fog, wind and heat: life in the Namib Desert. *New Scientist*, 127, 46–50.

Aronson, J. and Shmida, A. (1992). Plant species diversity along a Mediterranean-desert gradient and its correlation with interannual rainfall fluctuations. *Journal of Arid Environments*, 23, 235–47.

Aronson, J., Kigel, J., and Shmida, A. (1990). Comparative plant sizes and reproductive strategies in desert and Mediterranean populations of ephemeral plants. *Israel Journal of Botany*, 39, 413–30.

Aronson, J., Kigel, J., Shmida, A., and Klein, J. (1992). Adaptive phenology of desert and Mediterranean populations of annual plants grown with and without water stress. *Oecologia*, 89, 17–26.

Arrhenius, O. (1921). Species and area. *Journal of Ecology*, **9**, 95–9.

Avni, Y., Porat, N., Plakht, J., and Avni, G. (2006). Geomorphic changes leading to natural desertification versus anthropogenic land conservation in an arid environment, the Negev Highlands, Israel. *Geomorphology*, **82**, 177–200.

Axelrod, D.I. (1950). Evolution of desert vegetation in western North America. *Carnegie Institute of Washington Publication*, **590**, 216–306.

Ayal, Y. (1994). Time-lags in insect response to plant productivity: significance for plant–insect interactions in deserts. *Ecological Entomology*, **19**, 207–14.

Ayal, Y. and Izhaki, I. (1993). The effect of the mirid bug *Capsodes infuscatus* on fruit production of the geophyte *Asphodelus ramosus* in a desert habitat. *Oecologia*, **93**, 518–23.

Ayal, Y., Polis, G.A., Lubin, Y., and Goldberg, D.E. (2005). How can high animal diversity be supported in low-productivity deserts? The role of macrodetritivory and habitat physiognomy. In M. Shachak, J.R. Gosz, S.T.A. Pickett, and A. Perevolotsky, eds. *Biodiversity in drylands: toward a unified perspective*, pp. 15–29. Oxford University Press, Oxford.

Bagnold, R.A. (1941). *The physics of blown sand and desert dunes*. Methuen Press, London.

Bakken, G.S. (1980). The use of standard operative temperature in the study of the thermal energetics of birds. *Physiological Zoology*, **53**, 108–19.

Barnard, P., Brown, C.J., Jarvis, A.M., and Robertson, A. (1998). Extending the Namibian protected areas network to safeguard hotspots of endemism and diversity. *Biodiversity and Conservation*, **7**, 531–47.

Bartholomew, C. and Casey, T. (1977). Endothermy during terrestrial activity in large beetles. *Science*, **195**, 882–3.

Beadle, H.C.W. (1981). *The vegetation of Australia*. Gustav Fischer, Stuttgart.

Beatley, J.S. (1974). Phenological events and their environmental triggers in Mojave Desert ecosystems. *Ecology*, **55**, 856–63.

Becerra, J.X. (1994). Squirt-gun defense in *Bursera* and the chrysomelid counterploy. *Ecology*, **75**, 1991–6.

Becerra, J.X. (1997). Insects on plants: macroevolutionary chemical trends in host use. *Science*, **276**, 253–6.

Becerra, J.X. (2003). Synchronous coadaptation in an ancient case of herbivory. *Proceedings of the National Academy of Sciences USA*, **100**, 12804–7.

Becerra, J.X. and Venable, D.L. (1990). Rapid-terpene-bath and 'squirt-gun' defense in *Bursera schlechtendalii* and the counterploy of chrysomelid beetles. *Biotropica*, **22**, 320–3.

Beckett, R.P. (1998). Some aspects of the water relations of the lichen *Xanthomaculina hottentotta* (Ach.) Hale from the Namib Desert. *South African Journal of Botany*, **64**, 346–9.

Behnke, R. and Abel, N. (1996). Revisited: the overstocking controversy in semi-arid Africa. *World Animal Review*, **87**, 4–27.

Belnap, J. and Harper, K.T. (1995). Influence of cryptobiotic soil crusts on elemental content of tissue in two desert seed plants. *Arid Soil Research and Rehabilitation*, **9**, 107–15.

Belnap, J. and Warren, S.D. (2002). Patton's tracks in the Mojave Desert, USA: an ecological legacy. *Arid Land Research and Management*, **16**, 245–58.

Belnap, J., Rosentreter, R., Leonard, S., Kaltenecker, J.H., Williams, J., and Eldridge, D.J. (2001). *Biological soil crusts: ecology and management*. U.S. Department of the Interior and Bureau of Land Management, Denver. Technical Reference 1730–2.

Belnap, J., Phillips, S.L., Herrick, J.E., and Johansen, J.R. (2007). Wind erodibility of soils at Fort Irwin, California (Mojave Desert), USA, before and after trampling disturbance: implications for land management. *Earth Surface Processes and Landforms*, **32**, 75–84.

Ben-David, R. and Mazor, E. (1988). Stages in the evolution of Makhtesh Ramon and its drainage system. *Israel Journal of Earth Sciences*, **37**, 125–35.

Ben-Natan, G., Abramsky, Z., Kotler, B.P., and Brown, J.S. (2004). Seeds redistribution in sand dunes: a basis for coexistence for two gerbil species. *Oikos*, **105**, 325–35.

Bennett, A.F. and John-Alder, H. (1986). Thermal relations of some Australian skinks (Sauria: Scincidae). *Copeia*, **1986**, 57–64.

Bennett, A.F., Huey, R.B., John-Alder, H., and Nagy, K.A. (1984). The parasol tail and thermoregulatory behavior of the Cape ground squirrel *Xerus inauris*. *Physiological Zoology*, **57**, 57–62.

Berger, J. (1997). Population constraints associated with the use of black rhinos as an umbrella species for desert herbivores. *Conservation Biology*, **11**, 69–78.

Berger, J. and Cunningham, C. (1994). Phenotypic alteration, evolutionarily significant structures, and rhino conservation. *Conservation Biology*, **8**, 833–40.

Blaustein, L. and Margalit, J. (1996). Priority effects in temporary pools: nature and outcome of mosquito larva–toad tadpole interactions depend on order of entrance. *Journal of Animal Ecology*, **65**, 77–84.

Blydenstein, J., Hungerford, C.R., Day, G.I., and Humphrey, R. (1957). Effect of domestic livestock exclusion on vegetation in the Sonoran Desert. *Ecology*, **38**, 522–6.

Boaz, M., Plitmann, U. and Heyn, C.C. (1994). Reproductive effort in desert *versus* mediterranean crucifers: the allogamous *Erucaria rostrata* and *E. hispanica* and the autogamous *Erophila minima*. *Oecologia*, **100**, 286–92.

Bock, C.E., Bock, J.H., Jepson, K.L., and Ortega, J.C. (1986). Ecological effects of planting African lovegrasses in Arizona. *National Geographic Research*, **2**, 456–63.

Bock, C.E., Bock, J.H., Kennedy, L., and Jones, Z.F. (2007). Spread of nonnative grasses into grazed versus ungrazed desert grasslands. *Journal of Arid Environments*, **71**, 229–35.

Bodmer, R. and Ward, D. (2006). Frugivory in large mammalian herbivores. In K. Danell, R. Bergström, P. Duncan and J. Pastor, eds. *Large mammalian herbivores, ecosystem dynamics, and conservation*, pp. 232–60. Cambridge University Press, Cambridge.

Boeken, B. (1989). Life histories of desert geophytes: the demographic consequences of reproductive biomass partitioning patterns. *Oecologia*, **80**, 278–83.

Boeken, B. (1990). Life histories of two desert species of the bulbous genus *Bellevalia*: the relation between biomass partitioning and water availability. *Oecologia*, **82**, 172–9.

Boeken, B. (1991). Above-ground emergence in the desert tulip *Tulipa systola* Stapf. in the Negev Desert of Israel. *Functional Ecology*, **5**, 705–12.

Boeken, B. and Gutterman, Y. (1986). The effect of temperature in different habitats on flowering time of *Sternbergia clusiana* in the Negev Desert. In Z. Dubinsky and Y. Steinberger, eds. *Environmental quality and ecosystem stability*, volume 3, pp. 151–7. Bar-Ilan University Press, Ramat Gan.

Boeken, B. and Shachak, M. (1998). The dynamics of abundance and incidence of annual plant species during colonization in a desert. *Ecography*, **21**, 63–73.

Boeken, B., Shachak, M., Gutterman, Y., and Brand, S. (1995). Patchiness and disturbance: plant community responses to porcupine diggings in the central Negev. *Ecography*, **18**, 410–21.

Boeken, B., Lipchin, C., Gutterman, Y., and Van Rooyen, N. (1998). Annual plant community responses to density of small-scale soil disturbances in the Negev Desert of Israel. *Oecologia*, **114**, 106–17.

Bohrer, G., Kagan-Zur, V., Roth-Bejerano, N., and Ward, D. (2001). Effects of environmental variables on vesicular–arbuscular mycorrhizal abundance in wild populations of *Vangueria infausta*. *Journal of Vegetation Science*, **12**, 279–88.

Bohrer, G., Kagan-Zur, V., Roth-Bejerano, N., Ward, D., Beck, G., and Bonifacio, E. (2003). Effects of different Kalahari-Desert VA mycorrhizal communities on mineral acquisition and depletion from the soil by host plants. *Journal of Arid Environments*, **55**, 193–208.

Bouskila, A. (1995). Interactions between predation risk and competition: a field study of kangaroo rats and snakes. *Ecology*, **76**, 165–78.

Bowie, M. and Ward, D. (2004). Water and nutrient status of the mistletoe *Plicosepalus acaciae* parasitic on isolated Negev Desert populations of *Acacia raddiana* differing in level of mortality. *Journal of Arid Environments*, **56**, 487–508.

Boyko, H. (1947). On the role of plants as quantitative climate indicators and the geoecological law of distribution. *Journal of Ecology*, **35**, 1–27.

Brinkman, R. (1980). Saline and sodic soils. In Land reclamation and water management. pp 62–8. International Institute for Land Reclamation and Improvement (ILRI), Wageningen, The Netherlands.

Bristow, C.S., Lancaster, N., and Duller, G.A.T. (2005). Combining ground penetrating radar surveys and optical dating to determine dune migration in Namibia. *Journal of the Geological Society*, **162**, 315–22.

Bristow, C.S., Duller, G.A.T., and Lancaster, N. (2007). Age and dynamics of linear dunes in the Namib Desert. *Geology*, **35**, 555–8.

Britz, M-L. and Ward, D. (2007). Dynamics of woody vegetation in a semi-arid savanna, with a focus on bush encroachment. *African Journal of Range and Forage Science*, **24**, 131–40.

Brock, K.E. and Kelt, D.A. (2004). Keystone effects of the endangered Stephens' kangaroo rat (*Dipodomys stephensi*). *Biological Conservation*, **116**, 131–9.

Bronstein, J.L. (2001). The costs of mutualism. *American Zoologist*, **41**, 825–39.

Brown, J.H. and Davidson, D.W. (1977). Competition between seed-eating rodents and ants in desert ecosystems. *Science*, **196**, 880–2.

Brown, J.H. and Heske, E.J. (1990a). Control of a desert–grassland transition by a keystone rodent guild. *Science*, **250**, 1705–4707.

Brown, J.H. and Heske, E.J. (1990b). Temporal changes in a Chihuahuan Desert rodent community. *Oikos*, **59**, 290–302.

Brown, J.R. and Archer, S. (1989). Woody plant invasion of grasslands: establishment of honey mesquite (*Prosopis glandulosa* var. *glandulosa*) on sites differing in herbaceous biomass and grazing history. *Oecologia*, **80**, 19–26.

Brown, J.R. and Archer, S. (1999). Shrub invasion of grassland: recruitment is continuous and not regulated by herbaceous biomass or density. *Ecology*, **80**, 2385–96.

Brown, J.S. (1988). Patch use as an indicator of habitat preference, predation risk, and competition. *Behavioral Ecology and Sociobiology*, **22**, 37–47.

Brown, J.S. (1989). Desert rodent community structure: a test of four mechanisms of coexistence. *Ecological Monographs*, **59**, 1–20.

Brown, J.S. and Rosenzweig, M.L. (1986). Habitat selection in slowly regenerating environments. *Journal of Theoretical Biology*, **123**, 151–71.

Brown, J.S., Kotler, B.P., and Mitchell, W.A. (1997). Competition between birds and mammals: a comparison of giving-up densities between crested larks and gerbils. *Evolutionary Ecology*, **11**, 757–71.

Brown, W.V. and Smith, B.N. (1972). Grass evolution, the Kranz syndrome, $^{13}C/^{12}C$ ratios, and continental drift. *Nature*, **239**, 345–6.

Bruelheide, H., Manegold, M., and Jandt, U. (2004). The genetical structure of *Populus euphratica* and *Alhagi sparsifolia* stands in the Taklimakan Desert. In M. Runge and X. Zhang, eds. *Ecophysiology and habitat requirements of perennial plant species in the Taklimakan Desert*, pp. 153–60. Contributions to a 'Workshop on sustainable management of the shelterbelt vegetation of river oases in the Taklimakan Desert'; Urumqi, Mongolia, April 2–3, 2003.

Buffington, L.C. and Herbel, C.H. (1965). Vegetational changes on a semidesert grassland range from 1858 to 1963. *Ecological Monographs*, **35**, 139–64.

Bull, W.B. (1979). Threshold of critical power in streams. *Geological Society of America*, **90**, 453–64.

Bull, W.B. (1981). Soils, geology and hydrology of deserts. In D.D. Evans and J.L. Thames, eds. *Water in desert ecosystems*, pp. 42–58. Dowden, Hutchinson and Ross, Stroudsburg, PA.

Burke, A. (1995). *Geigeria alata* in the Namib Desert: seed heteromorphism in an extreme arid environment. *Journal of Vegetation Science*, **6**, 473–8.

Burke, A. (2004). A preliminary account of patterns of endemism in Namibia's Sperrgebiet—the succulent karoo. *Journal of Biogeography*, **31**, 1613–22.

Cable, J.M. and Huxman, T.E. (2004). Precipitation pulse size effects on Sonoran Desert soil microbial crusts. *Oecologia*, **141**, 317–24.

Cade, T.J. and Greenwald, L. (1966). Nasal gland excretion by falconiform birds. *Condor*, **68**, 338–50.

Cade, T.J. and Maclean, G.L. (1967). Transport of water by adult sandgrouse to their young. *Condor*, **69**, 323–43.

Calder, W.A. (1984). *Size, function, and life history*. Harvard University Press, Cambridge.

Calder, W.A. and Schmidt-Nielsen, K. (1966). Evaporative cooling and respiratory alkalosis in the pigeon. *Proceedings of the National Academy of Sciences USA*, **55**, 750–6.

Caldwell, M.M., White, R.S., Moore, R.T., and Camp, L.B. (1977). Carbon balance, productivity, and water use of cold-winter desert shrub communities dominated by C_3 and C_4 species. *Oecologia*, **29**, 275–300.

Caldwell, M.M., Manwaring, J.H., and Durham, S.L. (1991). The microscale distribution of neighboring plant roots in fertile soil microsites. *Functional Ecology*, **5**, 765–72.

Caldwell, M.M., Dawson, T.E., and Richards, J.H. (1998). Hydraulic lift: consequences of the efflux of water from plants. *Oecologia*, **113**, 151–61.

Callaway, R.J. (1995). Positive interactions among plants. *Botanical Review*, **61**, 306–49.

Campos, C.M. and Ojeda, R.A. (1997). Dispersal and germination of *Prosopis flexuosa* (Fabaceae) seeds by desert mammals in Argentina. *Journal of Arid Environments*, 35, 707–14.

Carrick, P.J. (2003). Competitive and facilitative relationships among three shrub species, and the role of browsing intensity and rooting depth in the Succulent Karoo, South Africa. *Journal of Vegetation Science*, 14, 761–72.

Caswell, H. (2001). *Matrix population models: construction, analysis and interpretation*. Sinauer, Sunderland, MA.

Catenazzi, A. and Donnelly, M.A. (2007). The *Ulva* connection: marine algae subsidize terrestrial predators in coastal Peru. *Oikos*, 116, 75–86.

Chapple, D.G. and Keogh, J.S. (2004). Parallel adaptive radiations in arid and temperate Australia: molecular phylogeography and systematics of the *Egernia whitii* (Lacertilia: Scincidae) species group. *Biological Journal of the Linnean Society*, 83, 157–73.

Charley, J.L. and Cowling, S.W. (1968). Changes in soil nutrient status resulting from overgrazing and their consequences in plant communities in semi-arid areas. *Proceedings of the Ecological Society of Australia*, 3, 23–8.

Cheal, D.C. (1993). Effects of stock grazing on the plants of semi-arid woodlands and grasslands. *Proceedings of the Royal Society of Victoria*, 105, 57–65.

Chesson, P. (2000). Mechanisms of maintenance of species diversity. *Annual Review of Ecology and Systematics*, 31, 343–66.

Chesson, P. and Huntly, N. (1989). Short-term instabilities and long-term community dynamics. *Trends in Ecology and Evolution*, 4, 293–8.

Chesson, P., Gebauer, R.L.E., Schwinning, S., Huntly, N., Wiegand, K., Ernest, M.S.K., Sher, A., Novoplansky, A., and Weltzin, J.F. (2004). Resource pulses, species interactions, and diversity maintenance in arid and semi-arid environments. *Oecologia*, 141, 236–53.

Chesson, P.L. and Warner, R.R. (1981). Environmental variability promotes coexistence in lottery competitive systems. *American Naturalist*, 117, 923–43.

Clapperton, R. (1993). *Quarternary geology and geomorphology of South America*. Elsevier, Amsterdam.

Coddington, J.A. (1988). Cladistic tests of adaptational hypotheses. *Cladistics*, 4, 3–22.

Cody, M.L. (1970). Chilean bird distribution. *Ecology*, 51, 455–64.

Cody, M.L. (1986). Diversity, rarity, and conservation in mediterranean-climate regions. In M.E. Soulé, ed. *Conservation biology: the science of scarcity and diversity*. Sinauer, Sunderland, MA.

Cody, M.L. (1993). Bird diversity components within and between habitats in Australia. In R.E. Ricklefs and D. Schluter, eds. *Species diversity in ecological communities: historical and geographical perspectives*, pp. 147–58. University of Chicago Press, Chicago.

Cogger, H.G. (1992). *Reptiles and amphibians of Australia*. 4th ed. Reed, Sydney.

Cohen, D. (1966). Optimizing reproduction in a randomly varying environment. *Journal of Theoretical Biology*, 12, 119–29.

Cohen, D. (1967). Optimizing reproduction in a randomly varying environment when a correlation may exist between the conditions at the time a choice has to be made and the subsequent outcome. *Journal of Theoretical Biology*, 16, 1–14.

Cohen, J.E. (1989). Food webs and community structure. In J. Roughgarden, R.M. May, and S.A. Levin, eds. *Perspectives in ecological theory*, pp. 181–202. Princeton University Press, Princeton.

Cohn, J.P. (2001). Sonoran Desert conservation. *BioScience*, **51**, 606–10.

Colwell, R.K. and Winkler, D.W. (1984). A null model for null models in biogeography. In D.R. Strong, D. Simberloff, L.G. Abele, and A.B. Thistle, eds. *Ecological communities: conceptual issues and the evidence*, pp. 344–59. Princeton University Press, Princeton.

Connell, J.H. (1978). Diversity in tropical rain forests and coral reefs. *Science*, **199**, 1302–10.

Cousins, S.H. (1980). A trophic continuum derived from plant structure, animal size and a detritus cascade. *Journal of Theoretical Biology*, **82**, 607–18.

Cousins, S.H. (1987). The decline of the trophic level concept. *Trends in Ecology and Evolution*, **2**, 312–6.

Cowling, R.M. and Hilton-Taylor, C. (1999). Plant biogeography, endemism and diversity. In W.R.J. Dean and S.J. Milton, eds. *The Karoo: ecological patterns and processes*, pp. 42–56. Cambridge University Press, Cambridge.

Cowling, R.M., Gibbs Russell, G.E., Hoffman, M.T., and Hilton-Taylor, C. (1989). Patterns of plant species diversity in southern Africa. In B.J. Huntley, ed. *Biotic diversity in southern Africa: concepts and conservation*, pp. 19–50. Oxford University Press, Cape Town.

Cowling, R.M., Holmes, P.M., and Rebelo, A.G. (1992). Plant diversity and endemism. In R.M. Cowling, ed. *The ecology of fynbos: nutrients, fire and diversity*, pp. 62–112. Oxford University Press, Cape Town.

Cowling, R.M., Rundel, P.W., Desmet, P.G., and Esler, K.J. (1998). Extraordinarily high regional-scale plant diversity in southern African arid lands: subcontinental and global comparisons. *Diversity and Distributions*, **4**, 27–36.

Cowling, R.M., Pressey, R.M., Lombard, A.T., Desmet, P.G., and Ellis, A.G. (1999). From representation to persistence: requirements for a sustainable system of conservation areas in the species-rich mediterranean-climate desert of southern Africa. *Diversity and Distributions*, **5**, 51–71.

Cracraft, J. (1973). Continental drift, paleoclimatology, and the evolution and biogeography of birds. *Journal of Zoology (London)*, **169**, 455–545.

Crawford, C.S. and Gosz, J.R. (1982). Desert ecosystems: their resources in space and time. Environmental Conservation, **9**, 181–95.

Crawford, E.C. and Schmidt-Nielsen, K. (1967). Temperature regulation and evaporative cooling in the ostrich. *American Journal of Physiology*, **212**, 347–53.

Crawley, M.J. (1983). *Herbivory. The dynamics of animal plant interactions*. Blackwells, Oxford.

Crawley, M.J. (1989). Insect herbivory and plant population dynamics. *Annual Review of Entomology*, **34**, 531–64.

Creagh, C. (1992). Understanding arid Australia. *Ecos*, **73**, 15–20.

Crisp, M.D., Laffan, S., Linder, H.P., and Monro, A. (2001). Endemism in the Australian flora. *Journal of Biogeography*, **28**, 183–98.

Croizat, L. (1962). *Space, time, form: the biological synthesis*. Self-published, Caracas.

Croizat, L. (1982). Vicariance/vicariism, panbiogeography, 'vicariance biogeography', etc.: a clarification. *Systematic Zoology*, **31**, 291–304.

Cronk, Q.C.B. and Fuller, J.L. (2001). *Plant invaders: the threat to natural ecosystems*. 2nd edn. Earthscan, London.

Cronquist, A. (1981). *An integrated system of classification of flowering plants.* Columbia University Press, New York.

Cross, A.F. and Schlesinger, W.H. (1999). Plant regulation of soil nutrient distribution in the northern Chihuahuan Desert. *Plant Ecology*, **145**, 11–25.

Cui, Y. and Shao, J. (2005). The role of ground water in arid/semiarid ecosystems, Northwest China. *Ground Water*, **43**, 471–7.

Dabous, A.A. and Osmond, J.K. (2001). Uranium isotopic study of artesian and pluvial contributions to the Nubian Aquifer, Western Desert, Egypt. *Journal of Hydrology*, **243**, 242–53.

Dafni, A., Shmida, A., and Avishai, M. (1981). Leafless autumnal-flowering geophytes in the Mediterranean region: phytogeographical, ecological and evolutionary aspects. *Plant Systematics and Evolution*, **137**, 181–93.

Dafni, A., Bernhardt, P., Shmida, A., Ivri, Y., and Greenbaum, S. (1990). Red bowl-shaped flowers: convergence for beetle pollination in the Mediterranean region. *Israel Journal of Botany*, **39**, 81–92.

Dahlgren, R.M.T., Clifford, H.T., and Yeo, P.F. (1985). *The families of the monocotyledons: structure, evolution and taxonomy.* Springer, Berlin.

Dallas, H.F., Curtis, B.A., and Ward, D. (1991). Water exchange, temperature tolerance, oxygen consumption and activity of the Namib Desert snail, *Trigonephrus* sp. *Journal of Molluscan Studies*, **57**, 359–66.

Daniels, S., Hamer, M., and Rogers, C. (2004). Molecular evidence suggests an ancient radiation for the fairy shrimp genus *Streptocephalus* (Branchiopoda: Anostraca). *Biological Journal of the Linnean Society*, **82**, 313–27.

Danin, A. (1991). Plant adaptation to desert dunes. *Journal of Arid Environments*, **21**, 193–212.

Danin, A. (1996). *Plants of desert dunes.* Springer, Berlin.

Danin, A. and Orshan, G. (1990). The distribution of Raunkiaer life forms in Israel in relation to the environment. *Journal of Vegetation Science*, **1**, 41–8.

Darlington, J.P.E.C. (1987). How termites keep their cool. *Entomological Society of Queensland News Bulletin*, **15**, 45–6.

Darlington, J.P.E.C., Zimmerman, P.R., Greenberg, J., Westberg, C., and Bakwin, P. (1997). Production of metabolic gases by nests of the termite *Macrotermes jeaneli* in Kenya. *Journal of Tropical Ecology*, **13**, 491–510.

Davidowitz, G. (2002). Does precipitation variability increase from mesic to xeric biomes? *Global Ecology and Biogeography*, **11**, 143–54.

Davidson, D.W. and Morton, S.R. (1981). Myrmecochory in some plants (Chenopodiaceae) of the Australian arid zone. *Oecologia*, **50**, 357–66.

Davidson, D.W., Samson, D.A., and Inouye, R.S. (1985). Granivory in the Chihuahuan Desert: interactions within and between trophic levels. *Ecology*, **66**, 486–502.

Davis, J.R. and DeNardo, D.F. (2007). The urinary bladder as a physiological reservoir that moderates dehydration in a large desert lizard, the Gila monster *Heloderma suspectum*. *Journal of Experimental Biology*, **210**, 1472–80.

Dawkins, R. and Krebs, J.R. (1979). Arms races between and within species. *Proceedings of the Royal Society of London, Series B*, **205**, 489–511.

Dawson, T.E. (1993). Hydraulic lift and water use by plants: implications for water balance, performance and plant–plant interactions. *Oecologia*, **95**, 565–74.

Day, A.D. and Ludeke, K.L. (1993). *Plant nutrients in desert environments.* Springer, Berlin.

Dayan, T., Tchernov, E., Yom-Tov, Y., and Simberloff, D. (1989). Ecological character displacement in Saharo-Arabian Vulpes: outfoxing Bergmann's rule. *Oikos*, 55, 263–72.

Dayan, T., Simberloff, D., Tchernov, E., and Yom-Tov, Y. (1990). Feline canines: community-wide character displacement among the small cats of Israel. *American Naturalist*, 136, 39–60.

Degen, A.A. (1988). Ash and electrolyte intakes of the fat sand rat, *Psammomys obesus*, consuming saltbush, *Atriplex halimus*, containing different water content. *Physiological Zoology*, 61, 137–41.

Degen, A.A., Pinshow, B., and Alkon, P.U. (1984). Summer water turnover rates on free-living chukars and sand partridges in the Negev Desert. *Condor*, 85, 333–7.

Degen, A.A., Kam, M., Khokhlova, I.S., and Zeevi, Y. (2000). Fiber digestion and energy utilization of fat sand rats (*Psammomys obesus*) consuming the chenopod *Anabasis articulata*. *Physiological and Biochemical Zoology*, 73, 574–80.

Diaz, S., Noy-Meir, I., and Cabido, M. (2001). Can grazing response of herbaceous plants be predicted from simple vegetative traits? *Journal of Applied Ecology*, 38, 497–508.

Dobson, A.P. and Crawley, M.J. (1987). What's special about desert ecology? *Trends in Ecology and Evolution*, 2, 145–6.

Dobzhansky, T. (1964). Biology: molecular and organismic. *American Zoologist*, 4, 443–52.

Dong, Z., Wang, T., and Wang, X. (2004). Geomorphology of the megadunes in the Badain Jaran Desert. *Geomorphology*, 60, 191–203.

Donovan, L.A., Linton, M.J., and Richards, J.H. (2001). Predawn plant water potential does not necessarily equilibrate with soil water potential under well-watered conditions. *Oecologia*, 129, 328–35.

Downs, C.T. and Perrin, M.R. (1990). Thermal parameters of four species of *Gerbillurus*. *Journal of Thermal Biology*, 15, 291–300.

Downs, C.T. and Ward, D. (1997). Does shading behavior of incubating shorebirds in hot environments cool the eggs or the adults? *Auk*, 114, 717–24.

Du Toit, E. (1942). The spread of prickly pear in the Union. *Farming in South Africa*, 17, 300–4.

Dunai, T.J., González López, G.A., and Juez-Larréet, J. (2005). Oligocene-Miocene age of aridity in the Atacama Desert revealed by exposure dating of erosion-sensitive landforms. *Geology*, 33, 321–4.

Dunning, J.B. (1986). Shrub-steppe bird assemblages revisited: implications for community ecology. *American Naturalist*, 128, 82–98.

Dunning, J.B., Danielson, B.J., and Pulliam, H.R. (1992). Ecological processes that affect populations in complex landscapes. *Oikos*, 65, 169–74.

Dyksterhuis, E.J. (1949). Condition and management of range land based on quantitative ecology. *Journal of Range Management*, 2, 104–15.

Eadie, J.M., Broekhoven, L., and Colgan, P. (1987). Size ratios and artifacts: Hutchinson's rule revisited. *American Naturalist*, 129, 1–17.

Eckardt, F.D. and Schemenauer, R.S. (1998). Fog water chemistry in the Namib Desert, Namibia. *Atmospheric Environment*, 32, 2595–9.

Eckardt, F.D., Drake, N.A., Goudie, A.S., White, K., and Viles, H. (2001). The role of playas in the formation of pedogenic gypsum crusts of the Central Namib Desert. *Earth Surface Processes and Landforms*, 26, 1177–93.

Eckert, R.E., Wood, M.K., Blackburn, W.H., and Peterson, F.F. (1979). Impacts of off-road vehicles on infiltration and sediment production of two desert soils. *Journal of Range Management*, 32, 394–7.

Edney, E.B. (1971). Body temperatures in tenebrionid beetles in the Namib Desert of southern Africa. *Journal of Experimental Biology*, 55, 253–72.

Edwards, G.E., Furbank, R.T., Hatch, M.D., and Osmond, C.B. (2001). What does it take to be C_4?: lessons from the evolution of C_4 photosynthesis. *Plant Physiology*, 125, 46–9.

Ehleringer, J.R. (1993). Carbon and water relations in desert plants: an isotopic perspective. In J.R Ehleringer, A.E. Hall, and G.D. Farquhar, eds. *Stable isotopes and plant carbon/water relations*, pp. 155–72. Academic Press, San Diego.

Ehleringer, J.R. and Forseth, I. (1980). Solar tracking by plants. *Science*, 210, 1094–8.

Ehleringer, J.R. and Monson, R.K. (1993). Evolutionary and ecological aspects of photosynthetic pathway variation. *Annual Review of Ecology and Systematics*, 24, 411–39.

Ehrlich, P.R. and Raven, P.H. (1964). Butterflies and plants: a study in coevolution. *Evolution*, 18, 586–608.

Eickmeier, W.G. (1978). Photosynthetic pathway distributions in Big Bend National Park, and implications for enhanced resource partitioning. *Photosynthetica*, 12, 290–7.

Eldridge, D.J. and Greene, R.S.B. (1994). Microbiotic soil crusts: a review of their roles in soil and ecological processes in the rangelands of Australia. *Australian Journal of Soil Research*, 32, 389–415.

Ellis, A.G. and Weis, A.E. (2006). Coexistence and differentiation of 'flowering stones': the role of local adaptation to soil microenvironment. *Journal of Ecology*, 94, 322–35.

Ellis, A.G., Weis, A.E., and Gaut, B.S. (2006). Evolutionary radiation of 'stone plants' in the genus *Argyroderma* (Aizoaceae): unraveling the effects of landscape, habitat and flowering time. *Evolution*, 60, 39–55.

Ellis, J.E. and Swift, D.M. (1988). Stability of African pastoral ecosystems: alternate paradigms and implications for development. *Journal of Range Management*, 41, 450–9.

Ellis, L.M. (1995). Bird use of salt cedar and cottonwood vegetation in the middle Rio Grande valley of New Mexico, USA. *Journal of Arid Environments*, 30, 339–49.

Ellis, R.P., Vogel, J.C., and Fuls, A. (1980). Photosynthetic pathways and the geographical distribution of grasses in South West Africa/Namibia. *South African Journal of Science*, 76, 307–14.

Ellner, S.P. and Shmida, A. (1981). Why are adaptations for long-range seed dispersal rare in desert plants? *Oecologia*, 53, 133–44.

Emanuel, W.R., Shugart, H.H., and Stevenson, M.P. (1985). Climatic change and the broad-scale distribution of terrestrial ecosystem complexes. *Climate Change*, 7, 29–43.

Ernest, S.K.M., Brown, J.H., and Parmenter, R.R. (2000). Rodents, plants, and precipitation: spatial and temporal dynamics of consumers and resources. *Oikos*, 88, 470–82.

Esler, K.J., Rundel, P.W., and Vorster, P. (1999). Biogeography of prostrate-leaved geophytes in semi-arid South Africa: hypotheses on functionality. *Plant Ecology*, 142, 105–20.

Esparza-Olguin, L., Valverde, T., and Vilchis-Anaya, E. (2002). Demographic analysis of a rare columnar cactus (*Neobuxbaumia macrocephala*) in the Tehuacan Valley, Mexico. *Biological Conservation*, **103**, 349–59.

Ettershank, G., Ettershank, J., Bryant, M., and Whitford, W.G. (1978). Effects of nitrogen fertilization on primary production in a Chihuahuan Desert ecosystem. *Journal of Arid Environments*, **1**, 135–9.

Evenari, M. (1985). Adaptations of plants and animals to the desert environment. In M. Evenari, I. Noy-Meir, and D.W. Goodall, eds. *Hot deserts and arid shrublands*, volume 12A, pp. 79–92. Elsevier, Amsterdam.

Evenari, M., Shanan, L., and Tadmor, N. (1982). *The Negev: the challenge of a desert*. 2nd ed. Harvard University Press, Cambridge, MA.

Ewens, W.J., Brockwell, P.J., Gani, J.M., and Resnick, S.I. (1996). Minimum viable population size in the presence of catastrophes. In M. Soulé, ed. *Viable populations for conservation*, pp. 59–68. Cambridge University Press, Cambridge.

Ewer, R.F. (1973). *The carnivores*. Cornell University Press, Ithaca, NY.

Ezcurra, E. (ed.) (2006). *Global deserts outlook*. United Nations Environment Program, Nairobi.

Facelli, J.M., Chesson, P., and Barnes, N. (2005). Differences in seed biology of annual plants in arid lands: a key ingredient of the storage effect. *Ecology*, **86**, 2998–3006.

Feh, C., Boldsukh, T., and Tourenq, C. (1994). Are family groups in equids a response to cooperative hunting by predators? The case of Mongolian kulans. *Revue Ecologie (Terre Vie)*, **49**, 11–20.

Felsenstein, J. (1985). Phylogenies and the comparative method. *American Naturalist*, **125**, 1–15.

Fielden, L.J., Waggoner, J.P., Perrin, M.R., and Hickman, G.C. (1990). Thermoregulation in the Namib Desert golden mole, *Eremitalpa granti namibensis* (Chrysochloridae). *Journal of Arid Environments*, **18**, 221–37.

Fielden, L.J., Duncan, F.D., Lighton, J.R.B., and Rechav, Y. (1993). Ventilation in the adults of *Amblyomma hebraeum* and *A. marmoreum* (Atari, Ixodidae), vectors of heartwater in southern Africa. *Revue d'Elevage et de Medecine Veterinaire des Pays Tropicaux*, **46**, 335–8.

Fireman, M. and Hayward, H.E. (1952). Indicator significance of some shrubs in the Escalente Desert, Utah. *Botanical Gazette*, **114**, 143–55.

Fisher, F.M., Zak, J.C., Cunningham, G.L., and Whitford, W.G. (1988). Water and nitrogen effects in growth allocation patterns of creosotebush in the northern Chihuahuan Desert. *Journal of Range Management*, **41**, 387–91.

Flegg, J. (1993). *Deserts: a miracle of life*. Facts on File, New York.

Fleming, T.H. and Holland, J.N. (1998). The evolution of obligate pollination mutualism: senita cactus and senita moth. *Oecologia*, **114**, 368–74.

Floret, C., Pontanier, R., and Rambal, S. (1982). Measurements and modelling of primary productivity on water use for a south Tunisian steppe. *Journal of Arid Environments*, **5**, 77–90.

Flowers, T.J. and Yeo, A.R. (1986). Ion relations of plants under drought and salinity. *Australian Journal of Plant Physiology*, **13**, 75–91.

Flowers, T.J., Troke, P.F., and Yeo, A.R. (1977). The mechanism of salt tolerance in halophytes. *Annual Review of Plant Physiology*, **28**, 89–21.

Foden, W., Midgley, G.F., Hughes, G., Bond, W.J., Thuiller, W., Hoffman, M.T., Kaleme, P., Underhill, L.G., Rebelo, A., and Hannah, L. (2007). A changing climate is eroding the geographical range of the Namib Desert tree *Aloe* through population declines and dispersal lags. *Diversity and Distributions*, **13**, 645–53.

Fonteyn, P.J. and Mahall, B.E. (1978). Competition among desert perennials. *Nature*, **275**, 544–5.

Fowler, N. (1986). The role of competition in plant communities in arid and semi-arid regions. *Annual Review of Ecology and Systematics*, **17**, 89–110.

Franchesci, V.R. and Horner, H.T. (1980). Calcium oxalate in plants. *Botanical Review*, **46**, 361–427.

Franco, A.C. and Nobel, P.S. (1989). Effect of nurse plants on the microhabitat and growth of cacti. *Journal of Ecology*, **77**, 870–86.

Franco-Pizaña, J., Fulbright, T., and Gardiner, D. (1995). Spatial relations between shrubs and *Prosopis glandulosa* canopies. *Journal of Vegetation Science*, **6**, 73–8.

Freeman, D.C. and Emlen, J.M. (1995). Assessment of interspecific interactions in plant communities: an illustration of the cold desert saltbush grasslands of North America. *Journal of Arid Environments*, **31**, 179–98.

Fretwell, S.D. (1977). The regulation of plant communities by the food chains exploiting them. *Perspectives in Biology and Medicine*, **20**, 169–85.

Fretwell, S.D. and Lucas, H.L. (1970). On territorial behavior and other factors influencing habitat distribution in birds. I. Theoretical development. *Acta Biotheoretica*, **14**, 16–36.

Friedel, M.H., Cellier, K.M., and Nicolson, K.P. (1980). Nutrient deficiencies in central Australian semi-desert rangelands, with reference to decline in range condition. *Australian Rangeland Journal*, **2**, 151–61.

Friedel, M.H., Foran, B.D., and Stafford Smith, D.M. (1990). Where the creeks run dry or ten feet high: pastoral management in Australia. *Proceedings of the Ecological Society of Australia*, **16**, 185–94.

Friedman, J. (1971). The effect of competition by adult *Zygophyllum dumosum* Boiss. on seedlings of *Artemisia herba-alba* Asso in the Negev Desert of Israel. *Journal of Ecology*, **59**, 775–82.

Friedman, J. and Stein, Z. (1980). The influence of seed dispersal mechanisms on the dispersion of *Anastatica hierochuntica* (Cruciferae) in the Negev Desert, Israel. *Journal of Ecology*, **68**, 43–50.

Fuller, B. (1993). *Institutional appropriation and social change among agropastoralists in central Namibia, 1916–1988*. Unpublished PhD thesis, Boston University, Boston, MA.

Fuller, W.H. (1975). *Soils of the desert southwest*. University of Arizona Press, Tucson, AZ.

Gadgil, M. and Vartak, V.D. (1975). Sacred groves of India—a plea for their continuous conservation. *Journal of the Bombay Natural History Society*, **72**, 313–20.

Gadgil, M. and Vartak, V.D. (1994). The sacred uses of nature. In R. Guha, ed. *Economic botany*, pp. 82–9. Oxford University Press, Delhi.

Galil, J. (1980). Kinetics of bulbous plants. *Endeavour*, **5**, 15–20.

Galil, J. (1983). Morpho-ecological studies of lowering in the seedling of the geophyte *Ixilirion tataricum* (Pall.) Herb. *New Phytologist*, **93**, 143–50.

Garland, T., Huey, R.B., and Bennett, A.F. (1991). Phylogeny and coadaptation of thermal physiology in lizards: a re-analysis. *Evolution*, **45**, 1969–75.

Garland, T., Harvey, P.H., and Ives, A.R. (1992). Procedures for the analysis of comparative data using phylogenetically independent contrasts. *Systematic Biology*, **41**, 18–32.

Gates, D.M. (2003). *Biophysical ecology.* Dover, Mineola, NY.

Geiger, R. (1961). *Das Klima der Bodennahen Luftschicht.* 4th ed. Friedrich Vieweg and Sohn, Braunschweig.

Ghazanfar, S.A. (1991). Vegetation structure and phytogeography of Jabal Shams, an arid mountain in Oman. *Journal of Biogeography,* **18,** 399–409.

Gilad, O., Grant, W.E., and Saltz, D. (2008). Simulated dynamics of Arabian Oryx (*Oryx leucoryx*) in the Israeli Negev: effects of migration corridors and post-reintroduction changes in natality on population viability. *Ecological Modelling,* **210,** 169–78.

Gillespie, J.H. (1977). Natural selection for variance in offspring numbers: a new evolutionary principle. *American Naturalist,* **111,** 1010–14.

Glen, A.S. and Dickman, C.R. (2005). Complex interactions among mammalian carnivores in Australia, and their implications for wildlife management. *Biological Review,* **80,** 387–401.

Glen, A.S., Dickman, C.R., Soulé, M.E., and Mackey, B.G. (2007). Evaluating the role of the dingo as a trophic regulator in Australian ecosystems. *Austral Ecology,* **32,** 492–501.

Glenn, E.P., Watson, M.C., O'Leary, J.W., and Axelson, R.D. (1992). Comparison of salt tolerance and osmotic adjustment of low-sodium and high-sodium subspecies of the C_4 halophyte, *Atriplex canescens. Plant, Cell and Environment,* **15,** 711–18.

Godínez-Alvarez, H., Valiente-Banuet, A., and Banuet, L.V. (1999). Biotic interactions and the population dynamics of the long-lived columnar cactus *Neobuxbaumia tetetzo* in the Tehuacán Valley, Mexico. *Canadian Journal of Botany,* 77, 203–8.

Gold, A.G. and Gujar, B.R. (1989). Of gods, trees and boundaries. *Asian Folklore Studies,* **48,** 211–29.

Goldberg, D. and Turner, R.M. (1986). Vegetation change and plant demography in permanent plots in the Sonoran Desert. *Ecology,* **67,** 695–712.

Goldberg, D.E. (1990). Components of resource competition in plant communities. In J. Grace and D. Tilman, eds. *Perspectives in plant competition,* pp. 27–49. Academic Press, San Diego.

Goldberg, D.E. and Novoplansky, A. (1997). On the relative importance of competition in unproductive environments. *Journal of Ecology,* **85,** 409–18.

Goldberg, D.E., Turkington, R., Olsvig-Whittaker, L., and Dyer, A.R. (2001). Density dependence in an annual plant community: variation among life history stages. *Ecological Monographs,* **71,** 423–46.

Goldblatt, P. and Manning, J.C. (1996). Phylogeny and speciation in *Lapeirousia* subgenus *Lapeirousia* (Iridaceae: Ixiodidae). *Annals of the Missouri Botanical Garden,* **83,** 346–61.

González-Megías, A. and Sánchez-Piñero, F. (2004). Response of host species to brood parasitism in dung beetles: importance of nest location by parasitic species. *Functional Ecology,* **18,** 914–24.

Goudie, A.S. (1983). Dust storms in space and time. *Progress in Physical Geography,* 7, 502–30.

Green, R.L. (2007). Trends in golf course water use and regulation in California. http://ucrturf.ucr.edu [Date accessed: 17 December 2007].

Gries, D., Zeng, F., Foetzki, A., Arndt, S., Bruelheide, H., Thomas, F., Zhang, X., and Runge, M. (2003). Growth and water relations of *Tamarix ramosissima* and *Populus euphratica* on Taklamakan Desert dunes in relation to depth to a permanent water table. *Plant, Cell and Environment*, **26**, 725–36.

Griffin, G.F., Stafford Smith, D.M., Morton, S.R., Allan, G.E., and Masters, K.A. (1989). Status and implications of the invasion of Tamarisk (*Tamarix aphylla*) on the Finke river, Northern Territory, Australia. *Journal of Environmental Management*, **29**, 297–315.

Grigory, S.C. (2007). Golf course water use. http://hillcountrywater.org/GolfCourse.htm [Date accessed: 17 December 2007].

Grime, J.P. (1977). Evidence for the existence of three primary strategies in plants and its relevance to ecological and evolutionary theory. *American Naturalist*, **111**, 1169–94.

Groner, E. and Ayal, Y. (2001). The interaction between bird predation and plant cover in determining habitat occupancy of darkling beetles. *Oikos*, **93**, 22–31.

Gross, J.E., Alkon, P.U., and Demment, M.W. (1996). Nutritional ecology of dimorphic herbivores: digestion and passage rates in Nubian ibex. *Oecologia*, **107**, 170–8.

Groves, C.P. (1986). The taxonomy, distribution, and adaptation of recent equids. In R.H. Meadow and H. Uerpmann, eds. *Equids in the ancient world*, pp. 11–51. Ludwig Reichert, Wiesbaden, Germany.

Günster, A. (1992). Aerial seed banks of the central Namib: the distribution of serotinous plants in relation to climate and habitat. *Journal of Biogeography*, **19**, 563–72.

Günster, A. (1993a). Does the timing and intensity of rain events affect resource allocation in serotinous desert plants? *Acta Oecologia*, **14**, 153–59.

Günster, A. (1993b). Microhabitat differentiation of serotinous plants in the Namib Desert. *Journal of Vegetation Science*, **4**, 585–90.

Günster, A. (1994). Seed bank dynamics: longevity, viability and predation of seeds of serotinous plants in the central Namib. *Journal of Arid Environments*, **28**, 195–205.

Guo, L.B. and Gifford, R.M. (2002). Soil carbon stocks and land use change: a meta-analysis. *Global Change Biology*, **8**, 345–60.

Guo, Q. (1996). Effects of banner-tailed kangaroo rat mounds on small-scale plant community structure. *Oecologia*, **106**, 247–56.

Guo, Z.T., Ruddiman, W.F., Hao, Q.Z., Wu, H.B., Qiao, Y.S., Zhu, R.X., Peng, S.Z., Wei, J.J., Yuan, B.Y., and Liu, T.S. (2002). Onset of Asian desertification by 22 Myr ago inferred from loess deposits in China. *Nature*, **416**, 159–63.

Gutierrez, J.R. and Whitford, W.G. (1987). Chihuahuan Desert annuals: importance of water and nitrogen. *Ecology*, **68**, 2032–45.

Gutierrez, J.R., DaSilva, O.A., Pagani, M.I., Weems, D., and Whitford, W.G. (1988). Effects of different patterns of supplemental water and nitrogen fertilization on productivity and composition of Chihuahuan Desert annual plants. *American Midland Naturalist*, **119**, 336–43.

Gutierrez, M., Gracen, V.E., and Edwards, G.E. (1974). Biochemical and cytological relationships in C_4 plants. *Planta*, **119**, 279–300.

Gutterman, Y. (1993). *Seed germination in desert plants*. Springer, Berlin.

Gutterman, Y. (1994). Strategies of seed dispersal and germination in plants inhabiting desert. *Botanical Review*, **60**, 373–416.

Gutterman, Y. (2000). Environmental factors and survival strategies of annual plant species in the Negev Desert, Israel. *Plant Species Biology*, **15**, 113–25.

Gutterman, Y. (2002). *Survival strategies of annual desert plants*. Springer, Berlin.

Gutterman, Y. and Ginott, S. (1994). Long-term protected 'seed bank' in dry inflorescences of *Asteriscus pygmaeus*: achene dispersal mechanism and germination. *Journal of Arid Environments*, **26**, 149–63.

Gutterman, Y. and Herr, N. (1981). Influences of porcupine (*Hystrix indica*) activity on the slopes on the northern Negev mountains: germination and vegetation renewal in different geomorphological types and slope directions. *Oecologia*, **51**, 332–4.

Gutterman, Y. and Shem-Tov, S. (1997). Mucilaginous seed coat structure of *Carrichtera annua* and *Anastatica hierochuntica* from the Negev Desert highlands of Israel, and its adhesion to the soil crust. *Journal of Arid Environments*, **35**, 695–705.

Hadar, L., Noy-Meir, I., and Perevolotsky, A. (1999). The effect of shrub clearing and grazing on the composition of a Mediterranean plant community: functional groups versus species. *Journal of Vegetation Science*, **10**, 673–82.

Hadley, N.F. (1970). Water relations of the desert scorpion, *Hadrurus arizonensis*. *Journal of Experimental Biology*, **53**, 547–58.

Hadley, N.F. (1979). Wax secretion and color phases of the desert tenebrionid beetle *Cryptoglossa verrucosa* (LeConte). *Science*, **203**, 367–9.

Hagadorn, J.W. and Waggoner, B. (2000). Ediacaran fossils from the southwestern Great Basin, United States. *Journal of Paleontology*, **74**, 349–59.

Haines, H., MacFarlane, W.V., Setchell, C., and Howard, B. (1974). Water turnover and pulmocutaneous evaporation of Australian desert dasyurids and murids. *American Journal of Physiology*, **227**, 958–63.

Hairston, N.G. and Hairston, N.G. (1993). Cause-effect relationships in energy flow, trophic structure, and interspecific interactions. *American Naturalist*, **142**, 379–411.

Hairston, N.G., Smith, F.E., and Slobodkin, L.B. (1960). Community structure, population control and competition. *American Naturalist*, **94**, 421–5.

Halvorson, W.L. and Patten, D.T. (1974). Moisture stress in Upper Sonoran Desert shrubs in relation to soil moisture and topography. *Ecology*, **55**, 173–7.

Hamer, M., Brendonck, L., Coomans, A., and Appleton, C.C. (1994a). A review of African Streptocephalidae (Crustacea: Branchiopoda: Anostraca). Part 1: south of Zambesi and Kunene rivers. *Archiv für Hydrobiologie*, **Supplement 99**, 235–77.

Hamer, M., Brendonck, L., Appleton, C.C., and Coomans, A. (1994b). A review of African Streptocephalidae (Crustacea: Branchiopoda: Anostraca). Part 2: north of Zambesi and Kunene rivers, and Madagascar. *Archiv für Hydrobiologie*, **Supplement 99**, 279–311.

Hamilton, W.D. (1971). Geometry for the selfish herd. *Journal of Theoretical Biology*, **31**, 295–311.

Hamilton, W.J. (1975). Coloration and its thermal consequences for diurnal desert insects. In N.F. Hadley, ed. *Environmental physiology of desert organisms*, pp. 67–89. Dowden, Hutchinson and Ross, Stroudsburg, PA.

Hamilton, W.J. and Seely, M.K. (1976). Fog basking by the Namib Desert beetle *Onymacris unguicularis*. *Nature*, **262**, 284–5.

Hammer, S.A. (1993). *The genus Conophytum*. Succulent Plant Publications, Pretoria, South Africa.

Hanan, N.P., Prevost, Y., Diouf, A., and Diallo, O. (1991). Assessment of desertification around deep wells in the Sahel using satellite imagery. *Journal of Applied Ecology*, **28**, 173–86.

Hardin, G. (1968). The tragedy of the commons. *Science*, **162**, 1243–8.

Hartsock, T.L. and Nobel, P.S. (1976). Watering converts a CAM plant to daytime CO_2 uptake. *Nature*, **262**, 574–6.

Hattersley, P.W. (1983). The distribution of C_3 and C_4 grasses in Australia in relation to climate. *Oecologia*, **57**, 113–28.

Hazard, L.C. (2001). Ion secretions by salt glands of desert iguanas (*Dipsosaurus dorsalis*). *Physiological and Biochemical Zoology*, **74**, 22–31.

Heinrich, B. (1977). Why have some animals evolved to regulate a high body temperature? *American Naturalist*, **111**, 623–40.

Heinrich, B. (1993). *Hot-blooded insects: strategies and mechanisms of thermoregulation*. Harvard University Press, Cambridge, MA.

Heinrich, B. (1994). Of Bedouins, beetles and blooms. *Natural History*, **103**, 52–9.

Hendricks, H., Bond, W., Midgley, J., and Novellie, P. (2005). Plant species richness and composition a long livestock grazing intensity gradients in a Namaqualand (South Africa) protected area. *Plant Ecology*, **176**, 19–33.

Henke, S.E. and Bryant, F.C. (1999). Effect of coyote removal on the faunal community in western Texas. *Journal of Wildlife Management*, **63**, 1066–81.

Hennessy, J.T., Gibbens, R.P., Tromble, J.M., and Cardenas, M. (1983). Vegetation changes from 1935 to 1980 in mesquite dunelands and former grasslands of southern New Mexico. *Journal of Range Management*, **36**, 370–4.

Henschel, J.R. (1990). Spiders wheel to escape. *South African Journal of Science*, **86**, 151–2.

Henschel, J.R. and Lubin, Y.D. (1992). Environmental factors affecting the web and activity of a psammophilous spider in the Namib Desert. *Journal of Arid Environments*, **22**, 173–89.

Henschel, J.R. and Lubin, Y.D. (1997). A test of habitat selection at two spatial scales in a sit-and-wait predator: a web spider in the Namib Desert dunes. *Journal of Animal Ecology*, **66**, 401–13.

Hermony, I., Shachak, M., and Abramsky, Z. (1992). Habitat distribution in the desert snail *Trochoidea seetzenii*. *Oikos*, **64**, 516–22.

Herron, M., Waterman, J.M., and Parkinson, C.L. (2005). Phylogeny and historical biogeography of African ground squirrels: the role of climate change in the evolution of *Xerus*. *Molecular Ecology*, **14**, 2773–88.

Heske, E.J., Brown, J.H., and Guo, Q. (1993). Effects of kangaroo rat exclusion on vegetation structure and plant species diversity in the Chihuahuan Desert. *Oecologia*, **95**, 520–4.

Heske, E.J., Brown, J.H., and Mistry, S. (1994). Long-term experimental study of a Chihuahuan Desert rodent community: 13 years of competition. *Ecology*, **75**, 438–45.

Hesla, B.I., Tieszen, H.L., and Boutton, T.W. (1985). Seasonal water relations of savanna shrubs and grasses in Kenya, East Africa. *Journal of Arid Environments*, **8**, 15–31.

Hesse, P.P., Magee, J.W., and van der Kaars, S. (2004). Late Quaternary climates of the Australian arid zone: a review. *Quaternary International*, **118/119**, 87–102.

Higgins, S.I., Bond, W.J., and Trollope, S.W. (2000). Fire, resprouting and variability: a recipe for grass–tree coexistence in savanna. *Journal of Ecology*, **88**, 213–29.

Hilton-Taylor, C. (1996). Patterns and characteristics of the flora of the Succulent Karoo biome, southern Africa. In L.J.E. van der Maesen, X.M. van der Burgt, and J.M. van Medenbach de Rooy, eds. *The biodiversity of African plants*, pp. 58–72. Kluwer, Dordrecht.

Hinsley, S.A., Ferns, P.N., Thomas, D.H., and Pinshow, B. (1993). Black-bellied sandgrouse and pin-tailed sandgrouse: closely related species with differing bioenergetic adaptations to arid zones. *Physiological Zoology*, **66**, 20–42.

Hoffman, M.T. and Ashwell, A. (2001). *Nature divided: land degradation in South Africa*. University of Cape Town Press, Cape Town.

Hoffman, M.T. and Cowling, R.M. (1990a). Desertification in the lower Sundays River Valley, South Africa. *Journal of Arid Environments*, **19**, 105–17.

Hoffman, M.T. and Cowling, R.M. (1990b). Vegetation change in the semi-arid, eastern Karoo over the last two hundred years: an expanding Karoo—fact or fiction? *South African Journal of Science*, **86**, 286–94.

Hoffman, M.T., Bond, W.J., and Stock, W.D. (1995). Desertification of the eastern Karoo, South Africa: conflicting palaeoecological, historical and soil isotopic evidence. *Environmental Monitoring and Assessment*, **37**, 159–77.

Holland, J.N. and Fleming, T.H. (1999). Mutualistic interactions between *Upiga virescens* (Pyralidae), a pollinating seed-consumer, and *Lophocereus schottii* (Cactaceae). *Ecology*, **80**, 2074–84.

Holland, J.N., DeAngelis, D.L., and Bronstein, J.L. (2002). Population dynamics and mutualism: functional responses of benefits and costs. *American Naturalist*, **159**, 231–44.

Holland, J.N., DeAngelis, D.L., and Schultz, S.T. (2004). Evolutionary stability of mutualism: interspecific population regulation as an evolutionarily stable strategy. *Proceedings of the Royal Society of London, Series B*, **271**, 1807–14.

Holt, R.D. and Kotler, B. (1987). Short-term apparent competition. *American Naturalist*, **130**, 412–30.

Horn, H.S. (1975). Markovian properties of forest succession. In M.L. Cody and J.M. Diamond, eds. *Ecology and evolution of communities*, pp. 196–211. Belknap Press, Cambridge, MA.

Howes, D.A. and Abrahams, A.D. (2003). Modeling runoff and runon in a desert shrubland ecosystem, Jornada Basin, New Mexico. *Geomorphology*, **53**, 45–73.

Huey, R.B. (1982). Temperature, physiology, and the ecology of reptiles. In C. Gans and F.H. Pough, eds. *Biology of the reptilia*, volume 12, pp. 25–91. Academic Press, New York.

Huey, R.B. and Bennett, A.F. (1987). Phylogenetic studies of coadaptation: preferred temperatures versus optimal performance temperatures of lizards. *Evolution*, **41**, 1098–115.

Huey, R.B. and Stevenson, R.D. (1979). Integrating thermal physiology and ecology of ectotherms: a discussion of approaches. *American Zoologist*, **19**, 357–66.

Huey, R.B., Pianka, E.R., Egan, M.E., and Coons, L.W. (1974). Ecological shifts in sympatry: Kalahari fossorial lizards (*Typhlosaurus*). *Ecology*, **55**, 304–16.

Hughes, J.J. and Ward, D. (1993). Predation risk and distance to cover affect foraging behaviour in Namib Desert gerbils. *Animal Behaviour*, **46**, 1243–5.

Hughes, J.J., Ward, D., and Perrin, M.R. (1994). Predation risk and competition affect habitat selection and activity of Namib Desert gerbils. *Ecology*, **75**, 1397–405.

Humphrey, R.R. (1958). The desert grassland. *Botanical Review*, **24**, 193–253.

Humphreys, W.F. (1973). *The environment, biology, and energetics of the wolf spider Lycosa godeffroyi (L. Koch 1865)*. Unpublished PhD thesis, Australian National University, Canberra.

Huschke, R.E. (1959). *Glossary of meteorology*. American Meteorological Society, Boston, MA.

Hutchinson, G.E. (1959). Homage to Santa Rosalia, or why are there so many kinds of animals? *American Naturalist*, **93**, 145–9.

Huxman, T.E. and Monson, R.K. (2003). Stomatal responses of C_3, C3-C4 and C_4 *Flaveria* species to light and intercellular CO_2 concentration: implications for the evolution of stomatal behaviour. *Plant, Cell and Environment*, **26**, 313–22.

Idso, S.B. (1992). Shrubland expansion in the American Southwest. *Climate Change*, **22**, 85–6.

Ihlenfeldt, H.-D. (1994). Diversification in an arid world: the Mesembryanthemaceae. *Annual Reviews of Ecology and Systematics*, **25**, 521–46.

Illius, A.W. and O'Connor, T.G. (2000). Resource heterogeneity and ungulate population dynamics. *Oikos*, **89**, 283.

Iverson, R.M. (1980). Processes of accelerated pluvial erosion on desert hillslopes modified by vehicular traffic. *Earth Surface Processes*, **5**, 369–88.

Jackson, R.B., Banner, J.L., Jobbágy, E.G., Pockman, W.T., and Wall, D.H. (2002). Ecosystem carbon loss with woody plant invasion of grasslands. *Nature*, **418**, 623–6.

Jackson, R.C. and Crovello, T.J. (1971). A comparison of numerical and biosystematic studies in *Haplopappus*. *Brittonia*, **23**, 54–70.

Jacobson, K.M. and Lester, E.A. (2003). A first assessment of genetic variation in *Welwitschia mirabilis* Hook. *Journal of Heredity*, **94**, 212–17.

Jacobson, P.J., Jacobson, K.M., and Seely, M.K. (1995). *Ephemeral rivers and their catchments: sustaining people and development in western Namibia*. Desert Research Foundation of Namibia, Windhoek.

James, C.D. and Shine, R. (2000). Why are there so many coexisting species of lizards in Australian deserts? *Oecologia*, **125**, 127–41.

James, C.D., Hoffman, M.T., Lightfoot, D.C., Forbes, G.S., and Whitford, W.G. (1994). Fruit abortion in *Yucca elata* and its implications for the mutualistic association with yucca moths. *Oikos*, **69**, 207–16.

James, C.D., Landsberg, J., and Morton, S.R. (1999). Provision of watering points in the Australian arid zone: a review of effects on biota. *Journal of Arid Environments*, **41**, 87–121.

James, D.W. and Jurinak, J.J. (1978). Nitrogen fertilization of dominant plants in the northeastern Great Basin desert. In N.E. West and J. Skujins, eds. *Nitrogen in desert ecosystems*, pp. 219–43. Dowden, Hutchinson and Ross, Stroudsburg, PA.

Jauffret, S. and Lavorel, S. (2003). Are plant functional types relevant to describe degradation in arid, southern Tunisian steppes? *Journal of Vegetation Science*, **14**, 399–408.

Jeltsch, F., Milton, S.J., Dean, W.R.J., and Van Rooyen, N. (1996). Tree spacing and coexistence in semiarid savannas. *Journal of Ecology*, **84**, 583–95.

Jeltsch, F., Milton, S.J., Dean, W.R.J., and Van Rooyen, N. (1997). Simulated pattern formation around artificial waterholes in the semi-arid Kalahari. *Journal of Vegetation Science*, **8**, 177–81.

Jeltsch, F., Weber, G., Dean, W.R.J., and Milton, S.J. (1998). Disturbances in savanna ecosystems: modelling the impact of a key determinant. In J.L. Usó, C.A. Brebbia, and H. Power, eds. *Ecosystems and sustainable development*, pp. 233–42. Computational Mechanics Publications, Southampton.

Jeltsch, F., Weber, G.E., and Grimm, V. (2000). Ecological buffering mechanisms in the savannas: a unifying theory of long-term tree–grass coexistence. *Plant Ecology*, **150**, 161–71.

Jennings, C.M.H. (1974). *The hydrology of Botswana*. Unpublished PhD thesis, University of Natal, Pietermaritzburg, South Africa.

Jesson, R.A. and Maclean, G.L. (1976). Salt glands in neonatal Australian Pratincole. *Emu*, **76**, 227.

Jiménez-Sierra, C., Mandujano, M.C., and Eguiarte, L.E. (2007). Are populations of the candy barrel cactus (*Echinocactus platyacanthus*) in the desert of Tehuacan, Mexico at risk? Population projection matrix and life table response analysis. *Biological Conservation*, **135**, 278–92.

Johnson, C.N. and Wroe, S. (2003). Causes of extinction of vertebrates during the Holocene of mainland Australia: arrival of the dingo, or human impact? *The Holocene*, **13**, 941–8.

Johnson, C.N., Isaac, J.L., and Fisher, D.O. (2007). Rarity of a top predator triggers continent-wide collapse of mammal prey: dingoes and marsupials in Australia. *Proceedings of the Royal Society B*, **114**, 341–6.

Johnson, H.B. (1975). Gas exchange strategies in desert plants. In D.M. Gates and R.B. Schmerl, eds. *Perspectives of biophysical ecology. Ecological studies*, volume 12, pp. 105–20. Springer, New York.

Johnson, S.D. and Steiner, K.E. (2000). Generalization versus specialization in plant pollination systems. *Trends in Ecology and Evolution*, **15**, 140–3.

Jones, C.G. and Shachak, M. (1990). Fertilization of the desert soil by rock-eating snails. *Nature*, **346**, 839–41.

Jones, C.G., Lawton, J.H., and Shachak, M. (1994). Organisms as ecosystem engineers. *Oikos*, **69**, 373–86.

Jönsson, K.I. and Järemo, J. (2003). A model on the evolution of cryptobiosis. *Annales Zoologica Fennici*, **40**, 331–40.

Jordan, P.W. and Nobel, P.S. (1984). Thermal and water relations of roots of desert succulents. *Annals of Botany*, **54**, 705–17.

Joubert, C.S.W. and Maclean, G.L. (1973). The structure of the water-holding feathers of the Namaqua sandgrouse. *Zoologica Africana*, **8**, 141–52.

Jürgens, N. (1986). Untersuchungen zur Ökologie sukkulenter Pflanzen des südlichen Afrika. *Mitteilungen aus dem Institut für Allgemeine Botanik Hamburg*, **21**, 129–365.

Jürgens, N., Gunster, A., Seely, M.K., and Jacobson, K.M. (1997). Desert. In R.M. Cowling, D.M. Richardson, and S.M. Pierce, eds. *Vegetation of southern Africa*, pp. 189–215. Cambridge University Press, Cambridge.

Kade, A. and Warren, S.D. (2002). Soil and plant recovery after historic military disturbances in the Sonoran Desert, USA. *Arid Land Research and Management*, **16**, 231–43.

Kam, M. and Degen, A.A. (1989). Efficiency of use of saltbush (*Atriplex halimus*) for growth by fat sand rats (*Psammomys obesus*). *Journal of Mammalogy*, **70**, 485–93.

Kam, M., Degen, A.A., and Nagy, K.A. (1987). Seasonal energy, water, and food consumption of Negev chukars and sand partridges. *Ecology*, **68**, 1029–37.

Kamenetsky, R. and Gutterman, Y. (1994). Life cycles and delay of germination in some geophytes inhabiting the Negev Desert highlands of Israel. *Journal of Arid Environments*, 27, 337–45.

Kappen, L., Lange, O.L., Schulze, E.-D., Evenari, M., and Buschbom, U. (1972). Extreme water stress and photosynthetic activity of the desert plant *Artemisia herba-alba* asso. *Oecologia*, 10, 177–82.

Kappen, L., Lange, O.L., Schulze, E.-D., Evenari, M., and Buschbom, U. (1976). Distributional pattern of water relations and net photosynthesis of *Hammada scoparia* (Pomel) Iljin in a desert environment. *Oecologia*, 23, 323–34.

Katjiua, M.L.K. and Ward, D. (2007). Pastoralists' perceptions and realities of vegetation change and browse consumption in the northern Kalahari, Namibia. *Journal of Arid Environments*, 69, 716–30.

Kelly, R.D. and Walker, B.H. (1977). The effects of different forms of land use on the ecology of a semi-arid region in south-eastern Rhodesia. *Journal of Ecology*, 62, 553–74.

Kelt, D.A. and Valone, T.J. (1995). Effects of grazing on the abundance and diversity of annual plants in Chihuahuan Desert scrub habitat. *Oecologia*, 103, 191–5.

Kelt, D.A., Brown, J.H., Heske, E.J., Marquet, P.A., Morton, S.R., Reid, J.R.W., Rogovin, K.A., and Shenbrot, G. (1996). Community structure of desert small mammals: comparisons across four continents. *Ecology*, 77, 746–61.

Kerley, G.I.H. (1991). Seed removal by rodents, birds and ants in the semi-arid Karoo, South Africa. *Journal of Arid Environments*, 20, 63–9.

Kitching, J.W. (1977). *The distribution of the Karoo vertebrate fauna*. Memoir No. 1, Bernard Price Institute for Paleontological Research. University of the Witwatersrand, Press, Johannesburg.

Knoop, W.T. and Walker, B.H. (1985). Interactions of woody and herbaceous vegetation in a southern African savanna. *Journal of Ecology*, 73, 235–53.

Koch, C. (1962). The Tenebrionidae of southern Africa. XXXI. Comprehensive notes on the tenebrionid fauna of the Namib Desert. *Annals of the Transvaal Museum*, 24, 61–106.

Koller, D. and Roth, N. (1964). Studies on the ecology and physiological significance of amphicarpy in *Gymnarrhena micrantha* (Compositae). *American Journal of Botany*, 51, 26–35.

Köppen, W. (1931). *Die Klimate der Erde*. de Gruyter, Berlin.

Koteja, P. (1991). On the relation between basal and field metabolic rates in birds and mammals. *Functional Ecology*, 5, 56–64.

Kotler, B.P. (1984). Risk of predation and the structure of desert rodent communities. *Ecology*, 65, 689–701.

Kotler, B.P. and Brown, J.S. (1988). Environmental heterogeneity and the coexistence of desert rodents. *Annual Review of Ecology and Systematics*, 19, 281–307.

Kotler, B.P., Brown, J.S., and Subach, A. (1993). Mechanisms of species coexistence of optimal foragers: temporal partitioning by two species of sand dune gerbils. *Oikos*, 67, 548–56.

Kotler, B.P., Ayal, Y., and Subach, A. (1994). Effects of predatory risk and resource renewal on the timing of foraging activity in a gerbil community. *Oecologia*, 100, 391–6.

Kotler, B.P., Brown, J.S., and Bouskila, A. (2004). Apprehension and time allocation in gerbils: the effects of predatory risk and energetic state. *Ecology*, 85, 917–22.

Kotliar, N.B. and Wiens, J.A. (1990). Multiple scales of patchiness and patch structure: a hierarchical framework for the study of heterogeneity. *Oikos*, **59**, 253–60.

Kraaij, T. and Ward, D. (2006). Effects of rain, nitrogen, fire and grazing on tree recruitment and early survival in bush-encroached savanna, South Africa. *Plant Ecology*, **186**, 235–46.

Krasnov, B.R., Shenbrot, G.I., Medvedev, S.G., Vatschenok, V.S., and Khokhlova, I.S. (1997). Host–habitat relation as an important determinant of spatial distribution of flea assemblages (Siphonaptera) on rodents in the Negev Desert. *Parasitology*, **114**, 159–73.

Krasnov, B.R., Shenbrot, G.I., Medvedev, S.G., Khokhlova, I.S., and Vatschenok, V.S. (1998). Habitat-dependence of a parasite–host relationship: flea assemblages in two gerbil species of the Negev Desert. *Journal of Medical Entomology*, **35**, 303–13.

Krasnov, B.R., Shenbrot, G.I., and Khokhlova, I.S. (2003). Density-dependent host selection in ectoparasites: an application of isodar theory to fleas parasitizing rodents. *Oecologia*, **134**, 365–72.

Krasnov, B.R., Stanko, M., Miklisova, D., and Morand, S. (2006). Habitat variation in species composition of flea assemblages on small mammals in central Europe. *Ecological Research*, **21**, 460–9.

Krivokhatsky, V.A. and Fet, V.Y. (1982). The spiders (Aranei) from rodent burrows in east Kara Kum. *Problems of Desert Development (USSR)*, **4**, 68–75.

Kwarteng, A.Y. (1999). Remote sensing assessment of oil lakes and oil-polluted surfaces at the Greater Burgan oil field, Kuwait. *International Journal of Applied Earth Observation and Geoinformation*, **1**, 36–47.

Lafferty, K.D. and Kuris, A.M. (2002). Trophic strategies, animal diversity and body size. *Trends in Ecology and Evolution*, **17**, 507–13.

Lamoreaux, P.E., Memon, B.A., and Idris, H. (1985). Groundwater development, Kharga Oases, Western Desert of Egypt: a long-term environmental concern. *Environmental Geology and Water Sciences*, **7**, 129–49.

Lamprey, H.F. (1983). Pastoralism yesterday and today: the overgrazing problem. In F. Bourliere, ed. *Tropical savannas*, pp. 643–66. Elsevier, Amsterdam.

Lancaster, N. (1995). *The geomorphology of desert dunes*. Routledge, London.

Lande, R., Engen, S., and Saether, B.-E. (1995). Optimal harvesting of fluctuating populations with a risk of extinction. *American Naturalist*, **145**, 728–45.

Landsberg, J., Lavorel, S., and Stol, J. (1999a). Grazing response groups among understorey plants in arid rangelands. *Journal of Vegetation Science*, **10**, 683–96.

Landsberg, J., O'Connor, T., and Freudenberger, D. (1999b). The impacts of livestock grazing on biodiversity in natural ecosystems. In H.J.G. Jung and G.C. Fahey, eds. *Fifth international symposium on the nutrition of herbivores*, pp. 752–77. American Society of Animal Science, Savoy, IL.

Lane, J.E., Swanson, D.L., Brigham, R.M., and McKechnie, A.E. (2004). Physiological responses to temperature in Whip-poor-wills: more evidence for the evolution of low metabolic rates in Caprimulgiformes. *Condor*, **106**, 921–5.

Lange, R.T. (1969). The piosphere: sheep track and dung patterns. *Journal of Range Management*, **22**, 396–400.

Lau, B. (ed.) (1989). *Charles John Andersson: trade and politics in central Namibia 1860–1864*, volume 2. Archives Service Division, Windhoek, Namibia.

Le Houérou, H.N. (1984). Rain use efficiency: a unifying concept in arid-land ecology. *Journal of Arid Environments*, 7, 213–47.

Lee, A.K. and Mercer, E.H. (1967). Cocoon surrounding desert-dwelling frogs. *Science*, 157, 87–8.

Leishman, M., Wright, I.J., Moles, A.T., and Westoby, M. (2000). The evolutionary ecology of seed size. In M. Fenner, ed. *Seeds—the ecology of regeneration in plant communities*. 2nd edn., pp. 31–57. CAB International, Wallingford.

Leishman, M.R. and Westoby, M. (1994). Hypotheses on seed size: tests using the semiarid flora of western New South Wales, Australia. *American Naturalist*, 143, 890–906.

Li, X.-R., Xiao, H.-L., Zhang, J.-G., and Wang, X.-P. (2004). Long-term ecosystem effects of sand-binding vegetation in the Tengger Desert, northern China. *Restoration Ecology*, 12, 376–90.

Lighton, J.B. and Fielden, L.J. (1996). Gas exchange in wind spiders: evolution of convergent respiratory strategies in solphugids and insects. *Journal of Insect Physiology*, 42, 347–57.

Lindemann, R.L. (1942). The trophic-dynamic aspect of ecology. *Ecology*, 23, 399–418.

Linder, H.P. (2000). Plant diversity and endemism in sub-Saharan Africa. *Journal of Biogeography*, 28, 169–82.

Liu, T.-S., Gu, Z.-S., An, Z.-S., and Fan, B.-Y. (1981). The dustfall in Beijing, China, on April 18, 1980. *Geological Society of America Special Paper*, 186, 149–58.

Lloyd, P. (2004). Variation in nest predation among arid-zone birds. *Ostrich*, 75, 228–35.

Lloyd, P. (2007). Predator control, mesopredator release, and impacts on bird nesting success: a field test. *African Zoology*, 42, 180–6.

Loope, L.L., Sanchez, P.G., Tarr, P.W., and Anderson, R.L. (1988). Biological invasions of arid land reserves. *Biological Conservation*, 18, 197–206.

Loria, M. and Noy-Meir, I. (1981). Dynamics of some annual populations in a desert loess plain. *Israel Journal of Botany*, 28, 211–25.

Lotem, A., Nakamura, H., and Zahavi, A. (1995). Constraints on egg discrimination and cuckoo–host co-evolution. *Animal Behaviour*, 49, 1185–209.

Louw, G.N. and Seely, M.K. (1980). Exploitation of fog water by a perennial dune grass, *Stipagrostis sabulicola*. *South African Journal of Science*, 76, 38–9.

Louw, G.N. and Seely, M.K. (1982). *Ecology of desert organisms*. Longmans, London.

Louw, G.N., Belonje, P.C., and Coetzee, H.J. (1969). Renal function, respiration, heart rate, and thermoregulation in the ostrich (*Struthio camelus*). *Scientific Papers of the Namib Desert Research Station*, 42, 43–54.

Lovegrove, B.G. (2000). The zoogeography of mammalian basal metabolic rate. *American Naturalist*, 156, 201–19.

Lovegrove, B.G. (2003). The influence of climate on the basal metabolic rate of small mammals: a slow–fast metabolic continuum. *Journal of Comparative Physiology B*, 173, 87–112.

Lovegrove, B.G., Lawes, M.J., and Roxburgh, L. (1999). Confirmation of pleisiomorphic daily torpor in mammals: the round-eared elephant shrew *Macroscelides proboscideus* (Macroscelidea). *Journal of Comparative Physiology B*, **169**, 453–60.

Lubin, Y.D. and Henschel, J.R. (1990). Foraging at the thermal limit: burrowing spiders (*Seothyra*, Eresidae) in the Namib Desert dunes. *Oecologia*, 84, 461–7.

Lubin, Y.D., Ellner, S.P., and Kotzman, M. (1993). Web relocation and habitat selection in a desert widow spider. *Ecology*, 74, 1915–28.

Lubin, Y.D., Henschel, J.R., and Baker, M.B. (2001). Costs of aggregation: shadow competition in a sit-and-wait predator. *Oikos*, 95, 59–68.

Ludwig, J.A. and Flavill, P. (1979). Productivity patterns of *Larrea* in the northern Chihuahuan Desert. In E.C. Lopez, T.J. Mabry, and S.F. Tavizon, eds. *Larrea*. Centro de Investigacion en Quimica Aplicada, pp. 139–50. Saltillo, Mexico.

Ludwig, J.A. and Tongway, D.J. (1995). Spatial organisation of landscapes and its function in semi-arid woodlands, Australia. *Landscape Ecology*, 10, 51–63.

Ludwig, J.A., Cunningham, G.L., and Whitson, P.D. (1988). Distribution of annual plants in North American deserts. *Journal of Arid Environments*, 15, 221–7.

Lüscher, M. (1961). Air conditioned termite nests. *Scientific American*, 238, 138–45.

Ma, J.-Y., Chen, K., Xia, D.-S., Wang, G., and Chen, F.-H. (2007). Variation in foliar stable carbon isotope among populations of a desert plant, *Reaumuria soongorica* (Pall.) Maxim. in different environments. *Journal of Arid Environments*, 69, 365–74.

MacArthur, R.H. and MacArthur, J.H. (1961). On bird species diversity. *Ecology*, 42, 594–8.

MacArthur, R.H. and Pianka, E.R. (1966). On optimal use of a patchy environment. *American Naturalist*, 100, 603–9.

MacArthur, R.H. and Wilson, E.O. (1964). *The dynamical theory of island biogeography*. Princeton University Press, Princeton.

MacDougal, D.T. and Spalding, E.S. (1910). *The water-balance of succulent plants*. Carnegie Institution of Washington, Washington, DC.

Mack, R.N. (1981). Invasion of *Bromus tectorum L.* into western North America: an ecological chronicle. *Agro-Ecosystems*, 7, 145–65.

Mackay, W.P., Loring, S.J., Frost, T.M., and Whitford, W.G. (1990). Population dynamics of a playa community in the Chihuahuan Desert. *Southwestern Naturalist*, 35, 393–402.

Maclean, G.L. (1967). The breeding biology of the Double-banded Courser *Rhinoptilus africanus* (Temminck). *Ibis*, 109, 556–9.

Maclean, G.L. (1976). A field study of the Australian Dotterel. *Emu*, 76, 207–15.

Maclean, G.L. (1996). *Ecophysiology of desert birds*. Springer, Berlin.

MacMillen, R.E. (1972). Water economy of noctural desert rodents. *Symposium of the Zoological Society of London*, 31, 147–74.

Maeda-Martínez, A.M. (1991). Distribution of species of Anostraca, Notostraca, Spinicaudata, and Laevicaudata in Mexico. *Hydrobiologia*, 212, 209–19.

Mahoney, S.A. and Jehl, J.R. (1985a). Adaptations of migratory shorebirds to highly saline and alkaline lakes: Wilson's phalarope and American avocets. *Condor*, 87, 520–7.

Mahoney, S.A. and Jehl, J.R. (1985b). Physiological ecology and salt loading of California gulls at an alkaline, hypersaline lake. *Physiological Zoology*, 58, 553–63.

Main, B.Y. (1956). Observations on the burrow and natural history of the trap-door spider *Missulena* (Ctenizidae). *Western Australian Naturalist*, 5, 73–80.

Malallah, G., Afzal, M., Kurian, M., Gulshan, S., and Dhami, M.S.I. (1998). Impact of oil pollution on some desert plants. *Environment International*, 24, 919–24.

Maloiy, G.M.O., Kamau, J.M.Z., Shkolnik, A., Meir, M., and Arieli, R. (1982). Thermoregulation and metabolism in a small desert carnivore: the fennec fox (*Fennecus zerda*, Mammalia). *Journal of Zoology*, 198, 279–91.

Mares, M.A. (1983). Desert rodent adaptation and community structure. In O.J. Reichman and J.H. Brown, eds. *Biology of desert rodents. Great Basin Naturalist Memoirs*, 7, 30–43.

Mares, M.A. and Rosenzweig, M.L. (1977). Seeds–seed eater systems. In G.H. Orians and O. Solbrig, eds. *Convergent evolution in warm deserts*, pp. 196–204. Dowden, Hutchinson and Ross, Stroudsburg, PA.

Mares, M.A. and Rosenzweig, M.L. (1978). Granivory in North and South American deserts: rodents, birds and ants. *Ecology*, 59, 235–41.

Mares, M.A., Blair, W.F., Enders, F.A., Greegor, D., Hulse, A.C., Hunt, J.H., Otte, D., Sage, R.D., and Tomoff, C.S. (1977). The strategies and community patterns of desert animals. In G.H. Orians and O.T. Solbrig, eds. *Convergent evolution in warm deserts*, pp. 107–63. Dowden, Hutchinson and Ross, Inc., Stroudsburg, PA.

Mares, M.A., Willig, M.R., and Lacher, T.E. (1985). The Brazilian Caatinga in South American zoogeography: tropical mammals in a dry region. *Journal of Biogeography*, 12, 57–69.

Mares, M.A., Ojeda, R.A., Borghi, C.E., Giannoni, S.M., Diaz, G.B., and Braun, J.K. (1997). How desert rodents overcome halophytic plant defenses. *Bioscience*, 47, 699–704.

Marquet, P.A. (1994). Diversity of small mammals in the Pacific coastal desert of Peru and Chile and adjacent Andean area: biogeography and community structure. *Australian Journal of Zoology*, 42, 527–42.

Marr, D.L., Brock, M.T., and Pellmyr, O. (2001). Coexistence of mutualists and antagonists: exploring the impact of cheaters on the yucca–yucca moth mutualism. *Oecologia*, 128, 454–63.

Marshall, T.C. and Spalton, J.A. (2000). Simultaneous inbreeding and outbreeding depression in reintroduced Arabian oryx. *Animal Conservation*, 3, 241–8.

Martinez-Meza, E. and Whitford, W.G. (1996). Stemflow, throughfall, and channelization of stemflow by three Chihuahuan Desert shrubs. *Journal of Arid Environments*, 32, 271–87.

Masoud, A.A. and Koike, K. (2006). Arid land salinization detected by remotely-sensed landcover changes: a case study in the Siwa region, NW Egypt. *Journal of Arid Environments*, 66, 151–67.

Mayhew, W.W. (1965). Adaptations of the amphibian, *Scaphiopus couchi*, to desert conditions. *American Midland Naturalist*, 74, 95–109.

Maynard Smith, J. (1982). *Evolution and the theory of games*. Cambridge University Press, Cambridge.

Mbatha, K.R. and Ward, D. (2006). Determining spatial and temporal variability in quantity and quality of vegetation for estimating the predictable sustainable stocking rate in semi-arid savanna. *African Journal of Range and Forage Science*, 23, 131–45.

McAuliffe, J.R. (1984). Sahuaro-nurse tree associations in the Sonoran Desert: competitive effects of sahuaros. *Oecologia*, **65**, 82–5.

McAuliffe, J.R. (1988). Markovian dynamics of simple and complex desert plant communities. *American Naturalist*, **131**, 459–90.

McAuliffe, J.R. (1994). Landscape evolution, soil formation, and ecological patterns and processes in Sonoran Desert bajadas. *Ecological Monographs*, **64**, 111–48.

McClain, E.S., Seely, M.K., Hadley, N.F., and Gray, V. (1985). Wax blooms in tenebrionid beetles of the Namib Desert: correlations with environment. *Ecology*, **66**, 112–19.

McClaran, M.P. and Anable, M.E. (1992). Spread of introduced Lehmann lovegrass along a grazing intensity gradient. *Journal of Applied Ecology*, **29**, 92–8.

McIntyre, S. and Lavorel, S. (2001). Livestock grazing in sub-tropical pastures: steps in the analysis of attribute response and plant functional types. *Journal of Ecology*, **89**, 209–26.

McKechnie, A. and Lovegrove, B.G. (2003). Facultative hypothermic responses in an Afrotropical arid-zone passerine, the red-headed finch (*Amadina erythrocephala*). *Journal of Comparative Physiology B*, **173**, 339–46.

McNab, B.K. and Morrison, P. (1963). Body temperature and metabolism in subspecies of *Peromyscus* from arid and mesic environments. *Ecological Monographs*, **33**, 63–82.

McPherson, G. (1995). The role of fire in the desert grasslands. In M.P. McClaran and T.R. Van Devender, eds. *The desert grassland*, pp. 130–51. University of Arizona Press, Tucson.

Medvedev, H.S. (1965). Adaptations of leg structure in desert darkling beetles (Coleoptera: Tenebrionidae). *Entomological Review*, **44**, 473–85.

Menge, B.A. (1995). Indirect effects in marine rocky intertidal interaction webs: patterns and importance. *Ecological Monographs*, **65**, 21–74.

Meserve, P.L. (1981). Trophic relationships among small mammals in a Chilean semiarid thorn scrub community. *Journal of Mammalogy*, **62**, 304–14.

Meserve, P.L., Gutierrez, J.R., Yunger, J.A., Contreras, L.C., and Jaksic, F.M. (1995). Role of biotic interactions in a small mammal assemblage in semiarid Chile. *Ecology*, **77**, 133–48.

Meyer, K.M., Ward, D., Moustakas, A., and Wiegand, K. (2005). Big is not better: small *Acacia mellifera* shrubs are more vital after fire. *African Journal of Ecology*, **43**, 131–6.

Middleton, N.J. (1986). Dust storms in the Middle East. *Journal of Arid Environments*, **10**, 83–96.

Middleton, N.J. and Thomas, D.S.G. (eds.) (1997). *World Atlas of Desertification*. 2nd ed. Edward Arnold, London.

Midgley, G.F. and Thuiller, W. (2007). Potential vulnerability of Namaqualand plant diversity to anthropogenic climate change. *Journal of Arid Environments*, **70**, 615–28.

Milchunas, D.G. and Lauenroth, W.K. (1993). Quantitative effects of grazing on vegetation and soils over a global range of environments. *Ecological Monographs*, **63**, 327–66.

Milchunas, D.G., Sala, O.E., and Lauenroth, W.K. (1988). A generalized model of the effects of grazing by large herbivores on grassland community structure. *American Naturalist*, **132**, 87–106.

Milchunas, D.G., Lauenroth, W.K., Chapman, P.L., and Kazempour, K. (1989). Effects of grazing, topography, and precipitation on the structure of a semi-arid grassland. *Vegetatio*, **80**, 11–23.

Milich, L. (1997). Deserts of the world. http://ag.arizona.edu/~lmilich/desert1. html [Date accessed: 26 August 2007].

Miller, J.A. (1995). Moths escape from evolutionary dead end. *Bioscience*, **45**, 741–2.

Miller, T.E.X. (2007). Does having multiple partners weaken the benefits of facultative mutualism? A test with cacti and cactus-tending ants. *Oikos*, **116**, 500–12.

Mills, L.S., Soulé, M.E., and Doak, D. (1993). The keystone-species concept in ecology and conservation. *BioScience*, **43**, 219–24.

Milton, S.J. (1991). Plant spinescence in arid southern Africa: does moisture mediate selection by mammals? *Oecologia*, **87**, 279–87.

Milton, S.J., Zimmerman, H.G., and Hoffman, J.H. (1999). Alien plant invaders of the Karoo: attributes, impacts and control. In W.R.J. Dean and S.J. Milton, eds. *The Karoo: ecological patterns and processes*, pp. 274–87. Cambridge University Press, Cambridge.

Milton, S.J. and Dean, W.R.J. (1995). How useful is the keystone species concept, and can it be applied to *Acacia erioloba* in the Kalahari Desert? *Zeitschrift für Ökologie und Naturschutz*, **4**, 147–56.

Milton, S.J. and Dean, W.R.J. (2000). Disturbance, drought and dynamics of desert dune grassland, South Africa. *Plant Ecology*, **150**, 37–51.

Milton, S.J., Dean, W.R.J., du Plessis, M.A., and Siegfried, W.R. (1994). A conceptual model of arid rangeland degradation. *Bioscience*, **44**, 70–6.

Milton, S.J., Dean, W.R.J., and Jeltsch, F. (1999). Large trees, fertile islands, and birds in arid savannas. *Journal of Arid Environments*, **41**, 61–78.

Minckley, R.L., Cane, J.H., and Kervin, L. (2000). Origins and ecological consequences of pollen specialization among desert bees. *Proceedings of the Royal Society, Biological Sciences*, **267**, 265–71.

Miriti, M.N. (2006). Ontogenetic shift from facilitation to competition in a desert shrub. *Journal of Ecology*, **94**, 973–9.

Misak, R.F., Abdel Baki, A.A., and El-Hakim, M.S. (1997). On the causes and control of the waterlogging phenomenon, Siwa Oasis, northern Western Desert, Egypt. *Journal of Arid Environments*, **37**, 23–32.

Mitchell, B.D. and Banks, P.B. (2005). Do wild dogs exclude foxes? Evidence for competition from dietary and spatial overlaps. *Austral Ecology*, **30**, 581–91.

Mitchell, W.A. (2000). Limits to species richness in a continuum of habitat heterogeneity: an ESS approach. *Evolutionary Ecology Research*, **2**, 293–316.

Mitchell, W.A., Abramsky, Z., Kotler, B.P., Pinshow, B., and Brown, J.S. (1990). The effect of competition on foraging activity in desert rodents—theory and experiments. *Ecology*, **71**, 844–54.

Mitchell, W.A., Kotler, B.P., Brown, J.S., Blaustein, L., and Dall, S.R.X. (2005). Species diversity, environmental heterogeneity, and species interactions. In M. Shachak, J.R. Gosz, S.T.A. Pickett, and A. Perevolotsky, eds. *Biodiversity in drylands: toward a unified perspective*, pp. 57–69. Oxford University Press, Oxford.

Monson, R.K. and Smith, S.D. (1982). Seasonal water potential components of Sonoran Desert plants. *Ecology*, **63**, 113–23.

Monson, R.K. and Szarek, S.R. (1981). Life cycle characteristics of *Machaeranthera gracilis* (Compositae) in desert habitats. *Oecologia*, **50**, 50–5.

Mooney, H.A., Troughton, I., and Berry, I. (1974). Arid climates and photosynthetic systems. *Carnegie Institute Washington Year Book*, 73, 792–805.

Mooney, H.A., Bjorkman, O., and Berry, J.A. (1975). Photosynthetic adaptations to high temperatures. In N.F. Hadley, ed. *Environmental physiology of desert organisms*, pp. 138–51. Dowden, Hutchinson and Ross, Stroudsburg, PA.

Morris, D.W. (1988). Habitat-dependent population regulation and community structure. *Evolutionary Ecology*, 2, 253–69.

Morton, S.R. (1985). Granivory in arid regions: comparison of Australia with North and South America. *Ecology*, 66, 1859–66.

Morton, S.R. (1993). Determinants of diversity in animal communities in arid Australia. In R.E. Ricklefs and D. Schluter, eds. *Species diversity in ecological communities: historical and geographical perspectives*, pp. 159–69. University of Chicago Press, Chicago.

Morton, S.R. and Davidson, D.W. (1988). Comparative structure of harvester ant communities in arid Australia and North America. *Ecological Monographs*, 58, 19–38.

Morton, S.R. and James, C.D. (1988). The diversity and abundance of lizards in arid Australia: a new hypothesis. *American Naturalist*, 132, 237–56.

Mueller, P. and Diamond, J. (2001). Metabolic rate and environmental productivity: well-provisioned animals evolved to run and idle fast. *Proceedings of the National Academy of Science USA*, 98, 12550–4.

Mulroy, T.W. and Rundel, P.W. (1977). Annual plants: adaptations to desert environments. *Bioscience*, 27, 109–14.

Mun, H.T. and Whitford, W.G. (1998). Changes in mass and chemistry of plant roots during long-term decomposition on a Chihuahuan Desert watershed. *Biology and Fertility of Soils*, 26, 16–22.

Munzbergova, Z. and Ward, D. (2002). *Acacia* trees as keystone species in Negev Desert ecosystems. *Journal of Vegetation Science*, 13, 227–36.

Murdoch, W.W. (1966). Population stability and life history phenomena. *American Naturalist*, 100, 5–11.

Murie, M. (1961). Metabolic characteristics of mountain, desert and coastal populations of *Peromyscus. Ecology*, 42, 723–40.

Mzilikazi, N. and Lovegrove, B.G. (2004). Daily torpor in free-ranging rock elephant shrews, *Elephantulus myurus*: a year-long study. *Physiological and Biochemical Zoology*, 77, 285–96.

Nash, M.H. and Whitford, W.G. (1995). Subterranean termites: regulators of organic matter in the Chihuahuan Desert. *Biology and Fertility of Soils*, 19, 15–18.

Naveh, Z. and Whittaker, R.H. (1979). Measurements and relationships of plant species diversity in Mediterranean shrublands and woodlands. In F. Grassle, G.P. Patil, W. Smith, and C. Taillie, eds. *Ecological diversity in theory and practice*, pp. 219–39. International Co-operative Publishing House, Fairland, MD.

Nevo, E. (1998). Genetic diversity in wild cereals: regional and local studies and their bearing on conservation *ex situ* and *in situ. Genetic Resources and Crop Evolution*, 45, 355–70.

Nevo, E., Beiles, A., Gutterman, Y., Storch, N., and Kaplan, D. (1984). Genetic resources of wild cereals in Israel and vicinity. I. Phenotypic variation within and between populations of wild wheat, *Triticum dicoccoides. Euphytica*, 33, 717–35.

Newman, E.I. (1973). Competition and diversity in herbaceous vegetation. *Nature*, 244, 310–11.

Newman, W.A. (1991). Origins of Southern Hemisphere endemism, especially among marine Crustacea. *Memoirs of the Queensland Museum*, 31, 51–76.

Newsome, A.E. (2001). The biology and ecology of the dingo. In C.R. Dickman and D. Lunney, ed. *A symposium on the dingo*, pp. 20–3. Royal Zoological Society of New South Wales, Sydney, Australia.

Nicholson, S.E. (1978). Climatic variations in the Sahel and other African regions during the past five centuries. *Journal of Arid Environments*, 1, 3–24.

Nobel, P.S. (1976). Water relations and photosynthesis of a desert CAM plant, *Agave deserti*. *Plant Physiology*, 58, 576–82.

Nobel, P.S. (1977). Water relations and photosynthesis of a barrel cactus, *Ferocactus acanthodes*, in the Colorado Desert. *Oecologia*, 27, 117–33.

Nobel, P.S. and Sanderson, J. (1984). Rectifier-like activities of roots of two desert succulents. *Journal of Experimental Botany*, 35, 727–37.

Nobel, P.S., Zaragoza, L.J., and Smith, W.K. (1975). Relation between mesophyll surface area, photosynthetic rate, and illumination level during development for leaves of *Plectranthus parviflorus* Henckel. *Plant Physiology*, 55, 1067–70.

Norrdahl, K. and Korpimäki, E. (2002). Seasonal changes in the numerical responses of predators to cyclic vole populations. *Ecography*, 25, 428–38.

Noy-Meir, I. (1973). Desert ecosystems: environment and producers. *Annual Review of Ecology and Systematics*, 4, 25–51.

Noy-Meir, I. (1982). Stability of plant–herbivore models and possible application to savanna. In B.J. Huntley and B.H. Walker, eds. *Ecology of tropical savannas*, pp. 591–609. Springer, Berlin.

Noy-Meir, I., Gutman, M., and Kaplan, Y. (1989). Responses of mediterranean grassland plants to grazing and protection. *Journal of Ecology*, 77, 290–310.

Nunney, L. (1993). The influence of mating system and non-overlapping generations on effective population size. *Evolution*, 47, 1329–41.

O'Connor, T.G. (1985). *A synthesis of field experiments concerning the grass layer in the savanna regions of southern Africa*. CSIR, Pretoria, South Africa. South African National Scientific Programmes Report, 114.

O'Connor, T.G. (1991). Local extinction in perennial grasslands: a life-history approach. *American Naturalist*, 137, 753–73.

O'Neill, A. (2002). *Living with the dingo*. Envirobook, Annandale, Australia.

Oksanen, L. and Oksanen, T. (2000). The logic and realism of the hypothesis of exploitation ecosystems (EEH). *American Naturalist*, 155, 703–23.

Oksanen, L., Fretwell, S.D., Arruda, J., and Niemela, P. (1981). Exploitation ecosystems in gradients of primary productivity. *American Naturalist*, 118, 240–61.

Ollier, C.D. (2005). Australian landforms and their history. http://www.ga.gov.au/education/facts/landforms/auslform.htm [Date accessed: 03 September 2007].

Onorato, D.P., Hellgren, E.C., Van Den Bussche, R.A., Doan-Crider, D.L., and Skiles, J.R. (2007). Genetic structure of American black bears in the desert southwest of North America: conservation implications for recolonization. *Conservation Genetics*, 8, 565–76.

Or, K. and Ward, D. (2003). Three-way interactions between *Acacia*, large mammalian herbivores and bruchid beetles-a review. *African Journal of Ecology*, 41, 257–65.

Orians, G.H. and Milewski, A.V. (2007). Ecology of Australia: the effects of nutrient-poor soils and intense fires. *Biological Reviews*, 82, 393–423.

Orshan, G. (1986). Plant form as describing vegetation and expressing adaptation to environment. *Annals of Botany*, 44, 7–38.

Osborn, T.G., Wood, J.G., and Paltridge, T.B. (1932). On the growth and reaction to grazing of the perennial saltbush (*Atriplex versicarium*). An ecological study of the biotic factor. *Proceedings of the Linnean Society of New South Wales*, 57, 377–402.

Osem, Y., Perevolotsky, A., and Kigel, J. (2004). Site productivity and plant size explain the response of annual species to grazing exclusion in a Mediterranean semi-arid rangeland. *Journal of Ecology*, 92, 297–309.

Osem, Y., Perevolotsky, A., and Kigel, J. (2007). Interactive effects of grazing and shrubs on the annual plant community in semi-arid Mediterranean shrublands. *Journal of Vegetation Science*, 18, 869–78.

Ostrowski, S., Williams, J.B., and Ismael, K. (2003). Heterothermy and the water economy of free-living Arabian oryx (*Oryx leucoryx*). *Journal of Experimental Biology*, 206, 1471–8.

Ovalle, C., Aronson, J., Avendaño, J., Meneses, R., and Moreno, R. (1993). Rehabilitation of degraded ecosystems in central Chile and its relevance to the arid 'Norte Chico'. *Revista Chilena de Historia Natural*, 66, 291–303.

Owen, L.A., Richards, B., Rhodes, E.J., Cunningham, W.D., Windley, B.F., Badamgarav, J., and Dorjnamjaa, D. (1998). Relic permafrost structures in the Gobi of Mongolia: age and significance. *Journal of Quaternary Science*, 13, 539–47.

Owuor, E.D., Fahima, T., Beharav, A., Korol, A., and Nevo, E. (1999). RAPD divergence caused by microsite edaphic selection in wild barley. *Genetica*, 105, 177–92.

Pacala, S.W., Hurtt, G.C., Baker, D., Peylin, P., Houghton, R.A., Birdsey, R.A., Heath, L., Sundquist, E.T., Stallard, R.F., Ciais, P., Moorcroft, P., Caspersen, J.P., Shevliakova, E., Moore, B., Kohlmaier, G., Holland, E., Gloor, M., Harmon, M.E., Fan, S.-M., Sarmiento, J.L., Goodale, C.L., Schimel, D., and Field, C.B. (2001). Consistent land- and atmosphere-based U.S. carbon sink estimates. *Science*, 292, 2316–20.

Page, J. (1984). *Arid lands*. Time-Life Books, Arlington, VA.

Pagel, M. (1994). Detecting correlated evolution on phylogenies: a general method for the comparative analysis of discrete characters. *Proceedings of the Royal Society of London, Series B*, 255, 37–45.

Paine, R.T. (1966). Food web complexity and species diversity. *American Naturalist*, 100, 65–75.

Paine, R.T. (1980). Food webs: linkage, interaction strength and community infrastructure. *Journal of Animal Ecology*, 49, 667–85.

Pake, C.E. and Venable, D.L. (1995). Is coexistence in Sonoran Desert annuals mediated by temporal variability in reproductive success? *Ecology*, 76, 246–61.

Pake, C.E. and Venable, D.L. (1996). Seed banks in desert annuals: implications for persistence and coexistence in variable environments. *Ecology*, 77, 1427–35.

Palgi, N., Vatnick, I., and Pinshow, B. (2005). Oxalate, calcium and ash intake and excretion balances in fat sand rats (*Psammomys obesus*) feeding on two different diets. *Comparative Biochemistry and Physiology A*, 141, 48–53.

Palmer, A.R. and Cowling, R.M. (1994). An investigation of topo-moisture gradients in the eastern Karoo, South Africa, and the identification of factors responsible for species turnover. *Journal of Arid Environments*, 26, 135–47.

Pankova, Y.I. and Dokuchaev, V.V. (2006). *Soil salinity in the Gobi (Mongolia)*. 18th World Congress of Soil Science, Philadelphia, PA.

Pantastico-Caldas, M. and Venable, D.L. (1993). Competition in two species of desert annuals along a topographic gradient. *Ecology*, 74, 2192–203.

Parker, C. (1989). Nurse plant relationships of columnar cacti in Arizona. *Physical Geography*, 10, 322–55.

Parker, G.A. (1984). Evolutionarily stable strategies. In J.R. Krebs and N.B. Davies, eds. *Behavioural ecology*. 2nd edn., pp. 30–61. Blackwells, Oxford.

Parker, L.W., Santos, P.F., Phillips, J., and Whitford, W.G. (1984). Carbon and nitrogen dynamics during decomposition of litter and roots of a Chihuahuan Desert annual, *Lepidium lasiocarpum*. *Ecological Monographs*, 54, 339–60.

Parnes, A. (1962). The geology of Makhtesh Ramon (Negev, Israel). Part 3a: Triassic ammonites from Israel. *Geological Survey of Israel Bulletin*, 33, 1–78.

Passioura, J.B. (1991). Soil structure and plant growth. *Australian Journal of Soil Research*, 29, 717–28.

Patten, D.T. and Dinger, B.E. (1969). Carbon dioxide exchange patterns of cacti from different environments. *Ecology*, 50, 686–8.

Peel, M.C., Finlayson, B.L., and McMahon, T.A. (2007). Updated world map of the Köppen-Geiger climate classification. *Hydrology and Earth System Sciences*, 11, 1633–44.

Pellmyr, O. (1996). Evolution of pollination and mutualism in the yucca moth lineage. *American Naturalist*, 148, 827–47.

Pellmyr, O. (2003). Yuccas, yucca moths and coevolution: a review. *Annals of the Missouri Botanical Gardens*, 90, 35–55.

Pellmyr, O. and Huth, C.J. (1994). Evolutionary stability of mutualism between yuccas and yucca moths. *Nature*, 372, 257–60.

Pellmyr, O. and Krenn, H.W. (2002). Origin of a complex key innovation in an obligate insect–plant mutualism. *Proceedings of the National Academy of Sciences USA*, 99, 5498–502.

Pellmyr, O., Leebens-Mack, J., and Huth, C.J. (1996). Non-mutualistic yucca moths and their evolutionary consequences. *Nature*, 380, 256–7.

Pellmyr, O., Massey, L.K., Hamrick, J.L., and Feist, M.A. (1997). Genetic consequences of specialization: yucca moth behavior and self-pollination in yuccas. *Oecologia*, 109, 273–8.

Penning de Vries, F.W.T., and Djiteye, M.A. (1982). *La productivite des Paturages Saheliens*. Centre for Agricultural Publishing and Documentation, Wageningen, the Netherlands.

Penrith, M.J. (1984). New taxa of *Onymacris* Allard and relationships within the genus (Coleoptera: Tenebrionidae). *Annals of the Transvaal Museum*, 33, 511–33.

Perevolotsky, A. and Seligman, N.G. (1998). Role of grazing in Mediterranean rangeland ecosystems. *BioScience*, 48, 1007–17.

Perkins, J.S. and Thomas, D.S.G. (1993). Spreading deserts or spatially confined environmental impacts: land degradation and cattle ranching in the Kalahari desert of Botswana. *Land Degradation and Rehabilitation*, 4, 179–94.

Phillips, J.E. (1964). Rectal absorption in the desert locust, *Schistocerca gregaria* Forskal. I. Water. *Journal of Experimental Biology*, 41, 15–38.

Pianka, E.R. (1969). Habitat specificity, speciation, and species density in Australian desert lizards. *Ecology*, 50, 498–502.

Pianka, E.R. (1972). Zoogeography and speciation of Australian desert lizards: an ecological perspective. *Copeia*, **1972**, 127–45.

Pianka, E.R. (1981). Diversity and adaptive radiations of Australian desert lizards. In A. Keast, ed. *Ecological biogeography of Australia*, pp. 1375–92. Junk, The Hague.

Pianka, E.R. (1986). *Ecology and natural history of desert lizards*. Princeton University Press, Princeton.

Pianka, E.R. and Huey, R.B. (1971). Bird species density in the Kalahari and Australian deserts. *Koedoe*, **14**, 123–9.

Pickup, G. and Chewings, V.H. (1994). A grazing gradient approach to land degradation assessment in arid areas from remotely-sensed data. *International Journal of Remote Sensing*, **15**, 597–617.

Pickup, G. and Stafford Smith, D.M. (1993). Problems, prospects and procedures for assessing the sustainability of pastoral land management in arid Australia. *Journal of Biogeography*, **20**, 471–87.

Pimm, S.L. (1991). *The balance of nature: ecological issues in the conservation of species and communities*. University of Chicago Press, Chicago.

Pinshow, B., Bernstein, M.H., Lopez, G.E., and Kleinhaus, S. (1982). Regulation of brain temperature in pigeons: effects of corneal convection. *American Journal of Physiology*, **242**, R577–R581.

Pinshow, B., Degen, A.A., and Alkon, P.U. (1983). Water intake, existence energy, and responses to water deprivation in the sand partridge (*Ammoperdix heyi*) and the chukar (*Alectoris chukar*): two phasianids of the Negev Desert. *Physiological Zoology*, **56**, 281–9.

Plakht, J. (1996). Mapping of Quaternary units in Makhtesh Ramon, central Negev. *Israel Journal of Earth Sciences*, **45**, 217–22.

Polis, G.A. (1991). Complex trophic interactions in deserts: an empirical critique of food-web theory. *American Naturalist*, **138**, 123–55.

Polis, G.A. (1994). Food webs, trophic cascades and community structure. *Australian Journal of Ecology*, **19**, 121–36.

Polis, G.A. and Hurd, S.D. (1996). Linking marine and terrestrial food webs: allochthonous input from the ocean supports high secondary productivity on small islands and coastal land communities. *American Naturalist*, **147**, 396–423.

Polis, G.A. and McCormick, S.J. (1986). Scorpions, spiders and solpugids: predation and competition among distantly related taxa. *Oecologia*, **71**, 111–16.

Polis, G.A. and Yamashita, T. (1991). The ecology and importance of predaceous arthropods in desert communities. In G.A. Polis, ed. *The ecology of desert communities*, pp. 180–222. Arizona University Press, Tucson.

Pople, A.R., Grigg, G.C., Cairns, S.C., Alexander, P., Beard, L.A., and Alexander, P. (2000). Trends in numbers of kangaroos and emus on either side of the South Australian dingo fence: evidence for predator regulation. *Wildlife Research*, **27**, 269–76.

Power, M.E., Tilman, D., Estes, J.E., Menge, B.A., Bond, W.J., Mills, L.S., Daily, G., Castilla, J.C., Lubchenco, J., and Paine, R.T. (1996). Challenges in the quest for keystones. *Bioscience*, **46**, 609–20.

Prakash, I. (1963). Zoogeography and evolution of the mammalian fauna of Rajasthan desert, India. *Mammalia*, **27**, 342–51.

Prakash, I. (1974). The ecology of vertebrates of the Indian desert. In M.S. Mani, ed. *Ecology and biogeography in India*, pp. 369–429. Dr. W. Junk, The Hague.

Prange, H.D. and Pinshow, B. (1994). Thermoregulation of an unusual grasshopper in a desert environment: the importance of food source and body size. *Journal of Thermal Biology*, **19**, 75–8.

Prellwitz, J., Rech, J., Michalski, G., Buck, B., Howell, M.S., and Brock, A. (2006). *Nitrate concentrations in Atacama Desert soils and their implications for the antiquity of the Atacama Desert.* 18th World Congress of Soil Science, Philadelphia, PA.

Price, M.V., Waser, N.W., and Bass, T.A. (1984). Effects of moonlight on microhabitat use by desert rodents. *Journal of Mammalogy*, **65**, 353–6.

Price, R.A. (1996). Systematics of the Gnetales: a review of morphological and molecular evidence. *International Journal of Plant Sciences*, **157**, S40–S49.

Primack, R.B. (2006). *Essentials of conservation biology.* 4th ed. Sinauer, Sunderland, MA.

Pulliam, H.R. (1988). Sources, sinks, and population regulation. *American Naturalist*, **132**, 652–61.

Pye, K. (1984). Loess. *Progress in Physical Geography*, **8**, 176–217.

Pye, K. (1987). *Aeolian dust and dust deposits.* Academic Press, London.

Rasa, O.A.E. and Heg, D. (2004). Individual variation and prior experience affect the discrimination of a brood-parasite by its subsocial beetle host. *Behavioural Ecology and Sociobiology*, **57**, 155–63.

Raunkiaer, C. (1934). *The life forms of plants and statistical plant geography.* Clarendon Press, Oxford.

Raven, P.A. (1963). Amphitropical relationships in the floras of North and South America. *Quarterly Review of Biology*, **38**, 151–77.

Recher, H.F. (1969). Bird species diversity and habitat diversity in Australia and North America. *American Naturalist*, **103**, 75–80.

Reid, R. and Ellis, J.E. (1995). Impacts of pastoralists on woodlands in South Turkana, Kenya: livestock-mediated tree recruitment. *Ecological Applications*, **5**, 978–92.

Repasky, R.E. and Schluter, D. (1996). Habitat distributions of wintering sparrows: foraging success in a transplant experiment. *Ecology*, **77**, 452–60.

Reynolds, J.F., Kemp, P.R., and Tenhunen, J.D. (2000). Effects of long-term rainfall variability on evapotranspiration and soil water distribution in the Chihuahuan Desert: a modelling analysis. *Plant Ecology*, **150**, 145–59.

Reynolds, J.F., Kemp, P.R., Ogle, K., and Fernández, R.J. (2004). Modifying the 'pulse-reserve' paradigm for deserts of North America: precipitation pulses, soil water, and plant responses. *Oecologia*, **141**, 194–210.

Richards, J.H. and Caldwell, M.M. (1987). Hydraulic lift: substantial nocturnal water transport between soil layers by *Artemisia tridentata* roots. *Oecologia*, **73**, 486–9.

Richer, J. (1995). Willingness to pay for desert protection. *Contemporary Economic Policy*, **13**, 93–104.

Riechert, S.E. (1981). The consequences of being territorial: spiders, a case study. *American Naturalist*, **117**, 871–92.

Riechert, S.E. and Harp, J. (1987). Nutritional ecology of spiders. In F. Slansky and J.G. Rodriguez, eds. *Nutritional ecology of insects, mites and spiders*, pp. 645–72. John Wiley and Sons, New York.

Rijke, A.M. (1972). The water-holding mechanism of sandgrouse feathers. *Journal of Experimental Biology*, **56**, 195–200.

Rissing, S.W. (1981). Foraging specializations of individual seed-harvester ants. *Behavioral Ecology and Sociobiology*, **9**, 149–52.

Rissing, S.W. (1986). Indirect effects of granivory by harvester ants: plant species composition and reproductive increase near ant nests. *Oecologia*, **68**, 231–4.

Robbins, P. (1998). Authority and environment: institutional landscapes in Rajasthan, India. *Annals of the Association of American Geographers*, **88**, 410–35.

Roberts, C.S., Seely, M.K., Ward, D., Mitchell, D., and Campbell, J.D. (1991). Body temperatures of Namib Desert tenebrionid beetles: their relationship in laboratory and field. *Physiological Entomology*, **16**, 463–75.

Robinson, M. (1999). *A field guide to frogs of Australia*. New Holland Publishers, Sydney, Australia.

Robinson, R. (ed.) (2001). *Plant sciences*. Macmillan Reference USA, New York.

Rödl, T. and Ward, D. (2002). Host recognition in a desert mistletoe: early stages of development are influenced by substrate and host origin. *Functional Ecology*, **16**, 128–34.

Rohner, C. and Ward, D. (1997). Chemical and mechanical defense against herbivory in two sympatric species of desert *Acacia*. *Journal of Vegetation Science*, **8**, 717–26.

Rohner, C. and Ward, D. (1999). Large mammalian herbivores and the conservation of arid *Acacia* stands in the Middle East. *Conservation Biology*, **13**, 1162–171.

Romney, E.M., Wallace, A., and Hunter, R.B. (1978). Plant responses to nitrogen fertilization in the northern Mojave Desert and its relationship to water manipulation. In N.E. West and J. Skujins, eds. *Nitrogen in desert ecosystems*, pp. 232–43. Dowden, Hutchinson and Ross, Stroudsburg, PA.

Rose, M. and Polis, G.A. (1997). The distribution and abundance of coyotes: the importance of subsidy by allochthonous foods coming from the sea. *Ecology*, **79**, 998–1007.

Rosenzweig, M.L. (1985). Some theoretical aspects of habitat selection. In M.L. Cody, ed. *Habitat selection in birds*, pp. 517–40. Academic Press, New York.

Rosenzweig, M.L. (1995). *Species diversity in space and time*. Cambridge University Press, Cambridge.

Rosenzweig, M.L. and Abramsky, Z. (1986). Centrifugal community organization. *Oikos*, **46**, 339–48.

Rosenzweig, M.L. and Abramsky, Z. (1993). How are diversity and productivity related? In R.E. Ricklefs and D. Schluter, eds. *Species diversity in ecological communities: historical and geographical perspectives*, pp. 52–65. University of Chicago Press, Chicago.

Rotenberry, J.T. (1980). Dietary relationships among shrubsteppe passerine birds: competition or opportunism in a variable environment? *Ecological Monographs*, **50**, 93–110.

Rubidge, B.S. (2005). Re-uniting lost continents: fossil reptiles from the ancient Karoo and their wanderlust. *South African Journal of Geology*, **108**, 135–72.

Ruiz, N., Ward, D., and Saltz, D. (2001). Crystals of calcium oxalate in leaves: constitutive or induced defense? *Functional Ecology*, **16**, 99–105.

Ruiz, N., Ward, D., and Saltz, D. (2002). Responses of *Pancratium sickenbergeri* to simulated bulb herbivory: combining defense and tolerance strategies. *Journal of Ecology*, **90**, 472–9.

Ruiz, N., Saltz, D., and Ward, D. (2006a). The effects of herbivory and resource variability on the production of a second inflorescence by the desert lily, *Pancratium sickenbergeri*. *Plant Ecology*, **186**, 47–55.

Ruiz, N., Ward, D., and Saltz, D. (2006b). Population differentiation and the effects of herbivory and sand compaction on the subterranean growth of a desert lily. *Journal of Heredity*, **97**, 409–16.

Ruiz, N., Saltz, D., and Ward, D. (2006c). Signal selection in a desert lily, *Pancratium sickenbergeri*. *Evolutionary Ecology Research*, **8**, 1461–74.

Rundel, P.W. (1978). Ecological relationships of desert fog zone lichens. *The Bryologist*, **81**, 277–93.

Ryel, R.J., Beyschlag, W., and Caldwell, M.M. (1994). Light field heterogeneity among tussock grasses: theoretical considerations of light harvesting and seedling establishment among tussock and uniform tiller distributions. *Oecologia*, **98**, 241–8.

Rzóska, J. (1984). Temporary and other waters. In J.L. Cloudsley-Thompson, ed. *Key environments: Sahara desert*, pp. 105–14. Pergamon Press, Oxford.

Saiko, T.A. and Zonn, I.S. (2000). Irrigation expansion and dynamics of desertification in the Circum-Aral region of Central Asia. *Applied Geography*, **20**, 349–67.

Saltz, D. and Rubenstein, D.I. (1995). Population dynamics of a reintroduced Asiatic wild ass (*Equus hemionus*) herd. *Ecological Applications*, **5**, 327–35.

Saltz, D. and Ward, D. (2000). Responding to a three-pronged attack: desert lilies subject to herbivory by dorcas gazelles. *Plant Ecology*, **148**, 127–38.

Saltz, D., Schmidt, H., Rowen, M., Karnieli, A., Ward, D., and Schmidt, I. (1999). Assessing grazing impacts by remote sensing in hyper-arid environments. *Journal of Range Management*, **52**, 500–7.

Saltz, D., Rowen, M., and Rubenstein, D.I. (2000). The effect of space-use patterns of reintroduced Asiatic wild ass on effective population size. *Conservation Biology*, **14**, 1852–61.

Saltz, D., Ward, D., Kapofi, I., and Karamata, J. (2004). Population estimation and harvesting potential for game in arid Namibia. *South African Journal of Wildlife Research*, **34**, 153–61.

Saltz, D., Rubenstein, D.I., and White, G.C. (2006). The impact of increased environmental stochasticity due to climate change on the dynamics of asiatic wild ass. *Conservation Biology*, **20**, 1402–9.

Samson, D.A., Philippi, T.E., and Davidson, D.W. (1992). Granivory and competition as determinants of annual plant diversity in the Chihuahuan Desert. *Oikos*, **65**, 61–80.

Sanborn, A.F., Heath, M.S., Heath, J.E., and Phillips, P.K. (1990). Evaporative cooling in the cicada *Okanagodes gracilis* (Homoptera: Cicadidae). *Physiologist*, **33A**, 106.

Sandquist, D.R. and Ehleringer, J.R. (1998). Intraspecific variation of drought adaptation in brittlebrush: leaf pubescence and timing of leaf loss vary with rainfall. *Oecologia*, **113**, 162–9.

Sauer, E.G.F. and Sauer, E.M. (1967). Yawning and other maintenance activities in the South African Ostrich. *Auk*, **84**, 571–87.

Savory, A. (1988). *Holistic resource management*. Island Press, Covelo, CA.

Schall, J.J. and Pianka, E.R. (1978). Geographical trends in numbers of species. *Science*, **201**, 679–86.

Schemenauer, R.S. and Cereceda, P. (1992a). The quality of fogwater collected for domestic and agricultural use in Chile. *Journal of Applied Meteorology*, **31**, 275–90.

Schemenauer, R.S. and Cereceda, P. (1992b). Monsoon cloudwater chemistry on the Arabian peninsula. *Atmospheric Environment*, **26A**, 1583–7.

Schlesinger, W.H. and Pilmanis, A.M. (1998). Plant–soil interactions in deserts. *Biogeochemistry*, **42**, 169–87.

Schlesinger, W.H., Reynolds, J.F., Cunningham, G.L., Huenneke, L.F., Jarrell, W.M., Virginia, R.A., and Whitford, W.G. (1990). Biological feedbacks in global desertification. *Science*, **247**, 1043–8.

Schlesinger, W.H., Raikes, J., Hartley, A.E., and Cross, A.F. (1996). On the spatial pattern of soil nutrients in desert ecosystems. *Ecology*, **77**, 364–74.

Schlesinger, W.H., Palmer Winkler, J., and Megonigal, J.P. (2000). Soils and the global carbon cycle. In Wigley, T. M. L. and D.S. Schimel, eds. *The global carbon cycle*, pp. 93–101. Cambridge University Press, Cambridge.

Schlesinger, W.H., Tartowski, S.L., and Schmidt, S.M. (2006). Nutrient cycling within an arid ecosystem. In K.M. Havstad, L.E. Huenneke, and W.H. Schlesinger, eds. *Structure and function of a Chihuahuan Desert ecosystem: the Jornada Basin LTER*, pp. 133–49. Oxford University Press, Oxford.

Schluter, D. and Ricklefs, R.E. (1993). Species diversity: an introduction to the problem. In R.E. Ricklefs and D. Schluter, eds. *Species diversity in ecological communities: historical and geographical perspectives*, pp. 1–10. University of Chicago Press, Chicago.

Schmidly, D.J., Wilkins, K.T., and Derr, J.N. (1983). Biogeography. In H.H. Genoways and J.H. Brown, eds. *Biology of the Heteromyidae. American Society of Mammalogists*, pp. 319–56. Provo, Utah. Special publication No. 10.

Schmidt-Nielsen, K., Schmidt-Nielsen, B., Jarnum, S.A., and Houpt, T.R. (1956). Body temperature of the camel and its relation to water economy. *American Journal of Physiology*, **188**, 103–12.

Schmidt-Nielsen, K., Taylor, C.R., and Shkolnik, A. (1971). Desert snails: problems of heat, water and food. *Journal of Experimental Biology*, **55**, 385–98.

Schmidt-Nielsen, K., Crawford, E.C., and Hammel, H.T. (1981). Respiratory water loss in camels. *Proceedings of the Royal Society of London, Series B*, **211**, 291–303.

Schmiedel, U. and Jürgens, N. (1999). Community structure on unusual habitat islands: quartz-fields in the Succulent Karoo, South Africa. *Plant Ecology*, **142**, 57–69.

Schodde, R. (1982). Origin, adaptation and evolution of birds in arid Australia. In Barker, W.R. and P.J.M. Greenslade, eds. *Evolution of the flora and fauna of arid Australia*, pp. 191–224. Peacock Press, Adelaide.

Schoener, T.W. (1989). Food webs from the small to the large. *Ecology*, **70**, 1559–89.

Scholes, R.J. and Archer, S.R. (1997). Tree–grass interactions in savannas. *Annual Review of Ecology and Systematics*, **28**, 517–44.

Scholes, R.J. and Walker, B.H. (1993). *An African savanna: synthesis of the Nylsvley study.* Cambridge University Press, Cambridge.

Scholnick, D.A. (1994). Seasonal variation and diurnal fluctuations in ephemeral desert pools. *Hydrobiologia*, **294**, 111–16.

Schulze, E.-D. (1982). Plant life forms and their carbon, water and nutrient relations. In O.L. Lange, P.S. Nobel, C.B. Osmond, and H. Ziegler, eds. *Water relations and carbon assimilation: physiological plant ecology II. Encyclopedia of plant physiology*, pp. 615–76. Springer, Berlin. New series volume 12B.

Schulze, E.-D. and Schulze, J. (1976). Distribution and control of photosynthetic pathways in plants growing in the Namib Desert, with special regard to *Welwitschia mirabilis* Hook. fil. *Madoqua*, **9**, 5–13.

Schulze, E.-D., Caldwell, M.M., Canadell, J., Mooncy, H.A., Jackson, R.B., Parsons, D., Scholes, R., Sala, O.E., and Trimborn, P. (1998). Downward flux of water through roots (i.e. inverse hydraulic lift) in dry Kalahari sands. *Oecologia*, **115**, 460–2.

Schuster, M., Duringer, P., Ghienne J.-F., Vignaud, P., Mackaye, H.T., Likius, A., and Brunet, M. (2006). The age of the Sahara Desert. *Science*, **311**, 821.

Schwinning, S., Sala, O.E., Loik, M.E., and Ehleringer, J.R. (2004). Thresholds, memory, and seasonality: understanding pulse dynamics in arid/semi-arid ecosystems. *Oecologia*, **141**, 191–3.

Scott, J.K. and Panetta, F.D. (1993). Predicting the Australian weed status of southern African plants. *Journal of Biogeography*, **20**, 87–93.

Seely, M.K. and Mitchell, D. (1987). Is the subsurface environment of the Namib Desert dunes a thermal haven for chthonic beetles? *South African Journal of Zoology*, **22**, 57–61.

Seely, M.K., de Vos, M.P., and Louw, G.N. (1977). Fog imbibition, satellite fauna and unusual leaf structure in a Namib Desert dune plant, *Trianthema here-roensis*. *South African Journal of Science*, **73**, 169–72.

Seely, M.K., Lewis, C.J., O'Brien, K.A., and Suttle, A.E. (1983). Fog response of tenebrionid beetles in the Namib Desert. *Journal of Arid Environments*, **6**, 135–43.

Seymour, R.S. and Seely, M.K. (1996). The respiratory environment of the Namib golden mole. *Journal of Arid Environments*, **32**, 453–61.

Shachak, M. (1980). Feeding, energy flow and soil turnover in the desert isopod, *Hemilepistus reaumuri*. *Oecologia*, **21**, 57–69.

Shachak, M., Chapman, E.A., and Steinberger, Y. (1976). Feeding, energy flow and soil turnover in the desert isopod, *Hemilepistus reaumuri*. *Oecologia*, **24**, 57–69.

Shachak, M., Safriel, U.N., and Hunum, R. (1981). An exceptional event of predation on desert snails by migratory thrushes in the Negev Desert, Israel. *Ecology*, **62**, 1441–9.

Shachak, M., Brand, S., and Gutterman, Y. (1991). Porcupine disturbances and vegetation pattern along a resource gradient in a desert. *Oecologia*, **88**, 141–7.

Shantz, H.L. (1927). Drought resistance and soil moisture. *Ecology*, **8**, 145–57.

Sharon, D. (1972). The spottiness of rainfall in a desert area. *Journal of Hydrology*, **17**, 161–75.

Sharon, D. (1981). The distribution in space of local rainfall in the Namib Desert. *International Journal of Climatology*, **1**, 69–75.

Shenbrot, G. (2004). Habitat selection in a seasonally variable environment: test of the isodar theory with the fat sand rat, *Psammomys obesus*, in the Negev. *Oikos*, **98**, 393–402.

Shenbrot, G., Rogovin, K.A., and Heske, E.J. (1994). Comparison of niche-packing and community organization in Asia and North America. *Australian Journal of Zoology*, **42**, 479–99.

Shenbrot, G., Krasnov, B., Khokhlova, I., Demidova, T., and Fielden, L. (2002). Habitat-dependent differences in architecture and microclimate of the burrows of Sundevall's jird (*Meriones crassus*) (Rodentia: Gerbillinae) in the Negev Desert, Israel. *Journal of Arid Environments*, 51, 265–79.

Sher, A.A., Goldberg, D.E., and Novoplansky, A. (2004). The effect of mean and variance in resource supply on survival of annuals from Mediterranean and desert environments. *Oecologia*, 141, 353–62.

Sher, A.A., Wiegand, K., and Ward, D. (submitted). Competition for water in *Acacia raddiana* and *Tamarix* species. *Journal of Arid Environments*.

Shkedy, Y. and Saltz, D. (2000). Characterizing core and corridor use by Nubian Ibex in the Negev Desert, Israel. *Conservation Biology*, 14, 200–6.

Shmida, A. (1972). *The vegetation of Gebel Maghara, North Sinai*. Unpublished MSc thesis, Hebrew University, Jerusalem.

Shmida, A. (1985). Biogeography of the desert flora. In M. Evenari, I. Noy-Meir, and D.W. Goodall, eds. *Ecosystems of the world*, volume 12A, pp. 23–77. Elsevier, Amsterdam.

Shmida, A. and Darom, D. (1986). *Handbook of wildflowers of Israel: desert flora*. Keter Press, Jerusalem.

Shmida, A. and Whittaker, R.H. (1985). Trends of species diversity and growth forms in arid regions. Unpublished manuscript. Hebrew University of Jerusalem, Israel.

Shrestha, M.K., Golan-Goldhirsh, A., and Ward, D. (2002). Population genetic structure in isolated populations of *Acacia raddiana* investigated by random amplified polymorphic DNA (RAPD) markers. *Biological Conservation*, 108, 119–27.

Shreve, F. (1942). The desert vegetation of North America. *Botanical Review*, 8, 195–246.

Shreve, F. and Wiggins, I.L. (1964). *Vegetation and flora of the Sonoran Desert*, volumes 1 and 2. Stanford University Press, Palo Alto, CA.

Sierra, C., Ortega, E., Quirantes, J., Lozano, J., and Martinez, J. (1990). *Proyecto LUCDEME Mapa de suelos Baza 994*. M.A.P.A.-ICONA, Madrid.

Sinclair, A.R.E. and Fryxell, J.M. (1985). The Sahel of Africa: ecology of a disaster. *Canadian Journal of Zoology*, 63, 987–94.

Singh, G. (1988). History of aridland vegetation and climate: a global perspective. *Biological Reviews*, 63, 159–95.

Sinitzin, V.M. (1962). *Palaeogeography of Asia*. USSR Academy of Sciences Press, Moscow.

Skarpe, C. (1990a). Shrub layer dynamics under different herbivore densities in an arid savanna, Botswana. *Journal of Applied Ecology*, 27, 873–85.

Skarpe, C. (1990b). Structure of the woody vegetation in disturbed and undisturbed arid savanna. *Vegetatio*, 87, 11–18.

Skarpe, C. (2000). Desertification, no-change or alternative states: can we trust simple models on livestock impact in dry rangelands? *Applied Vegetation Science*, 3, 261–8.

Smet, M. and Ward, D. (2005). A comparison of the effects of different rangeland management systems on plant species composition, diversity and vegetation structure in a semi-arid savanna. *African Journal of Range and Forage Science*, 22, 59–71.

Smet, M. and Ward, D. (2006). Soil quality gradients around water-points under different management systems in a semi-arid savanna, South Africa. *Journal of Arid Environments*, 64, 251–69.

Smit, G.N., Rethman, N.F.G., and Moore, A. (1996). Vegetative growth, reproduction, browse production and response to tree clearing of woody plants in
African savanna. *African Journal of Range and Forage Science*, **13**, 78–88.

Smith, S.D., Anderson, J.E., and Monson, R.K. (1997). *Physiological ecology of
North American desert plants*. Springer, Berlin.

Snyder, C.T., Frickel, D.G., Hadley, R.F., and Miller, R.F. (1976). Effects of off-road
vehicle use on the hydrology and landscape of arid environments in central
and southern California. *U.S. Geological Survey Water Resources Investigations*,
76–99.

Solbrig, O. (1973). The floristic disjunctions between Monte in Argentina and
the Sonoran Desert in Mexico and the United States. *Annals of the Missouri
Botanical Gardens*, **59**, 218–33.

Spalton, J.A., Brend, S.A., and Lawrence, M.W. (1999). Arabian oryx reintroduction in Oman: successes and setbacks. *Oryx*, **33**, 168–75.

Specht, R.L. and Specht, A. (1999). *Australian plant communities: dynamics of
structure, growth, and biodiversity*. Oxford University Press, Oxford.

Stafford Smith, D.M. and Morton, S.R. (1990). A framework for the ecology of arid
Australia. *Journal of Arid Environments*, **18**, 255–78.

Stamp, N.E. (1984). Self-burial behaviour of *Erodium cicutarium* seeds. *Journal of
Ecology*, **72**, 611–20.

Stanley-Price, M.R. (1989). *Animal re-introductions: the Arabian oryx in Oman*.
Cambridge University Press, Cambridge.

Stearns, S.C. (1992). *The evolution of life histories*. Oxford University Press,
Oxford.

Steenbergh, W.F. and Lowe, C.H. (1977). Ecology of the Saguaro: II. Reproduction,
germination, establishment, growth, and survival of the young plant. US
National Park Service, *Monograph Series Number 8*, US Government Printing
Office, Washington, DC.

Stephens, G. and Whitford, W.G. (1993). Responses of *Bouteloua eriopoda* to irrigation and nitrogen fertilization in a Chihuahuan Desert grassland. *Journal of
Arid Environments*, **24**, 415–421.

Stiling, P.D. (2002). *Ecology: theories and applications*. 4th ed. Prentice-Hall, New
Jersey.

Stowe, L.G. and Teeri, J.A. (1978). The geographic distribution of C_4 species of the
Dicotyledonae in relation to climate. *American Naturalist*, **112**, 609–23.

Strahler, A.N. (1976). *Principles of earth science*. Harper and Row, New York.

Strauss, S.Y. (1991). Indirect effects in community ecology: their definition, study,
and importance. *Trends in Ecology and Evolution*, **6**, 206–10.

Sun, J. and Liu, T. (2006). The age of the Taklimakan Desert. *Science*, **312**,
1621.

Suzán, H., Nabhan, G.P., and Patten, D.T. (1996). The importance of *Olneya
tesota* as a nurse plant in the Sonoran Desert. *Journal of Vegetation Science*,
7, 635–44.

Swap, R., Garstang, M., Greco, S., Talbot, R., and Kâllberg, P. (1992). Saharan dust
in the Amazon Basin. *Tellus B*, **44**, 133–49.

Tang, Q.C. and Zhang, J.B. (2001). Water resources and eco-environment
protection in the arid regions in northwest of China. *Progress in Geography*,
20, 227–33.

Tchabovsky, A.V., Krasnov, B.R., Khokhlova, I.S., and Shenbrot, G.I. (2001). The effect of vegetation cover on vigilance and foraging tactics in the fat sand rat, *Psammomys obesus. Journal of Ethology*, **19**, 107–15.

Teague, W.R. and Smit, G.N. (1992). Relations between woody and herbaceous components and the effects of bush-clearing in southern African savannas. *Journal of the Grassland Society of South Africa*, **9**, 60–71.

Terborgh, J. (1973). On the notion of favorableness in plant ecology. *American Naturalist*, **107**, 481–501.

Thoday, D. (1926). The contractile roots of *Oxalis incarnata. Annals of Botany*, **40**, 571–83.

Thoday, D. and Davey, A.J. (1932). Contractile roots. II. On the mechanism of root contraction in *Oxalis incarnata. Annals of Botany*, **46**, 993–1005.

Thompson, J.N. (1998). Rapid evolution as an ecological process. *Trends in Ecology and Evolution*, **13**, 329–32.

Thompson, J.N. and Pellmyr, O. (1992). Mutualism with pollinating seed parasites amid co-pollinators: constraints on specialization. *Ecology*, **73**, 1780–91.

Thompson, W.R. (1939). Biological control and the theories of the interaction of populations. *Parasitology*, **31**, 299–388.

Thorne, R.F. (1973). Major disjunctions in the geographic ranges of seed plants. *Quarterly Review of Biology*, **47**, 365–411.

Thornthwaite, C.W. (1948). An approach to the rational classification of climate. *Geographical Review*, **38**, 55–94.

Tielborger, K. and Kadmon, R. (2000). Indirect effects in a desert plant community: is competition among annuals more intense under shrub canopies? *Plant Ecology*, **150**, 53–63.

Tieleman, B.I., Williams, J.B., and Buschur, M.E. (2002). Physiological adjustments to arid and mesic environments in larks (Alaudidae). *Physiological and Biochemical Zoology*, **75**, 305–13.

Tieleman, B.I., Williams, J.B., and Bloomer, P. (2003a). Adaptation of metabolism and evaporative water loss along an aridity gradient. *Proceedings of the Royal Society, London, Series B*, **270**, 207–14.

Tieleman, B.I., Williams, J.B., Buschur, M.E., and Brown, C.R. (2003b). Phenotypic variation of larks along an aridity gradient: are desert birds more flexible? *Ecology*, **84**, 1800–15.

Tilman, D. (1982). *Resource competition and community structure*. Princeton University Press, Princeton.

Tilman, D. (1988). *Plant strategies and the dynamics and structure of plant communities*. Princeton University Press, Princeton.

Tinsley, R.C. (1999). Parasite adaptation to extreme conditions in a desert environment. *Parasitology*, **119**, S31–S36.

Tinsley, R.C., Cable, J., and Porter, R. (2002). Pathological effects of *Pseudodiplorchis americanus* (Monogenea: Polystomatidae) on the lung epithelium of its host, *Scaphiopus couchii. Parasitology*, **125**, 143–53.

Tomlinson, S., Withers, P.C., and Cooper, C. (2007). Hypothermia versus torpor in response to cold stress in the native Australian mouse *Pseudomys hermannsburgensis* and the introduced house mouse *Mus musculus. Comparative Biochemistry and Physiology A*, **148**, 645–50.

Toolson, E.C. (1987). Water profligacy as an adaptation to hot deserts: water loss and evaporative cooling in the Sonoran Desert cicada, *Diceroprocta apache* (Homoptera: Cicadidae). *Physiological Zoology*, **60**, 379–85.

Treydte, A.C., Williams, J.B., Bedin, E., Ostrowski, S., Seddon, P.J., Marschall, E.A., Waite, T.A., and Ismail, K. (2001). In search of the optimal management strategy for Arabian oryx. *Animal Conservation*, **4**, 239–49.

Trivers, R.L. and Willard, D.E. (1973). Natural selection of parental ability to vary sex ratio of offspring. *Science*, **179**, 90–2.

Turner, B.L. (1977). Fossil history and geography of Compositae. In V.H. Heywood, J.B. Harborne, and B.L. Turner, eds. *The biology and chemistry of the Compositae*, pp. 21–41. Academic Press, New York.

Turner, J.S. (1994). Ventilation and thermal constancy in a colony of a south African termite (*Odontotermes transvaalensis*: Macrotermitinae). *Journal of Arid Environments*, **28**, 231–48.

Turner, J.S. (2001). On the mound of *Macrotermes michaelseni* as an organ of respiratory gas exchange. *Physiological and Biochemical Zoology*, **74**, 798–822.

Turner, J.S. and Lombard, A.T. (1991). Body color and body temperatures in white and black Namib Desert beetles. *Journal of Arid Environments*, **19**, 303–15.

Turner, J.S. and Picker, M.D. (1993). Thermal ecology of an embedded dwarf succulent from southern Africa (*Lithops* spp: Mesembryanthemaceae). *Journal of Arid Environments*, **24**, 361–85.

Turner, J.S., Henschel, J.R., and Lubin, Y.D. (1993). Thermal constraints on a burrowing spider in a hot environment. *Behavioral Ecology and Sociobiology*, **33**, 35–43.

United Nations Environment Program (1992). *World atlas of desertification*. Edward Arnold, Sevenoaks.

United Nations Environment Program (1996). *Indicators of sustainable development: guidelines and methodologies*. United Nations, New York.

Valentine, K.A. (1947). Distance from water as a factor in grazing capacity of rangeland. *Journal of Forestry*, **45**, 749–54.

Valiente-Banuet, A. and Ezcurra, E. (1991). Shade as a cause of the association between the cactus *Neobuxbaumia tetetzo* and the nurse plant *Mimosa luisiana* in the Tehuacan valley, Mexico. *Journal of Ecology*, **79**, 961–72.

Valone, T.J., Brown, J.H., and Heske, E.J. (1994). Interactions between rodents and ants in the Chihuahuan Desert: an update. *Ecology*, **75**, 252–5.

Van de Koppel, J., Rietkerk, M., and Weissing, F.J. (1997). Catastrophic vegetation shifts and soil degradation in terrestrial grazing systems. *Trends in Ecology and Evolution*, **12**, 352–6.

Van der Pijl, L. (1972). *Principles of dispersal in higher plants*. Springer, Berlin.

Van Rheede Van Oudtshoorn, K. and Van Rooyen, M.W. (1999). *Dispersal biology of desert plants*. Springer, Berlin.

Van Rooyen, N., Bredenkamp, G.J., and Theron, G.K. (1991). Kalahari vegetation: veld condition trends and ecological status of species. *Koedoe*, **33**, 63–88.

Van Valen, L. (1977). The red queen. *American Naturalist*, **111**, 809–10.

Vasek, F.C. (1980). Creosote bush: long-lived clones in the Mojave Desert. *American Journal of Botany*, **67**, 246–55.

Veech, J.A. (2001). The foraging behavior of granivorous rodents and short-term apparent competition among seeds. *Behavioral Ecology*, **12**, 467–74.

Venable, D.L. (1985). The evolutionary ecology of seed heteromorphism. *American Naturalist*, **126**, 577–95.

Venable, D.L. (2007). Bet hedging in a guild of desert annuals. *Ecology*, **88**, 1086–90.

Venable, D.L., Pake, C.E., and Caprio, A.C. (1993). Diversity and coexistence of Sonoran Desert winter annuals. *Plant Species Biology*, **8**, 207–16.

Venable, D.L., Dyerson, E., and Morales, E. (1995). Population dynamic consequences and evolution of seed traits of *Heterosperma pinnatum* (Asteraceae). *American Journal of Botany*, **82**, 410–20.

Venter, J., Liggitt, B., Tainton, N.M., and Clarke, G.P.M. (1989). The influence of different land use practices on soil erosion, herbage production, and grass species richness and diversity. *Journal of the Grassland Society of Southern Africa*, **6**, 89–98.

Vernon, C. (1999). Biogeography, endemism and diversity of animals in the Karoo. In W.R.J. Dean and S.J. Milton, eds. *The Karoo: ecological patterns and processes*, pp. 57–85. Cambridge University Press, Cambridge.

Vesk, P.A., Leishman, M.R., and Westoby, M. (2004). Simple traits do not predict grazing response in Australian shrublands and woodlands. *Journal of Applied Ecology*, **41**, 22–31.

Vishnevetsky, S. and Steinberger, Y. (1997). Bacterial and fungal dynamics and their contribution to microbial biomass in desert soil. *Journal of Arid Environments*, **37**, 83–90.

Vitt, L.J. and Pianka, E.R., eds. (1994). *Lizard ecology: historical and experimental perspectives*. Princeton University Press, Princeton.

Vogel, J.C. and Seely, M.K. (1977). Occurrence of C_4 plants in the central Namib Desert. *Madoqua*, **10**, 75–8.

Vogel, S. (1994). *Life in moving fluids*. Princeton University Press, Princeton.

Volis, S. (2007). Correlated patterns of variation in phenology and seed production in populations of two annual grasses along an aridity gradient. *Evolutionary Ecology*, **21**, 381–93.

Volis, S., Mendlinger, S., Safriel, U.N., Olsvig-Whittaker, L., and Orlovsky, N. (1998). Phenotypic variation and stress resistance in core and peripheral populations of *Hordeum spontaneum*. *Biodiversity and Conservation*, 7, 799–813.

Volis, S., Yakubov, B., Shulgina, I., Ward, D., Zur, V., and Mendlinger, S. (2001). Tests for adaptive RAPD variation in population genetic structure of wild barley, *Hordeum spontaneum* Koch. *Biological Journal of Linnean Society*, **74**, 289–303.

Volis, S., Mendlinger, S., and Ward, D. (2002). Adaptive traits of wild barley plants of Mediterranean and desert origin. *Oecologia*, **133**, 131–8.

Volis, S., Mendlinger, S., Ward, D., and Verhoeven, K. (2004). Phenotypic selection and regulation of reproduction in different environments in wild barley. *Journal of Evolutionary Biology*, **17**, 1121–31.

Von Willert, D.J., Eller, B.M., Brinckmann, E., and Baasch, R. (1982). CO_2 gas exchange and transpiration of *Welwitschia mirabilis* Hook. fil. in the central Namib Desert. *Oecologia*, **55**, 21–9.

Von Willert, D.J., Brinckmann, E., Scheitler, B., and Eller, B.M. (1985). Availability of water controls crassulacean acid metabolism in succulents of the Richtersveld (Namib Desert, South Africa). *Planta*, **164**, 44–55.

Von Willert, D.J., Eller, B.M., Werger, M.J.A., Brinckmann, E., and Ihlenfeldt, H.-D. (1992). *Life strategies of succulents in deserts, with special reference to the Namib Desert.* Cambridge University Press, Cambridge.

Wadia, D.N. (1960). *The post-glacial desiccation of central Asia.* Monograph, National Institute of Science (India), 1–25.

Waisel, Y. (1972). *Biology of halophytes.* Academic Press, New York.

Walker, B.H. and Noy-Meir, I. (1982). Aspects of the stability and resilience of savanna ecosystems. In B.J. Huntley and B.H. Walker, eds. *Ecology of tropical savannas*, pp. 556–90. Springer, Berlin.

Walker, B.H., Ludwig, D., Holling, C.S., and Peterman, R.M. (1981). Stability of semi-arid savanna grazing systems. *Journal of Ecology*, **69**, 473–98.

Walter, H. (1939). Grassland, savanna and bush of arid regions of Africa and its ecological conditions. *Yearbook for Scientific Botany*, **87**, 750–860. [in German]

Walter, H. (1954). The encroachment, the appearance of subtropical savanna regions, and their ecological causes. *Vegetatio*, **5/6**, 6–10. [in German]

Walter, H. (1971). *Ecology of tropical and subtropical vegetation.* Oliver and Boyd, Edinburgh.

Walter, H. (1973). *Vegetation of the earth in relation to climate and the ecophysiological conditions.* Springer, Berlin.

Ward, D. (1991). A test of the 'maxithermy' hypothesis with three species of tenebrionid beetles. *Journal of Arid Environments*, **21**, 331 6.

Ward, D. (2001). Plant species diversity and population dynamics in Makhtesh Ramon. In B. Krasnov and E. Mazor, eds. *The Makhteshim Country: a laboratory of nature*, pp. 171–86. Pensoft, Sofia, Bulgaria.

Ward, D. (2002). Do we understand the causes of bush encroachment? In A.W. Seydack, T. Vorster, W.J. Vermeulen, and I.J. Van Der Merwe, eds. *Multiple use management of natural forests and woodlands: policy refinements and scientific progress*, pp. 189–201. Department of Water Affairs and Forestry, Pretoria.

Ward, D. (2005a). The effects of grazing on plant biodiversity in arid ecosystems. In M. Shachak, S.T.A. Pickett, J.R. Gosz, and A. Perevolotsky, eds. *Biodiversity in drylands: toward a unified framework*, pp. 233–49. Oxford University Press, Oxford.

Ward, D. (2005b). Do we understand the causes of bush encroachment in African savannas? *African Journal of Range and Forage Science*, **22**, 101–5.

Ward, D. (2006). Long-term effects of herbivory on plant diversity and functional types in arid ecosystems. In K. Danell, R. Bergström, P. Duncan, and J. Pastor, eds. *Large mammalian herbivores, ecosystem dynamics, and conservation*, pp. 142–69. Cambridge University Press, Cambridge.

Ward, D. and Blaustein, L. (1994). The overriding influence of flash floods on species-area curves in ephemeral Negev Desert pools: a consideration of the value of island biogeography theory. *Journal of Biogeography*, **21**, 595–603.

Ward, D. and Henschel, J.R. (1992). Experimental evidence that a desert parasitoid keeps its host cool. *Ethology*, **92**, 135–42.

Ward, D. and Lubin, Y.D. (1993). Habitat selection and the life history of a desert spider, *Stegodyphus lineatus* (Eresidae). *Journal of Animal Ecology*, **62**, 353–63.

Ward, D. and Ngairorue, B.T. (2000). Are Namibia's grasslands desertifying? *Journal of Range Management*, **53**, 138–44.

Ward, D. and Olsvig-Whittaker, L. (1993). Plant species diversity at the junction of two desert biogeographic zones. *Biodiversity Letters*, 1, 172–85.

Ward, D. and Rohner, C. (1997). Anthropogenic causes of high mortality and low recruitment in three *Acacia* tree taxa in the Negev Desert, Israel. *Biodiversity and Conservation*, 6, 877–93.

Ward, D. and Saltz, D.G. (1994). Foraging at different spatial scales: dorcas gazelles foraging for lilies in the Negev Desert. *Ecology*, 75, 48–58.

Ward, D. and Seely, M.K. (1996a). Competition and habitat selection in Namib Desert tenebrionid beetles. *Evolutionary Ecology*, 10, 341-–59.

Ward, D. and Seely, M.K. (1996b). Adaptation and constraint in the evolution of the physiology and behavior of the Namib Desert tenebrionid beetle genus *Onymacris*. *Evolution*, 50, 1231–40.

Ward, D. and Seely, M.K. (1996c). Behavioral thermoregulation in six Namib Desert tenebrionid beetle species (Coleoptera). *Annals of the Entomological Society of America*, 89, 442–51.

Ward, D. and Slotow, R.H. (1992). The effects of water availability on the life history of the desert snail, *Trochoidea seetzeni*. *Oecologia*, 90, 572–80.

Ward, D. and Smith, J.N.M. (2000). Interhabitat differences in parasitism frequency by Brown-headed Cowbirds in the Okanagan Valley, British Columbia. In J.N.M. Smith, T.L. Cook, S.I. Rothstein, S.K. Robinson, and S.G. Sealy, eds. *Ecology and management of cowbirds and their hosts*, pp. 210–19. University of Texas Press, Austin.

Ward, J.D., Seely, M.K., and Lancaster, N. (1983). On the antiquity of the Namib. *South African Journal of Science*, 79, 175–83.

Ward, D., Olsvig-Whittaker, L., and Lawes, M.J. (1993). Vegetation-environment relationships in a Negev Desert erosion cirque. *Journal of Vegetation Science*, 4, 83–94.

Ward, D., Lindholm, A.K., and Smith, J.N.M. (1996). Multiple parasitism of the red-winged blackbird: further experimental evidence of evolutionary lag in a common host of the brown-headed cowbird. *Auk*, 113, 408–13.

Ward, D., Spiegel, M., and Saltz, D. (1997). Gazelle herbivory and interpopulation differences in calcium oxalate content of leaves of a desert lily. *Journal of Chemical Ecology*, 23, 333–46.

Ward, D., Ngairorue, B.T., Kathena, J., Samuels, R., and Ofran, Y. (1998). Land degradation is not a necessary outcome of communal pastoralism in arid Namibia. *Journal of Arid Environments*, 40, 357–71.

Ward, D., Saltz, D., and Olsvig-Whittaker, L. (2000a). Distinguishing signal from noise: long-term studies of vegetation in Makhtesh Ramon erosion cirque, Negev Desert, Israel. *Plant Ecology*, 150, 27–36.

Ward, D., Ngairorue, B.T., Apollus, A., and Tjiveze, H. (2000b). Perceptions and realities of land degradation in arid Otjimbingwe, Namibia. *Journal of Arid Environments*, 45, 337–56.

Ward, D., Feldman, K., and Avni, Y. (2001). The effects of loess erosion on soil nutrients, plant diversity and plant quality in Negev Desert wadis. *Journal of Arid Environments*, 48, 461–73.

Ward, D., Saltz, D., and Ngairorue, B.T. (2004). Spatio-temporal rainfall variation and stock management in arid Namibia. *Journal of Range Management*, 57, 130–40.

Waser, N.M., Chittka, L., Price, M.V., Williams, N.M., and Ollerton, J. (1996). Generalization in pollination systems, and why it matters. *Ecology*, 77, 1043–60.

Webb, R.H. (1982). Off-road motorcycle effects on a desert soil. *Environmental Conservation*, 9, 197–208.

Webb, R.H. and Wilshire, H.G. (1980). Recovery of soils and vegetation in a Mojave Desert ghost town, Nevada. *Journal of Arid Environments*, 3, 291–303.

Webb, R.H., Ragland, H.C., Godwin, W.H., and Jenkins, D. (1978). Environmental effects of soil property changes with off-road vehicle use. *Environmental Management*, 2, 219–33.

Weber, G.E., Moloney, K., and Jeltsch, F. (2000). Simulated long-term vegetation response to alternative stocking strategies in savanna rangelands. *Plant Ecology*, 150, 77–96.

Wegener, A.L. (1966). *The origin of continents and oceans*. Dover Publications, London.

Welker, J.M., Briske, D.D., and Weaver, R.W. (1991). Intraclonal nitrogen variation in the bunchgrass *Schizachyrium scoparium* Hubb.: an assessment of the physiological individual. *Functional Ecology*, 5, 433–50.

Wells, P.V. and Hunziker, J.H. (1976). Origin of the creosote bush (*Larrea*) deserts of southwestern North America. *Annals of the Missouri Botanical Gardens*, 63, 843–61.

Weltzin, J.F. and McPherson, G.R. (1997). Spatial and temporal soil moisture resource partitioning by trees and savannas in a temperate savanna, Arizona, USA. *Oecologia*, 112, 156–64.

Went, F.W. (1955). The ecology of desert plants. *Scientific American*, 192, 68–75.

Werger, M.J.A. (1978). *Biogeography and ecology of South Africa*. Junk, The Hague.

Werk, K.S., Ehleringer, J.R., Forseth, I.N., and Cook, C.S. (1983). Photosynthetic characteristics of Sonoran Desert winter annuals. *Oecologia*, 59, 101–5.

Werner, E.E. and Anholt, B.R. (1996). Predator-induced behavioral indirect effects: consequences to competitive interactions in anuran larvae. *Ecology*, 77, 157–69.

West, N.E. (1983). Great Basin-Colorado Plateau sagebrush semi-desert. In N.E. West, ed. *Temperate deserts and semi-deserts*, pp. 331–74. Elsevier, New York.

West, N.E. (1990). Structure and function of soil microphytic crusts in wildland ecosystems of arid and semi-arid regions. *Advances in Ecological Research*, 20, 179–223.

West, N.E. and Skujins, J. (1978). *Nitrogen in desert ecosystems*. Dowden, Hutchinson and Ross, Stroudsburg, PA.

Westoby, M. (1980). Elements of a theory of vegetation dynamics in arid rangelands. *Israel Journal of Botany*, 28, 169–94.

Westoby, M. (1989). Selective forces exerted by vertebrate herbivores on plants. *Trends in Ecology and Evolution*, 4, 115–17.

Westoby, M. (1993). Biodiversity in Australia compared with other continents. In R.E. Ricklefs and D. Schluter, eds. *Species diversity in ecological communities: historical and geographical perspectives*, pp. 170–7. University of Chicago Press, Chicago.

Westoby, M. (1999). A leaf-height-seed (LHS) plant ecology strategy scheme. *Plant and Soil*, 199, 213–27.

White, M.E. (1993). *After the greening: the browning of Australia*. Kangaroo Press, Kenthurst, Australia.

Whitford, W.G. (1996). The importance of the biodiversity of soil biota in arid ecosystems. *Biodiversity and Conservation*, 5, 185–95.

Whitford, W.G. (1999). Contribution of pits dug by goannas (*Varanus gouldii*) to the banded mulga landscapes in eastern Australia. *Journal of Arid Environments*, **40**, 453–7.

Whitford, W.G. (2002). *Ecology of desert systems*. Academic Press, San Diego.

Whitford, W.G. and Kay, F.R. (1999). Biopedturbation by mammals in deserts: a review. *Journal of Arid Environments*, **41**, 203–30.

Whitford, W.G., Steinberger, Y., MacKay, W., Parker, L.W., Freckman, D., Wallwork, J.A., and Weems, D. (1986). Rainfall and decomposition in the Chihuahuan Desert. *Oecologia*, **68**, 512–15.

Whittaker, R.H. (1975). *Communities and ecosystems*. MacMillan, New York.

Whittaker, R.H. (1977). Evolution of species diversity in land communities. *Evolutionary Biology*, **10**, 1–67.

Whittaker, R.H. and Niering, W.A. (1975). Vegetation of the Santa Catalina Mountains, Arizona. V. Biomass, production, and diversity along the elevation gradient. *Ecology*, **56**, 771–90.

Wiegand, K., Jeltsch, F., and Ward, D. (1999). Analysis of the population dynamics of *Acacia* trees in the Negev Desert, Israel with a spatially-explicit computer simulation model. *Ecological Modelling*, **117**, 203–24.

Wiegand, K., Jeltsch, F., and Ward, D. (2000). Do spatial effects play a role in the spatial distribution of desert dwelling *Acacia raddiana*? *Journal of Vegetation Science*, **11**, 473–84.

Wiegand, K., Jeltsch, F., and Ward, D. (2004). Minimum recruitment frequency in plants with episodic recruitment. *Oecologia*, **141**, 363–72.

Wiegand, K., Ward, D., and Saltz, D. (2005). Bush encroachment dynamics in an arid environment with a single soil layer. *Journal of Vegetation Science*, **16**, 311–20.

Wiegand, K., Saltz, D., and Ward, D. (2006). A patch-dynamics approach to savanna dynamics and woody plant encroachment—insights from an arid savanna. *Perspectives in Plant Ecology, Evolution and Systematics*, 7, 229–42.

Wiens, J.A. (1991). Similarity of shrub–desert avifaunas of Australia and North America. *Ecology*, **72**, 479–95.

Wiens, J.A. and Rotenberry, J.T. (1981). Habitat associations and community structure of birds in shrubsteppe environments. *Ecological Monographs*, **51**, 21–41.

Wiens, J.A., Stenseth, N.C., Van Horne, B., and Ims, R.A. (1993). Ecological mechanisms and landscape ecology. *Oikos*, **66**, 369–80.

Wilby, A., Boeken, B., and Shachak, M. (2001). Integration of ecosystem engineering and trophic effects of herbivores. *Oikos*, **92**, 436–44.

Wilby, A., Boeken, B., and Shachak, M. (2005). The impact of animals on species diversity in arid-land plant communities. In M. Shachak, J.R. Gosz, S.T.A. Pickett, and A. Perevolotsky, eds. *Biodiversity in drylands: toward a unified perspective*, pp. 189–205. Oxford University Press, Oxford.

Williams, J.B. (2001). Energy expenditure and water flux of free-living dune larks in the Namib: a test of the reallocation hypothesis on a desert bird. *Functional Ecology*, **15**, 175–85.

Williams, J.B., Siegfried, W.R., Milton, S.J., Adams, N.J., Dean, W.R.J., du Plessis, M.A., Jackson, S., and Nagy, K.A. (1993). Field metabolism, water requirements, and foraging behaviour of wild ostriches in the Namib. *Ecology*, **74**, 390–404.

Williams, J.B., Ostrowski, S., Bedlin, E., and Ismail, K. (2001). Seasonal variation in energy expenditure, water flux and food consumption of Arabian oryx, *Oryx leucoryx*. *Journal of Experimental Biology*, **204**, 2301–20.

Williams, J.B., Lenain, D., Ostrowski, S., Tieleman, B.I., and Seddon, P.J. (2002). Energy expenditure and water flux of Rüppell's foxes in Saudi Arabia. *Physiological and Biochemical Zoology*, 75, 479–88.

Williams, J.B., Muñoz-Garcia, A., Ostrowski, S., and Tieleman, B.I. (2004). A phylogenetic analysis of basal metabolism, total evaporative water loss, and life-history among foxes from desert and mesic regions. *Journal of Comparative Physiology B*, **174**, 29–39.

Williams, W.D. (1985). Biotic adaptations in temporary lentic waters, with special reference to those in semi-arid and arid regions. *Hydrobiologia*, **125**, 85–110.

Willmer, P., Stone, G., and Johnston, I. (2000). *Environmental physiology of animals*. Blackwells, Oxford.

Wilshire, H.G. and Nakata, J.K. (1976). Off-road vehicle effects on California's Mojave Desert. *California Geologist*, **29**, 123–32.

Wilson, M.V. and Shmida, A. (1984). Measuring beta diversity with presence-absence data. *Journal of Ecology*, **72**, 1055–64.

Winemiller, K.O. and Polis, G.A. (1996). Food webs: what can they tell us about the world? In G.A. Polis and K.O. Winemiller, eds. *Food webs: integration of patterns and dynamics*, pp. 1–22. Chapman and Hall, New York.

Winter, K. (1979). $\delta^{13}C$ values of some succulent plants from Madagascar. *Oecologia*, **40**, 103–12.

Winter, K., Lüttge, U., Winter, E., and Troughton, J.H. (1978). Seasonal shift from CO_2 photosynthesis to crassulacean acid metabolism in *Mesembryanthemum crystallinum* growing in its natural environment. *Oecologia*, **34**, 225–37.

Yeaton, R.I. (1978). A cyclical relationship between *Larrea tridentata* and *Opuntia leptocaulis* in the northern Chihuahuan Desert. *Journal of Ecology*, **66**, 651–6.

Yoder, C.K. and Nowak, R.S. (1999). Hydraulic lift among native plant species in the Mojave Desert. *Plant and Soil*, **215**, 93–102.

Yodzis, P. (1988). The indeterminacy of ecological interactions as perceived through perturbation experiments. *Ecology*, **69**, 508–15.

Young, D.R. and Nobel, P.S. (1986). Predictions of soil–water potentials in the north-western Sonoran Desert. *Journal of Ecology*, **74**, 143–54.

Zaady, E., Gutterman, Y., and Boeken, B. (1997). The germination of mucilaginous seeds of *Plantago coronopus*, *Reboudia pinnata*, and *Carrichtera annua* on cyanobacterial soil crust from the Negev Desert. *Plant and Soil*, **190**, 247–52.

Zaret, T. (1980). *Predation and freshwater communities*. Yale University Press, New Haven.

Ziv, Y., Abramsky, Z., Kotler, B.P., and Subach, A. (1993). Interference competition and temporal and habitat partitioning in two gerbil species. *Oikos*, **66**, 237–46.

Ziv, Y., Kotler, B.P., Abramsky, Z., and Rosenzweig, M.L. (1995). Foraging efficiencies of competing rodents: why do gerbils exhibit shared-preference habitat selection? *Oikos*, **73**, 260–8.

Ziv, Y., Rosenzweig, M.L., and Holt, R.D. (2005). Shalom: a landscape simulation model for understanding animal biodiversity. In M. Shachak, J.R. Gosz, S.T.A. Pickett, and A. Perevolotsky, eds. *Biodiversity in drylands: toward a unified perspective*, pp. 70–88. Oxford University Press, Oxford.

Zohary, M. (1937). The dispersal ecological circumstances of the plants of Palestine. *Beihefte zum Botanischen Zentralblatt*, **A56**, 1–155. [in German]

Zohary, M. (1962). *Plant life of Palestine (Israel and Jordan)*. Ronald Press, New York.

Zohary, M. (1973). *Geobotanical foundations of the Middle East*. Gustav Fischer, Stuttgart.

Zonn, I.S. (1993). The Aral's problem in the light of new geopolitics. *Problems of Desert Development*, **3**, 9–17. [in Russian]

Index

Note: page numbers in *italics* refer to Figures and Tables.

abiotic factors
  effect on biodiversity 145-7
  effect on flea species 138
  fire 27-8
  geology 20-1
    mountains 26, *27*
    plateau landscapes 26
    rock landscapes 25
    sand landscapes 214
    stone substrates 25
  precipitation
    fog 15
    oases 14-15
    rainfall 11-14
    run off 15-17
    soil salinity 17-19
    see also rainfall
  temperature 19-20
Abramsky, Z. *et al.* 116, 124
Abramsky, Z. and Rosenzweig, M.L. 199, *200*
Acacia species 248
  A. caven 218
  A. erioloba (camelthorn) 30, 119
    facilitation of other plant species *64*
  A. mellifera germination, influencing
      factors 232
  A. raddiana
    dispersal 211-12
    distribution, influencing factors 250-1
    genotype by environment
        interactions 261, *262*
    herbivory 153, *154*
    as keystone species *119*
    mortality in Negev desert wadis *221*
  A. reficiens 189
    germination 187
    root depth *62-3*
    seed scarification 168
Acanthaceae *210*
Acinonyx jubatus (cheetah) 137
Acocks, J.P.H. 245
Acomys cahirinus, snail predation 124
adaptations, animals 66-7
  endurers 87-92
    phylogenetically controlled studies 92

larks 98-9
  Peromyscus species 99-101
  skinks 97-8
  small carnivores 101
  tenebrionid beetles 93-7
  physiological cooling mechanisms 80-4
  salt glands 84-5
  to halophyte consumption 85-7
  to temporary pools 87
evaders 68-72
  burrowing spiders 76-7
  Cape ground squirrel *78-9*
  dasyurids and murids, water
      turnover 79-80
  frogs 74, *75*
  jirds 75, *76*
  kangaroo rats 74-5, *76*
  snails 72-4
  termites *77-8*
  vizcacha rat 75
adaptive characteristics, desert plants *35*
Addicott, J.F. and Tyre, A.J. 161-2
Adelostoma grande 125
Adesmia dilatata, predation 125
Adesmia metallica syriaca 125
Adondakis, S. and Venable, D.I. 104
aeolian layers, Asia 24
aerial transfer of nutrients 184
aestivation 80
  frogs and toads 74, *75*
Afghanistan desert 9
Afik, D. and Pinshow, B. 101
African wild dog (*Lycaon pictus*) 137
Agavaceae 36, 204, *210*
Agave deserti 58
  photosynthetic pathways *36*
  water uptake 63
age of deserts 3-4
Agelenopsis aperta 130
Aizoaceae 203, *204, 210*, 212, 214
Akodon genus 215
albedo, effect of overgrazing 218, *219*
Alectoris chukar (chukars) 82-3
Alhagi maurorum (now A. *graecorum*),
      rooting depth 63

Alhagi sparsifolia, clonality 49
Allenby's gerbil (*Gerbillus andersoni allenbyi*), predation risk 125–6
allelopathy 104
alluvial fans 12, *14*
Aloe species 36, 59
α diversity (local species richness) 11, 192
  birds 198
  granivores 197
  lizards 195
  plants 193
  small mammals 216
  in Succulent Karoo 254
Amadina erythrocephalus (red-headed finch), hypothermia 81
Amaranthaceae *210*
Amaryllidaceae 212
Amazon rainforests, aerial nutrient transfer 184
Ambrosia dumosa
  competition 105–6, *107*
  facilitation 106–*7*
American black bear (*Ursus americanus*), recolonization 260
Ammoperdix heyi (sand partridge) 82–3
amphicarpy 43, 45
Amphiocoma species, attraction to red flowers 171–2
amphiphytic plants 40–1
Anabasis articulata 31, 153–4
Andersson, Charles John 224, 231
Andira humilis, rooting depth 63
animals
  adaptations 66–7
    endurers 87–92
    evaders 68–72
      burrowing spiders 76–7
      Cape ground squirrel *78–9*
      dasyurids and murids 79–80
      frogs 74, *75*
      jirds 75, *76*
      kangaroo rats 74–5, *76*
      snails 72–4
      termites *77*–8
      vizcacha rat 75
    phylogenetically controlled studies 92
      larks 98–*9*
      Peromyscus species 99–101
      skinks 97–8
      small carnivores 101
      tenebrionid beetles 93–7
    physiological cooling mechanisms 80–4
    salt glands 84–5
    to halophyte consumption 85–7
    to temporary pools 87
  biodiversity 194–5
    birds 198
    in ephemeral pools 198–9
    granivores 197–8

lizards 195–7
competition
  granivores 115–17
  habitat selection models 109–12
  macroarthropod detrivores 112–15
  patch scale 107–9
  size, relationship to method of heat endurance 66–7
annual plants 29, 31, 40–1
  adaptive characteristics *35*
  diversity 193
  comparisons with mesic annuals 41–2
  competition 103–5
  delayed germination 46
  facilitation by shrubs 106, 107
  germination mechanisms *43*, 44
  grazing effects 152–3, 154
  Picris damascena 32
  rarity of long-range dispersal 44–6
  seed dispersal strategies 42–3
  seed heteromorphism 47–8
Anostraca 204
Antarctic deserts 4, *5*
  reasons for formation *9*, 10
  temperature 20
ant herbivory, seeds 44
anticlines 26
antitelechory 45
  possible reasons for 46
ant–plant mutualisms 157–8
ants
  biodiversity 197–8
  competition with rodents 116
  ecosystem engineering 189
  indirect interaction with rodents 118, 120
  seed dispersal 169–70
Aphodius tersus 143–4
apparent competition 120–2
aquatic systems, trophic levels 180
aquifer pumping 239–40
aquifers 15
Arabian desert 20
  age 3
  location *5*
  reasons for formation *9*
  seed heteromorphism 47
Arabian oryx (*Oryx leucoryx*) 261
  reintroduction 259–60
Arad, Z. *et al.* 73
Aral Sea region, desertification 240, *241*
Arctic deserts 4
  reasons for formation *9*, 10
Argyroderma species 194, 213, *214*
arid belts 4
arid deserts, definition 7
arid ecosystems, attributes 184
aridity vii. 1, 2, 4–5
aridity indices 5–7
Aristida adscensionis, seed predation *167*
Arizona, military manoeuvres 237

armadillo 216
arms races 141
Artemisia species 214
  A. herba-alba
    competition 106
    water potentials 49
  A. ordosica 260
  A. tridentata, hydraulic lift 63, 65
artesian wells 15
arthropod diversity, ephemeral
    pools 198–9
Artiodactyla 216
Asclepiadaceae *210*
Asiatic wild ass (*Equus hemionus*),
    reintroduction 256–8
aspartate formation, C$_4$ photosynthesis 38
Asphodelus ramosus 156
  insect herbivory 155
Asteraceae *210*, 214
Astragalus armatus 153
Astragalus cicer, apparent
    competition 121–2
Atacama-Sechura desert 15, 218
  age 3
  location *5*
  reasons for formation 8, *9*
atelechory 45, 46
Athene cunicularia (burrowing owls) 183
Athens, climate 6
atmospheric circulation 7
Atriplex species
  A. halimus 60–1
  consumption by fat sand rat 126
  salt glands 86
Augrabies waterfall *13*
Auliscomys genus 215
Australia 2, *5*, 20, *211*
  absence of Solifugae *203*, 215
  age of deserts 3
  bird diversity 198
  desertification 218
  endemism 208
  extinctions 135–6
  fire 28
  granivore diversity 197–8
  grazing responses 154–5
  invasive species 234
  limiting nutrients 20, 187–8
  lizard diversity 195–7
  photosynthesis pathways 37
  piosphere effects 223
  reasons for formation 9
  shield desert 26
  small mammals 215
Australian skinks, phylogenetically
    controlled studies 97–8
autarchoglossans 134
Avena barbatus, biodiversity 263
Avena sterilis, comparison of desert
    and mesic races 42

Avni, Y. *et al.* 219, 220–1
Ayal, Y. 155, 177
Ayal, Y. *et al.* 180–1
Ayal, Y. and Izhaki, I. 155
Azizia, record temperature 19

Badain Jaran desert, dunes 22
Bagnold, R.A. 21
Baja California desert system 183–4
bajadas (alluvial fans) 12, *14*
Balnford's fox (*Vulpes cana*), carnassial
    teeth 205–6
banner-tailed kangaroo rat (*Dipodomys
    spectabilis*) 120
barchan dunes *22*
barrel cactus (*Ferocactus
    acanthodes*) 57–8
barrens, polar regions 10
basal metabolic rate
  larks 98–9
  Peromyscus species *100*
Beatley, J.S. 187
Becerra, J.X. 156, 172–3
Becerra, J.X. and Venable, D.L. 157
bees, pollination of creosote bush 159
beetles, body temperature 67
behavioural thermoregulation 68, *69*
Bellevalia species, hysteranthy 52–3
Belnap, J. and Warren, S.D. 237–9
benefit-cost model, senita cactus-senita
    moth mutualism 165–6
Ben-Natan, G. *et al.* 116, *117*
Berger, J. 247–8
Berger, J. and Cunningham, C. 248
Bergmann's rule 205
β diversity (species turnover) 192–3
  granivores 197
  plants 194
  small mammals 215, 216
bet hedging, desert annuals 48
biodiversity 192–3
  animals 194–5
    birds 198
    in ephemeral pools 198–9
    granivores 197–8
    lizards 195–7
  effect of rainfall variability 11
  plants 193–4, 209
  productivity-diversity
    relationships 199–202
  Succulent Karoo 254–5
biogeography, large scale patterns 208
  animals 215–16
  plants 209–15
biological soil crusts 39–*40*, 186
  recovery after military
    manoeuvres 238–9
  in revegetated lands 261
biotic interactions 1
bipedality, rodents 205

birds
  biodiversity 198
  competition with rodents 116–17
  cooling mechanisms 80, 81, 82–4
    ostrich 91–2
  larks, phylogenetically controlled
    studies 98–9
  salt glands 84–5
  tenebrionid beetle predation 125
black-backed jackal (*Canis
    mesomelas*) 136–7
black rhinoceros *Diceros bicornis* 247–8
black widow spiders
  Latrodectus indistinctus 183
  Latrodectus revivensis 129–30, 177
bladder, water storage in Gila monster 92
Blaustein, L. and Margalit, J. 123
Blepharida leaf beetles 156–7
  coevolution with *Bursera* trees 172–3
Blepharis, germination mechanism *43*
Bodmer, R. and Ward, D. 252
body size
  medium-sized mammals 101
  rodents *178*
  tenebrionid beetles 180
Boeken, B. 52–3, 54
Boeken, B. *et al.* 168–9
Bohrer, G. *et al.* 262
Boraginaceae *210*
Boscia albitrunca (shepherd's tree) 30
  rooting depth 62, 63
Bouskila, A. 134
Bouteloua eriopoda, effect of
    irrigation 189
Bowie, M. and Ward, D., active water
    uptake by mistletoes 31
bradyspory *43*
Brassicaceae *210*
Bristow, C.S. *et al.* 22
Brock, K.E. and Kelt, D.A. *120*
Bromus madritensis, indirect
    interactions *120*
Bromus tectorum (cheatgrass),
    invasion 234–5
Bronstein, J.L. 164–5
brood parasites 137, 141–4
brown-headed cowbirds (*Molothrus ater*) 142
brown hyaenas (*Hyaena brunnea*) 137
Brown, J.H. and Heske, E.J. 120, 167
Brown, J.S. 107–8, 111
Brown, J.S. *et al.* 117
Brown, J.S. and Rosenzweig, M.I. 114
Brown, W.V. and Smith, B.N. 38–9
Bruelheide, H. *et al.* 48–9
Brunsvigia species *213*
Bufo viridis, priority effects 123
bulbs 51–*2*
  depth of 54–6, 174–5
  herbivory 53–4, 149
Bull, W.B. *13–4*

bunch grasses 51
Burhinus oedicnemus (stone curlews),
    beetle predation 125
buried litter, decomposition 191
Burke, A. 208
burrowing owls (*Athene cunicularia*)
    183
burrowing spiders 76–7
burrow temperatures 75, *76*
Bursera trees
  B. schlechtendalii 156–7
  coevolution with *Blepharida* leaf
    beetles 172–3
bush encroachment *229–34*
  impact of climate change 236
  Magersfontein *243–4*
bushy tail, Cape ground squirrel *78–9*

C$_3$ photosynthesis 34–5
C$_4$ photosynthesis 35–6
  aspartate and malate formation 38
Cactaceae 203, 204, *210*
  invasive species 234
cacti 36
  flowering 58
Cactoblastis cactorum 234
cactus ferruginous owl 249
cactus-tending ants 157–8
calcium oxalate crystals (raphide)
    production, lilies *175–6*
Caldwell, M.M. *et al.* 64
California, willingness to pay for
    conservation 264
Callaway, R.J. 106
camels 89–91, *90*
  as keystone species 248
camelthorn (*Acacia erioloba*) 30
CAM photosynthesis 36–7
CAM recycling 39
CAM succulents, adaptive
    characteristics *35*
candy barrel cactus (*Echinocactus
    platyacanthus*) 249–50
canine tooth structure, felines 206–7
Canis latrans (coyote) 135
Canis lupus dingo (dingo) 136
Canis mesomelas (black-backed
    jackal) 136–7
cannibalism 183
Cape ground squirrel (*Xerus
    inauris*) *78–9*
Capparidaceae *210*
Capra ibex nubiana (Nubian ibex)
  body size 101
  metapopulation dynamics 253
Capsodes infuscatus, herbivory 155
caracal (*Felis caracal*) 136–7
Caragana korshinskii 260
carbon storage, woody plants 236–7
carnassial tooth lengths, foxes 205–6

Carnegiea gigantea (saguaro cactus)
  facilitation 106
  flowering 58
carotid *rete mirabile* 80
Carparachne aureoflava 141
Carrichtera annua 44
Carrick, P.J. 105
Caryophyllaceae *210*
cascade model, food webs 181
Catapyrenium squamulosum, recovery
  after military manoeuvres 239
Catenazzi, A. and Donnelly, M.A. 184
cats (*Felis catus*), as cause of Australian
  extinctions 135–6
caviomorphs 215
centrifugal community
  organization 110–*11*, 113, 114
Certhilauda erythrochlamys (dune larks),
  cooling mechanism 83
chain length, food webs 181, 182
chamaephytes 32, 152
  quartz field specialists 213–14
character displacement 205–8
Charley, J.I. and Cowling, S.W. 187–8
cheatgrass (*Bromus tectorum*), invasion 234–5
cheating behaviour, in yucca–yucca moth
  mutualism 161–3
cheetah (*Acinonyx jubatus*) 137
chemical soil crusts 39–40
Chenopodiaceae *210*, 212, 214
  invasive species 234
Chesson, P. 104, 148
Chihuahuan desert 20
  bush encroachment 236
  grazing effects 223
  indirect interactions 118
  keystone species 119–20
  nitrogen limitation 187, 189
  photosynthetic pathways 37
  reasons for formation *9*
  run-off and run-on 16–17
Chilean deserts 2
China
  revegetation 260–1
  soil salinization 221–2
chisel-toothed kangaroo rat (*Dipodomys
  microps*) 86
chlorenchyma, *Ferocactus acanthodes* 57
chukars (*Alectoris chukar*) 82–3
cicadas, body temperature 67
Ciconia ciconia (white storks), beetle
  predation 125
Cladocera 204
climate change 217, 235–7
  effect on habitats 253
clonality, desert plants 48–9
closed macrotermite mounds *76*–7
clustering, spiders 130–1
Coachella Valley, scorpion study 131–*2*
Coachella Valley food web 182

coalface of evolution (genotype by
  environment interactions) 261
coastal deserts, fog 15
coevolution
  Bursera trees and *Blepharida* leaf
    beetles 172–3
  dorcas gazelle and lilies 173–6
  mutualism 160, 170
    senita and yucca systems 171
  red Negev flowers 171–2
Cogger, H.G. 196
Cohen, D. 46
Cohen, J.E., food web laws 181–3
Cohn, J.P. 249
cold deserts 4–5, 20
Collema tenax, recovery after military
  manoeuvres 239
Colorado River, oases 15
comb-eared skinks (*Ctenotus* genus),
  species richness 196–7
'common garden' experiments, *Peromyscus*
  species 92, 99–101
community fallows, Rajasthan *265, 266*
community-level density dependence,
  annual plants 103–4
competition 44
  between animals
    granivores 115–17
    habitat selection models 109–12
    macroarthropod detrivores 112–15
    patch scale 107–9
    see also indirect interactions
  'honeycomb rippling' model 232
  interspecific, scale effects 177–8
  in plant communities 102–3
    annuals 103–5
    shrubs 105–6
  productivity-diversity
    relationships 201–2
complexity of food webs 177–8
Conchostraca 204
connectivity, food webs 181, 182
Conophytum species 59
conservation
  approaches 246
  finance and control 264–7
  of habitats 253–6
  of metapopulations 252–3
  recolonization, American black bear 260
  reintroductions of species
    Arabian oryx 259–60
    Asiatic wild ass 256–8
  revegetation 260–*1*
  of single populations 249–51
  SLOSS debate 251–2
  of species 246–7
    focal species 249
    keystone species 248–9
    umbrella species 247–8
  value 246

continental drift 39
contracted vegetation 146, 192
contractile roots, geophytes 54–6
control of land, Rajasthan 265–7
convectively coupled organisms 67
convergent evolution 203–5
convergent regulation model, habitat
        selection 127–8
Convolvulaceae 210
cooling mechanisms 80–4
corms 52
costs, mutualistic relationships 164–5
countercurrent cooling system,
        kangaroo rats 75, 76
countercurrent multipliers, loops of
        Henle 70, 72
Cowling, R.M. et al. 255–6
Cowling, R.M. and Hilton-Taylor, C. 193,
        194
coyotes (Canis latrans), keystone
        predation 135
Crassulaceae 203, 210, 212
Crassula genus 36, 39, 59
Crawley, M.J. 155
'cream skimming', crested larks 117
Crematogaster opuntiae, association with
        cacti 157–8
creosote bush (Larrea tridentata) 31, 189
    clonality 48
    competition 105–6
    pollination 159
crested lark (Galerida cristata),
        competition 117
cricetines 215
Crisp, M.D. et al. 208
critical power threshold 12, 13, 14
critical temperatures
    CTMax, Australian skinks 97–8
    tenebrionid beetles 93, 96
Crocuta crocuta (spotted hyaenas) 137
crossover regulation model, habitat
        selection 127–8, 129
Crotalus cerastes (sidewinder snakes) 134
crowned plovers (Vanellus coronatus),
        cooling mechanisms 83
cryptobiosis 87
Cryptoglossa verrucosa, cuticular water
        loss 69
cryptophytes 33
Ctenotus genus (comb-eared skinks),
        species richness 196–7
Cucurbitaceae 210
Culiseta longiareolata, priority effects 123
curled belly feathers, sandgrouse 83–4
Cuscuta 33
cyanobacteria, biological
        soil crusts 39, 40
cycles (looping), food webs 181, 182, 183
cyclical succession 106
cyclicity, bush encroachment 231

Cyclorana platycephala 74, 75
Cyperaceae 210

Dabous, A.A. and Osmond, J.K. 240
Dactylopius opuntiae 234
Dafni, A. et al. 52, 172
Dallas, H.F. et al. 72–3
Damara people, Namibia 224
dandelion, seed dispersal mechanism 47
Daniels, S. et al. 204–5
Danin, A. 41, 61
Danthonia genus 214
darkling beetles see tenebrionid beetles
Darlington, J.P.E.C. 77
Dasycercus cristicauda 79
Dasypeltis scabra 137
Dasyuridae 215
Dasyuroides byrnei 79
Dasyurids, water turnover 79–80
Davidowitz, G. 2–3
Davidson, D.W. et al. 118
Davidson, D.W. and Morton, S.R. 169
Dayan, T. et al. 205–8
Death Valley, California, photosynthesis
        pathways 37
deciduous shrubs, adaptive
        characteristics 35
decomposition 191
decreasers 151
deep-rooted trees, adaptive
        characteristics 35
definition of deserts vii. 1, 2
    rainfall 4–5
dehorning, black rhinoceros 248
delayed germination, annual plants 46
density-dependence
    annual plants 103–4
    flea host selection 139, 140
    isodars 126–9
density-dependent effects, grazing 228
descriptive food webs 181
desert grasslands, fire 28
desertification 217–18
    in Aral Sea region 240, 241
    effects on nutrients 219, 220
    in Negev desert 219–21
    in the Sahel 218–19
    soil salinization 221–2
desert locust (Schistocerca gregaria), water
        conservation 70, 71
desert mouse (Pseudomys
        hermannsburgensis),
        hypothermia 81
desert patina (desert varnish) 25, 26
desert pavements 25
desert spinifex 51
desiccation tolerance 87
devil's claw (Ibicella lutea), seed dispersal
        mechanism 47
Diaz, S. et al. 151

Diceros bicornis (black rhinoceros) *247*–8
dietary information, inadequacy 183
differentiation diversity 193
diffuse vegetation 192
dingoes (*Canis lupus dingo*), keystone
    predation 136
Dipodidae 215
Dipodomys species (kangaroo rats) 74–5,
    76, 215
    D. merriami, foraging behaviour 121–2
    D. microps 86
    D. ordii 135
    keystone effects 119–20
    predation by snakes *134*–5
    seed predation 167–8
Dipsosaurus dorsalis, potassium chloride
    secretion *85*
direct mortality effect, predation 124–5
dispersal strategies, seeds 42–3, *47*
    heteromorphism 47–8
    rarity of long-range dispersal 44–6
disturbance hypotheses, bush
    encroachment 232–3, 234
disturbances 189–91
divergent evolution 202–3
divergent regulation models, habitat
    selection *127*
diversity *see* biodiversity
diversity rules, desert vegetation 209
donor-controlled interactions 183–4
Donovan, L.A. *et al.* 49
Dorcas gazelle (*Gazella dorcas*) *174*, 177,
    190–1
    bulb herbivory 54–5, 149
    coevolution with lilies 173–6
dormancy, *Sphincterochila boisseri* 73
double-banded coursers (*Rhinoptilus
    cursorius*) 83
downpours, effects 12–13
Downs, C.T. and Perrin, M.R. 80
Downs, C.T. and Ward, D. 83
drought enduring plants 30
drought escapers
    animals 87
    plants 29
drought evading plants 30
drought resistors
    animals 87
    plants 30–1
drought stress 31
drought tolerators
    animals 87
    plants 30–31
        halophytes 61–2
dry sub-humidity 7
dune formation 22–4, 218
dune larks (*Certhilauda erythrochlamys*),
    cooling mechanism 83
dune systems 20
dung beetles, brood parasites 143–4

Dunning, J.B. 116–17
duricrusts 18
dust storms 24
Du Toit, E. 234
Dyksterhuis, E.J. 151

Echinocactus platyacanthus (candy barrel
    cactus) 249–50
Echinops polyceras, herbivory 153
Eckardt, F.D. *et al.* 18
Eckardt, F.D. and Schemenauer, R.S. 15
ecological character displacement 205–8
ecosystem engineering 189–91
ectoparasites 137
    fleas 137–9
ectothermic organisms 67
edaphic heterogeneity 209
Edentata 216
Edney, E.B. 93–4
effective population size (N_e), reintroduced
    species 257
Ehleringer, J.R. and Forseth, I. 41
Ehleringer, J.R. and Monson, R.K. 39
Eickmeier, W.G. 37
Eilat mountains 253, *254*
Ekhiin-Gol oasis, solonchaks 19
elaiosomes 169
electrical conductivity, measurement of
    salinity 18
elephant *249*
    as keystone species *248*
Eligmodontia genus 215
Ellis, A.G. and Weis, A.E. 213–14
Ellis, J.E. and Swift, D.M. 228
Ellis, R.P. *et al.* 38, 39
Ellner, S.P. and Shmida, A. 45–6
El Niño effect 8–9, 12
Emanuel, W.R. *et al.* 217, 235
Emex spinosa 43
    seed heteromorphism 47
emmer wheat (*Triticum dicoccoides*),
    biodiversity 263
Encelia farinosa, leaf pubescence 49–50
enclosures, Rajasthan *265*, 266
endemism 208
    in Succulent Karoo 254–5
endoparasites 137
    Pseudodiplorchis americanus 139–40
endothermic organisms 67
endurers 66, 87–92
energetics, in study of food webs 179–80,
    181
energy expenditure, chukars and sand
    partridges 82–3
Epacridaceae *210*
Ephedraceae 212
Ephedra genus 212
ephemeral pools 87
    biodiversity 198–9
    fauna 204, 215

Equus hemionus 88
Equus hemionus onager (*see also* Asiatic
        wild ass), herbivory
        effects 149, *150*
    reintroduction 256–8
Eragrostis species
    E. lehmanniana, seed predation *167*
    invasion 234
Eremina desertorum 74
    water loss 73
Eremitalpa granti namibensis (Namib
        desert golden mole), body
        temperature 67
Eremostibes opacus 142–3
Erodium species
    indirect interactions *120*
    seeds *43*
erosional cirque (makhtesh) 26, *27*
erosion effects, downpours 12
escape strategy, seeds 42
Esler, K.J. *et al.* 213
Eucalyptus marginata, rooting depth 63
Euchondrus species, water loss 73–4
Euphorbiaceae 36, *210*
    convergence 203
evaders 66, 68–72
    burrowing spiders 76–7
    Cape ground squirrel *78–9*
    dasyurids and murids, water
            turnover 79–80
    frogs 74
        Cyclorana platycephala 75
    jirds 75, *76*
    kangaroo rats 74–5, *76*
    snails 72–4
    termites *77–8*
    vizcacha rat 75
evaporation potential 5
evaporative cooling 66, 68
    camels 90
    gerbil species 80, *81*
    limitations 80
Evenari, M. 39
evergreen shrubs, adaptive
            characteristics *35*
evolution
    convergent 203–5
    divergent 202–3
Evolutionarily Stable Strategy (ESS) models
    productivity–diversity
            relationships 201–2
    senita cactus–senita moth
            mutualism 167
    yucca–yucca moth mutualism 162
evolutionary approach vii–viii
evolutionary equilibrium 141, 143–4
evolutionary lag 141, 143–4
excretory systems 70
exhaled air temperature, kangaroo
        rats 75, *76*

exploitation competition 118
    annual plants 103, 104
extinctions, in Australia 135–6

Fabaceae *210*
    invasive species 234
Facelli, J.M. *et al.* 104
facilitation
    islands of fertility 29, 189
    nurse plant effects 106–7
Fagonia species 41
Falco tinnunculus (Rock Kestrel) 177
fat reserves, camels 91
fat sand rat (*Psammomys obesus*) 127
    habitat selection 126, *128–9*
    halophyte consumption 61, 86–7
favourability rules, desert vegetation 209
fecundity comparisons, geometric
            mean 47
feedback mechanisms *14*
felines, canine tooth structure 206–7
Felis caracal (caracal) 136–7
Felis catus (cats), as cause of Australian
            extinctions 135–6
fenceline contrasts *223*
fennec fox (*Fennecus zerda*), panting 82
Ferocactus acanthodes (barrel cactus) 57–8
field metabolic rate (FMR), *Peromyscus*
            species 100
fire 27–8
    in Australia 188
    role in bush encroachment 232
flash floods 4, 12, 199
fleas 137–9, *138*
Fleming, T.H. and Holland, J.N. 164, 171
Floret, C. *et al.* 187
flowering, cacti 58
fluvial system *13*
focal species 247, 249
fog basking, tenebrionid beetles 94–5, *96*
fog deserts *8*
fog as water source 15
Fonteyn, P.J. and Mahall, B.E. 105–6
food webs 177–9
    Cohen's laws 181
        Polis and Ayal's problems 181–3
    donor-recipient habitat
            interactions 183–4
    HSS (Hairston, Smith and Slobodkin)
            model 179–81
foraging behaviour, effect of predation
            risk 108, 125–6
forest department enclosures,
            Rajasthan *265*, 266
fossils 3
Fouquieriaceae *210*
foxes
    carnassial tooth lengths 205–6
    as cause of Australian extinctions 135–6
    cooling mechanisms 82

fennec fox (*Fennecus zerda*), panting 82
see also Vulpes species
Franco, A.C. and Nobel, P.S. 106
Franseria deltoidea, water
potential 49, *50*
Fretwell, S.D. and Lucas, H.L. 109
Friedel, M.H. *et al.* 188
Friedman, J. 106
Friedman, J. and Stein, Z. 44
frogs 74
Cyclorana platycephala 75
Fuller, B. *225*
functional diversity, birds 198

gabar goshawk (*Micronisus gabar*), salt
glands 84–5
Galerida cristata (crested lark),
competition 117
Galil, J. 54
game theory model, seed
heteromorphism 47–8
γ diversity (regional species
diversity) 193
birds 198
lizards 195, 196–7
in Succulent Karoo 254
Gandanimeno eresus 132
gape-limitation hypothesis 131
Garryaceae 204
Gazella dorcas (dorcas gazelle) *174*, 177,
190–1
bulb herbivory 54–5, 149
coevolution with lilies 173–6
Geiger, R. 5
generalization, pollination 158
genotype by environment (G X E)
interactions 261–3
geocarpy 45
Geococcyx californianus (roadrunner),
salt glands 84
Geoffroea decorticans 218
geographical locations 4, *5*
geology 20–1
mountains 26, *27*
plateau landscapes 26
rock landscapes 25
sand landscapes 21–4
stone substrates 25
Geolycosa godeffroyi 130
geometric mean, fecundity
comparisons 47
geophytes 29, *33*, 51–2
contractile roots 54–6
hysteranthy 52–4
resistance to grazing 154
Geraniaceae *210*
gerbil (*Gerbillus*) species 215
Gerbillurus competition *115*
Gerbillus competition 116–7
foraging behaviour 108–9, 132–3

G. andersoni allenbyi, predation
risk 125–6
G. dasyurus, snail predation 124
parasitism by fleas 138–9, *140*
thermoregulation 80
germination
delayed, annual plants 46
triggering factors 187
germination mechanisms, annual
plants *43*, 44, 46
germination of seeds, effect of seed
herbivory 168
Ghazanfar , S.A. 199, *200*
Gibbaeum species 213
Gibson desert
location *5*
reasons for formation *9*
Gila monsters (*Heloderma
suspectum*) 92
giving-up density (GUD) 108
global warming *see* climate change
goannas (*Varanus gouldii*) 191
Gobi desert 218
age 3
location *5*
reasons for formation *9*
soil salinity variation 18–19
temperature 20
gochers 265–6
Goegap nature reserve, floral dispersal
types *45*
Goldberg, D.E. *et al.* 103–4
Goldberg, D.E. and Novoplansky, A. 102–3
Goldberg, D. and Turner, R.M. 148–9
golf courses 239, 242
Gondwana
Loranthaceae distribution *202*
Streptocephalus genus
distribution 205
González-Megías, A. and
Sánchez-Piñero, F. 143–4
Goodeniaceae *210*
gopher snakes (*Pituophis catenifer
deserticola*) 183
Goudie, A.S. 24
Gram Panchayat *gochers* 265–6
granivores 167–8, 215
biodiversity 197–8
competition 115–17
role in seed dispersal 168–70
grasses 51
amphiphytic 41
fog as water source 50, 51
grazing effects 151–2
invasive species 234–5
Namib desert 38
photosynthetic pathways 38–9
seed predation *167–8*
grasshoppers, temperature
regulation 67, *68*

grazing
  as cause of desertification 218, *219*, 222
  in Otjimbingwe, Namibia 224–6
  piosphere effects 222–4
  role in bush encroachment 231,
      233, 234
  see also herbivory
grazing ecosystems
  bush encroachment 229–34
  vegetation and herbivore population
      oscillations 227–9
grazing responses *147*–8, 151
  in Australia 154–5
Great Basin desert 4, 20, *211*
  age 3
  location 5
  photosynthesis pathways 37
  reasons for formation 9
Great Grey Shrike (*Lanius excubitor*) 177
Great Sandy desert
  location 5
  reasons for formation 9
green world 179, 180
Grime, J.P. 103
Grime–Tilman debate 103
Groner, E. and Ayal, Y. 125
ground-truthing 245
gular fluttering 83
Günster, A. 43
Guo, Z.T. *et al.* 24
Gutterman, Y. 42
Gymnarrhena micrantha 43
gypsum deposits 18

habitat conservation 253–6
habitat selection, spiders 129–31
habitat selection models 109–12
Hadley cells 7, 10
Haines, H. *et al.* 79
Hairston, N.G. *et al.* 179–80
halophytes 33, 60–2, 214
  consumption by mammals 85–7
  leaf succulents 59
Hamilton, W.J. 96
Hamilton, W.J. and Seely, M.K. 94–5
Hammada scoparia 30, 153
  photosynthetic rate 49
Hanan, N.P. *et al.* 224
Hardin, G. 219
Hartmann's mountain zebra (*Equus zebra hartmannae*) 87, *88*
Hartsock, T.L. and Nobel, P.S. 36
harvester ants
  biodiversity 197–8
  ecosystem engineering 189
  seed dispersal 169–70
Hattersley, P.W. 37
Haworthia species 59
Hazard, L.C. 85
heat conservation, ostrich 92

heat gain control, physiological
    mechanisms 80–4
Hedysarum scoparium 260
height of plants
  annuals 41
  effect of grazing pressure 151, 154–5
Heinrich, B. 93, 96
Heloderma suspectum (Gila monster) 92
hemicryptophytes 33
Hemilepistus reaumuri 131
  soil turnover 21
Hendricks, H. *et al.* 223
Henke, S.E. and Bryant, F.C. 135
Henle, loops of 70, *71*
  countercurrent multipliers *72*
Henschel, J.R. 141
Henschel, J.R. and Lubin, Y.D. 131
herbivory 145–8
  Australia, grazing responses 154–5
  beneficial effects on seed
      germination 251
  by insects 155–8
  effects on relationships among plant
      functional types 150–4
  effects on species composition 148
  halophyte consumption 85–7
  long-term studies 148–*50*
  of *Pancratium sickenbergeri* 53–4
  seed dispersal 168–70
  seed predation 167–8
  see also grazing
Herero people, Namibia 224
Hermony, I. *et al.* 124
Heske, E.J. *et al.* 167–8
Heteromyidae 215
heterotherms (poikilotherms) 67
heterothermy, camels 89
hibernation 80
Hirpicium alienatum, competition 105
Hoffman, M.T. 194
Hoffman, M.T. *et al.* 244–5
Holland, J.N. *et al.* 165–7
Holland, J.N. and Fleming, T.H. 164
Holt, R.D. and Kotler, B. 120–1
homeotherms (homoiotherms) 67
'honeycomb rippling' model of
    competition 232
honey mesquite (*Prosopis glandulosa*),
    recruitment 231
Hordeum spontaneum (wild barley)
  comparison of desert and mesic races 42
  genotype by environment
      interactions 263
hot deserts 19–20
Howes, D.A. and Abrahams, A.D. 16
HSS (Hairston, Smith and Slobodkin)
    model 179–81
Huangtu (Loess) Plateau 24
Huey, R.B. and Bennett, A.F. 97–8
Hughes, J.J. *et al.* 115

Hughes, J.J. and Ward, D. 133
human impact 1, 217
   military manoeuvres 237–9
   oil pollution 240, 242
   role in bush encroachment 232
   water use 239–40
hummock grasses 51
Humphrey, R.R. 28
hump-shaped curves, productivity-
       diversity relationship 199–*200*
Hutchinsonian size differences 207
hyaenas 137, 177
hydraulic lift, phreatophytes 63–5
Hydrophyllaceae *210*
hyperaridity 5, *7*
hypothermia survival 81
hysteranthous plants 52–4
Hystrix indica (Indian crested porcupine),
   diggings, effect on plant
   diversity 168, *169*, 190

Ibicella lutea (devil's claw), seed dispersal
   mechanism *47*
ice 4–5
ice plants (Aizoaceae) 36
Ideal Free Distribution 109, 126
Ihlenfeldt, H.-D. 194
Illius, A.W. and O'Connor, T.G. 228
inactivity, role in heat endurance 87
inbreeding depression, in yucca 161
increasers 151
indicator species 247
indirect interactions 118–19
   keystone species 119–20
   priority effects 122–3
   short-term apparent
       competition 120–2
insect herbivory 155–8
insectivores
   Namib golden mole (*Eremitalpa granti*
      namibensis) 67
   round-eared elephant shrew
      (*Macroscelides*
      proboscideus) 80–1
insects 216
   adaptations to heat 68–70
   halophyte consumption 85
interactions
   indirect 118–19
      keystone species 119–20
      priority effects 122–3
      short-term apparent
         competition 120–2
   see also competition; facilitation
interaction webs 181
interference competition
   annual plants 103–4
   gerbil species *116*
interpulse periods 103
   effect on plant survival 187, *188*

interspecific competition
   effect on habitat selectivity 109, *110*
   scale effects 177–8
   tenebrionid beetles 112–15
intraguild predation,
      scorpions 131
intraspecific competition, tenebrionid
     beetles 112
invaders 151
invasive species 234–5
inverse hydraulic lift 65
ion concentrations,
     fog water 15
Iranian desert 20
   location *5*
   reasons for formation *9*
Irano-Turanian region *211*
Iridaceae *210*, 212
'Irish bridges', Negev desert 221
irrigation experiments, Chihuahuan
     desert 189
'islands of fertility' 21, 189
isodars 126–9, *127*
isolegs 109, *110*, *111*
Isometroides vescus 131
isopods, effects on soil 21
Israeli flora, dispersal types *45*
Ixiolirion tataricum 54

Jackson, R.B. *et al.* 236–7
James, C.D. *et al.* 223
James, C.D. and Shine, R. 196, 197
Janusia gracilis 148–9
Jauffret, S. and Lavorel, S. 152, 153
Jeltsch, F. *et al.* 153, 224, 231
Jimenez-Sierra, C. *et al.* 249–50
jirds (*Meriones crassus*) 75, *76*
Johnson, C.N. *et al.* 135–6
Johnson, H.B. 39
Jones, C.G. and Shachak, M. 20–1
Jordana experimental range, bush
     encroachment *230*
Jürgens, N. 194

Kade, A. and Warren, S.D. 237
Kalahari desert 2, 20
   bird diversity 198
   lizards 196
   location *5*
   reasons for formation *9*
Kam, M. and Degen, A.A. 61
Kamenetsky, R. and Gutterman, Y. 52
kangaroo rats (*Dipodomys* species) 74–5,
     76, 215
   foraging behaviour 121–2
   keystone effects 119–20
   Ord's kangaroo rat 135
   predation by snakes *134*–5
   seed predation 167–8
Kappen, L. *et al.* 49

Karoo desert 2
  age 3
  evidence for expansion 245
  invasive species 234
  plant species richness 193, 194
  reasons for formation 9
  shrub–shrub competition 105
  see also Succulent Karoo
Kelt, D.A. *et al.* 197, 205
Kelt, D.A. and Valone, T.J. 153
key links, food webs 181–2
keystone predation 135–7
keystone species 119–20, 247, 248–9
kidneys 70, *71*
  adaptations, to halophyte
    consumption 86
Knersvlakte 213
Köppen, W. 5
Kotler, B.P. 132–3
Kotler, B.P. *et al.* 116, 125–6
Kotliar, N.B. and Wiens, J.A. 178
Kraaij, T. and Ward, D. 232
Krameriaceae 204
Krameria grayi 148–9
Kranz anatomy 35
Krasnov, B.R. *et al.* 138–9
kulans (*Equus hemionus onager*),
    herbivory effects 149, *150*
Kuwait, oil pollution 240, 242
Kwarteng, A.Y. 242

Lagomorpha 216
Lake Chad, desertification *244*
Lamiaceae *210*
Lamoreaux, P.E. *et al.* 239–40
land ownership 264–6
Landsberg, J. *et al.* 151–2, 153, 155
landscapes
  desert pavements *25*
  mountains 26, *27*
  plateau 26
  rock 25
  sand 21–4
Lange, R.T. 223
Lanius excubitor (Great Grey
    Shrike) 177
larks, phylogenetically controlled
    studies 98–9
Larrea tridentata (creosote bush) 31, 189
  clonality 48
  competition 105–6
  pollination 159
Latrodectus species (black widow spiders)
  L. hesperus 131
  L. indistinctus 183
  L. revivensis 129–30, 177
leaf adaptations, annual plants 41
leaf hairs 49–50
leafhoppers, halophyte consumption 85
leaf pubescence, desert shrubs 49–50

leaf size, effect of grazing pressure 151,
    153, *154*
leaf succulents 59–60
leaf temperatures, *Lithops*
    species 59–60
leaves, drought avoidance 30
Lee, A.K. and Mercer, E.H. 74
leg length, tenebrionid beetles *93*, 97
Le Houérou, H.N. 2
Leipoldtia schultzei, competition 105
Lennoaceae 204
leopards (*Panthera pardus*) 137, 177
Leporillus conditor 79
Levahim housing development, Negev
    desert 242
lichens 15, *16*
  nitrogen inputs 20–1
  recovery after military manoeuvres 239
light intensity, effect on decomposition 191
light-use efficiency, photosynthetic
    pathways 36–7
Liliaceae *210*
lilies, coevolution with dorcas gaz-
    elle 173–6
limestone deserts 20
limiting nutrients 2, 20
Limnodynastes spenceri 74
Linder, H.P. 208
linear (longitudinal) dunes 22–3
links, food webs 181
Liometopum apiculatum,
    cactus-tending 157–8
lions (*Panthera leo*) 137
Lithops genus (stone plants) 59–60
little pocket mice (*Perognathus
    longimembris*) 121–2
Liu, T.-S. *et al.* 24
Li, X.-R. *et al.* 260–1
lizards
  biodiversity 195–7
  subterranean 196
  thermoregulation 92
Lloyd, P. 136–7
Loasaceae *210*
local species richness (α diversity) 192
  birds 198
  granivores 197
  lizards 195
  plants 193
  small mammals 216
  in Succulent Karoo 254
loess 24
Loess Plateau (China) 24
longevity, creosote bushes 48
longitudinal (linear) dunes 22–3
looping, food webs 181, 182, 183
looping mutual predation, arachnids 132
Lophocerus schottii (senita cactus),
    mutualism with senita
    moth 163–7

Loranthaceae, Gondwanan
    distribution *202*
Lotka–Volterra models *122*, 123
lottery model of coexistence *104*, 148
Louw, G.N. and Seely, N.K. 50–1
Lovegrove, B.G. 99
Lovegrove, B.G. *et al.* 80–1
Lubin, Y.D. *et al.* 129, 130
Lubin, Y.D. and Henschel, J.R. 76
Ludwig, J.A. and Flavill, P. 187
Lüscher, M. *77–8*
Lycaon pictus (African wild dog) 137

Ma, J.-Y. *et al.* 61
MacArthur, R.H. and
    Pianka, E.R. 109, *110*
MacArthur, R.H. and Wilson, E.O. 251
MacDougal, D.T. and Spalding, E.S. 58
Machaeranthera gracilis, desert and
    foothills races 42
Maclean, G.L. 83
macropores, production by termites 189
Macroscelides proboscideus (round-eared
    elephant shrew), torpor 80–1
Macrotermes michaelseni
macrotermite mounds *76–7*
Magersfontein, bush encroachment *243–4*
makhtesh (erosional cirque) 26, *27*
Makhtesh Ramon 199
Malallah, G. *et al.* 242
malate formation, C_4 photosynthesis 38
Maloiy, G.M.O. *et al.* 101
Malpighian tubules 70
Malvaceae *210*
mammals, halophyte consumption 85–7
Mares, M.A. 205
Mares, M.A. *et al.* 216
marine systems, interaction with desert
    food webs 183–4
Marr, D.L. *et al.* 163
marsupials 215
mass tree recruitment 229–31
    role of rainfall *232–3*
maternal allocation hypothesis 257
matrix models, single populations 249–50
maxithermy hypothesis, tenebrionid
    beetles 96
McAuliffe 106, 189
McClain, E.S. *et al.* 96
McKechnie, A. and Lovegrove, B.G. 81
McNab, B.K. and Morrison, P. 99
McPherson, G. 27–8
mechanical soil crusts 39–40
Medvedev, H.S. 93
megadunes 22
Melastomataceae *210*
Meriones crassus (jirds) 75, *76*
    parasitism by fleas 138
Merriam's kangaroo rat (*Dipodomys
    merriami*) 121–2

Mesembryanthema *204*, 254
    competition 105
Messor species
    M. ebeninus, seed transportation 189,
        190
    seed dispersal 169
metabolism, low energy, chukars
    and sand partridges 82–3
metapopulations, conservation 252–3
Meyer, K.M. *et al.* 28
microbial decomposition 191
Micronisus gabar (gabar goshawk), salt
    glands 84–5
Middle Eastern deserts 2
Middleton, N.J. and Thomas, D.S.G. 222
Midgley, G.F. and Thuiller, W. 235
Milchunas, D.G. *et al.* 147
military training areas 237–9
Miller, T.E.X. 157–8
Milton, S.J. 153
Milton, S.J. *et al.* 234, 235
mimicry, brood parasites 142
Minosiella intermedia 131
Miocene, desertification 3
Miriti, M.N. *107*
missed opportunity costs (MOC) 108
mistletoes 31, *32*, 33, 202
    genotype by environment
        interactions 261–2, *263*
    infection of *Acacia raddiana* 250–1
Mitchell, W.A. *et al.* 108–9, *201*
Mojave desert 20
    photosynthetic pathways 37
    reasons for formation 9
    shrub-shrub competition 105–6
Molothrus ater (brown-headed
    cowbirds) 142
Monson, R.K. and Smith, S.D. *30*
Monte desert 218
    biodiversity 216
    location *5*
    reasons for formation 9
moonlit nights, foraging behaviour 108,
    132–3, 135
Morton, S.R. and Davidson, D.W. 197–8
Morton, S.R. and James, C.D. 196
mosquito larvae, priority effects 123
'mother-site' theory, Zohary 44, 46
mountain-and-basin desert 26
mountain landscapes 26, *27*
Mueller, P. and Diamond, J. 99–101
Munzbergova, Z. and Ward, D. *119*
Muridae 215
    water turnover 79–80
Murie, M. 99
mutualism *158*
    ant–plant 157–8
    coevolution 170
      senita and yucca systems 171
    costs 164–5

mutualism (*Continued*)
  pollination 158–9
    senita cactus–senita moth 163–7
    yucca–yucca moth 159–63
Myoporaceae *210*
myrmecochory 169–70
Myrtaceae *210*
myxospermy 44

Nabatean people 16, *17*
Nama Karoo, plant species
      richness 193, 194
Namib desert 2, 20
  age 4
  annual plants, seed preservation
      strategies 43
  black rhinoceros *247*–8
  competition between granivores 115
  dunes 22–*3*
  fenceline contrasts *223*
  fog water 15, 50
  gypsum duricrusts 18
  large herbivore populations *248*
  lichens *16*
  location *5*
  mountains *27*
  photosynthesis pathways 38
  plant species 212
  plant species richness 194
  rainfall variability 11
  reasons for formation 8, *9*
  seed heteromorphism 47
  snails 72
Namib golden mole (*Eremitalpa
      granti namibensis*) 67
Namibia
  bush encroachment 231
  Otjimbingwe, grazing effects 224–6
Narcissus effect 147
nasal countercurrent heat exchanger 80
natural selection 1
nearest-neighbour distance, shrubs 105
Negev desert *220*
  Acacia raddiana populations 211–*12*
  annual plants, seed preservation
      strategies 43
  competition between granivores 116,
      117
  desertification 219–21
  ephemeral pools, arthropod
      diversity 198–*9*
  erosional cirque *27*
  fleas 137–9
  Hemilepistus reaumuri, soil turnover 21
  insect herbivory 155
  keystone species 119
  Levahim housing development *242*
  Nabatean people 16, *17*
  NDVI values 245
  nitrogen inputs 20–1

predation risk 125–6
rainfall *2*
  variability 11
red flowers 171–2
rodent–snail interactions 124–5
shrub–shrub competition 106
snails 72, 73
tenebrionid beetle predation 125
wadis 13
Negev highlands 253, *254*
Neobatrachus pictus 74
net primary productivity, *Peromyscus*
      species 99–101, *100*
Nevo, E. 263, *264*
niche compression 109, *110*, 111, 114, 115
niche partitioning, lizards 195
niche separation, roots 105, 231
Nile River
  oases 15
  sugar farms *222*
nitrogen
  effect on *Acacia mellifera*
      germination 232
  effects of desertification 219, *220*
  effects of erosion 220
nitrogen fixation
  Acacia species 119
  biological soil crusts 40
nitrogen inputs 20–1
nitrogen limitation 185, 187–9
Nobel, P.S. and Sanderson, J. 63
nocturnal flower opening, yucca and
      senita cactus 171
nomadism *219*, 222
Normalized Difference Vegetation Indices
      (NDVI) *244*, 245
North America
  bird diversity 198
  desertification 217
  granivore diversity 197–8
  grasslands, fire 28
  lizard diversity 195–7
  small mammals 215
Nosopsyllus iranus 138–9
Notomys species 79, 215
Notostraca 204
Noy-Meir, I. 184–5, 187
Noy-Meir, I. *et al.* 151
Nubian ibex (*Capra ibex nubiana*)
  body size 101
  metapopulation dynamics 253
nurse plant effects 106–7, 119
nutrient limitation 2, 20, 187–9
nutrients
  aerial transfer 184
  effects of desertification 219, *220*
  effects of erosion 220

oases 14–15
oceans, circulation patterns 7–9

Octodon genus 215
Octodontomys genus 215
Octomys, kidney *71*
Odontotermes transvaalensis 77
odour mimicry, brood parasites 142
Oenotheraceae 204
off-road motor vehicle use 219, 237
    effect on soils 238–9
oil pollution 240, 242
Oksanen, L. *et al.* 180
Olneya tesota 119
Oman, reintroduction of Arabian oryx 259
omnivory 182
onager (*Equus hemionus onager*),
            herbivory effects 149, *150*
Onagraceae *210*
Onorato, D.P. *et al.* 260
Onthophagus merdarius 143–4
Onymacris species
    fog basking *94–5*
    O. rugatipennis, competition 112–15
    size distribution patterns 205, *206*
    wax blooms *94*, 96
    white abdomen *95*
Opatroides punctulatus 125
open macrotermite mounds 76
Opuntia genus
    invasive species 234
    O. imbricata, protection by ants 157–8
    O. leptocaulis 189
orans, Rajasthan *265*, 266
Orchidaceae *210*
Ord's kangaroo rat (*Dipodomys ordii*) 135
Orians, G.H. and Milewski, A.V. 188
Orobanche aegyptiaca 33, 34
Oryx species 87–9, *88*
    O. leucoryx 259–60, 261
Oryzopsis hymenoides, apparent
            competition 121–2
Osborn, T.G. *et al.* 222
Osem, Y. *et al.* 107
osmotic potentials, relationship to drought
            avoidance *30*
ostrich (*Struthio camelus*) 91–2
    seed herbivory 168
Otjimbingwe, Namibia, grazing
            effects 224–6
overgrazing
    as cause of desertification 218, *219*, 222
    in Otjimbingwe, Namibia 224–6
    piosphere effects 222–4
    role in bush encroachment 231
ownership of land 264–6
oxalate consumption, adaptations 86–7
Oxalidaceae *210*
oxaloacetate 35
oxygen consumption rates, snails 72

Paine, R.T. 135
Pake, C.E. and Venable, D.I. 104

palatability of plants 153–4
Palpimanus stridulator 131
Pancratium genus 214
    P. sickenbergeri 52, 190–1
    herbivory 53–6, *55*, 149
    'source' and 'sink' populations 252
Pangaea 202
Panicum genus 214
Panthera leo (lions) 137
Panthera pardus (leopards) 137, 177
panting as cooling mechanism 82, 83
parallel regulation model, habitat
            selection *127*
parasites 137–40
    brood parasites 141–4
parasitoids 137, 140–1
Parastizopus armaticeps 142–3
Parategeticula species, mutualism with
            yucca 159–63
Paruroctonus mesaensis 131
pastoralism 218, *219*, 222–7
    bush encroachment 229–34
    as cause of desertification 217, *218*
    in Otjimbingwe, Namibia 224–6
    vegetation and herbivore population
            oscillations 227–9
Patagonian desert 20
    location *5*
    reasons for formation *9*
patch scale 107–9, 111
Pellmyr, O. 159, 161, 163
Pellmyr, O. *et al.* 162–3
Peltohyas australis 84
Penning de Vries, F.W.T. and Djiteye,
            M.A. 187
PEP carboxylase 35
perennial grasses, adaptive
            characteristics 35
permafrost 10
Perognathus longimembris (little
            pocket mouse), foraging
            behaviour 121–2
Peromyscus species, phylogenetically
            controlled studies 99–101
phanerophytes 32
phenotypic plasticity, birds 99
Phillips, J.E. 70
phosphorus, aerial transfer 184
phosphorus limitation 20, 187–8
photosynthetic pathways 36–9
    C_3 34–5
    C_4 35–6
    CAM 36
    Ferocactus acanthodes 57
    Welwitschia mirabilis 56
photosynthetic rates 49
    annual plants 41
    effects of climate change 236
    tussock grasses 51
Phragmites communis 61

phreatophytes 33, 62–3
  hydraulic lift 63–5
Phyllotis genus 215
phylogenetically controlled studies 92
  larks 98–9
  Peromyscus species 99–101
  skinks 97–8
  small carnivores 101
  tenebrionid beetles 93–7
Physadesmia globosa, competition 112–15
phytogeographical desert regions 209, *211*
Pianka, E.R. 195, 196–7
Pianka, E.R. and Huey, R.B. 198
Pickup, G. and Chewings, V.H. 245
Picris babylonica, effects of oil pollu-
    tion 242
Picris damascena 32
pigeons, *rete mirabile ophthalmicum* 80
Pimelia grandis, predation 125
Pinshow, B. *et al.* 80
pioneer roots 54
piosphere grazing effects 222–4, 225, *226*
Pituophis catenifer deserticola (gopher
    snakes) 183
Plantago coronopus 44
Plantago insularis, seed dispersal 169
plant–animal interactions 145
  coevolution 170
    Bursera trees and *Blepharida* leaf
      beetles 172–3
    dorcas gazelle and lilies 173–6
    red Negev flowers 171–2
    senita and yucca systems 171
  see also herbivory; pollination; seed
    dispersal
plants 29
  annuals 40–1
    comparisons with mesic annuals 41–2
    delayed germination 46
    germination mechanisms *43*, 44
    rarity of long-range dispersal 44–6
    seed dispersal strategies 42–3
    seed heteromorphism 47–8
  biodiversity 193–4
    effect of abiotic factors 145–7
  classification 29–33
    structural/functional groups *35*
  clonality 48–9
  competition 102–3
    annuals 103–5
    shrubs 105–6
  cyclical relationships 189
  fog as water source 50–1
  geophytes 51–2
    contractile roots 54–6
    hysteranthy 52–4
  grasses 51
  halophytes 60–2
  leaf pubescence 49–50
  leaf succulents 59–60

nurse plant effects 106–7
photosynthesis 34–9, 49
phreatophytes 62–3
  hydraulic lift 63–5
stem succulents 56–8
vegetation type, effect of rainfall 192
plateau landscapes 26
Platysaurus broadleyi, thermoregulation *69*
playa lakes 12–14, 18
Plectrachne species 51
Plicosepalus acaciae (mistletoe) 31, 33, 202,
    262
  genotype by environment
    interactions 261–2, *263*
Plumbaginaceae *210*
Pniel Estates, satellite photography *244*
Poaceae *210*
  invasive species 234
poaching, black rhinoceros 248
Poekilocerus bufonius, body temperature
    regulation 67, *68*
Pogonomyrmex rugosus, seed dispersal 169
poikilohydric organisms 40
poikilotherms (heterotherms) 67
polar deserts 4
  reasons for formation *9*, 10
Polemoniaceae 204, *210*
Polis, G.A. 180, 181–3
Polis, G.A. and Hurd, S.D. 183
Polis, G.A. and McCormick, S.J. 131–2
pollination 158–9
  by *Amphiocoma* beetles 171–2
  senita cactus–senita moth
    mutualism 163–7
  yucca–yucca moth mutualism
    159–63
pollination strategies, hysteranthy 52
Polygonaceae *210*
polyphenism 46
pompilid wasps 140–1
population density, effect on mutualistic
    relationships 165–6
Populus euphratica, clonality 48–9
porcupine diggings, effect on plant diver-
    sity 168, *169*, 190
Portulacaceae 214
potassium limitation 20
potassium secretion, reptiles 85
potential evapotranspiration 6, 7
Prange, H.D. and Pinshow, B. 67
precipitation 11–19, 184–7
  see also rainfall
predation
  direct mortality effect 124–5
  on fat sand rat 129
  keystone predation 135–7
  short-term apparent competition 120–1
  see also seed predation
predation risk, behavioural effects 107–8,
    125–6

predators
  keystone species 248–9
  scorpions 131–2
  snakes 134–5
  spiders 129–31
  visual hunting 132–3
preferred body temperature
  Australian skinks 97–8
  tenebrionid beetles 93, 95–6
prey:predator ratio 182
priority effects 122–3
productivity–diversity relationships 193,
    199–202
Prosopis species
  P. glandulosa (honey mesquite),
    recruitment 231
  rooting depth 63
  seed dispersal 168
prostrate-leaved geophytes 212–13
Proteaceae 210
protection strategies, seeds 42–4, 46
Psammomys obesus (fat sand rat) 127
  habitat selection 126, 128–9
  halophyte consumption 61, 86–7
psammophilous plants 214–15
Pseudodiplorchis americanus 139–40
Pseudomys species 79, 215
  P. hermannsburgensis (desert mouse),
    hypothermia 81
Pseudopompilus humboldti 140
Pterocles species (sandgrouse) 83–4
pulse–reserve models 185–6
pulses, rainfall 12
Pye, K. 24

quartz fields 213–14

radiation coupled organisms 67
rainfall 4–5, 11–14, 184–7
  effect in grazed ecosystems 228
  effect on vegetation 192, 209
  El Niño effect 8–9
  influencing factors 7–10
  relationship to dust storm frequencies 24
  role in bush encroachment 232–3
  seasonal effects 6
  variation 2–3
rainfall pulses 186
rain shadow (relief) deserts 8, 9
Rajasthan, control of land 265–7
rangeland studies 243–5
Ranunculus species, flower colours 171
raphide production, lilies 175–6
rapid bath response, *Bursera*
    schlechtendalii 156–7
raptors, salt glands 84–5
Rasa, O.A.E. and Heg, D. 142
Raunkiaer, C., classification of plant
    functional types 31–3
Reaumuria soongorica 61

Reboudia pinnata 44
  effect of harvester ants 189, *190*
  seed dispersal 170
recolonization, American black bear 260
rectal fluid production, desert
    locusts 70
rectifiers 63
Red Data Book species, Succulent
    Karoo 255
red flower colouration, Negev desert 171–2
red foxes (*Vulpes vulpes*), as cause of
    Australian extinctions 135–6
red-headed finch (*Amadina*
    erythrocephalus),
    hypothermia 81
Red Queen hypothesis 170
red vizcacha rat (*Tympanoctomys*
    barrerae) 75, *86*
reg (desert pavement) 25
regional species diversity
    (γ diversity) 193
  birds 198
  lizards 195, 196–7
  in Succulent Karoo 254
reintroductions of species
  Arabian oryx 259–60
  Asiatic wild ass 256–8
relief (rain shadow) deserts 8, 9
Repasky, R.E. and Schluter, D. 117
reproductive strategies, annual plants,
    seed size 42
reptiles, salt glands 85
resource allocation models *122*, 123
resource-limited fruit set, yucca and
    senita cactus 171
resources
  two-phase pulse hypothesis 102–3
  see also nutrients
respiratory alkalosis 83
Retama raetam, rooting depth 63
rete mirabile 80
revegetation 260–1
reverse flow, roots 63
Reynolds, J.F. *et al.* 185–6, 230–1
Rhabdomys pumilio (striped field mice),
    competition with gerbils *115*
Rhinoptilus cursorius (double-banded
    coursers) 83
rhizomes 52
Richards, J.H. and Caldwell, M.M. 63, 65
Richer, J. 264
Riechert, S.E. 130
Riechert, S.E. and Harp, J. 130
Rio Grande River, oases 15
Rissing, S.W. 169
roadrunner (*Geococcyx californianus*),
    salt glands 84
Robbins, P. 265–7
Rock Kestrel (*Falco tinnunculus*) 177
rock landscapes 25

rodents
  body size *178*
  convergence 205
  desert mouse (*Pseudomys
    hermannsburgensis*) 81
  ecosystem engineering 189
  indirect interaction with ants 118
  little pocket mice (*Perognathus
    longimembris*) 121–2
  red vizcacha rat (*Tympanoctomys
    barrerae*) 75, 86
  snail predation 124–5
  striped field mice (*Rhabdomys
    pumilio*) 115
  see also gerbil (*Gerbillus* and
    Gerbillurus) species; kangaroo rats
    (*Dipodomys* species); fat sand rat
    (*Psammomys obesus*)
Rohner, C. and Ward, D. 153–4, 251
rooting depth, phreatophytes 62–3
root parasites 33, *34*
roots, niche separation 105, 231
root systems
  hydraulic lift 63–5, *64*
  succulent plants 58
Rosaceae *210*
Rosenzweig, M.L. 126
Rosenzweig, M.L. and Abramsky,
    Z. 109–*11*, 199, 200
round-eared elephant shrew (*Macroscelides
    proboscideus*), torpor 80–1
Rub' al-Khali (Empty Quarter, Middle
    East) 82
Rubiaceae *210*
Rubisco (RuBP carboxylase-oxygenase)
    reactions 34, 35, 36
Ruiz, N. *et al.* 53–4, 55–6, 149
run-off 15–17
  seed anchorage 46
run-off harvesting 219, 220–1
run-on 15–7
Rüppell's fox (*Vulpes rueppellii*)
  carnassial teeth 205–6
  cooling mechanism 82
  phylogenetically controlled studies 101
Ruschia caroli, projected impact of climate
    change *235*
Ruschia robusta
  competition 105
  projected impact of climate change *235*
Ryel, R.J. *et al.* 51

sacrifice zone, water points 223
saguaro cactus (*Carnegiea gigantea*),
    flowering 58
Sahara desert 26
  age 4
  location *5*
  nitrogen limitation 187
  plant species 212

rainfall 2
  reasons for formation *9*
  temperature 19–20
Saharo-Arabian region *211*
Sahel
  desertification 218–*19*
  piosphere effects 224
Sahelian (Sudano-Decanian)
    region *211*
Saiko, T.A. and Zonn, I.S. 240
saline oases 15
saline soils 17–19
salinity tolerance, halophytes 61–2
salt accumulation 60
salt excretor plants 61
salt glands 84–5
  in plants 86
Salton Sea 13
Saltz, D. *et al.* 149, 245, 257
Saltz, D. and Ward, D. 149
sand compaction, effect on bulb
    depth 55–6
sandgrouse (*Pterocles* species) 83–4
sand landscapes 21–4
sand partridges (*Ammoperdix heyi*) 82–3
Sandquist, D.R. and Ehleringer, J.R.
    49–50
sandstorms 21–2
Santalum acuminatum 33
Sarcobatus vermiculatus 61
Sarcophilus harrisii (devil, Tasmanian
    devil) 136
Sarcopoterium spinosum, facilitation 107
satellite photography *244*, 245
Saudi Arabia, reintroduction of Arabian
    oryx 259–60
scale invariance, food webs 181
scaling effects, food webs 177–9
Scaphiopus couchii (spadefoot toad) 74,
    139–40
scarification of seeds 168, *252*
  Acacia raddiana 251
scent-hunting predators 134–5
Schismus arabicus
  seed dispersal 169
  seed size 42
Schistocerca gregaria (desert locust),
    water conservation 70, *71*
Schlesinger, W.H. *et al.* 219
Schmidt-Nielsen, K. *et al.* 73, 91
Schmiedel, U. and Jürgens, N. 213
Schulze, E.-D. and Schulze, J. 56
Scorpio maurus 131
scorpions 131–2
scouring effects, downpours 12
Scrophulariaceae *210*
sea, circulation patterns 7–9
seasonal effects
  habitat selection, fat sand rat 126, *128–9*
  rainfall 6

seed dispersal 42–3, *47*
  Acacia raddiana 211–12, 251
  by herbivores 168–*70*
seed heteromorphism, annual
      plants 47–8
seed predation 167–8
seed protection strategies
  annual plants 42–4
  hysteranthous plants 52
seed size 42
Seely, M.K. *et al.* 94–5
seifs 22–3
selective abortion, yucca 160, 164
self-incompatibility, yucca and senita
      cactus 171
'selfish herd' effect, spiders 131
self-pollination, yucca 160–1
semi-aridity 5, *7*
senita cactus–senita moth mutual-
      ism 163–7
  coevolution 171
Seothyra henscheli, shadow
      competition 130
serotiny 43
Shachak, M. *et al.* 21
shadow competition, spiders 130–1
Shantz, H.I., classification of desert
      plants 29–31
shared-preference model 115, 116
Sharon, D. 11, *12*
Shenbrot, G. 126, 128
Shenbrot, G. *et al.* 75
shepherd's tree (*Boscia albitrunca*) 30
Sher, A.A. *et al.* 187
shield desert 26
Shkedy, Y. and Saltz, D. 253
Shmida, A. 192, 209, *211*
short-term apparent competition 120–2
Shrestha, M.K. *et al.* 211–12, 261
shrub encroachment *229–34*
  impact of climate change 236
  Magersfontein *243–4*
shrubs
  clonality 48–9
  competition 105–6
  grazing effects 152
  'islands of fertility' 21
  leaf pubescence 49–50
  nurse plant effects 106–7
  photosynthesis 49
shuttling, burrowing spiders 77
sidewinder snakes (*Crotalus
      cerastes*) *134*
Simpson desert
  location *5*
  reasons for formation *9*
  wadis 13
Sinai desert, shield desert 26
Sinclair, A.R.E. and Fryxell, J.M. 218–19
single populations, conservation 249–51

'sink' populations, *Pancratium
      sickenbergeri* 252
Siwa oasis, soil salinization 222
skinks, phylogenetically controlled
      studies 97–8
SLOSS (Single Large Or Several Small)
      conservation debate 251–2
small mammals, biogeography 215–16
Smet, M. and Ward, D. 223
Sminthopsis crassicaudata 79
Smith, S.D. *et al.* 40
snails 72–4
  nitrogen inputs 20–1
  predation 124–5
snakes 134–5
  Dasypeltis scabra 137
snow 4–5
soil
  effect of off-road vehicles 238–9
  effects of organisms 21
  saline 17–19, 217, 218, 221–2
  salt accumulation 60
soil heterogeneity 219
soil organic matter, relationship to
      termite abundance 191
soil water, two-layer theory 229–31
Solanaceae *210*
solar tracking, annual plants 41
Solifugae (sun spiders)
  absence from Australia *203*, 215
  ventilation cycle 69
solonchaks 19
Somali-Chalbi (Ogaden)
      desert
  location *5*
  reasons for formation *9*
Sonoran desert 20, *211*
  biodiversity 216
  cactus ferruginous owl 249
  delayed germination 46
  keystone species 119
  photosynthetic pathways 37
  reasons for formation *9*
  seed heteromorphism 47
  senita cactus–senita moth
      mutualism 163–7
  wadis 13
'source' populations, *Pancratium
      sickenbergeri* 252
South Africa, desertification 217–18
South America, small
      mammals 215, 216
South American region *211*
southern African region *211*
spadefoot toad (*Scaphiopus couchii*) 74,
      139–40
Spalton, J.A. *et al.* 259
spatially explicit models 250–1
spatial variation, rainfall 11, *12*
specialization, arachnids 131

specialized pollination
systems 158–9
species-area curve 193
species composition, effects of grazing 148
species diversity, representation
in food webs 183
species richness
animals 194–5
in ephemeral pools 198–9
granivores 197–8
lizards 195–7
birds 198
plants 193–4
species turnover (β diversity) 192–3
granivores 197
plants 194
small mammals 215, 216
specific leaf area (SLA), high, advantage in
grazed areas 151, 154
Spergularia diandra, seed size 42
Sphincterochila boisseri 73
Sphincterochila zonata, water loss 73
spiders
burrowing 76–7
interaction with parasitoids 140
predation by scorpions 131, 132
web relocation 129–31
see also Latrodectus and *Stegodyphus*
species
spinescence of plants 153
spinifex grasslands *196*
fire 28
spiracle opening, insects and
solifugids 69
spotted hyaenas (*Crocuta crocuta*) 137
Stafford Smith, D.M. and
Morton, S.R. 188
Stefan–Boltzmann law 90
Stegodyphus lineatus 130
interaction with pompilid wasps 140
web relocation 129–30
stem succulents 56–8
Stenocara gracilipes 93
Stenocereus thurberi, facilitation 106
Stenoponia tripectinata 138–9
Sternbergia clusiana, facilitation *106*
Stiltia isabella 84
stilting behaviour, tenebrionid beetles *93*,
96–7
Stipa capensis
ant herbivory 169–70
comparison of desert and mesic races 42
Stipagrostis species 41, 214
S. sabulicola, fog as water source 50, 51
stomata, drought avoidance 30
stomatal opening
Agave deserti 58
Ferocactus acanthodes 57
stone curlews (*Burhinus oedicnemus*),
beetle predation 125

stone plants (*Lithops* genus) *59–60*
stone substrates 25
storage effect, annual plants 104
Stowe, L.G. and Teeri, J.A. 39
Streptocephalus genus, geographical
distribution 204–5
stress tolerance 103
striped field mice (*Rhabdomys pumilio*),
competition with gerbils *115*
striped hyaenas (*Hyaena hyaena*) 177
structural/functional classification, desert
plants 33, *35*
Struthio camelus (ostrich) 91–2
seed herbivory 168
Sturt's Stony desert
location *5*
reasons for formation *9*
subterranean lizards 196
Succulent Karoo
conservation 253–6
geophytes 212–13
invasive species 235
plant species richness 193, 194
succulent plants 214
CAM photosynthesis 36
convergent evolution *203*
leaf succulents 59–60
stem succulents 56–8
Sudano-Decanian (Sahelian) region *211*
sugar farms, Nile River *222*
sulphur limitation 188
summer annuals 41
sun spiders (Solifugae)
absence from Australia *203*, 215
ventilation cycle 69
surface area:volume ratios 66
insects 68
Sus scrofa (wild boar), seed herbivory 168
Swakop river, water flow *226*
synanthous plants 52
synclines 26
Synosternus cleopatrae 139, *140*

tadpoles, priority effects 123
Taklamakan desert 218
age 3
location *5*
reasons for formation *9*
takyrs 19
Tamarix species 234
T. aphylla 61
rooting depth 63
T. nilotica 214–15
Tegeticula species
mutualism with yucca 159–63
T. carnerosanella 160
Tehuacan desert, insect herbivory 156
telechory, rarity 44–6
temperature vii. 2, 19–20
temporal niches, annual plants 104

temporal variability
  plant abundance *146–7*
  rainfall 12
temporary pools 87
  biodiversity 198–9
  fauna 204, 215
tenebrionid beetles
  body size 180
  brood parasites *142–3*
  competition 112–15
  phylogenetically controlled
    studies 93–7
  predation 125
  size distribution patterns 205, *206*
  wax blooms 69, *70*
termite mounds *77–8*
termites
  ecosystem engineering 189
  role in decomposition 191
  in spinifex grasslands 196
terpene resin release, *Bursera* spe-
    cies 156–7, *172–3*
Thar desert 211, 216
  age 3
  location *5*
  reasons for formation 9
thermoneutral zones, gerbil species 80
thermoregulation 67
  endurers 87–92
  evaders 68–72
  parasitoids 140
  physiological mechanisms 80–4
thermosiphon effect, termite mounds *77–8*
therophytes 31
Thorne, R.F. 214
Thornthwaite, C.W. 6
threshold of critical power 12, *13, 14*
Thylacinus cyanocephalus (thylacine) 136
Thylamys elegans 216
Thymelea hirsuta 153
ticks, ventilation strategy 69
Tieleman, B.I. *et al.* 98–9
Tilman, D. 103, 105
  resource allocation model *122*, 123
toads 74
  endoparasites 139–40
Tomlinson, S. *et al.* 81
'top-down' control, HSS model 179–80
torpor 80–1
total evaporative water loss (TEWL)
  foxes 82, *101*
  larks 98–9
Trachyderma philistina, predation 125
trade-offs, *Pancratium sickenbergeri 53*
tragedy of the commons 219
trampling
  around water points 223
  effects on soils 238
transpiration rates, *Welwitschia*
    mirabilis 57

tree–grass coexistence, two-layer
    theory 229–31, 233–4
Treydte, A.C. *et al.* 259–60
Trianthema hereroenisis, fog as water
    source 50–1
Trigonephrus species 72–3
Triodia species 51
Triticum dicoccoides (emmer wheat),
    biodiversity 263
Trochoidea seetzenii 73
Trochoidea simulata, water loss 73
trophic levels 179, 180, 182
tubers 52
Tulipa species
  flower colours 171
  T. systola 33, 168
    above ground emergence 54
Turkana region, Kenya, herbivore and plant
    populations *228*
Turkestan desert 20
  age 3
  location *5*
  reasons for formation 9
Turner, J.S. 77, 78
Turner, J.S. and Lombard, A.T. 97
Turner, J.S. and Picker, M.D. 59–60
tussock features, relationship to
    grazing 151–2
tussock grasses 51
two-layer theory, tree–grass
    coexistence 229–31, 233–4
two-phase resource pulse
    hypothesis 102–33
Tympanoctomys species
  kidney *71*
  T. barrerae (red vizcacha rat) 75, *86*

umbrella species 247–8
  Nubian ibex 253
United Nations Environment Programme,
    definition of aridity 6–7
Upiga virescens (senita moth), mutualism
    with senita cactus 163–7
upwelling *8*
Urginea maritima 154
uric acid excretion 70, 82
Uroplectes otjimbinguensis 132
Ursus americanus (American black bear),
    recolonization 260

Valentine, K.A. 223
Valone, T.J. *et al.* 120
Vanellus coronatus (crowned plovers),
    cooling mechanisms 83
Vangueria infausta 262
Van Rheede van Oudtshoorn and Van
    Rooyen, M. 42–3, *45*
Varanus gouldii (goannas) 191
vascular hemiparasitic plants 33
vascular parasitic plants 33

Vasek, F.C. 48
Veech, J.A. 121–2
vein-cutting behaviour, *Bursera*
    species 156–7
Venable, D.I. 47–8
Venable, D.I. *et al.* 46
ventilation cycles, discontinuous 69
Venturi effect, open termite mounds 77
Veromessor pergandei, seed dispersal 169
vesicular arbuscular mycorrhizae (VAM)
    species, genotype by
    environment interactions 262–3
Vesk, P.A. *et al.* 154–5
Victoria desert
    location 5
    reasons for formation 9
Vishnevetsky, S. and Steinberger, Y. 191
visually hunting predators 132–3
vizcacha rat (*Tympanoctomys barrerae*) 75,
    86
Volis, S. 42
Volis, S. *et al.* 263
Von Willert, D.J. *et al.* 56–7
Vulpes species
    carnassial tooth lengths 205–6
    V. rueppellii (Rüppell's fox)
      cooling mechanism 82
      phylogenetically controlled
      studies 101
    V. vulpes (red fox), as cause of Australian
      extinctions 135–6

wadi plants, photosynthetic rates 49
wadis 12, 13
    Acacia raddiana mortality *221*
    erosion 219–21, *220*
Walter correlation 209
Walter, H. 229
Ward, D. 205
Ward, D. and Blaustein, L. 198–9
Ward, D. *et al.* 2, 45, 53, 146, 149, *150*,
    153, 199, 219–21, 224–5
Ward, D. and Henschel, J.R. 140
Ward, D. and Lubin, Y.D. 129–30
Ward, D. and Ngairorue, B.T. 227
Ward, D. and Olsvig-Whittaker, L. 192,
    199
Ward, D. and Rohner, C. 250
Ward, D. and Saltz, D. 149, 173–4
Ward, D. and Seely, M.K. 93–7, 112–13
water accumulation, frogs 74
water balance
    camels 89–91
    Gila monsters 92
water conservation
    excretory systems 70
    mammals 80
    snails 72
water deficiency 6
water loss, snails 73–4

water points, piosphere grazing
    effects 222–4, 225, *226*
water potentials 49
    desert shrubs 49, *50*
water relations, and flowering of cacti 58
water stress (water deficit) 31
water transportation, sandgrouse 83–4
water turnover, dasyurids and
    murids 79–80
water use 239–40, 242–3
water-use efficiency, photosynthetic
    pathways 37
wax blooms, tenebrionid beetles 69, *70*,
    94, *96*
Webb, R.H. 238
Weber, G.E. *et al.* 228
web relocation, spiders 129–31
Welwitschia genus 212
    W. mirabilis 56–7
Wheeling spider (*Carparachne
    aureoflava*) 141
white abdomen, tenebrionid beetles *95*, *97*
white storks (*Ciconia ciconia*), beetle
    predation 125
Whitford, W.G. 184, 187, 191, 204
Whittaker law 209
widow spiders (*Latrodectus*) 129–30, 177,
    183
Wiegand, K. *et al.* 187, 232, 250–1
Wiens, J.A. 198
Wiens, J.A. and Rotenberry, J.T. 117
Wilby, A. *et al.* 169, 189
wild barley (*Hordeum spontaneum*)
    comparison of desert and mesic races 42
    genotype by environment
      interactions 263
wild boar (*Sus scrofa*), seed herbivory 168
wild oats
    biodiversity 263
    comparison of desert and mesic races 42
Williams, J.B. *et al.* 101
willingness to pay for conservation 264
Willmer, P. *et al.* 66, 68
Windhoek, water use by
    neighbourhood *239*
window of variable opacity, *Lithops*
    species *59*
winter annuals 41
Winter, K. *et al.* 37
wolves, phylogenetically controlled
    studies 101

Xenopsylla species 138–9, *140*
    X. dipodilla 138
Xerus species
    geographical distribution *195*
    X. inauris (Cape ground squirrel) *78–9*

Yeaton, R.I. 106
Yoder, C.K. and Nowak, R.S. 65

Yucca schidigera, hydraulic lift 65
yucca–yucca moth mutualism 159–61
   cheating behaviour 161–3
   coevolution 171
   costs 164–5

Zaady, E. *et al.* 44
Ziv, Y. *et al.* *116*, 178

Zohary, M., 'mother-site'
      theory 44, 46
Zophosis punctata 125
Zygophyllaceae *210*, 214
Zygophyllum album 215
Zygophyllum
      dumosum 31
   competition 106